Educational management:
strategy, quality and resources

COMPANION VOLUMES

The companion volumes in this series are:

Organizational Effectiveness and Improvement in Education, edited by Alma Harris, Nigel Bennett and Margaret Preedy

Professional Development for Educational Management, edited by Lesley Kydd, Megan Crawford and Colin Riches

Leadership and Teams in Educational Management, edited by Megan Crawford, Lesley Kydd and Colin Riches

All four of these readers are part of a course, Effective Leadership and Management in Education, that is itself part of the Open University MA Programme.

THE OPEN UNIVERSITY MA IN EDUCATION

The Open University MA in Education is now firmly established as the most popular postgraduate degree for education professionals in Europe, with over 3,500 students registering each year. The MA in Education is designed particularly for those with experience of teaching, the advisory service, educational administration or allied fields.

Structure of the MA

The MA is a modular degree, and students are therefore free to select from a range of options the programme which best fits in with their interests and professional goals. Specialist lines in management and primary education are also available. Study in the Open University's Advanced Diploma and Certificate Programmes can also be counted towards the MA, and successful study in the MA programme entitles students to apply for entry into the Open University Doctorate in Education programme.

COURSES CURRENTLY AVAILABLE:

- Management
- Child Development
- Primary Education
- Curriculum, Learning and Assessment
- Special Needs
- Language and Literacy
- Mentoring

- Education, Training and Employment
- Gender
- Educational Research
- Science Education
- Adult Learners
- Maths Education

OU supported open learning

The MA in Education programme provides great flexibility. Students study at their own pace, in their own time, anywhere in the European Union. They receive specially prepared study materials, supported by tutorials, thus offering the chance to work with other students.

How to apply

If you would like to register for this programme, or simply to find out more information, please write for the *Professional Development in Education* prospectus to the Course Reservations and Sales Centre, PO Box 724, The Open University, Walton Hall, Milton Keynes, MK7 6ZS, UK (Telephone 01908 653231).

Educational management: strategy, quality and resources

Edited by
MARGARET PREEDY, RON GLATTER
AND ROSALIND LEVAČIĆ
at The Open University

OPEN UNIVERSITY PRESS
Buckingham . Philadelphia

Open University Press
Celtic Court
22 Ballmoor
Buckingham MK18 1XW

and 1900 Frost Road, Suite 101
Bristol, PA 19007, USA

First published 1997
Reprinted 1998

A catalogue record of this book is available from the British Library

ISBN 0 335 19797 3 (pbk)   0 335 19798 1 (hbk)

Library of Congress Cataloging-in-Publication Data

Educational management: strategy, quality, and resources/edited by
   Margaret Preedy, Ron Glatter, and Rosalind Levačić.
        p.   cm.—(Leadership and management in education)
   Includes bibliographical references and index.
   ISBN 0-335-19798-1.   ISBN 0-335-19797-3 (pbk.)
   1. School management and organizations—United States. 2. Total
quality management—United States.   I. Preedy, Margaret.
II. Glatter, Ron.   III. Levačić, Rosalind.   IV. Series.
LB2805.E3476   1996
371'.2'00973–dc20   96-32325
                                                                CIP

Typeset by Type Study, Scarborough, North Yorkshire
Printed and bound in Great Britain by Redwood Books, Trowbridge

Contents

Acknowledgements

Very grateful acknowledgement is made to Sindy York for her invaluable secretarial support.

The chapters listed below come from the following sources, to whose publishers grateful acknowledgement is made.

2 Cuttance, P. (1994) 'Monitoring Educational Quality Through PIs for School Practice', *School Effectiveness and School Improvement,* 5(2): 101–26 with kind permission from Swets & Zeitlinger Publishers.

3 Riley, K. (1994) 'Quality and Equality: competing or complementary objectives', Chapter 1 in Riley, K. *Quality and Equality,* London, Cassell PLC.

4 The Further Education Development Agency (FEDA) for granting permission to reproduce material from *Continuous Improvement and Quality Standards,* Further Education Unit (1994).

5 Aspinwall, K. *et al.* (1992) 'Using success criteria', Chapter 7 in Aspinwall *et al., Managing Evaluation in Education,* London, Routledge.

6 Hopkins, D. *et al.* (1994) 'Making sense of change', Chapter 3 in Hopkins *et al., School Improvement in an Era of Change,* London, Cassell PLC.

7 West, N. (1995) 'A framework for curriculum development, policy implementation and monitoring quality', Chapter 3 in N. West, *Middle Management in the Primary School,* London, David Fulton Publishers.

8 Dean, J. (1993) 'Organising learning', Chapter 6 in *Managing the Secondary School,* London, Routledge.

9 Holland, P. and Hamerton, P. (1994) 'Balancing school and individual approaches' in P. Gray, *et al.* (eds) *Challenging Behaviour in Schools,* London, Routledge.

10 Reprinted with permission from the author. Coles, M. (1993) 'Curriculum evaluation as review and development', revised version of Chapter 7 in C. Day, *et al.,*

Leadership and Curriculum in the Primary School, London, Paul Chapman Publishing Limited.

11 This material is a revised version of Chapter 3, 'The locally managed school as an open system' by Rosalind Levačić which originally appeared in *Local Management of Schools*, Buckingham, Open University Press 1995.

12 Glover, D. *Resourcing education: linking educational objectives and budgeting*, based on current research (commissioned article).

13 Knight, B. (1993) 'Budget analysis and construction', Chapter 7 in B. Knight, *Financial Management for Schools*, Oxford, Heinemann.

14 Sutton, M. (1994) 'Allocating budgets for curriculum support', commissioned paper based on 'Sharing the purse strings' which first appeared in *Managing Schools Today*, 4(7): 14–16 published by The Questions Publishing Company, 27 Frederick Street, Birmingham B1 3HH.

15 Carr, J. G. (1994) 'Unit costing in colleges' originally published as 'Effective Financial Management in FE and HE', *ACCA Technical Bulletin* No. 29, reproduced with the permission of the Certified Accountants Educational Trust.

16 Bailey, A. and Johnson, G. (1992) 'How strategies develop in organisations', Chapter 8 in Faulkner and Johnson (eds) *The Challenge of Strategic Management*, London, Kogan Page Ltd.

17 National Audit Office (1994) *Value for money at grant-maintained schools: a review of performance*, HMSO. Parliamentary copyright is reproduced with the permission of the Controller of HMSO.

18 Drodge, S. and Cooper, N. 'Strategy and management in the further education sector' (commissioned article).

19 Weindling, D. 'Strategic planning in schools: some practical techniques' (commissioned article).

20 Reprinted with permission from the author. MacGilchrist, B. *et al.* (1995) 'The impact of development planning in primary schools', from Chapters 14 and 15 in B. MacGilchrist *et al.*, *Planning Matters*, London, Paul Chapman Publishing Ltd.

21 This extract is from *Leading Projects: a manager's pocket guide* by T. Young published by the Industrial Society, London and reproduced with permission.

22 Bagley, C., Woods, P. and Glatter, R. (1995) 'Scanning the market: school strategies for discovering parental perspectives', *Educational Management and Administration*, 24(2): 125–38.

23 James, C. and Phillips, P. (1995) 'The practice of educational marketing in schools', *Educational Management and Administration*, 23(2).

24 Goldring, E. (1995) 'Educational Leadership: schools, environments and boundary spanning' (commissioned article).

1 | Introduction: managing quality, resources and strategy

MARGARET PREEDY, RON GLATTER AND ROSALIND LEVAČIĆ

This collection of readings explores three central and interrelated tasks for the educational manager: developing and maintaining quality in processes and outcomes, using resources effectively, and establishing a strategic overview and direction for the institution. In examining these themes, this selection aims to help educational managers to improve their own practice, by encouraging critical reflection on management processes and on how conceptual frameworks and research evidence can contribute to more effective professional performance in schools and colleges.

Many educational managers have traditionally been somewhat sceptical of 'theory', claiming that management is an essentially practical activity. However, all management decisions and actions are based on participants' assumptions and expectations, be they implicit or explicit, about organizational events and behaviours. This collection is based on the premise that there is an interactive relationship between theory and action (see Fullan 1991); examining our understandings and perspectives, and exploring alternative views, can help us to explore our organizational context in new ways, providing the basis for changes in practice. Similarly, trying out new forms of action can lead us to question our existing understandings and perspectives.

This selection of readings is also based on the belief that developing an understanding of current educational management practice is important for *all* teachers, whether or not they hold designated management posts. As the research evidence shows (see, for example, Louis and Miles 1990; Nias *et al.* 1992), shared understanding, among all staff, about the purposes of educational organizations and collaborative ways of working towards these purposes, are of major importance in managing the context for effective learning and teaching.

The collection has a strongly practical flavour, focusing on frameworks, ideas and approaches that teachers can test out and develop in their own schools and colleges. It draws on material taking a range of perspectives and approaches – theoretical overviews, applications of conceptual frameworks to management practice, research evidence and case examples. Some of the chapters take a generic approach, others are based in particular educational sectors – primary, secondary and further education. It is important for teachers as managers to transcend sector boundaries in their thinking: there is much to be learned from reflecting on one's own perspectives in the light of insights drawn from other sectors.

The following sections of this chapter outline some of the main issues involved in managing quality, resources and strategy, and provide a brief overview of later chapters.

Quality

Efforts to improve quality in education are not new, but in recent years have received increasing attention. External pressures have played an important part here, in particular three main factors (see Stuart 1994):

1 educational issues – concerns about the performance of schools and colleges expressed by governments, the inspectorate and the public at large;
2 political issues – concerns about reducing public spending as a proportion of GDP, and the demands of education vis-à-vis other public expenditure priorities;
3 economic arguments – concerns about the links between educational spending and economic success, especially in comparison with competitor nations.

Legislative changes in the UK and elsewhere have brought increased autonomy for schools and colleges, accompanied by requirements making them more accountable for the quality of provision and spending decisions. These requirements include funding linked to pupil numbers, a prescribed national curriculum and testing arrangements, publication of performance data on test and examination results and attendance rates, and a cycle of regular external inspections in which institutions are assessed against explicit and detailed criteria.

This context raises a number of issues for schools and colleges seeking to enhance educational quality – issues about the nature, purpose, focus, content and control of attempts to improve quality. These issues arise because there is no simple recipe for educational quality that can be used across all contexts and at all times. If there were such a recipe, enhancing quality would be a relatively simple matter: combine the prescribed ingredients and await results. However, assessing quality is a complicated and value-laden task. There are many interacting factors which contribute to quality in education: 'students and their backgrounds, staff and their skills' [institutions] and their structure and ethos, curricula, and social expectations' (OECD 1989).

The nature of educational quality is contested (see, for example, Doherty 1994), but there is little argument that quality improvement should focus on learning and teaching, and creating a framework within which these activities can take place most effectively. Since the main purpose of schools and colleges is to enable pupils/students to learn, the needs of the learner must be the primary concern. Developing curriculum quality is therefore a key task. Later chapters in this volume examine the major elements of the curriculum management cycle – review, planning, implementation and evaluation – and the complex issues involved in curriculum change, which includes all stages of the management cycle.

However, focusing on learning quality raises questions about defining and prioritiz-ing the multiple needs of individual learners, e.g. academic, social, spiritual and moral development, preparation for working life, for citizenship and parenthood. Similarly, schools, and especially colleges, have multiple and often competing goals for different groups of learners. Given finite resources, it is difficult for institutions to improve the quality of provision equitably for all groups. For example, even within a relatively homogeneous course group, the teacher's aim may be to enable as many students as possible to achieve pass grades in the course examination. This may suggest focusing attention on borderline pass/fail students, which may entail less than equal treatment for those who are expected to achieve a pass score, but might (with extra help) have achieved a distinction or top grade.

There are also issues concerned with whose definition of quality is to count. Schools and colleges have multiple stakeholders – students, parents, employers, funding bodies, local and central authorities – each with differing quality definitions and emphases. Thus, for example, some parents may be largely concerned with examina-tion results, employers with work-related skills, funding bodies at least partly with cost-effectiveness and staff : student ratios. Similarly, decision makers at different levels in the educational system and in the institution are likely to have various quality concerns which are not necessarily compatible. Managing for quality therefore entails mediating between various quality agendas.

Another important concern for institutional managers and teachers is balancing the tension between external accountability demands to demonstrate or *prove* quality and internal development work aiming to enhance or *improve* quality. We can usefully dis-tinguish here between quality control and quality assurance. Quality control is con-cerned with checking outcomes after the educational process has occurred, to identify problems and weaknesses. External inspection, public examinations, internal tests and examinations, and annual department reviews, can be seen as examples of quality control. Quality assurance, on the other hand, is concerned with 'feed-forward' rather than feedback, i.e. with designing process and systems so that potential problems are anticipated and prevented from happening, e.g. planning a course – including its objectives, content, staffing, resources, teaching methods and expected outcomes – to ensure that, as far as possible, all students achieve the course objectives, i.e. matching intentions, processes and outcomes closely together.

It has been argued that external quality control mechanisms contribute little to inter-nal improvement purposes, and educational institutions therefore need to develop their own quality management approaches directed towards ongoing development and guided by professional values and judgements and professional accountability (see Nixon 1995). 'If schools wish to maximise control of their work, then they need to set their own quality agendas before others set them' (Freeman 1994: 23). Clearly, both quality control and assurance are important and necessary for effective manage-ment. Most quality management approaches combine both elements along with a com-mitment to continuing improvement. One such approach involves a local education authority (LEA)–school/college quality development partnership, which has three main purposes: (a) to support the development of institutions and the LEA as learning com-munities; (b) to improve teaching and learning; (c) to permit the institutions and the LEA to respond proactively to accountability demands (see Ribbins and Burridge 1994).

Since quality management is concerned with ongoing development, then per-formance indicators and criteria for judging success need to be adapted over time, as earlier targets are met. This raises questions about the design and use of indicators and success criteria. It is relatively easy to design and use quantitative indicators such as percentage attendance rates, and to adjust our expectations and targets as performance improves (or declines!). However, this is much more difficult with 'softer' qualitative indicators such as pupil satisfaction with school, and staff : student relationships. Also, given the 'unclear technology' (Cohen and March 1983) of learning and teaching, there are problems in defining and measuring the outcomes to be sought in terms of students' improved performance, particularly in more expressive areas such as social and moral development. Indeed, the institution's impact on these areas of student development may not be evident until they have reached adulthood, and there are, of course, many other intervening variables, e.g. family and peer group influences.

For all these reasons, there is a tendency for quantitative easy-to-measure performance indicators to dominate our thinking, despite the evidence from the school effectiveness and improvement literature (see, for example, NCE 1996) about the importance of the more qualitative aspects of school life (such as shared values and cultures, positive staff : student relationships) in successful schools.

Effective institutional arrangements for monitoring, maintaining and improving quality require the allocation of human, material and financial resources. This takes us to our second major theme.

Resources

Here we focus on financial and material resources; human resource management is explored in two companion volumes (Kydd *et al.* 1997; Crawford *et al.* 1997).

The overarching theme of this section is relating financial and resource management to the attainment of educational quality. A particular focus is the need to link budgeting to the achievement of school or college educational objectives. This linkage is problematic because of the nature of educational outputs: these are difficult to measure and often intangible. They are also contested. Furthermore, education is not like a manufacturing production process where inputs are clearly linked to outputs by means of an explicit and well understood technology. In contrast, knowledge of the link between the quantity and quality of teaching time, deployment of materials, size of class and other inputs on the one hand, and the amount of learning achieved by students on the other hand, is much more uncertain.

The problematic nature of the relationships between the amount and pattern of resource use and the processes for planning and managing resources, on the one hand, and educational effectiveness on the other, has become more prominent in recent years. Evidence from inspection reports, see for example HMCI (1995), have indicated a number of deficiencies in financial management, in particular a failure to target spending to areas of priority, a failure to assess the cost effectiveness of resource deployment decisions and to estimate costs of alternative plans, and over-cautiousness in carrying forward quite significant proportions of the budget for no clear purpose. These problems would seem to indicate a lack of integration between resource and curriculum management.

It is important that school/college resource policies are directed by the institution's overall goals and curriculum plans rather than, as is sometimes the case, the reverse, where resource considerations dictate educational priorities. It is therefore necessary for resource management to be proactive, using budgeting as a planning instrument, geared to future outcomes rather than taking an incremental approach based on replicating historical patterns of allocation. This implies a rational approach to resource management in which budget setting is explicitly informed by educational objectives. This in turn requires that annual budgeting be conducted within a longer term framework of strategic management and a broader framework of institutional development planning. Thus resource management provides a vital link between strategy and quality.

The rational approach is widely advocated as an essential aspect of the management of effective educational institutions and has received increasing emphasis from agencies such as the Office for Standards in Education (Ofsted) and the Further Education Funding Council. But it must be borne in mind that the rational perspective is much stronger as a normative model than as a description of actual practice. Alternative perspectives on organizations, which are represented in a companion volume (Harris et al. 1996) may offer a more realistic description of actual resource management practice in educational institutions. Among these alternatives, the micropolitical perspective is of particular salience since resources are a key instrument of power. Thus any competition between different interest groups within a school or college is likely to be focused on rival claims for finance and other resources. From a micropolitical perspective there is no agreed set of organizational objectives to be addressed through budgeting. The resource allocation decisions which finally emerge are the result of conflict, negotiation and compromise between different groups. Resource management is then the art of balancing interests and maintaining a degree of harmony. Another relevant perspective is ambiguity, particularly manifest in educational institutions by the absence of a clear technology relating resource inputs to educational outputs. Ambiguity is reflected in the absence of coupling between the budget on the one hand and educational objectives and outputs on the other.

Educational managers need to resolve the extent to which they can adapt a rational approach to resource management in their particular organizational contexts. The culture of the organization will influence what particular approach to resource management can be made effective and may itself need modifying in order to improve resource and strategic management practices.

Strategy

Strategic planning is a key management process, drawing together institutional values and goals, and providing the framework for the development of quality of provision and the deployment of resources. Until the early 1990s, strategic planning for both schools and further education in England and Wales was conducted largely at the local authority level of the education system. However, the devolution of greater powers of decision making and resource allocation to schools and the incorporation of colleges brought the need for institutions to plan strategically.

This entails looking at the medium and longer term direction of the organization, mapping out its future in an integrated way, taking account of expected trends and developments in the environment as well as internally. Each institution 'must interpret the environment in which it operates and define its own role within that environment. It will need to have a clear view of how it wishes to develop, and the means of securing that development' (FEU 1994: 5). Strategic planning provides the basis for translating decisions into actions in a proactive, rather than reactive way.

In the current political and economic context in which increased levels of efficiency and effectiveness and close links between funding and quality of provision are required, strategic management is important for external accountability as well as institutional development. Strategic planning raises many of the same dilemmas discussed earlier in relation to quality management, in particular, meeting the diverse and often competing expectations of different groups of clients and stakeholders and managing the tensions between external demands and internal priorities. The articles in this volume contribute to and take forward the debate on some of the main issues in strategic management. Three in particular should be mentioned briefly here.

First, as with managing quality and resources, much of the literature on strategy in educational organization takes a broadly rationalist stance. That is to say, it is assumed that: goals are clear and agreed, the planning process follows systematic and logical steps, that full information can be gained on the range of possible policy alternatives, enabling a logical choice of the best option, to which all organizational members are committed. However, organizations are in many ways 'non-rational' (see Patterson *et al.* 1986): goals and the means for reaching them are neither clear nor agreed, appropriate data necessary for logical decision making are rarely available, and choices may be determined as much by sectional interests as by institution-wide objectives. In this context, strategic planning is concerned with negotiating consent as well as establishing future direction.

This brings us to the second factor: organizational culture. Unless there is a large degree of shared staff commitment to the core values and mission underlying the strategic plan, it will not be put into practice successfully. Strategic planning must become embedded in the culture of the organization if all staff are to work together in the same direction towards common goals.

Involvement in formulating the plan and the associated mission statement may help to build staff ownership and identification. In this respect, the process of strategic planning can be as important as the product. However, as mentioned earlier, the notion of shared goals is problematic, and there are also questions about the nature and extent of staff consultation or participation in the planning process, and whether planning should start with an organization-wide 'grand design' (with details filled in later) or with individual plans formulated by subunits, which are then brought together and synthesized to form the overall plan.

A third important factor to note here is the rapid change and uncertainty in the school/college environment, making it very difficult to predict future external trends and demands. Educational institutions need to be able to scan the environment, to gain accurate market information, and to respond rapidly, in order to survive in a competitive climate. Given this ambiguous and swiftly changing context, strategic planning is both more difficult and more urgent and, it has been suggested, may need to be flexible or 'evolutionary' in form (see Louis and Miles 1990; Wallace and McMahon 1994). This means regularly modifying and adapting plans and expectations in response to changing circumstances and opportunities.

Overview of later chapters

We now turn to look at the later chapters in this volume in relation to our three major themes outlined above.

Chapters 2–5 are concerned with various aspects of quality in education. Cuttance (Chapter 2) examines a quality management system operated by a large Australian state, which has some useful messages for other contexts. The approach is designed to meet both accountability and improvement purposes. Using quite sophisticated performance indicators, an ongoing school review and monitoring programme provides continuous feedback on various areas of performance across the school system as a whole. The data provide information for decision making at system level and at the same time are fed back to the schools to contribute to internal development.

Riley (Chapter 3) addresses the problematic issue of how we can provide and improve quality equitably for different client groups. In exploring the tension between quality and equality, she argues that decision makers in local authorities and institutions should ensure that their notions of quality embrace the idea of equal opportunities; a limited view of quality as a standard service for all is not adequate to meet the needs of disadvantaged groups.

The Further Education Unit paper (Chapter 4) provides practical guidance on continuous quality improvement, while recognizing some of the problems involved, not least that quality improvement is unlikely to be successful without a supportive institutional culture. However, as the chapter acknowledges, cultural change is long term and problematic (see Fullan 1991).

Chapter 5 by Aspinwall *et al*. changes the focus from the institution-wide aspects of quality management to the more specific issue of developing and using performance indicators and success criteria. Arguing the need for both quantitative and qualitative criteria, the authors explore design issues and problems, and make the important point that performance information, if it is to be of value for development purposes, should be directed towards problem solving and action.

The next groups of chapters turn from general quality management issues to look at curriculum management, starting with an overview of curriculum change. In a wide ranging survey, Hopkins *et al*. (Chapter 6) identify a number of key issues emerging from the management of change literature and their relevance for curriculum management in particular. They highlight the complex and long term nature of curriculum change and the need to draw on multiple perspectives in understanding the innovation process. West (Chapter 7) points to some of the difficulties in managing externally-initiated change in the school. Examining the processes of planning, implementing and monitoring curriculum change, he argues the need to bridge the implementation gap between curriculum policy making and what actually happens in the classroom. West suggests that planning should include specifying in precise detail what we want to see in terms of the curriculum in action, as it is experienced by pupils.

Chapters 8 and 9 consider the organizational context for curriculum management. Dean (Chapter 8) argues that in order to promote effective learning we need to look afresh at the often taken-for-granted administrative arrangements such as use of space and equipment, and staff deployment, as well as equal opportunity strategies. Chapter 9, by Holland and Hamerton, suggests that the tension between meeting individual and group needs within the school's pastoral care provision can be addressed by a careful balancing of resources on a whole school basis.

Finally, in this section, Coles (Chapter 10) addresses the issues involved in curriculum evaluation. He argues that, to be effective, this process should be undertaken as a collaborative enquiry based on an ongoing commitment to the improvement of classroom practice by all staff.

Part 2 begins with a broad overview of financial and resource management, linking to the overall functioning of the educational institution. In Chapter 11 Levačić uses the open systems model to trace the links between the input of finance and resources, which depend on the institution's interaction with its external environment, and educational outputs and outcomes. The complexity of the intervening processes which link financial and resource inputs to educational outputs and outcomes explains why it is relatively easy for budget management to be decoupled from educational activities and objectives. However, the rational approach to resource management requires strong coupling between budget plans and educational objectives which is expressed in an institutional development plan. In Chapter 12, Glover considers the processes that are encompassed by a rational approach to resource management, using evidence from Ofsted inspections and qualitative research in schools. Particular emphasis is given to the view that the rational approach to the importance of strategic management and to relating this consistently to institutional development planning, which in turn is closely linked to budgeting. Glover argues that the rational approach can work effectively only in institutions where individuals and subunits have a clear and agreed understanding of their own contributions to strategic and development plans, and where both these plans and the budgeting decisions necessary to bring them about are regularly reviewed.

Having set budgeting within the broad context of the organization and its strategic management, the section then focuses on budget planning. Knight (Chapter 13) examines three major aspects of the budgeting process and a number of approaches to budget preparation, which vary in their degree of rationality. Knight stresses the importance of clarifying the purpose of the budget and identifying an appropriate strategy and format. The last two chapters in Part 2 focus on resource allocation within the institution. Sutton (Chapter 14) considers decentralized and centralized approaches in schools for allocating and managing subunit budgets, in particular finance for curriculum support. The choice of the best approach for a particular context depends on assessing the implications for efficiency and effectiveness, bearing in mind the size of the school, the competencies of its senior and middle managers and its culture and leadership style. Extending this theme within the context of further education colleges, Chapter 15 by Carr examines the technique of unit costing and the potential of activity based approaches. This is of particular relevance to costing educational programmes and managing through cost centres.

Moving to our third major theme, Part 3 opens with a number of articles exploring the complexities of strategic planning. Bailey and Johnson (Chapter 16) identify six main perspectives or alternative explanations of strategy development in organizations. The authors argue that to engage in effective strategy formulation, managers need to understand the process as seen by their colleagues, who may interpret it in a variety of different ways. The six different perspectives are not mutually exclusive. It is usually necessary to draw on several of them to provide an adequate explanation of the complexities of strategic decision making in organizations. Taking a contrasting, broadly rationalist, perspective, the National Audit Office (Chapter 17) outlines a systematic approach to strategic planning, including deriving the budget from the plan, providing another view of some of the issues addressed in the chapters in Part 2.

Drawing on a small scale study of three colleges, Drodge and Cooper (Chapter 18) identify distinct differences of style in the management of strategic planning, linked to different organizational cultures, with contrasts in the extent to which responsibility and decision making were devolved within the colleges. Chapter 19, by Weindling, explores some useful practical techniques for strategic planning, stressing the need to incorporate a strategic dimension into the school development plan as a means for managing multiple changes.

On the basis of an empirical study of development planning in primary schools, MacGilchrist et al. (Chapter 20) identify four different types of plan. Effective plans were those which developed clear links between pupil learning, teacher development and school-wide improvements, i.e. a whole school approach. Formulation of school development plans, the authors found, is more complex than much of the available guidance suggests. Chapter 21, by Young, changes the focus from institution-wide planning to explore similar themes and issues with respect to project teams, identifying the main tasks and process components in effective project management and interacting with stakeholders.

The final chapters in this volume examine various aspects of boundary management and environmental linkage, key elements of strategic analysis. Bagley et al. (Chapter 22) explore the extent to which schools scan and interpret parental perspectives and expectations, drawing on a large scale research study of the interrelationship between parental choice and school decision making and responsiveness. James and Phillips, in Chapter 23, discuss the results of an investigation to assess how far marketing principles are used by primary and secondary schools, both maintained and private. The authors found a general lack of a coherent marketing strategy and a piecemeal approach to this activity in most schools they surveyed.

In conclusion to the volume, Goldring (Chapter 24) explores the role of leadership in boundary spanning. She argues the need for institutional leaders to take an active stance in ensuring that schools/colleges maintain an equilibrium with their environments. This entails balancing the tension between the organization's need to be autonomous and to resist excessive demands, and at the same time to maintain linkages and ensure continuing external support.

Finally, we should add that this collection is inevitably partial, with many omissions. This volume is one of four readers linked to an Open University course, E838 *Effective Leadership and Management in Education*, and many themes not covered in this volume are addressed in the course material or in the three companion readers. It is hoped that this collection will serve to stimulate reflection and the review of practice in the central aspects of management in education which it addresses.

References

Cohen, M. and March, J. (1983) Leadership and ambiguity, in O. Boyd-Barrett, T. Bush, J. Goodey, I. McNay and M. Preedy (eds) *Approaches to Post-School Management*. London: Harper and Row.

Crawford, M., Kydd, L. and Riches, C. (eds) (1996) *Leadership and Teams in Educational Management*. Buckingham: Open University Press.

Doherty, G. D. (ed.) (1994) *Developing Quality Systems in Education*. London: Routledge.

Freeman, R. (1994) Quality assurance in secondary education, *Quality Assurance in Education*, 2 (1): 21–5.

Fullan, M. (1991) *The New Meaning of Educational Change*. London: Cassell.

Further Education Unit/Staff College (1994) *Strategic Planning Handbook*. London: FEU.

Harris, A., Bennett, N. and Preedy, M. (eds) (1996) *Organizational Effectiveness and Improvement in Education*. Buckingham: Open University Press.

HMCI (1995) *Standards and Quality in Education 1993–1994*, Annual Report of Her Majesty's Chief Inspector of Schools. London: HMSO.

Kydd, L., Crawford, M. and Riches, C. (eds) (1996) *Professional Development for Educational Management*. Buckingham: Open University Press.

Louis, K. and Miles, M. B. (1990) *Improving the Urban High School*. New York: Teachers College Press.

National Commission on Education (1996) *Success Against the Odds: Effective schools in disadvantaged areas*. London: Routledge.

Nias, J., Southworth, G. and Campbell, P. (1992) *Whole School Curriculum Development in the Primary School*. London: Falmer Press.

Nixon, J. (1995) Managing the school curriculum for the new millennium, in J. Bell and B. Harrison (eds) *Vision and Values in Managing Education*. London: David Fulton Publishers.

Patterson, J., Purkey, S. and Parker, J. (1986) *Productive School Systems for a Non-rational World*. Alexandria, VA: Association for Supervision and Curriculum Development.

Ribbins, P. and Burridge, E. (1994) Promoting improvement in schools, in P. Ribbins and E. Burridge (eds) *Improving Education: Promoting quality in schools*. London: Cassell.

Stuart, N. (1994) Quality in education, in P. Ribbins and E. Burridge (eds) *op. cit.*

Wallace, M. and McMahon, A. (1994) *Planning for Change in Turbulent Times*. London: Cassell.

PART 1

Developing quality

2 | Monitoring educational quality*

PETER CUTTANCE

Introduction

It is important to distinguish between quality management and quality control. Centralised systems have tended to depend on quality control as their primary means of quality assurance. Quality control in such systems can be characterised as:

- input orientated – as exemplified by its focus on administrative controls over inputs to the system. Most of the form-filling in bureaucratic systems is designed to meet the purpose of control over inputs.
- inspection orientated – that is, inspection of the outputs to select out or redesignate practices and items which do not meet pre-defined service or product standards.

Quality control systems

Most education systems have always exercised some control over the quality of their output. Typically this has taken the form of *inspection* of the outputs from the system. Inspection in education systems has taken one of two forms: the system-wide testing of student achievement, or the use of professional inspectors to assess the standard of student work [. . .].

In principle, classical inspection systems are not primarily designed to *assure* that quality outcomes are provided, but rather to control and certify the quality of the products produced for public consumption. They ascertain which 'goods' are defective and therefore require to be reworked. In education such 'reworking' is an aspect of processes such as the retention of students until they have reached a particular standard and the formal non-certification of some students. In terms of quality control,

* This material has been abridged and was originally published as 'Monitoring educational quality through performance indicators for school practice'.

uncertified students, that is, those who leave school without any formal credentials, are a parallel in the education system to defective goods produced by a manufacturer and sold as 'seconds'. The manufacturer does not stamp such goods with their premier (quality) marque. The existence of unlabelled lines of products (often referred to as 'specials') from manufacturers is usually a symptom of poor quality management.

Quality management systems

The alternative to sole reliance on input controls and inspection systems is to focus on *quality management* systems. Quality management systems attempt to *assure* quality through the introduction of appropriate processes for the management and monitoring of operations. That is, they attempt to integrate the process of work with the necessary mechanisms for assuring quality at each stage of the process. Plans indicating clear outcomes and strategies of how those are to be achieved, review systems and audit procedures are basic components of quality management approaches.

To be effective such approaches must be integrated into everyday work practices. The *quality system* itself also requires a meta level quality assurance mechanism. Systemic quality assurance is based on audit and review of operational units to ensure that they have effective quality management systems, plus the direct monitoring of the quality of outcomes. At the school-level this requires the introduction and maintenance of systems to continuously monitor the effectiveness of strategies and practices – a key function of *action plans*.

Monitoring systems should be designed to provide frequent assessments of progress so that action to correct any undesirable effects can be taken at the first sign of things not working the way they were expected to. It is more important that the monitoring system be simple and that observations be made frequently, than always be guaranteed to give the right answer.

Although the quality of outcomes themselves must be continuously monitored, the system is referred to as a quality management system because it aims to assure quality outcomes by monitoring that the processes implemented lead to the intended intermediate outcomes in every aspect of the system's operation.

Quality assurance in devolved systems

Devolved systems require the introduction of quality assurance processes, because they do not have recourse to the quality control mechanisms provided by centralised administrative systems. The lack of such control systems is not considered a disadvantage, however, because the emphasis they place on inputs is now considered inappropriate and counter productive. Management perspectives now almost universally emphasise the need to focus not on inputs, but on *outputs* and *outcomes*.

Effective management requires a well-developed statement of outcomes, clear responsibility structures and quality assurance systems designed to assess progress in meeting these outcomes. Unclear or undefined outcomes do not provide for clear delegation of responsibility. Individuals and groups can only be properly held accountable for achieving well defined outcomes. In the absence of clear objectives accountability becomes vague and unenforceable. Bureaucratic centralised systems fall back on the process of checking whether administrative instructions have been followed, rather than assessing how well educational outcomes have been met. A centralised system necessarily operates by rules, set procedures and statute in order to reduce the number of problematic decisions that officials at the centre have to take. In the case of the education system these rules are of major as well as of minor scale and they militate against the overall responsiveness of the system.

Such rules are frequently not only inappropriate and inflexible: they also create a multitude of administrative forms and bureaucratic arrangements which take time to produce, time to update, time to understand, and time to comply with (or avoid). Such an approach leads to a great deal of effort being devoted at all levels to rule making and rule breaking rather than to establishing goals and parameters for achievements and then setting out to achieve these.

Audit and review processes are fundamental to the delivery of high quality outcomes in devolved systems. Audit essentially serves accountability purposes, but also provides information from which specific types of systemic performance indicators can be constructed. Review processes are important throughout all stages of the process of delivering high quality education to students. In fact, review – through continuous work place monitoring by those doing the work – is a basic component of the management of quality outcomes.

There is a false belief held by some supporters of devolved systems that such systems can be held accountable on the basis of outcomes and outputs alone, thus substantially removing the need for the continuous review function. This belief assumes that clients will exercise judgement about the quality of the service provided and adjust their demand for the service in light of this. While this perspective is built on sound consumer demand theory it is somewhat less relevant to the production of a quality service in the public sector.

Three arguments can be put forward to substantiate the need for audit and review functions in a devolved state education system. First, accountability to parliament requires not only that useful service is provided to clients, but that the service is efficient and provides value for money – state education is essentially an oligopoly in terms of markets, therefore, changes in client demand do not accurately reflect efficiency. Further, the essentially 'free' nature of state education to the client means that any assessment based simply on consumer demand provides a poor guide to quality, because a 'free' service provides no opportunities to assess the elasticity of demand for that service.

Second, client-led accountability systems do not provide direct feedback as to why a service is providing or not providing quality service – that is, demand information does not contain data on the characteristics of quality to which clients are responding. This is true even in unconstrained markets. In fact, producers of goods and services in competitive markets find it more – not less – important to undertake substantial product and service delivery reviews. Consumer market research is a very substantial industry, particularly in highly competitive markets.

Third, the management – as opposed to the inspection – of quality requires continuous review throughout every aspect of development, production and delivery. An efficient system for assessing quality does not rely solely on inspection at the end of the production process as the primary means of indicating that a service is inferior – something, which incidentally, management has no interest in producing – and management cannot rely on a decline in demand, as clients turn to other providers' services, to tell them that their service is of inferior quality.

Accountability or development: two masters or one?

There is a duality in the concepts of accountability and development applicable to education systems. Accountability refers to the *proving* of quality and development to the *improving* of quality. Clearly, systems based on input controls and those with a specific focus on outputs address the issue of accountability directly, although from quite different perspectives. However, they pay little attention to the contribution that accountability processes might make to the development needs of an organisation. The advantage gained by adopting a quality management perspective is that of binding the process of accountability and development into a unified structure. Whilst it is important for operational reasons to maintain a distinction between accountability and development outcomes, it is important for the overall effectiveness of an organisation that accountability and development are seen as complementary. Accountability systems need to be established in a way which maximises their contribution to the development of the organisation.

Strategic planning for school development

One of the key processes bringing accountability and development together is strategic planning. Over [recent] years all Australian state education systems have developed strategic plans for the implementation of policies and programs. Such systemic plans have been further augmented by development and management plans for each of the operational units in the system.

Schools have also established plans for their own development. These are known as *school development plans*. School development plans are a statement of the key programs and activities that the school wants to change or improve (objectives); how these improvements are to be achieved (strategies); and what their impact will be (outcomes); to improve learning outcomes for students. A school development plan is only one aspect of a school's total planning process. It describes the school's priority areas for development, but it does not encompass the on-going maintenance activities of the school. The objectives as they are identified in the school development plan arise from two sources: the programs and policies which the government has mandated for implementation in schools, and the particular aspirations of schools and their communities. Action plans are developed by schools to address the objectives stated in their school development plans. The processes by which school development plans identify their objectives and implement them are crucial to their success. The objectives themselves and the implementation process must focus as directly as possible on increasing educational outcomes for students.

The systemic strategic plan, along with school development plans, normally have a three-year time horizon and each is rolled-forward after an annual review of progress.

Performance indicators in education

[. . .]

The quality management approach described in earlier sections of this paper is based on the perspective that within any part of the education system an operational unit or an individual worker is simultaneously a client of the services provided in support to them from other parts of the system and a producer of services or products to other parts of the system. Hence, at any one point in the structure the operation of a unit or an individual can be viewed as a performance in the context of the requirements of their clients.

Indicator systems in education have been proposed in order to address a range of different issues. The main uses that have been suggested for them include:

- assessing the impact of educational reforms
- informing policy makers of the practices that are most effective for improving education
- explaining causes of conditions and changes
- informing decision-making and management
- stimulating and focusing effort
- ensuring accountability
- defining educational objectives
- monitoring standards and trends
- forecasting future changes.

Each of the above uses of indicator systems in education is discussed in more detail in Cuttance (1989). Oakes (1986) has suggested that there are five types of information that indicators can provide at the operational level. These are:

- performance information in relation to the achievement of goals and objectives
- information on the features of the system that are most important in achieving particular goals and objectives
- policy relevant information
- problem orientated information
- information on *central* features of the system.

Table 2.1 cross-classifies these five types of information against the nine purposes set out earlier for education indicator systems. The five types of information can be subdivided into those which are derived from *evaluations* of the system and those which are derived from routine *monitoring* of the system. The category of 'policy relevant information' is applicable to information from both evaluation and monitoring sources. Also, a certain amount of 'problem orientated information' will be made available through the diagnostic and formative components of formal *evaluation* activities, but its main source will be from *monitoring* activities in the system. From Table 2.1 it is clear that some of the purposes put forward for education indicators draw more heavily on *monitoring* activities and others draw more heavily on *evaluation* activities. Thus, an indicator system which encompasses all nine purposes would need to gather information from both formal and informal evaluations and from routine monitoring of the system.

The purposes of performance indicators described above are subsumed under the more general functions of quality assurance, development and accountability in education systems discussed earlier in this chapter.

Table 2.1 Purposes of education indicator systems and the types of information they need to provide

Purpose of performance indicator	Type of information required				
	Evaluation			Monitoring	
	Achievement of goals and objectives	Features responsible for performance	Policy relevant information	Problem orientated information	Information about central features of the system
Assessing impact of reforms	X	X	X		
Assessing most effective practice	X	X	X	X	
Explaining causes and conditions	X	X	X	X	X
Decision-making and management	X	X	X	X	X
Stimulating and focusing effort	X	X	X	X	X
Ensuring accountability	X		X		X
Defining objectives		X	X		X
Monitoring standards and trends			X	X	X
Forecasting future change			X	X	X

Strategic information to assist the improvement of school systems

Cooley (1983) discusses the information requirements for improving education systems. [. . .] The 'rational' model of decision making posits that systems make decisions, and act on them, in response to data and frameworks for deliberative action. Action-based models, such as those embodied in change strategies involving a significant degree of stakeholder participation posit that the 'political' environment of the organisation is a determining factor in both shaping the data and the orientation to action.

The quality management literature, on the other hand, emphasises gradual or continuous improvement rather than structural or large scale change. Quality management approaches can be criticised for a failure to recognise the necessity for both continuous improvement and significant structural change in complex organisations (Cuttance 1993). Both continuous improvement and structural change require ongoing monitoring systems to assess progress towards desired outcomes.

Cooley (1983) provides a discussion of the key factors for successful monitoring in school systems. He argues that there are two primary features of such systems for the continuous monitoring of progress:

- a client orientation, and
- a systems approach to program improvement.

Client orientation

A client orientation is necessary if the data made available from the monitoring system are to influence the alternative perspectives that decision makers bring to the situation. Without a clear and agreed position of who the clients are, and there may be more than one type of client, the information gathered through the monitoring system will have little relevance to decisions that focus on improving the outcomes of the system. The value of information in relation to outcomes for clients is not that the data determine priorities to settle policy issues but that they permit those issues to be argued more productively (Cooley 1983). A client orientation in the monitoring system requires that the system itself allow for interaction with clients in the data gathering process.

[. . .]

A systems approach to improvement

The systems approach that Cooley describes is focussed on the continuous use of indicators to monitor performance and adapt practice to the requirements of the situation. This is contrasted with the alternative of employing periodic summative evaluations to assess the success of discrete programs. The approach of summative program evaluation provides a static view of the performance of a program. Programs, however, are dynamic and are continually impacted by other extant programs, new programs and general turbulence and influences in the system's environment. Further, program evaluations take a significant time to complete and it is not uncommon to hear that decision makers had to make the decision before the information from the evaluation that was available.

This does not mean that there is not a role for summative program evaluations in assessing the performance of school systems, rather that the role should not be seen as one which can provide responsive information of a dynamic nature as required for management decision making. Summative program evaluations aim to provide infrequent but accurate information, whereas the need of decision makers is for frequent information, even if it is somewhat less accurate at each occasion. The power of the data provided from a monitoring system is gained from its contribution of contextual understanding to the working knowledge of the decision maker and the corroborative information to flag situations where performance has moved out of the expected range in specific sectors of the system or over time. Such monitoring information allows the decision maker to take action as appropriate in response to information that things are not proceeding according to the way that they were expected to do so. The accumulation of information from such monitoring systems can provide the basis for establishing the areas in which a system needs to focus its attention in improving overall performance.

Monitoring systems can also provide an indication of the distribution of performance throughout the school system in relation to a particular indicator. This supports meta-level inferences indicating whether the system is performing uniformly or whether there are performance issues that require attention in particular parts of the system. For example, in a school system there may be particular performance issues in the high school sector that are not found in the primary school sector. The adaptiveness of teaching strategies to student learning styles is one such issue of relevance to Australian school systems.

Where monitoring over time provides information that performance is deteriorating or not meeting expectations after focussed corrective action has been taken, there is a need to establish a broader understanding as to the nature of the problem. This provides an important and fundamental role for program evaluation. The contribution of program evaluations to system performance rests less on summative information than on formative and diagnostic analysis of the issues responsible for performance. Clearly, an assessment of the summative performance of a program is required before any analysis of the issues impeding the achievement of program objectives can be undertaken, but this by itself is of little utility in managing the performance of a school system. Decision makers require an analysis of the potential responses they could make to particular performance problems. The solution should not be bound entirely by the program under evaluation, as management also requires to assess the likely impact of any response on other programs.

The outcome of an effective monitoring system, therefore, is guidance for priority setting and the provision of data to inform appropriate action, which may be focussed corrective action. Over time a monitoring system should also provide information about how the school system is responding to changes in its external environment. This information should be extrapolated to provide limited 'over the horizon radar'.

Monitoring the effectiveness of school practice and functioning

The remaining sections of this chapter report on a system that was established in an Australian state school system to monitor the practice and functioning in schools. The primary purpose of the monitoring system was to report on performance with respect to particular practices across the system as a whole in order to monitor the effectiveness of programs and policies in achieving the system's planned strategic outcomes. Ongoing reviews of practice were conducted in four *domains*: teaching and learning, organisation and management, ethos and culture, and equal opportunities and social justice. Each domain addressed five to eight *areas* of school activity. Three to five *aspects* of performance were developed to report on each of the areas of activity reviewed. In total this provides about 100 profiles of performance across the four domains of practice. In general, only one of the four domains of practice was reviewed in each school.

The monitoring statements were developed by teams of school-based teachers, principals and superintendents. In drawing up the statements of practice in each of the aspects to be reviewed these teams drew upon the research literature in the relevant area, the Department's guidelines and policy statements relevant to that aspect, and their own experience as educators in schools. The monitoring statements were then trialed in various reviews and revised before being incorporated into the regular development review process in schools. [. . .]

The gathering of the information in school reviews is context sensitive – in particular, consideration is given as to whether or not it is appropriate to expect a particular practice to occur in the situation being observed.

The monitoring data will be assessed also for its relationship to student learning. The purpose of such assessment will be to evaluate the relative importance of different practices for the educational development and progress of students.

The information obtained from the monitoring program will be used to diagnose systemic performance weaknesses and monitor trends in the school system as a whole. Further, it provides summative information on the standard of practice that exists in the system. This information provides important input into policy formulation, and strategic decision making and resource allocation.

The information from the monitoring program will also be linked to departmental programs and policies. A two dimensional matrix with programs and policies on one axis and practice indicators on the other establishes the linkage between individual aspects of effective practice and particular programs and policies. Thus, the monitoring program provides an on-going basis for monitoring the effectiveness of individual programs and policies. However, the range of practices monitored is broader than the set of systemic programs and policies. That is, various aspects of practice that are not specifically addressed by programs or policies are also monitored.

The monitoring statements may be prepared for use in other contexts in the system. In particular, some schools have expressed an interest in using them as an internal screening device in their own development and planning practices, and other schools have expressed an interest in using them in staff training and development sessions.

Reviewing performance of school practice and functioning

One domain of practice is monitored in each school review. Information is collected from staff and a cross-section of parents and students, mainly through interviews and discussions. In addition, relevant documents may be examined. However, direct observation also plays an important part in gathering information. Observation by the review team of the general environment of the school, student recreation and study areas, classrooms, staff-rooms, etc, is undertaken. Depending on the domain of practice being monitored in a particular school, discussions may also be held with specific individuals, such as those responsible for the financial management of the school, those with key responsibilities for curriculum development and implementation, etc. The types of documents that may be perused as part of the information gathering exercise include: school newsletters, parent and staff information booklets, teacher work plans, student records and reports, minutes of school meetings, etc.

The domains of management and organisation, ethos and culture, and equal opportunities and social justice use the school as the unit for reporting. Reporting on the domain of teaching and learning is based on the classroom as the unit of observation. This latter domain involves considerably more classroom observation than the other three domains. [. . .] There is discussion with the individual teacher before the observation period and again after the observation period. The purpose of the observation is to gather information about normal practice in schools. No special preparation is required by teachers. The observation is not linked to any process of teacher appraisal. Hence, no feedback is given about the general effectiveness of the teacher, although the review team member may discuss some aspects of practice that were observed during the session with the teacher, if the latter so desires.

Since the monitoring program has the specific purpose of improving the quality of practice and functioning in schools, the recording of information is based on categorical statements that relate to the extent of the implementation of practice in the situation observed. Three decisions have to be made by the observer about each aspect reviewed. The first is whether or not there is sufficient data on which to make an assessment of the effectiveness of the practice associated with that aspect. The second decision is whether the practice in that aspect is regarded as effective or not effective as described by the description in the practice indicator statement. The third decision requires a distinction to be made between levels of effectiveness (or ineffectiveness). The reviewer assesses whether the practice observed is regarded as effective at an outstanding level (EO) or at a satisfactory level (ES). Similarly practice which is regarded as ineffective is classified according to whether or not this has been recognised (by the teacher or the school) as an aspect of functioning which requires development and for which planning for improvement is in hand (NCP), or whether that aspect of functioning has not yet been acknowledged as requiring improvement (NN).

An annual report from the monitoring program is published for each of the four domains of practice. These reports do not identify individual schools or teachers. They highlight aspects of practice that have been found to be particularly effective and make recommendations where performance is considered to be in need of further development in schools, or where the practice appears to require further development in schools serving particular sections of the student population. These recommendations may lead to more indepth reviews of particular policies or programs which are responsible for supporting those areas of practice found to need the most improvement. Such further reviews may evaluate a particular program or policy, or a group of them, or they may focus on particular aspects of functioning and practice in schools. The analysis assists the effective utilisation of systemic resources for improvement in key areas and thus supports schools in their function of providing high quality education for students.

Findings for a state school system

[. . .]

The monitoring data presented here are for 128 schools reviewed in 1990 [. . .] The overall assessment from the reviews indicated that 42 percent of schools reviewed were well advanced in terms of their development planning and were able to effectively manage and sustain their own development. Thirty percent were found to be able to establish the necessary structures and processes for sustainable development with the normal assistance and support provided by area and system programs. Seventeen percent were found to be in need of early and continuing support to establish the necessary structures and processes for sustainable development. Twelve percent of schools were found to be in need of substantial support over a prolonged period in order to establish the structures and processes for sustainable development. Significant leadership and organisational development and change is likely to be necessary to establish the basis for effective development in this latter group of schools.

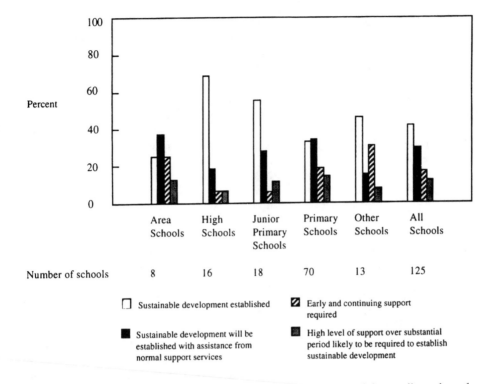

Figure 2.1 Development of schools by level of schooling. Because of the small number of schools reviewed at some levels of schooling, care must be exercised in interpreting the differences in these assessments. The estimates should be read as indicating the range of variation between different types of schools. These are aggregate group statistics, therefore they do not indicate the assessment pertaining to specific schools in a group.

Summary

The following is a summary of the data obtained from the reviews in 128 schools in 1990. It is presented for two domains of practice and functioning [teaching and learning, and management and organisation]. [. . .]

The monitoring program found that for most aspects of classroom functioning, practices were effective in the vast majority of classrooms, and in a considerable proportion, were very effective. The findings indicated that procedures for the systematic monitoring and review of the curriculum needed further development in at least 50 percent of classrooms. There is some evidence to suggest that practices which effectively supported students' development of learning strategies were less evident than those which supported their social development. There was also an indication in the findings that more attention was required in some classrooms to the use of a wider range of resources and teaching approaches to acknowledge and support student differences.

[. . .]

The performance of management in the use of resources beyond the direct school environment and of buildings and grounds was highly effective in most schools.

Aspects of management relating to staffing and students were performed effectively in more than half of all schools. Some specific aspects of general management – particularly those relating to decision making, staff training and development and the supervision and support of staff, required further development in more than half of all schools. Aspects of management relating to school planning, particularly, context setting for planning, school management planning and internal review processes for school development planning, also require further development in more than half of all schools. The areas requiring most comprehensive development across the system were those relating to curriculum management: curriculum review and relevance, and program evaluation.

Discussion

The system of monitoring practice and functioning that has been established had been developed as one component of the broader review and development structure.

The assessment of the information from the domains of *teaching and learning* and *management and organisation* indicated that the effectiveness of practice and functioning in the latter domain was in need of more development than in the former. The information available from the performance indicators for both domains indicated that strengths were found in the non-curriculum aspects of schooling and that future attention in the development of schools needed to be directed towards curriculum issues: particularly, planning, maintenance, development and review of curriculum and programs within schools; the organisation and strategies for the effective use within schools of resources to deliver the curriculum, including staff training and development; and the management and review of development in schools.

The monitoring program is undertaken as part of a school review program that provided direct assistance to schools in assessing their performance and areas for further development. As such, the monitoring program is undertaken in a non-threatening context and provides information directly relevant to decision making and resource allocation at the system level. It provides continuous feed-back on a wide range of aspects of performance and functioning across the system. Further, it provides the opportunity to continuously research the impact of a wide range of practices in schools on the improvement of student outcomes. These research analyses provide feedback to the teams working with schools to provide context sensitive information on what works in different situations. Although in the state in which this analysis was based the program had not impacted directly on priorities at the system level there is evidence from another state that such programs can have a powerful impact on both strategic decision making and resource allocation.

The type of indicators employed in this program are much more complex than the simple global indicators which are often the focus of indicator systems in education. The depth of information conveyed by these indicators provides the type of information that senior management in school systems require. They contain sufficient information to obviate the need to initiate an *ad hoc* investigation each time an indicator suggests that a program or policy is not having its intended impact, but are not so cumbersome and costly to operate that they are impractical.

References

Cooley, W. W. (1983) Improving the performance of an education system, *Educational Researcher*, 12: 4–12.

Cuttance, P. F. (1989) *Performance Indicators for Schooling*, report prepared for the Scottish Education Department. Edinburgh: Scottish Education Department.

Cuttance, P. F. (1993) Quality assurance and quality management: complementary but different functions, *Evaluation*, 218–23.

Oakes, J. (1986) *Education Indicators: A Guide for Policy Makers*. New Jersey: Centre for Policy Studies in Education, Rutgers University.

3 | Quality and equality: competing or complementary objectives?

KATHRYN A. RILEY

Quality and equality are interconnected: not separate entities but inseparable features of any good education provision. Fostering quality and equality requires an awareness of the obstacles which individuals face in achieving their potential and of the barriers which obstruct harmonious relationships between groups and individuals. Resolving such equality issues is a route to quality.

The equality issue facing pupils and teachers also needs to be viewed together. The differential educational experience offered to girls and boys, black and white pupils is connected to that offered to teachers – female and male, black and white. Equality in the classroom cannot be separated from equality in the staffroom. It is a shared agenda – a shared experience.

In seeking to develop a strategy which incorporates both quality and equality, tensions and dilemmas are bound to arise for providers and receivers of the education services because decisions about the nature of services, who receives them and how they are delivered are not neutral. They depend on value judgements made by those involved in education: teachers, governors, administrators and policy-makers. Each of these groups has varying degrees of discretion to influence educational processes and outcomes. Decisions that they make – or fail to make – will impact differentially on students and staff. This chapter explores the context of the debate on quality and equality and the scope which the key groups have to influence both educational processes and outcomes.

The quest for quality

Over the past decade quality has been the buzzword: *quality services*, a *quality educational experience*, total *quality management*. Quality has entered into the vocabulary of the educational professionals, politicians and the myriad individuals, groups and organizations that claim a stake in the education service.

But although quality in education has apparently become a national goal, definitions are elusive, or maybe illusory. A major OECD report on schools and quality has argued against providing one simple definition of quality in education and has suggested instead that we need a clearer understanding of how context – curriculum, school organization, resources and facilities, and evaluation of pupils, teachers and systems – can contribute to quality (OECD 1989). As with any value-laden concept, definitions of quality change over time and vary for different individuals and groups. Attempts to improve quality raise questions about the aims of society, the purposes of schooling and the nature of participation.

Much current thinking about the concept of quality has originated in the manufacturing sector. Concerns about manufacturing quality and standards stem from the late nineteenth- and early twentieth-century decline in skilled workers and the consequent difficulties caused for mass production. Quality control was introduced in the 1920s in an attempt to increase the percentage of sound products manufactured. After World War II there was a shift in emphasis from quality control to quality assurance, an activity which focused on the pre-production planning in an attempt to develop processes and procedures that would minimize faulty production.

The 'quality revolution' took place in Japan in the 1950s assisted by seminal figures such as Deming and Duran (Macdonald and Piggott, 1990). Deming emphasized quality assurance and the importance of creating a quality culture. He argued that until the 1950s definitions of quality in manufacturing had tended to rest on what the experts thought customers wanted, rather than on information about what customers actually wanted.

The rise of consumerism, particularly in the USA, shifted attention to the customer voice. Quality became everyone's business. Customers would make decisions about quality, insomuch as they could exercise choice by withholding their purchasing power. This approach has been sustained through the 1980s and into the 1990s by theorists such as Peters and Waterman (1982), who have argued that being 'closer to the customer' is a fundamental attribute of a successful company.

Quality in the public and private sectors

Manufacturing and other private sector notions of quality began to permeate the public sector in the UK at the national level with the election of the 1979 Conservative government, and [. . .] they have been linked to the development of measures to assess performance of public sector organizations. Many local authorities have responded to the quality drive by developing a new focus on services and customers and by finding new ways to evaluate the quality and impact of their services.

There are difficulties, however, in transferring private sector models about quality into the public sector. To begin with, the common language increasingly used in both the public and private sector masks some fundamental differences. The term 'customer', for example, is used today for shoppers as well as for users of services such as education.

But the education 'customer' hardly resembles the supermarket shopper. The purchasing power of the education consumer is limited. Only a minority have the financial power to exit from the public education service. And exercising this power will not pressurize the management to improve the service; indeed, if those who can afford to exit the service do so, the pressure for public sector resources for education falls, having lost the involvement of the wealthiest, most powerful and articulate parents. All parents as 'customers' of the education service supposedly have the right to choose a school, but not necessarily the possibility of exercising that choice. Indeed, there is increasing evidence to suggest that it is schools that are choosing parents and children. Furthermore, the education customer *has* to buy; the super-market customer can just walk out of the shop without purchasing.

The education service has become imbued with the language and concepts of quality. Many local education authorities have striven to develop the mechanisms and processes of inspection as one essential way of validating quality and of giving certain key stakeholders in education (headteachers and governors) a handle.

> The fundamental principle is that headteachers and governors must have a view about quality. The inspectors' role is to authenticate that view. It is essential that schools have an objective evaluation of quality . . . For these you need pro-cedures and competency.
>
> (Riley 1992a: 14)

Other local education authorities have set up quality assurance teams, or have described their activities in marketing or business terms: 'quality control', 'managing a franchise'. [. . .]

However, [. . .] in the light of recent legislation, local authorities will have to develop very different approaches to quality. Essential to any new framework [is] the need to integrate equality issues – the wider lessons from equalities work have rarely been incorporated into broader quality goals – and to have clarity about the differ-ences between quality in the public and private sectors.

Skelcher (1992) has argued that the differences between the way that the public and commercial sectors approach quality spring from their structural characteristics. There are differences in *accountability* (local authorities have a wider and more public range of accountability structures than the private sector); *choice* (local authorities work to enable local citizens to exercise choice: choice in commercial enterprises is linked to market concerns); and *purpose* (local authorities have a range of purposes: the pro-vision of services, regulation, facilitation of local needs: commercial purposes are not exclusively but are largely geared to profit). All of these differences, summarized in Table 3.1, govern the way the two kinds of enterprise deal with their customers.

Despite these differences, commercial and public sector are united in needing to get it right for both customers and staff. Skelcher argues, however, that local authorities have not been sufficiently customer-orientated in the past, nor had a clear enough focus on quality. A strategy for quality requires a clearer information base about ser-vice usage; improved access to services; the development of performance indicators which are customer-based; and changes in organizational culture so that professional differences do not create barriers to service provision.

Customer care initiatives (identifying who the customers are and what they want, and examining the impact of services on particular groups) have been one way in which local authorities have tried to focus more clearly on quality. Improving quality requires authorities to recognize the needs, background and experiences of individuals

Table 3.1   Comparison of local government and commercial sectors

	Local government	*Commercial*
Accountability	Extensive Open	Limited Closed
Choice	Wide value base Political process Customer also citizen	Narrow value base Managerial process Limited influence customer
Purpose	Multiple	Narrow

Source: Skelcher (1992)

and also to recognize that services are of value only if they are judged to be of value by recipients [. . .].

Creating a bridge between quality and equality

But quality strategies can succeed in meeting the needs of customers only if they take into account the diverse views and perspectives of a range of groups. Quality is not a universal concept: what represents quality for one user may not do so for another. 'Specifying service quality will always involve considering how users experience and evaluate a service and understanding the circumstances in which they will use it' (Stewart and Walsh 1990: 4).

In assessing the impact of services on particular groups, customer care initiatives have begun to grapple with the links between quality and equality. Stewart and Walsh have suggested that three essential elements contribute to a framework for quality:

- whether the core service fits the purpose for which it was designed;
- the physical surroundings in which the service is delivered;
- and the service relationship between those who provide and those who receive the service.

This framework is a useful one for examining the inter-relationship between quality and equality. The core services question, 'Does the service meet the requirements of those for whom it is provided?', cannot be answered without knowing who the customers are: their gender, ethnic background and age. Similarly, the physical and social conditions of provision have to be viewed in the context of whether the services are physically accessible and whether customers, or clients, are encouraged or discouraged from taking up the service. Finally, the quality of the service relationship depends on whether those who are delivering the service understand the needs of those who are receiving the service. The questions posed in Figure 3.1 apply not only to local authorities but also to schools and institutions.

The integration of equality issues within quality initiatives is, however, problematic. Tensions and dilemmas can be created by competing priorities about consumer satisfaction, effective use of resources and staff satisfaction.

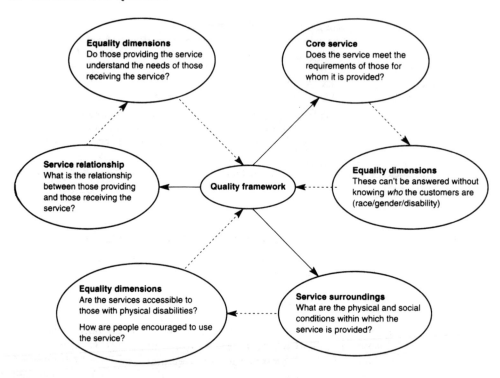

Figure 3.1 Quality and equality: an inter-related network

Evaluation of whether consumer satisfaction has been achieved highlights the tension between judging quality in terms of general levels of satisfaction and looking at quality from the perspective of disadvantaged groups. Satisfaction levels may vary between those who have experienced targeted improvement and other groups.

The objective of achieving the most effective use of resources has to be viewed within the context of diminishing resources for local authorities, colleges and schools. In striving for 'value for money' there is a tension between devoting resources to activities which will benefit the community at large and devoting resources to those which will provide most benefit to disadvantaged groups. For example, a 'One O'Clock' club may act as a general but time-limited amenity for parents in a locality but a day nursery will more effectively serve the needs of single parents who need to seek employment.

In introducing customer care initiatives as part of their core strategy to improve quality, many local authorities have also developed training packages for staff aimed at enhancing autonomy and job satisfaction. But local authorities have limited staff training budgets and will need to make decisions about the balance of resources: general staff training as against targeted training opportunities for disadvantaged groups who have had limited access to training. An emphasis on positive action training will advantage certain groups (women, black and ethnic minorities, people with disabilities) at the expense of the dominant group (white men). (These issues are summarized in Figure 3.2.) Schools and colleges will also have to look at similar issues when allocating training resources.

Objective	Quality	Equality
Consumer satisfaction	General level of consumer satisfaction	Activities may be focused on needs of specific groups
	Quality for one group of users may not be the same for all users	
Effective use of resources	Emphasis on 'value for money' for at large community	Emphasis on disadvantaged groups
	Limited resources may mean services need to be targeted to those in greatest need	
Staff satisfaction	Emphasis on 'customer care' can enhance staff autonomy and job satisfaction overall	Activities aimed at redressing past inequalities
	Emphasis on positive action training may appear to advantage certain groups at expense of dominant group (white men)	

Figure 3.2 Quality and equality: tensions and dilemmas

In resolving these tensions, local authorities, schools and colleges will have to make value judgements based on their assessments about competing priorities. In so doing, they will be exercising their discretion.

Pursuing equality: the art of the possible

The debate about equality has received less national government attention recently than the debate about quality and has often been disparate, fragmented and margina- lized at a local level. [. . .]

It is axiomatic that quality in education is a goal of governments. The pursuit of quality is the *raison d'être* of government: a basis of their mandate. The pursuit of equality, however, is a much more discretionary activity reflecting both the values of national government and the purposes of other policy-makers and practitioners in the system. Given that interpretations of quality are value-laden, it is therefore unsur- prising that national governments have varied significantly in the extent to which they supported equality as a national goal. [. . .]

In the UK the settings for equality policies have been set down in legislation through:

the Disabled Persons Employment Act 1944, which requires organizations of more than 20 people to employ at least 3 per cent registered disabled people (unless they gain an exemption from this duty);

the Sex Discrimination Act 1975 and the Race Relations Act 1976, which cover direct and indirect discrimination in employment and services: the latter also places a duty on local authorities to promote equality of opportunity;

and through the Equal Pay Act 1983, which requires women and men who carry out the same type of work, or work of equal value, to be paid the same.

But British governments over [recent years] have rarely intervened to pursue equality objectives. One notable exception has been in Northern Ireland, where the government has used the strongly interventionist policy of contract compliance to influence employment practices in respect of religious affiliation. The British government also reluctantly agreed to incorporate the concept of equal pay for work of equal value into UK legislation (through the 1983 Equal Pay Act) in response to the jurisdiction of the European courts. In general terms, however, the pursuit of equality objectives in the UK has largely been exercised through the discretionary activities of individuals and organizations.

Discretion is therefore a concept which needs some exploration. It can be defined in a number of ways: narrowly, as how key actors, in exceptional cases, depart from rules that they are expected to follow, [. . .] or, more broadly, as how 'a public officer has discretion within the effective limits of "his" powers to make a choice amongst possible courses of action, or inaction' (Davis 1969, quoted in Lidstrom, 1991).

According to Lidstrom, in this broader definition of discretion organizations, or actors within those organizations, possess a certain scope for choice which is exercised within effective limits. In exercising their discretion actors take into account their own knowledge, judgement, assessment, beliefs and values.

[. . .]

Manley-Casimir (1991) argued that an examination of discretion should be a critical focus of study for those looking at education administration. In his view both education and education administration are value-based normative activities. Decision-making undertaken by key actors in the system cannot be divided into the rational and the intuitive. The exercise of judgement is central to the exercise of decision-making.

[. . .]

In order to understand the significance of discretion in administration, Manley-Casimir suggested that concepts such as power, justice and responsibility needed clarifying and empirical and theoretical work on administrative decision-making from a variety of disciplines needed to be explored.

The issue of administrative discretion has engaged scholars from political theory, public administration, organizational theory, cognitive psychology, sociology, criminology and law. Political theorists have been concerned about discretionary power; criminologists with the presence of discretion in the justice system; administrative theorists with the exercise of discretion on a day-to-day basis. From these concerns two central issues have emerged, both of which are critical to our understanding of education administration: how to ensure that there are safeguards to prevent the abuse of power, and how to deal with the problems of bias in judgement.

[. . .]

Discretion is involved in the judgements and activities of educators at all levels of the system: from classroom teachers to chief education officers. [. . .] Education officers and elected members still have scope, even within the current context of the changes in educational powers and responsibilities, to exercise their discretion in ways that reflect the values and purposes of their organization.

A study of the exercise of discretion by local education authorities contrasted how very different LEAs chose to operate their discretion (Riley 1992b). One LEA used its discretion to maximize the redistribution of resources in pursuit of egalitarian goals. [. . .] A second authority exercised its discretion very differently: to develop its business planning activities in a way that would maximize market forces. [. . .]

[. . . In] the UK the *pursuit* of equal opportunities is largely a discretionary activity, although within a mandatory framework which forbids certain aspects of discrimination. Within this weak national framework, the key to equality of opportunity lies with the major actors in the education service: practitioners, policy-makers and governors. (How education 'consumers' will feature in this framework is as yet unclear.) These key actors can use their discretion to pursue equality, or not. Value concepts and judgements also inform different understandings about equality.

Equality: a contestable concept

Over [recent years], a number of large organizations in both the public and private sector – driven by various circumstances and pressures – have attempted to introduce equality programmes. In local authorities equality programmes have covered council employment policies and the delivery of services and have largely focused on issues of race, gender and disability. Some authorities have also included sexual orientation, class and/or age as further aspects of their policy.

[. . .] Resource maximization and social justice have been the two main arguments used in Britain, and elsewhere, to persuade organizations to tackle inequality. Arguments about social justice prevailed in the 1970s and to a lesser extent in the 1980s. In a number of inner-city areas, black parents' groups were instrumental in forcing questions about racial discrimination (e.g. the disproportionate rates of suspensions, or expulsions, of black students) on to the political agenda. A number of urban authorities were also influenced in the 1980s by the election of a new breed of councillors committed to equalities issues and determined to see significant changes in how local authority decisions were made and resources allocated (Riley 1992b). Many grassroots equality initiatives in education, particularly on gender, were influenced by the experience and activities of classroom teachers (Arnot 1986).

The drive to develop equality programmes in local authority education services was also influenced by evidence of the continuing discrimination experienced by disadvantaged groups:

- Hidden discrimination continued in schools.
- Parental concerns about the schooling of black children helped put issues about race on the education agenda.
- Many black students continued to under-perform in examinations.
- Female students still had unequal access to higher education.
- Female staff employed in the education service had unequal employment opportunities.
- Women in the labour force were still segregated into low-paid occupations.
- The gap between women's and men's pay was higher in the UK than almost any other European Community country.

In the harsher economic climate of the late 1980s and early 1990s arguments about social resource maximization [. . .] found greater favour than arguments about social justice. Equal opportunities arguments about resource maximization within the education service have focused on ensuring that scarce educational resources are used effectively. Equality strategies in education have emphasized the need to develop the potential of all pupils; to retain skilled staff in the organization and increase their effectiveness; and to attract key staff to shortage areas. But equal opportunities is an ambiguous and contested concept based on differing values and assumptions. Attempts to introduce equality policies have frequently led to confusion, misunderstanding and conflict (Riley 1990).

Equal opportunity strategies have largely been premissed on one of two interpretations of equality: *equality of opportunity* and *equality of outcome*. Each of these two approaches is based on differing assumptions about the nature of inequality, the action needed to tackle it and the goals. The liberal interpretation of equality, equality of opportunity, has been concerned with ensuring that the rules of the game (for employment, or access to courses, or examinations) are set out fairly. The assumption has been that rigorous administrative controls and formalized systems will ensure that fair play takes place and create the circumstances in which previously disadvantaged groups compete equally with other groups of students, or employees.

The more radical conception of equality, equality of outcome, has been concerned about widening access (to courses, or to employment) through action designed to redress past inequalities. It has been an essentially interventionist strategy aimed at redistributing resources and opportunities to disadvantaged groups. Its success or failure has been measured in terms of outcomes and the degree to which disadvantaged groups have achieved access to power and resources.

It has been suggested that both approaches are vulnerable to the accusation that they promise more than they can deliver but that elements of both are required for future developments [. . .]. Be that as it may, it is obvious that the context for tackling inequality has shifted dramatically over [recent] years. Public sector spending has gradually been reduced. Overall national spending on education, for example, has declined as a proportion of GDP [. . .]. Legislative and financial changes, in education and other areas of local government, have shifted power from local government to central government, and from local government to schools and institutions. The power to influence equality issues is increasingly with the new stakeholders in education [. . .].

Quality and equality

Quality and equality, as already stated, are not identical concepts, although they are interrelated. *Quality is about levels and standards: equality about power and resources.* A tension exists between the two which is based on values and ideology. Through the exercise of their discretion – based on values and judgements – key actors in the system can influence quality and equality outcomes in favour of different groups in the system (see Figure 3.3).

Posing the question *Quality for whom?* highlights the tension between quality and equality, and can result in radically different answers. At a time of financial constraints on public spending in education, the question of quality for whom becomes even more important.

- Is the objective of quality to further raise the standards of the high achievers in order to achieve limited economic imperatives?

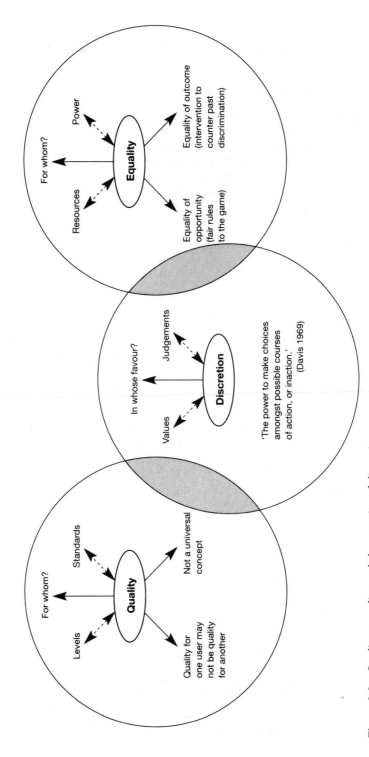

Figure 3.3 Quality, equality and the exercise of discretion

- Is it to raise the standards of low achievers and move the UK up the economic league table?
- Is it to raise the standards and opportunities of particular groups of children: girls, black and ethnic minorities, children with disabilities?
- Fundamentally, is quality rooted on assumptions about universal standards, or on the rights of particular groups?

[I would] argue that the notion of quality should also embrace a concept of equal opportunities which is focused not just on outcomes but on processes – *how* students experience and participate in the education system. Fundamental to this argument is the assertion that the organization and delivery of education services is more than the creation of a product for consumption.

Definitions of quality in education need to include consideration of standards but they also need to consider:

- Who is using the service?
- What are the range and diversity of needs?

If the providers of education services are driven to assuming that their goal is to achieve a common and standard service for all pupils, then we may well see the creation of an education service which is only suitable for a small number. A standard service may focus narrowly on the needs of middle-class, able-bodied white males, thereby ignoring the majority of students: female, black and ethnic minorities, people with disabilities. The organization and delivery of education needs to cater for diversity and changing needs: recognizing the individuality of students and those who deliver education services. A focus on quality and equality engaging those who are involved in education as users and as producers enables this complex process to take place.

> For all groups in society, access to influence and control over education, its contents and methods, is as important a dimension of equality with other groups as any quantitative measure of educational attainment. If equal participation in education by different groups will have any meaning as a measure of equality in educational terms, a precondition must be that the groups have equal share in deciding what education shall be about.
>
> (Eide 1978)

References

Arnot, M. (1986) Sex discrimination and educational change, *Module 4: Race, Gender and Education Policy-making* (Open University Course E333). Milton Keynes: Open University.

Davis, K. C. (1969) *Discretionary Justice*. Baton Rouge, USA: Louisiana State University Press.

Eide, K. (1978) Some key problems of equality in education. Paper for IIEP/Inter-agency seminar on educational development, 27–30 November.

Lidstrom, A. (1991) Discretion: an art of the possible, research report 1991, 5. Department of Political Science: University of Umeå, Sweden.

Manley-Casimir, M. (1991) Taking the road not taken: reframing education administration for another day in P. Ribbins, R. Glatter, T. Simkins and L. Watson (eds) *Developing Education Leaders*. Harlow: Longman/BEMAS.

OECD (1989) *Schools and Quality: an international report*. Paris: OECD.

Peters, T. and Waterman, R. (1982) *In Search of Excellence*. New York: Harper and Row.

Riley, K. (1990) Equality for women – the role of local authorities, *Local Government Studies*, Jan–Feb., pp. 49–68.

Riley, K. (1992a) *Education Indicators and the Search for Quality*. Luton: Local Government Management Board.

Riley, K. (1992b) The changing framework and purposes of education authorities, *Research Papers in Education, Policy and Practice*, 7 (1): 3–25.

Skelcher, C. (1992) Improving the quality of local public services, *Service Industries Journal*, 12 (4): 463–77.

Stewart, J. and Walsh, K. (1990) *In Search of Quality*. Luton: Local Government Management Board.

4 | Continuous improvement and quality standards*

FURTHER EDUCATION UNIT

Introduction

Continuous quality improvement is a subject about which much is currently written and spoken. It is a feature of the various approaches to quality commonly adopted by colleges. The practical guidance which follows is designed to assist colleges in improving the quality of the services they provide by:

- establishing continuous quality improvement within the mission and culture of the corporation;
- identifying priority areas for improvement of services within the strategic planning process;

Glossary
In this chapter the following terminology is used:

Desired features: those features of any service identified by its customers and agreed by the college as being important, e.g. speed is a desired feature in the return of marked work.

Quality standard: the level of performance that can be expected for any given feature of the service, e.g. all marked work should be returned within five working days of being handed in.

Measures: the ways in which actual performance is monitored against the quality standards, e.g. assignment records or a student survey could both measure whether the quality standard relating to the return of marked work, above, had been met.

Improvement target: an agreed specified improvement to be achieved by a given period, e.g. all marked work to be returned within four working days or an increase in satisfaction about the return of marked work from 85% to 90%.

---

* This material has been abridged.

- setting up quality councils and quality initiative groups (QIGs);
- using quality standards, measures and improvement targets.

It is intended for:

- senior college managers and those with responsibility for managing quality at college level;
- staff with responsibility for improving specified services within the college;
- staff development managers with responsibility for programmes to help staff develop the skills to contribute to continuous quality improvement and to become effective members of QIGs.

The context

The major challenge facing FE [Further Education] corporations is to increase participation and improve achievement. They must do this while maintaining and improving quality and making more efficient use of available resources.

Strategic and operational planning have acquired even greater significance since incorporation and colleges have now been through the process of submitting plans to the Further Education Funding Councils (FEFCs).

In order to meet the requirements of the funding councils for strategic planning, colleges will already have:

- a college mission;
- undertaken a needs analysis;
- a three-year strategic plan;
- an operational plan.

This means they will have:

Needs analysis
- found out, by market research, what people want and need from the college;
- considered current provision;
- identified gaps between needs and what is provided;

Vision
- decided on the kind of organisation they want to be and the values underpinning this;

Mission
- expressed the vision publicly in a mission statement, outlining the core purpose or business of the college, the services it offers, its values and goals.

They will also have prepared a strategic plan to enable them to move toward the vision and a more detailed operational plan showing what they intend to do in the next 12 months.

Most colleges now recognise that continuous quality improvement is essential if they are to survive and prosper. Often this is reflected in their mission statements and strategic and operational plans. A management philosophy with which many people in FE are familiar and feel comfortable is Total Quality Management (TQM). It has continuous quality improvement at its heart and is based on:

- the creation of a climate in which everyone shares responsibility for continuous quality improvement;
- a customer focus;

> The primary external customer in FE is the learner; sponsors, such as employers and parents are considered secondary customers. As well as external customers, however, there are also internal customers within a college. Thus for example staff providing programmes are internal customers of the centralised admissions process.

- managing by fact/data (rather than on the basis of history, or assumption);
- people-based management.
  [. . .]

A culture of improvement

While many colleges have written continuous quality improvement into their mission statements and strategic plans, the creation of such a shared culture is a more complex and longer term endeavour. As in other areas, for example equal opportunities, it is easier to write documents of intent than to ensure practice corresponds with it.

The experience of colleges which have embarked upon this route strongly suggests that a significant culture shift may be necessary from seeing quality as a vague 'good thing' to which everyone pays lip service, to:

- a college-wide goal of continuous quality improvement which involves everyone: support staff, corporation members, the principal, teaching staff and managers;
- meeting agreed needs, requirements and expectations of learners and their sponsors (the customers) which can be measured by the use of quality standards.

In other words a much more robust and rigorous definition of quality is needed. The significance of and difficulty in achieving such a shift in attitudes, values and behaviour should not be under-estimated. Many commentators suggest that without such a cultural shift, attempting to achieve quality improvement is unlikely to be successful and may even be counter-productive.

Cultural change within an organisation requires:

- change (in attitudes and behaviour) to start from the top;
- senior managers to lead by example and be seen to be genuine in their endeavour to improve quality;
- communicating and listening with respect to others' views – whoever they are;
- being open to praise and criticism;
- encouraging people to identify difficulties/barriers and suggest solutions i.e. seeing criticism as an opportunity for improvement rather than reacting defensively.

When these qualities and skills are present, shared values can become a reality and people will be encouraged to share ownership of the responsibility to strive toward improvement. Cultural change should thus be seen as a long-term goal.

A quality strategy

Having identified continuous quality improvement as part of the mission and begun to change the culture, the next stage for colleges is to plan how to move toward it.

Such a quality strategy typically includes:

- training for senior managers in the principles and practice of managing for quality, which can later be cascaded to other members of staff. It is crucial that there is seen to be genuine senior management commitment in practice to quality improvement, if the venture is to be successful;
- the establishment of a quality infrastructure, in particular a body or bodies with responsibility for promoting quality throughout the college.

Quality infrastructure

Many colleges set up quality councils or boards. Their remits are often to:

- support the college mission by establishing a quality policy;
- develop implementation strategies to ensure the policy is translated into practice;
- establish mechanisms by which specific improvement initiatives are selected and co-ordinated;
- ensure that improvement initiatives are separate from 'business as usual';
- organise and facilitate the setting up of QIGs or teams and allocating human and financial resources to them;
- ensure improvements are appropriately measured, recorded and reported;
- ensure that findings and standards are used and publicised appropriately;
- establish mechanisms by which successes can be recognised and communicated throughout the organisation;
- help embed a culture of continuous quality improvement throughout the college and ensure that interest is maintained.

The members of quality councils are keepers and users of all quality management information and data, and collectively manage the operation of the quality strategy.

If such a body is not set up, these responsibilities would lie with the SMT. While this has the advantage of ensuring senior commitment to it, it has the major disadvantage of being likely to be seen as the prerogative of the SMT alone, rather than something everyone shares.

Membership, then, is important. Clearly senior managers must be members:

- to demonstrate public commitment to quality improvement;
- because they are ultimately accountable for the quality of the service;
- because only they can manage the allocation of resources to improvement activities.

Beyond that, however, membership needs to be at a variety of levels and across functions and faculty structures. It could also include members of corporation boards, the student union, employers or parents. While some roles may be allocated, particularly the custody of computerised quality management information, the council members are generally seen as a working group, with each person leading on specified quality initiatives. Some members may receive training as internal facilitators to train, guide and support QIGs set up to address specific quality issues.

Once the quality council has been set up, it is likely to be given some priority areas for action by the SMT. These will have been identified by a variety of means, for example:

- the needs analysis;
- curriculum review and evaluation returns;
- surveys of potential customers;
- feedback from staff and learners;
- feedback from external agencies e.g. FEFC inspectors, verifiers, moderators.

Judgements will need to be made about which areas to work on first and this will depend upon the mission of the college and external pressures. However, it is important that the number tackled at once does not exceed the capacity to cope, and that small-scale tasks which have a greater chance of success are addressed before larger more complex ones.

[. . .] there has been a growing awareness of the central importance of the quality of services to learners. *Funding Learning* (FEFC, 1992), with its proposal that funding should follow activities associated with entry, on-programme and exit, and the funding methodology which followed it, has resulted in even greater importance being accorded to such services. These might include:

College services

BEFORE OR AT ENTRY

- information on access to the college
- consultancy services
- advice and guidance
- diagnostic assessment
- enrolment

ON-PROGRAMME

- Assessment/Accreditation of Prior Learning (APL)
- induction
- learner support e.g. advice, counselling, accommodation, child-care facilities, transport, physical access
- learning support e.g. action planning, study skills, workshop and library facilities, work experience, learning support for specific groups such as people with learning difficulties or second language speakers

AT TRANSITION/ACHIEVEMENT

- careers advice
- guidance on HE application
- interview skills

These are all examples of the kinds of services which could be improved by the use of quality standards.

Equally, however, more traditional aspects of college provision may also benefit from such an approach. Many colleges already have annual curriculum review and evaluation systems. Some have developed these to include the setting of quality standards in relation to, for example:

- tutorial provision;
- the return of marked work;
- the variety of teaching and learning strategies employed;
- equal opportunities.

For ease of expression, the term 'service' will be used to refer to any of the aspects of provision mentioned above.

Having decided upon the services to be the focus of attention, the quality council needs to set up a number of QIGs each of which will be charged with the task of analysing one specified service and improving it.

Quality initiative groups (QIGs)

QIGs are short-term task groups set up to improve a specified service. They are not responsible for the ongoing maintenance of that quality.

However, where the focus of the improvement is to be teaching and learning rather than cross-college services, the permanent programme/course team may be a more appropriate group to initiate and manage improvement. Many colleges now have cross-college curriculum review and evaluation systems and college-wide quality characteristics [. . .] which provide programme teams with a common college framework within which they set their own quality standards and targets. Such teams are often referred to as curriculum improvement teams.

Members of the group should be chosen on the basis of their ability to analyse the service in question and bring about improvements. They should thus include representatives from:

- all parts of the college that contribute to the service or supply services to it;
- a range of levels of seniority within the college;
- internal and, if possible, external customers of the service.

Facilitating such a group is a skilled task. Facilitators need to have expertise in managing group processes and a number of specific techniques such as flow-charting and root cause analysis [. . .]. If no member of the group possesses such skills it may be necessary to appoint someone from outside the group and/or to consider training. A more conventional group leader will also be required to convene and chair the meetings.

At its first meeting the group will need to:

- agree membership (including any specialist expertise that may be needed) and roles;
- agree on the task;
- agree a meeting schedule to achieve the task;
- clarify the group's level of decision making;
- agree communications procedures with the quality council/SMT and the level of resourcing being given to the group to achieve its task;
- remind itself of the college mission and values.

The task

The task, in relation to any given service, can be described briefly as:

- identifying the gaps between current and required practice;
- setting standards;
- analysing the difficulties;
- suggesting improvements;
- trialling and implementing the improvements and measuring their effectiveness;
- reporting to the quality council/SMT.

This will involve the [six] steps [described below].

Detailed guidelines for QIGs

Step 1 *Identifying current practice*

Staff generally think they know what current practice is. However, others may 'know' quite different things about the same set of activities. It is important therefore to arrive at a definition that all members can share.

Inevitably people will also have views on what is wrong with the service, but the emphasis at this stage should, as far as possible, be upon the description of current practice rather than some ideal.

This can be achieved by:

- defining the service and agreeing those aspects of it that should be included;

> For example, those aspects involved in providing a service to learners who want to change course might include:
>
> - tutor advice and assistance
> - careers adviser assistance
> - personal counselling
> - information on other available programmes/courses
> - advice and assistance from staff in new subject/programme areas
> - administrative arrangements.

- drawing a flowchart of the processes involved at present [. . .];
- testing the accuracy by 'walking through' the processes as if one were a student and modifying the flowchart if it does not reflect experience;
- identifying the internal and external customers;

> For example, 16 year old full-time students and part-time adult students are external primary customers of the admissions process. Employers and parents may be external secondary customers and college staff receiving students will be internal customers of the same process.

- identifying and grouping customers according to which parts of the process they use;

> For example, students, parents and staff will 'use' different aspects of the admissions process and access it at different points.

• identifying the internal and external suppliers to the process.

This is important because the quality of any service will be partly determined by the quality of the services supplied to it. The flowchart will enable inputs to the process, and thus suppliers, to be identified.

Step 2 Identifying what is required

When a QIG is set up to improve a specified service, there is often a view within the SMT about what is wrong with the service. In addition, individual QIG members may also have (often differing) views about what needs to be improved. Nonetheless it is important to understand what customers, both internal and external, want from the service; what they think of it at present and what their priorities are for improvement.

The group needs, therefore, to:

• agree a sample of customers, internal and external, to interview;

> For example, if the service under consideration is the provision of information about courses available in the college, customers might include prospective students, employers and parents (external) and guidance staff and the receptionists (internal). It might also be important to sample views at different sites.

• devise a questionnaire or interview schedule that will elicit the following information:
  – what customers want from the service
  – what they think about it currently (likes and dislikes)
  – what they would like to be changed;
• interview confidentially a small number of each type of customer to build up an indication of the requirements they have for the service;

> There may be other requirements for the service. For example there may be an internal of external requirement on the college to gather data for ethnic monitoring as part of the admissions process. This may not be identified by the customers, but should be added to the list of requirements. Equally some requirements may arise from the college mission.

• find out about best practice elsewhere. This is a process known as benchmarking;

> Benchmarking entails examining other people's practice to see how they do it. It may involve visiting and analysing in some detail:
>
> • other parts of the college undertaking similar processes to the service in question
> • the same process and service in other colleges
> • a similar process outside FE
>
> Effective benchmarking can make the difference between small incremental change and larger scale improvement. Lateral or creative thinking may enable colleges to learn valuable lessons from best practice in a wide variety of settings.

- use all this information to devise a two-dimensional survey;

> This should list the identified requirements for the service and ask respondents to rate the college's current performance of them and indicate their importance [. . .].

- ask a representative sample of customers to complete the survey;
- summarise the findings. One useful way of doing this is shown in Figure 4.1;
- agree and list all the requirements and features of the desired service, on the basis of:
  - the features identified by customers
  - the objectives of the service and any requirements the college and external bodies have of it
  - the feasibility of achieving them.

> For example, the following desired features may be agreed for the tutorial system in a college:
>
> - regular one-to-one meetings with tutor
> - extra emergency meetings when required
> - supportive of learners and their development
> - involve action planning and recording achievement.
>
> It is likely that the first three features would have been identified by students. The last one however may be a requirement the college has of the tutorial system, based on its strategic plan. Others may be required by external bodies.

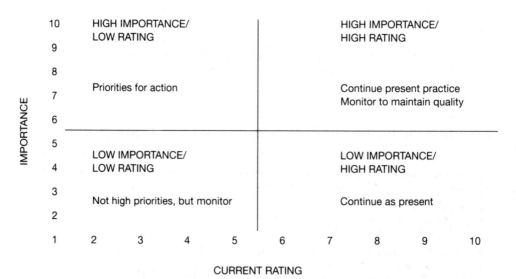

Figure 4.1   Survey summary

Step 3 *Setting standards*

Standards express the level of performance that can be expected for any given service. They are usually derived from the features and level of requirement identified by customers and others. Once established, institutional performance can be measured against them.

In the spirit of continuous improvement, standards should not be seen as static, but should become more rigorous over time.

QIGs should therefore:

- set standards for the agreed desired features.

For instance in the example above, regular individual tutorials were identified and agreed as a desired feature of the tutorial system. The standard set for this might be a 30-minute individual tutorial every two weeks. It may, however, be that this is only thought to be achievable for full-time students and that for part-time students the standard should be a 15-minute individual tutorial every four weeks. Thus the feature is common but the standards may differ for different groups of customers.

Standards should be realistic and expressed as clearly as possible. This is because the next task is to:

- agree measures for each standard.

Measures are the means by which actual performance is monitored and checked against set standards. They can comprise hard or perceptual data.

For example it is relatively easy to find a measure to monitor the frequency and duration of tutorials. Tutorial records would be a possible measure, another might be a student survey. However another desired feature of the tutorial system was that tutorials should be 'supportive'.

Despite its subjective nature, this might be considered so important that it was expressed as a quality standard, e.g. the provision of a supportive environment in which students can reflect on their progress. This is clearly more difficult to measure. However, a student satisfaction survey could ask students to evaluate the supportiveness of their tutorials on a scale of 1 to 4, where 1 is excellent and 4 is poor (see Figure 4.2).

Standards therefore should reflect the agreed desired features and measures should monitor actual performance against the standards [. . .]. It is important that the agreed desired features are the starting point, otherwise there is a danger that standards will be chosen because they are easy to measure. On the other hand, the need to measure performance against standards does add discipline to the setting of clear standards.

SERVICE: TUTORIALS	Excellent			Poor
FEATURES	1	2	3	4
1. supportive				
2.				

Figure 4.2

Step 4 Redesigning the process

The information gained from the flowchart describing the service (Step 1), the agreed desired features of the service, the summary survey giving priorities for action (Step 2), and the standards (Step 3) should all be used to inform the redesigning process. The group will need to:

- use the survey summary to identify features of high importance and low rating. These will give priorities for action, although they must be tempered by the ability of the college to tackle them;
- use the flowchart if necessary to identify where the difficulty occurs;
- express the difficulty simply, e.g. too long a delay between x and y;
- for each identified problem undertake a root-cause analysis [. . .] until the 'roots' of the problem are apparent;
- sometimes the roots of the problem will lie within the service itself. At other times, however, they may have their source with internal or external suppliers to the service;
- investigate ways to improve the service to overcome the problems and make it more like the desired service. It will be important to consider:
  - simplifying the process
  - new tools/equipment
  - staff awareness raising/training
  - improving communication
  - the cost of suggested improvements;
- discuss potential improvements with customers and/or suppliers;
- decide which improvements will be tried first and how they will be trialled;
- redesign the process.

Step 5 Implementing the new process

Bringing about institutional change is rarely easy. Indeed it is, conversely, only too easy for people to be suspicious of change; to prefer the status quo which they know and about which they feel comfortable.

Every QIG should include in its membership representatives of contributors to a service and its customers and suppliers. In addition, the work of the group should be more widely known about within the college. Nonetheless, it is crucial that everyone involved in delivering the new service should know clearly why it has been redesigned, what it now looks like, and what they are being expected to do differently.

Suppliers to the service, especially, may need to know why they are being asked to do things differently and their agreement sought.

There is an issue for QIGs here about authority. It is important that the QIG has, and is seen to have, the authority to suggest changes to well-established practices. This is why it is important when any QIG is set up, that the levels of decision-making are clear and the relationship of the QIG to the quality council and/or SMT is spelt out. For example, suggested changes may have to be referred to the quality council or SMT for final approval.

If the culture of continuous improvement has been established successfully in a college, the work of the QIG is accepted and transparent, and people have been included in the change process and consulted, such issues will be minimised. Nonetheless, QIG members should be aware of people's sensitivities when change is introduced and should take care to communicate the proposed changes to all those involved in helpful ways.

It may not be possible to trial a new process before implementing it fully. Nevertheless, wherever possible, QIGs should pilot the redesigned process. For example, it may be possible to pilot a new enrolment process on some roll-on roll-off programmes or short courses before full implementation in the new academic year. It should then be possible to:

- use the measures (Step 4) to see how successful the pilot process has been in relation to the standards set;
- identify any continuing difficulties;
- modify the process to address any problems identified, referring back to earlier steps as necessary (Step 3);
- modify the standards in the light of the pilot experience if appropriate;
- communicate the modified process to all participants;
- implement the new service fully.

Step 6 Evaluating success

Having implemented the new service fully the QIG will need to use the measures to see if the new service meets the standards.

Usually this is done by a student survey, but sometimes other measures are used [. . .]. Such surveys should relate only to those desired features considered to be important and should be designed to be quick to complete and to analyse.

Once the results have been collated and analysed:

- modify the standards if necessary;

> For example, if in [a student] survey it was found that only 30% of students answered [that they had received a regular 30 minute fortnightly tutorial], then the standard would clearly be too ambitious in the first instance.

- recommend improvement targets;

> For example, if 82% of students were satisfied with the supportiveness of their tutorials (scoring 1 or 2) the target might be set as 90% satisfaction within a year.

- report to the quality council, outlining the changes; the desired features, standards and measures; the extent to which the standards have been met and the recommendations for future improvement targets.

After the quality initiative

Once the QIG has reported to the quality council, its task is complete. Usually responsibility for the maintenance and further improvement of quality is given back to the people involved in the delivery of the new process.
Whatever decision is made the quality council will need to:

- adopt the standards formally;
- decide if, where and in what form they should be published e.g. in the college charter or annual reports;
- decide on improvement targets;
- communicate the achievements and decisions to the 'owners' of the new service and the members of the QIG;
- arrange for the survey to be administered at identified intervals and progress monitored.

More generally it will need to:

- consider whether the quality council or SMT could do things differently to improve the effectiveness of QIGs;
- review the QIG's work and learn from the experience for the next one.

In the longer term, as the obvious candidates for improvement have been tackled by QIGs, the quality council will have to decide which areas should be the next to be addressed. Customer surveys can help in establishing this. [. . .] Final decisions however will need to be taken in consultation with the SMT in the context of the college's strategic plans and any relevant national initiatives.

Conclusions

This chapter has:

- located quality standards within the philosophical framework of continuous quality improvement;
- shown how strategic planning for quality has its roots in such college values;
- illustrated the sort of culture and quality infrastructure necessary to operationalise the strategic priorities for quality;

- provided detailed guidance for groups charged with improving a specified service, with particular reference to the ways in which standards can be arrived at and improved over time.

Once standards have been set and measures developed to monitor their achievement, the results can be used in many different ways. This chapter has focused on their contribution to continuous quality improvement, but more specifically they may be used for internal management and external promotion purposes.

For example they may be used in internal management for quality to:

- provide evidence of quality standards reached;
- recognise and celebrate improvements made;
- inform planning for improvement work, e.g. by identifying those areas in which further work is necessary;
- provide baseline information upon which improvement targets may be set;
- allocate internal budgets for improvement initiatives;
- demonstrate senior management commitment to continuous quality improvement;

and in external promotion to:

- support submissions to awarding bodies for new programmes/courses;
- provide verifiable proof of internal quality assessment e.g. for FEFCs;
- promote, publicise and market the services provided by the college, e.g. in the college charter or in promotional materials;
- demonstrate the commitment of the college to continuous quality improvement to customers and funding and awarding bodies.

Thus 'managing by fact or data' through the use of service quality standards can enable a college to manage its own services more effectively, and to communicate its offer to prospective funders and learners more accurately. Moreover, the data will enable colleges to provide evidence that the offer will be delivered. As colleges seek to improve participation, retention and achievement rates in what may well become an increasingly competitive local environment, this is likely to have increasing significance in influencing learners' choice of institution.

Acknowledgement

This chapter is the result of an early draft on service standards prepared by Angela Cross-Durrant before she left the Unit. She is now a member of the FEFC Inspectorate.

Reference

FEFC (1992) *Funding Learning*. London: FEFC.

5 | Using success criteria*

KATH ASPINWALL, TIM SIMKINS, JOHN F. WILKINSON AND M. JOHN MCAULEY

[. . .] Terms such as success criteria, performance indicators and target setting have recently gained currency in the world of education. This kind of language is traditionally associated with the culture of commerce and industry, and is viewed with suspicion by many educationalists. Those who hold this view argue that this kind of language implies an emphasis on formal accountability, on a product-centred view of the task at hand, and a preoccupation with quantifiable findings, whereas educational organizations are dealing not with a product but with the complex process of educating and developing people which cannot be represented in such relatively simple ways.

There are many who view this apparent culture clash as irreconcilable. However, such a view often represents more a rejection of the language being used than a desire to be uncritical or unaccountable. Good professionals are invariably looking for evidence of success and indicators of their level of performance. In simple terms, they constantly pose the question 'How are we doing?' This question in turn implies a need for clarity about what we are trying to achieve and about how we shall know whether we have achieved it. This may lead to the design and use of fairly hard, quantitative 'performance indicators'; often, however, this will be inappropriate and softer approaches will be necessary. Whatever particular method is used, however, it needs to be based on a systematic approach. [. . .]

Designing and using success criteria and indicators

All evaluation is in some way comparative. Either explicitly or implicitly, information gathered through ongoing monitoring processes or from specific pieces of investigation will incorporate ideas about the standards or criteria against which performance

---

* This material has been abridged.

should be judged and about the kinds of information which represent evidence of success or otherwise in achieving these standards. This is the world of performance indicators. These may be specified in a fairly 'soft' or subjective way, or they may be embodied in apparently 'harder' and more objective measures. Hopkins and Leask offer the following definition of a performance indicator:

> A performance indicator is a statement against which achievement in an area or activity can be assessed; they are also useful for setting goals and clarifying objectives. For some performance indicators, a brief statement is sufficient; for others the statement should be more specific and refer to supplementary processes which would give a measure of depth, quality and/or commitment in a particular area. In our view there is a place for both quantitative and qualitative indicators.
>
> (Hopkins and Leask, 1989: 6–7)

The development and use of success criteria and indicators is not necessarily a complex technical task, although there are many examples of performance measures in education which do require a good deal of specialist knowledge for their application and interpretation. [. . .]

However, if success criteria are to be of maximum benefit, they need to be developed and used in a systematic way which takes account of the pitfalls that can arise. A systematic approach can best be developed by working through a number of key questions in relation to a programme or activity.

Question 1: What is it trying to achieve?

This is the central question, and will require considerable thought and discussion. It needs to be addressed within the context of the specific purposes for which the evaluation is being undertaken. So, for example, the criteria will be very different if the main concern is to monitor the implementation of a project over time than if it is to assess the impact of a change in teaching method on students' learning. [. . .] Two examples of approaches to the identification of performance areas are given in Figures 5.1 and 5.2. One is taken from the schools sector, and the other from further education.

---

1 *Academic progress*
  What proportion of pupils in the school have made above average levels of academic progress over the relevant time period?

2 *Pupil satisfaction*
  What proportion of pupils in the school are satisfied with the education they are receiving?

3 *Pupil–teacher relationships*
  What proportion of pupils in the school have good or 'vital' relationships with one or more teachers?

Figure 5.1   Sheffield University school success criteria
Source: Gray and Jesson (1990)

1 *The staff : student ratio* based on full-time equivalent (fte) student and academic staff numbers.

2 *Non-teacher cost* per enrolled student.

3 *Cost per fte student* enrolled on a course.

4 *Completion rates* for students enrolled on courses, and the cost per fte student completing a course.

5 *Rates of target qualifications* gained for students enrolled on a course, and the cost per qualified fte student.

6 *Rates of employment or progression* to further and higher education for students completing appropriate courses.

Figure 5.2 The Joint Efficiency Study's success criteria for further education
Source: DES (1987) The Joint Efficiency Study

It will be seen that the two approaches differ substantially in their emphasis. That proposed for schools explicitly identifies three performance areas and defines a focusing question for each one. In contrast, the Joint Efficiency Study moves straight to the specification of six performance areas: although these are based on two core performance areas, 'efficiency' and 'effectiveness'. The study defines efficiency as the relationship of inputs to outputs and effectiveness as the extent to which objectives are being achieved. Thus criteria 1 to 4 broadly relate to the area of efficiency and 5 and 6 to that of effectiveness.

There are other differences. The school criteria make no reference to resource utilization or cost, whereas three of the further education (FE) criteria, with their concern for efficiency, do. In contrast, two of the school criteria are concerned with process whereas none of the FE criteria is. And, whereas the FE criteria are all relatively straightforward to define and easy to quantify, two of the school criteria are quite difficult to represent other than in a qualitative way.

These differences, though important, should not be allowed to detract from the main point, which is that any success criteria should be based on an analysis of what the key dimensions of achievement are. Only when this is done is it safe to proceed to a consideration of more specific indicators of success.

Question 2: What would be appropriate indicators of success?

Having identified our area of concern, we need to identify one or more phenomena about which information can be gathered and which will help us to answer our chosen question: what would indicate success in this particular area? [. . .]

An example of how broad performance areas can be translated into more specific success indicators is the 'Quality of Learning and Teaching Profile' developed by the Scottish HMI in relation to further education (Scottish Education Department, 1990). This translates five areas – relevance, access, responsiveness, appropriateness and standards – into 17 'quality statements' (QS) (see Figure 5.3).

Relevance

QS1   There is a planned portfolio of programmes which is broadly consistent with the identified needs of clients.

QS2   The overall content of each individual programme is suited to its aims and purposes.

QS3   Programme content is accurate and up-to-date in its treatment of employment practice and new technology.

Access

QS4   Potential clients receive clear, accurate, and comprehensive information about programmes on offer and have the opportunity to clarify their goals in order that students enrol for a suitable programme.

QS5   The prior learning of students, whether certified or experiential, is adequately taken into account.

QS6   Circumstantial restrictions on access, such as those arising from the timing and location of courses, are minimized.

Responsiveness

QS7   Innovative programmes or modifications to existing programmes for employers and community users are provided with a minimum of lead time.

QS8   There is liaison and collaboration with employers and community users in the delivery of programmes.

QS9   Students have access to sources of information, advice, and support which assist them to meet their learning needs, cope with difficulties and progress satisfactorily from a programme.

QS10 Programmes are negotiable and components are selected to meet individual needs.

QS11 Students are able to progress at their own pace.

QS12 Clients have the opportunity to evaluate provision.

Appropriateness (of learning and teaching approaches)

QS13 There is a climate of purposefulness and rapport, and a concern for individual student achievement.

QS14 The learning resources and environment are well planned and organized with regard to the accomplishment of learning outcomes.

QS15 Learning and teaching methods are appropriate to learning outcomes, emphasize student activity and responsibility, and are varied.

Standards

QS16 Assessment approaches cover all the learning outcomes and performance criteria and are applied to the work of all students.

QS17 The standards, as set out in descriptors, are correctly applied and systematically moderated.

Note: Terminology tends to vary among different kinds of educational provision. In reading these quality statements 'programme' should be deemed to include 'courses', and 'learning outcomes' to include 'outcomes' and 'learning objectives' and so on.

Figure 5.3 Quality of Learning and Teaching (QLT) Profile
Source: Scottish Education Department (1990)

It is important that a systematic framework is developed for thinking about performance, so that all major performance areas are defined and suitable indicators are developed for each. This might be done in a number of ways, depending on the programme or activity being considered. The QLT Profile is just one approach. Another classification which is often advocated is that of 'input', 'process' and 'outcome'. Each of these three dimensions focuses on a different aspect of provision. *Input* concerns the scale and appropriateness of the resources devoted to a programme. It includes such considerations as expenditure, costs and the appropriateness of teacher skills. *Process* is concerned primarily with the quality of interactions between, and experiences undergone by, those involved in the programme. It might include, for example, the degree of active learning undertaken by pupils or the range of teaching methods used on a course in further education. Finally, *outcome* concerns the results of the programme – learning achieved, entry to further education or work, and so on. In each of these areas it is possible to think of indicators of success which are both quantitative and qualitative. Each of these three areas can be developed in a variety of ways, depending on the objectives and priorities of the programme under consideration. Such an approach can be used at a variety of levels from the individual activity or programme to the whole institution. [. . .]

The definition of performance areas and the derivation of indicators for each can best be considered as an iterative process. The systematic identification of performance areas can provide a framework for deriving indicators appropriate to each (for example, using the QLT Profile or the input/process/output model); on the other hand, the generation of a large number of indicators can lead to the refinement of performance areas or the identification of new ones. [. . .]

Question 3: How should data be gathered and processed?

There are usually many ways of gathering and processing data on a particular phenomenon. This may involve measuring things. Consider academic achievement, for example. One possible measure of this is examination performance, perhaps in GCSE, or test results. Is it sufficient to measure the number of passes, or passes at a particular level, or should different weightings be applied to different grades of pass? If the latter, what should the weightings be? As a measure of efficiency of staff utilization, too, the SSR can be measured in a variety of ways: for example, at different times in the year, or by weighting part-time students in particular ways. Where such choices exist, different measures are likely to show different patterns of performance.

To choose a suitable way of gathering and processing data we may need to refine our criteria of success. For example, is 'success' enabling a high proportion of less able students to obtain passes at GCSE, or is it maximizing the number of students who obtain passes at grades A and B? The former would best be assessed by a simple measure of total passes; the latter would need the results to be weighted heavily in favour of the higher grades. A department which performs well on one criterion may not do so on the other, and vice versa.

Statistics of examination results, of staff deployment or of anything else, are not the only kind of data which might be collected as indicators of success, however. In its work on the Quality of Learning and Teaching Profile, HMI suggest 10 evaluation instruments (EIs) which combine a variety of interviews, questionnaires and recording schedules (Scottish Education Department 1990: 20). These are:

EI 1   User Survey (postal questionnaire)
EI 2A   Student Survey: guidance (questionnaire)
EI 2B   Student Survey: learning and teaching (questionnaire)
EI 2C   Student Survey (interview)
EI 3A   Staff Survey: guidance (questionnaire)
EI 3B   Staff Survey: learning, teaching and assessment (questionnaire)

EI 4   Programme Analysis (recording schedule for analysis of documentation and
          interview findings by a team of evaluators)
EI 5   Module Analysis (recording schedule for analysis of 'extended' modules and
          findings from discussion by evaluators)
EI 6   Analysis of Student Work (recording schedule for analysis of assessed student
          work by evaluators)
EI 7   Analysis of Teaching (recording schedule for analysis of findings arising from
          observation of learning and teaching in classrooms, workshops, etc. by
          evaluators).

These evaluation instruments are then related to the 17 quality statements as shown in
Figure 5.4. Evidence from instruments such as these is just as valid as more traditional
statistics – indeed it may be more so for particular purposes. Data from such sources
will still need to be aggregated in a suitable way, however, to produce usable information. [. . .]

Question 4: With what can the results validly be compared?

However well the success criteria have been designed and however well the data have
been gathered and processed, information about performance in relation to a particular development at a given point in time is of little value on its own in answering the
question 'How are we doing?' It has to be placed in comparative perspective. The
statements 'We're doing OK' or 'We could do better' implies the existence of some
standard against which performance is being judged.

It is common to use three main types of standard for making judgements about
achievements:

- *Comparative:* How are we doing in comparison with similar developments elsewhere?
- *Progress:* How are we doing compared with how we have done previously?
- *Target:* How are we doing compared with a specific standard or target(s) which we
  have set ourselves, or which others have set for us?

Each of these approaches has its attractions. Comparison with similar programmes
elsewhere ensures an outward-looking approach to evaluation and guards against par-
ochialism. An emphasis on our own progress demonstrates the importance of development and potentially can be extremely motivating. The development and utilization of
specific targets encourages the development of clear links between plans and performance assessment. Perhaps the best advice is to use a combination of all three
approaches in an attempt to get the best of all worlds.

Question 5: What other information is necessary to put the results into context?

The availability of information which can be used for comparative purposes, while
essential, may not be sufficient to enable appropriate conclusions to be drawn from
evaluation data, however. The question still remains: 'Is the comparison valid?' or
'Is like being compared with like?' There may be many reasons why a comparison
with similar developments elsewhere may not be valid. Differences in examination

Quality statement (abbreviated)	Evaluation instrument									
	1	2A	2B	2C	3A	3B	4	5	6	7
Relevance										
QS1 Relevant portfolio of programmes	✓		✓				✓			
QS2 Appropriate programme content	✓		✓	✓		✓	✓	✓	✓	✓
QS3 Accurate, up-to-date content	✓		✓			✓		✓	✓	✓
Access										
QS4 Appropriate pre-entry guidance	✓	✓			✓					
QS5 Recognition of prior learning				✓	✓		✓			
QS6 Circumstantial restriction on access minimized	✓		✓	✓	✓		✓			
Responsiveness										
QS7 Innovative programmes provided quickly	✓						✓			
QS8 Collaboration with employers in programme delivery	✓		✓	✓			✓			
QS9 Appropriate continuing guidance		✓			✓					
QS10 Programme re-negotiation		✓			✓		✓			
QS11 Self-spaced learning		✓			✓			✓		
QS12 Evaluation by clients		✓			✓		✓	✓		
Appropriateness of learning and teaching methods										
QS13 Purposefulness and rapport; concern for individual achievement			✓	✓		✓		✓		✓
QS14 Appropriate learning environment and resources			✓	✓		✓		✓		✓
QS15 Appropriate learning and teaching methods			✓	✓		✓		✓		✓
Standards										
QS16 Comprehensive assessment approaches						✓		✓	✓	
QS17 Correct application of standards; moderation						✓	✓	✓	✓	

Figure 5.4 The quality statements addressed by each evaluation instrument
Source: Scottish Education Department (1990)

performance, for example, often reflect differences in student ability rather than teaching quality; or perhaps a relatively low SSR reflects the need to teach a higher than average proportion of students with special needs in small groups. Our own progress over time may have been affected by staff shortages or a changing student profile. And the targets we have set, or been set, may have been based on quite unrealistic expectations deriving from experience in very different circumstances.

It is essential that performance assessment takes account of such qualifications. It is important too, however, that they are used in a sensible way. Too often in education it is argued that our achievements cannot be assessed because our situation is unique. Interestingly, uniqueness is more often claimed to excuse apparently poor performance than to explain good! Where there are concerns about comparability, a number of strategies are possible:

- Use statistical techniques to attempt to take account of the sources of difference. For example, it may be possible to take account of differences in student ability in comparing examination results.
- Seek other comparators. For example, look for schools, colleges or departments whose characteristics most closely resemble your own. Or alternatively, move to a self-determined progress or target model rather than an externally imposed comparative one.
- Seek a wider variety of information which captures different aspects of achievement.

The discussion and development of these kinds of approaches not only increase the likelihood of drawing valid conclusions; they also enhance in a more general sense our understanding of the problem of assessing 'success'.

Question 6: What conclusions can legitimately be drawn?

We can now begin to put the elements of the development and use of success indicators together. These elements are:

- identification of *performance areas*, with one or more focusing questions for each;
- identification of a number of *success criteria* for each area;
- determination of the *kinds of data* which need to be collected and analysed to present evidence in relation to the chosen criteria;
- determination of the basis on which the level of performance is to be judged (the basis for *comparison*);
- consideration of any *particular circumstances* which may need to be taken into account in interpreting performance.

Figure 5.5 shows the process of analysis for two very different areas of concern. [. . .]
Once the analysis gets to this point, conclusions should be emerging. However, at this stage it is worth reviewing the process which has been undertaken so far:

- Have the correct areas of performance been identified?
- Have criteria been identified which adequately represent these areas?

	Example A (Primary school)	Example B (Further education)
Performance area	Pupil-centred learning	Efficiency of staff utilization
Success criterion	Pupil–pupil co-operation	Staff : student ratio
Data collection	1 Observation schedule 2 Teacher interview	Annual Monitoring Survey data
Comparator(s)	Progress over time	1 DFEE target 2 Other similar colleges
Contextual factors	Class sizes have increased	The college's work is biased towards staff-intensive subjects

Figure 5.5   Developing and using success criteria

- Have data been gathered and processed in appropriate ways to assess achievement against these criteria?
- Have comparisons been made with the right things?
- Has account been taken of particular circumstances that may limit the validity of comparisons?

It may be helpful to draw up in relation to each of these questions a list of the strengths and weaknesses of the process through which success criteria have been defined and in relation to which evidence has been gathered. While doing this, it is desirable to consider how far the information which has been obtained meets a number of basic quality tests:

- Is it *relevant* to the focusing question or questions? It is too easy to collect information on the basis of convenience or cost rather than in relation to clearly defined questions. There is also a danger of collecting far more information than is necessary to form judgements about the performance area in question. It is essential, therefore, that the most rigorous standards of relevance be applied. With resources scarce, it is not acceptable to collect information because it appears 'interesting'.
- Is it an *adequate* response to these questions, in the sense that it reflects the full range or complexity of the issue or does it present a limited view? We have already pointed out the danger of omitting important performance areas from the analysis. This is particularly likely to occur if only one stakeholder is involved in the discussion. For example, teachers may give quite a low priority to assessing the efficiency of a programme in which they are involved; conversely, administrators may not always be too concerned about educational quality provided the resource sums look right.
- Is it *valid*, in the sense that it adequately represents what it is supposed to represent? Perhaps the biggest, and most common, criticism of the performance indicators approach to collecting evidence for evaluative purposes is that quantifiable measures tend to drive out the less quantifiable dimensions of performance, and that the essence of educational quality cannot be captured by such measures either

at all (the extreme position) or alone. One problem here is that quantified and stan-dardized measures are much easier to treat comparatively, and external comparison is an important dimension of accountability in education.

- Is it *reliable?* Would similar conclusions be drawn if the information was obtained by somebody else or by some other method? This is a tricky area. Again, quantita-tive indicators are often more reliable than more qualitative ones, although as the previous paragraph suggests, their reliability may be bought at the expense of their validity. Where reliability is a problem, there is advantage in using more than one kind or source of data in relation to a particular criterion: [this is known as] 'trian-gulation'. [. . .]

Question 7: What action follows?

[There are] four ways in which information might be managed. Briefly, these [are] using information *symbolically,* or as a *scorecard,* or in an *attention-directing* way, or for *problem-solving.* Information arising from monitoring and evaluation processes, including that relating to success criteria, can serve any of these four purposes. It is often tempting to concentrate on collecting and providing symbolic and scorecard information, especially where this is sufficient to ensure a quiet life! However, such an approach is not consistent with the kinds of values outlined earlier. It will do little to encourage and facilitate processes of development and even the accountability function will be quite restricted. Performance information, if it is to be of value, must be attention-directing and it must be supplemented by processes which ensure a problem-solving approach to the identified areas of concerns. Such a philosophy, how-ever, is not a cosy one. It challenges and it may threaten. It is essential, therefore, to consider carefully the behavioural implications of information management.

Information and behaviour

A key characteristic of the management of information is that it affects behaviour. Often its effects are intended – when, for example, a teaching approach is changed in response to negative feedback by students. Frequently, though the methods used to collect or disseminate information have behavioural consequences which not only are unexpected but are the exact opposite of what was hoped for. It is essential, therefore, that those responsible for developing and using success indicators concern themselves not merely with the *technical* adequacy of their information – in terms of its relevance, validity, reliability and so on – but also with the *behavioural* appropriateness of the methods they are using to manage the evaluation process. Questions of perception, expectation and motivation are just as important as those of research design.

Individuals view information management processes, including monitoring and eva-luation, in terms of their impact on themselves and their work. They attempt to inter-pret the purposes of those who are managing the process and they also attempt to envisage the likely consequences of these processes for their position in the organiz-ation. They may accept the 'official' view about these things. Or they may develop their own alternative understandings on the basis of their previous experiences or their perceptions of how the process of monitoring and evaluation is proceeding. For those managing evaluation, therefore, it is important that the 'style' adopted is consistent with the philosophy espoused. Often this is not the case, and then a number of possible behavioural consequences follow. This can be illustrated by the kinds of responses which may arise in relation to success indicators whose design or use have been ill-judged (Lawler and Rhode 1976, Ch. 6). Some responses are legitimate, although they are not in the best interests of the organization and were not intended by those designing the evaluation process. For example:

- Individuals may respond in a *rigidly bureaucratic* way, changing their behaviour uncritically in response to the type of performance implied by the indicator. The often-cited fear of 'teaching to the test' is a good example of this.
- They may adopt *strategic behaviour* designed to make them look good in terms of the indicator. This may involve spending up at the end of the financial year on anything which is available, when 'spending to budget' is an indicator of success and funds cannot be carried over. Or it may mean limiting examination entries to the most able students to ensure a good pass rate.

Other responses are normally considered to be illegitimate, but may still be engaged in by those who feel their interests are threatened:

- *Reporting invalid data* which puts the performance of an individual or group in a good light. An example of this might be the marking of absent students as present on class registers when attendance is used as an indicator of success.
- Attempting to *subvert* the whole information-gathering process by ridiculing it, overloading it and so on.

Such responses arise because information is often used in situations where conflicts of interest exist and people are conscious of the potential impact of information on key decisions. These concerns can be addressed in part by ensuring that indicators cannot easily be manipulated in these ways – the design issue. But this is not always possible, especially where, as is often the case in education, the factor which is being assessed is complex. Furthermore, there is always the danger of a vicious cycle setting in, with 'unacceptable' responses giving rise to tighter restrictions, which led in turn to new methods of getting round the system being invented. Most of these examples relate to the use of success indicators for accountability purposes alone. Where the developmental dimension dominates, the dangers are fewer, but still they cannot be ignored. People may have differing views about what comprises desirable development. In these circumstances it is necessary to think about the behavioural as well as the technical dimension of information management.

Managing success indicators

If success indicators are to be used effectively, a number of issues need to be considered carefully before the process of designing them begins.

Keep them simple and clear

Success indicators can be developed at a number of levels and in a variety of ways. At the level of the organization, it is possible to develop very long lists, such as the list of school performance indicators promulgated by the DES (DES 1989) or the indicators developed by the Department of Employment for evaluating TVEI (Department of Employment 1991). The general consensus, however, is that such lists are of limited use except as stimuli to creative thinking. The aim should be to develop a relatively small number of indicators which capture the key dimensions of success for the programme or activity which is being monitored or evaluated.

The argument for simplicity, however, should not be used as an excuse for unjustifiable reductionism. For example, unadjusted examination scores do not 'speak for themselves'; and examination success will rarely be acceptable as the only dimension of performance which needs to be measured. The point being made here is about obtaining a realistic focus, not an inappropriate oversimplification.

Set them after discussion

The best success indicators are those which have been developed by or in partnership with those who work in the area where performance is to be assessed, or who have an interest in the area. Such a process ensures that the indicators have credibility and authority, and this in turn reduces the likelihood that the undesirable consequences outlined above will occur. Success indicators developed in this way will:

- be built upon the educational objectives of the programme which is to be assessed, although they may also take account of externally determined requirements;
- take account of local circumstances, although they will also take account of good practice in comparable circumstances elsewhere to ensure that expectations are not set unrealistically low (or high!).

Put another way, success criteria should take full account of what a programme is trying to do and the circumstances in which it is being done, but they should also put performance in the broader context of the expectations of others and the experience of what is being achieved elsewhere. Those running a programme are key stakeholders, but they are rarely the only ones.

Ensure openness

It is important that all those stakeholders who have a legitimate involvement have a shared understanding about the kinds of information that is being gathered and the purposes for which it will be used. This is not always the case. There is a need to be clear about:

- what criteria are to be used;
- why they were chosen;
- what information is to be collected in relation to them;
- how the outcomes of the process will be used.

Information about these things should be communicated in ways appropriate to the particular audience. This is not always easy, especially if the indicators involve a good deal of technical calculation or analysis. It should always be possible, however, with sufficient thought.

Use the indicators for developmental purposes

The driving force for the development of success indicators is commonly that of accountability. Those who manage us, or from whom we obtain resources, commonly set the pace or call the tune when indicators are being designed. Even when we take the initiative, it is because we wish to pre-empt the issue before others set the agenda for us. It is highly desirable, however, that indicators are viewed from a developmental perspective whoever takes the initiative and whatever the prime motivation for their development. The intelligent use and interpretation of information about performance can be a powerful influence for change and development.

It is important, therefore that the use of success indicators is seen as an integral part of the monitoring and evaluation *process*, not simply as a parallel activity which is necessary to meet external requirements.

Keep them under review

Success indicators may be used for monitoring and/or as part of a review or in-depth investigation. In either case, but particularly for monitoring, it will probably be appropriate to use the same indicators for a period of time, perhaps for a number of years. This has advantages. Not least, a consistent time series of information enables progress to be charted in a helpful way. On the other hand, there is always the danger that the same information will continue to be routinely gathered, despite the fact that objectives have been modified or external factors have changed so as to render any comparison of performance meaningless. It is important, therefore, that the success indicators being used are reviewed regularly.

[. . .]

Conclusion

[. . .] Some [readers of this chapter] will have been reinforced in their concerns about the dangers of adopting approaches to evaluation in education which are too hard-nosed and which embody dangers of serious misuse. As Mrs Angela Rumbold, Minister of State, said in introducing the DES's list of performance indicators for schools in 1989:

> Those of us advocating the use of performance indicators in education must always attach a 'Government Health Warning'. Considered in isolation they are open to misinterpretation and misuse and can damage the health of a school.
> (DES 1989)

We share these concerns. The view that all indicators should carry a 'health warning' is a valid one, and we have tried to indicate in this chapter the kinds of issues that such a warning might address. However, it is also our view that in a world where legitimate pressures for accountability in education are increasing, it is important that educators are as clear as possible about what they are trying to achieve and the ways in which they wish to demonstrate success. Such clarity is not just valuable in rendering an account, however; it can also provide the basis for gathering information which can really contribute to successful development.

References

DES (Department of Education and Science) (1987) *Managing Colleges Efficiently*. London: HMSO.

DES (Department of Education and Science) (1989) Performance Indicators: an aide-memoire from the DES, *Education*, 8 December: 514–15.

Department of Employment (1991) *Guidance on TVEI Performance Indicators*. London: HMSO.

Gray, J. and Jesson, J. (1990) The negotiation and construction of performance indicators: some principles, proposals and problems, *Evaluation and Research in Education*, 4 (2): 93–108.

Hopkins, D. and Leask, M. (1989) Performance indicators and school development, *School Organisation*, 9 (1): 3–20.

Lawler, E. E. and Rhode, J. G. (1976) *Information and Control in Organisations*. Pacific Palisades, CA: Goodyear.

Scottish Education Department (1990) *Measuring Up: performance indicators in further education*. London: HMSO.

6 | Making sense of change*

DAVID HOPKINS, MEL AINSCOW AND MEL WEST

On ways of thinking about change

Knowledge expands at such a rate that we need some way of classifying it and redu-cing it to manageable proportions. We also need to conceive of knowledge in ways that make sense and lead to action. This is why people often think in terms of *models*, because they often provide helpful frameworks for action. There is also a more profound way of viewing knowledge, in terms of underlying *values or assump-tions*. In this section we will explore further these two ways of thinking about change.

There are almost as many conceptions of the change process as there are writers on the subject, but despite this there are some broad areas of agreement. Hoyle's (1976) Open University unit, Strategies of Curriculum Change, for example, provides a help-ful review of the differing interpretations and facets of the term 'change', and an intro-duction to various change models from a UK perspective.

Our brief review serves to give a 'feel' for the area. Bennis *et al.* (1969) were the first to describe systematically the fundamental strategies of change. They identified three broad groupings which are said to comprise the range of approaches to change:

- *Power-coercive* refers to an approach which is direct, legalistic and authoritarian, and where the flow of communication is one way, from the initiator to the prac-titioner.
- *Normative re-educative* strategies are directed at the attitudes, norms and opinions of a group of practitioners, the mode of approach usually being made through group work with an emphasis on two-way interpersonal communication.
- *Rational-empirical* refers to an approach based on expertise which is aimed at the reason or intellect of the practitioner. The medium used is usually the book, lecture or advertisement, and communication is largely one-way.

* This material has been abridged.

In their book *The Planning of Change*, Bennis *et al.* (1969) provided a detailed rationale for each approach and gave examples of strategies under each of these three headings. The purpose of describing these three strategies or models is not merely taxonomic, but also to enable people, once having diagnosed a situation, to select the most appropriate change strategy for that particular change or setting.

The Bennis *et al.* approach, therefore, is about ordering the knowledge base in order to give researchers and practitioners more control over the process. Another interesting model that does just that was developed by Ray Bolam with his colleagues in Bristol during the mid-1970s while they were working on a succession of applied educational research projects. Bolam's conceptual framework for innovation provides a way of organizing a great deal of previous work, a way of thinking about the process of change, and an indication of how to go about doing it. It distinguishes between four major factors: the change agent, the innovation, the user system and the process of innovation over time. These four factors are presented (in Figure 6.1) as a two-dimensional conceptual framework. Bolam's framework, which merits closer attention, highlights the interactive nature of the innovation process, which is vitally important in any mature appreciation of how change comes about.

We have also found the distinction between 'adoptive' and 'adaptive' models of change helpful as a means of categorizing the literature (Hopkins 1984). The *adoptive* approach to change tends to disregard the variables existing within the individual school environment. These strategies are preoccupied with a top-down approach to change: they assume that change is linear and motivated by an authority figure. These models are often based on the (correct) assumption that it is usually the case that external pressure provides the motivation for change. [. . .] The best known of these approaches is probably the Research, Development and Dissemination (RD&D) model of educational change. As we have said, this is a top-down, or more accurately a centre-periphery, model of change that was developed to assist the implementation of centralized curriculum innovation in the mid-1960s and later. The ideas underlying the model are well known, but the most sophisticated description of

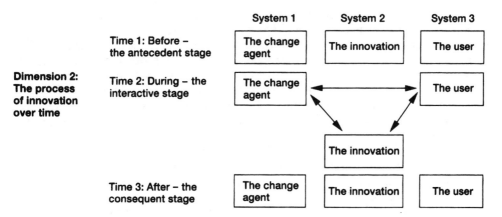

Figure 6.1 A conceptual framework for the study of innovation (Bolam, 1975, pp. 274–5)

Table 6.1   Guba and Clark's (1965) RD&D model

Method	Purpose
Research	To advance knowledge
Invention	To innovate
Design	To systematize the components of the innovation
Dissemination	To inform
Demonstration	To build conviction
Trial	To test
Installation	To operationalize
Institutionalization	To establish as an integral component of the system

Source: Quoted in Hoyle (1976: 40)

the model has been given by Guba and Clark (1965). Their classification is seen in Table 6.1.

This model, or variations of it, follows an almost irresistible logic. It represents the strategy used by most centralized curriculum development agencies, and by the same token policy makers, in implementing their 'products' or policies. It is recognizable as an 'ideal type' of approach, used in the UK, for example, by the Schools Council in the late 1960s and 1970s, and more recently by the National Curriculum Council (NCC). Ironically, [. . .] this approach to educational change has not proved very successful. Although this fact is now widely recognized by researchers and practitioners, it is still the preferred approach of policy makers and politicians – a situation unlikely to change in the near future.

There are other approaches to educational change that are more sensitive to the situation of the individual school and local context. They are appreciative of the environment in which they intervene, and demonstrate a concern for developing a capacity for change within the school situation rather than the adoption *per se* of the specific approach. These have been described as *adaptive* models of change (Lippitt *et al.* 1978). Interestingly, even Guba and Clark (1975) have publicly abandoned their advocacy for the RD&D approach, and ten years later proposed a more adaptive or cultural conceptualization of change.

If we stay with curriculum change for the moment, then a well-developed model which illustrates the adaptive approach has been provided by Malcolm Skilbeck's (1984) articulation of school-based curriculum development. Skilbeck outlines a five-stage model for this: situational analysis; goal formulation; programme building; interpretation and implementation; and monitoring, feedback assessment and reconstruction. Although there is a logical order to these stages, there may be sound reasons for intervening first at any one of them. Skilbeck also admits that, despite the technical appeal of such a model, teachers do not in fact proceed in such a linear fashion. His view is that the model should encourage groups of teachers involved in curriculum development to take into account different aspects of the process, to see it as an organic whole, and to work in a moderately systematic way.

School-based curriculum development is an appealing concept. Skilbeck's description, however, has a historical ring to it, especially to those of us enmeshed in the challenges of centrally imposed curricula and innovation overload. Certainly the model as it stands needs modifying to fit current circumstances. What, however, is interesting about [. . .] a National Curriculum is that, ironically, [it puts] more pressure on schools to develop their own version of a curriculum as a response to and elaboration of highly specific national criteria. [. . .] Successful schools are increasingly developing their own curriculum to reflect their own aspirations and the needs of their own pupils within the context of national criteria. This is where an adaptive model of curriculum change such as Skilbeck's could prove very helpful.

The distinction between adoptive and adaptive models of change is, of course, overly simplistic. At best these should be regarded as 'ideal types' and be open to modification. Mature responses to prescriptions of this type have been provided by Ronald Havelock, and by Gene Hall and Susan Loucks.

Havelock's (1975) linkage model embraces both adoptive and adaptive models of change, albeit at a structural level, and provides a more realistic approach to school autonomy in times of centralized change. He envisages a linkage process that mediates between RD&D agencies and the school. In the UK the best examples of these linking organizations would be teacher centres or LEA curriculum agencies. At present, such external support in the UK is in a hiatus. This, however, [. . .] is no reason to underestimate the importance of this function in facilitating the change process in schools.

The Levels of Use (LOU) instrument and the Concerns Based Adoption Model (CBAM) were originally developed by Hall and Loucks (1977, 1978) as a means of evaluating the level of implementation of a change in curriculum or teaching practice, and assessing the concerns of teachers as they move through the innovation process. These approaches were technically valid and extremely useful as evaluation tools. In this respect they fell into the 'adoption' category, as they had a specific and instrumental purpose. In later work (e.g. Loucks-Horsley and Hergert 1985; Hall and Hord 1987) these approaches have been used with great success, in a more adaptive way, in school-based development programmes. This is a good example of a well-developed and reliable approach to school development.

Beside the descriptions of specific approaches, what we are now beginning to see in these classifications of change strategies is not only ways of making change happen, but values about how change should be accomplished. Views on the complexity of change are value laden. The world view of those committed to change by adoption, for example, is most probably very different from that of those committed to an adaptive approach. To highlight this point, we provide examples of the value positions underpinning curriculum implementation which have been graphically contrasted by Ted Aoki (1984). He summarizes two polarized approaches to implementation: implementation as instrumental action as compared with practical action (Table 6.2). What Aoki is demonstrating so vividly here is the importance of people's values or view of the world in determining their approach to educational change or innovation. We see clearly in this example some of the reasons why a more instrumental approach to change has not always been overwhelmingly successful. These, of course, are the same values as underpin the adoption approaches to change we have just described [. . .]. There are, however, other similar, but more accessible, frameworks for clarifying the values underlying our approaches to change, as we see in the following section.

Three perspectives on planned change

Some years ago Ernest House (1979) wrote a 'state-of-the-art' paper on curriculum innovation. The organizing framework that he used in it contained three perspectives on educational change: the technological, the political and the cultural.

Table 6.2 Two contrasting views of curriculum implementation

As *instrumental action*	As *practical action*
With the researcher as the locus implies the following:	**With the teacher as the locus implies the following:**
Doing curriculum implementation is installing curriculum X.	Within this framework, to do curriculum implementation is to come to a deep understanding of curriculum X and to transform it based on the appropriateness to the situation.
The interest of the teacher is in placing curriculum X in a classroom or school faithfully and efficiently.	The implementer's interest is in the transformation of curriculum X within the situation based on disclosed underlying assumptions and conditions that make the transformation possible.
The implied view of curriculum is that of a commodity to be dispensed by teachers and consumed by students.	The implied view of curriculum X is that it is an object to be interpreted and critically reflected upon in an on-going transformation of curriculum and self.
The implied view of the good teacher is one who installs curriculum X efficiently and faithfully.	The implied view of the teacher is that of an actor who acts with and upon curriculum X as he/she reflects upon his/her own assumptions underlying action.
To explain 'implementation' within this framework is to give a cause–effect relationship.	Within this framework, to explain implementation is to trace it to underlying unreflected aspects which upon disclosure imply transformative action.
The implementer's subjectivity is irrelevant as implementing curriculum X is seen as an objective process.	The implementer's central activity is reflection upon his/her subjectively based action with and upon curriculum X.
The implied underlying relationship between theory and practice is one in which to implement is to put into practice curriculum-as-plan (that is, to apply to a practical situation an ideal construct).	The implied form of theory/practice relationship is that theory and practice are in dialectic relationship. To implement within this framework is to reflect critically upon the relationship between curriculum-as-plan and curriculum-in-use.
The typical approach to implementation studies is through examination of the degree of fidelity of the installed curriculum compared with the master curriculum.	To evaluate implementation within this framework is to examine the quality of the activity of discovering underlying assumptions, interests, values, motives, perspectives, root metaphors and implications for action to improve the human condition.

Source: Adapted from Aoki (1984: 112–13 and 116–17)

The *technological* perspective is best illustrated by the RD&D model, and has all the characteristics of the adoption approach to change we have already described. It has been, and continues to be, used by those concerned with centralized approaches to curriculum and educational change such as we have already described. In many countries, despite the apparent moves towards decentralization, the dominant *modus operandi* has been, as we have seen, technological.

The perspective assumes a rational view of the world. Yet as Jerry Patterson and his colleagues (1986) hint in the title of their book, *Productive School Systems for a Non-rational World*, things are not always like that. This is not to imply that schools are irrational or do not make sense, but rather that they are complex organizations operating in a disorderly environment. Although we live in a non-rational world, most educational policy assumes a rational logic: if A happens then B will follow. When the 'if-then' logic does not work, it is common to resort to 'if only' statements. If only X had not happened, then B would have occurred. The problem with 'if-then and if only' thinking is twofold: (1) it only rarely mirrors reality, and (2) it encourages individuals to externalize blame and not take action themselves. Be this as it may, the technological approach continues to be the dominant perspective, and by trying to pretend otherwise one also falls into the 'if only' trap. The approach, as we have already said, is logical, it makes sense; our approach to school improvement would be unrealistic unless it also embraced this perspective.

The *political* perspective emphasizes that educational change inevitably involves conflict. Change by its very nature involves certain individuals and groups doing new things which inevitably disturb the status quo. What for some is improvement may for others, initially at least, appear at best irrelevant and in some cases foolish. In many schools it is fairly easy to predict the reactions of certain groups and individuals. Often senior management in school will try different strategies to get the various groups and significant individuals to support their proposals. [. . .]

The micro-political aspects of educational change have received a great deal of attention [. . .] from British commentators. Educational sociologists like Eric Hoyle (1986), Stephen Ball (1987), Andy Hargreaves (1986) and Peter Woods (1986) have, in a series of books, and papers, illustrated aspects of the phenomenon. Studies in this area have introduced a number of very helpful concepts. The mid-1970s Rand study on educational change in the USA [. . .] introduced the notion of 'mutual adaption' whereby the successful implementation of national initiatives was characterized by both the school *and* the innovation changing through a process of mutual adaption. A similar concept, that of 'curriculum negotiation', was introduced by Barry Macdonald and Rob Walker (1976) in their study of curriculum innovation in England. They maintain that basic conflicts in values are camouflaged by a common rhetoric to which all subscribe. Their context is that of the Schools Council and similar centralized curriculum projects. Here, the gap between project intent and classroom practice is the consequence of trade-offs in meaning that are negotiated between developers and teachers on the one hand, and developers and academic critics on the other. Their argument is that with academics they negotiate an ideal version of the project, and with teachers a watered-down version that is 'do-able' in practice. Although the situation is different now (no one cares what academics think any more), the micro-political trade-offs survive, whatever the context.

The *cultural* perspective, in studies of educational change at least, is concerned with the social setting in which innovation intervenes. It demonstrates a commitment to the everyday reality, the cultural norms that are disturbed when innovation threatens. It is the antithesis of the adoptive models we reviewed earlier, and shares many of the values of the adaptive approach we described at the same time. We refer here also to Sarason (1982), where the problem of change is treated as essentially a cultural one.

There is a strong research tradition in the UK of in-depth studies that throw some light upon the impact of culture in schools and classrooms. Many of these studies take a sociological perspective and most involve ethnographic approaches to inquiry. Some of these studies help us to understand the way structures influence culture [. . .] within a school (e.g. Woods 1979; Ball 1981), whereas others focus on the sub-cultures of particular student groups (e.g. Hargreaves 1967; Willis 1977). Much of this literature is rich with accounts that reveal the complexities of school life, including the ways in which the culture of an organization impacts upon individual teachers and the way they go about their tasks.

[. . .]

We have [. . .] excellent examples of British work in this 'cultural' tradition. The work of Jean Rudduck, who, more than anyone else, has followed in the tradition of Lawrence Stenhouse, has exemplified a commitment to appreciating culture as a social phenomenon. Stenhouse (quoted in House 1979: 8) defined culture as 'a complex of shared understandings which serve as a medium through which individualized human minds interact'. Rudduck (1991) amplifies this definition through a series of research projects that embrace the 'cultural' perspective, including that of pupils. Jennifer Nias, Geoff Southworth and their colleagues have, in their long-term research into primary schools, given a great deal of texture to the perspective (e.g. Nias *et al.* 1989). Nias (1989: 143), besides complaining that the term 'culture' is applied with 'a wilful lack of precision' to schools, maintains on the basis of her and her colleagues' work that a school's culture does not have an existence independent of those who participate in it. The cultural phenomenon [. . .] deserves more attention.

This trinity of perspectives, besides being a helpful way of organizing the research literature, seems also to have a degree of universal applicability. In Table 6.3 we have summarized the three perspectives and compared them to some of the other interpretations of change reviewed in this chapter. Each of these perspectives affords a unique insight into the process of change. The important point is that no one perspective has a monopoly of the truth. It is through a holistic overview of all three that one is able to grasp the reality of *all* those involved in the process of change.

A striking example of this point is provided by the conclusions of a [. . .] study of curriculum innovation and change. On the basis of two qualitative studies of innovation involving seventeen schools, Corbett and Rossman (1989: 187–8) concluded that successful change requires the simultaneous use of multiple perspectives. Every school contains those susceptible to each of these perspectives. Focusing on all three 'increases the pool of potential implementors'.

The point that we are trying to emphasize is that each of these perspectives provides us with a valuable lens through which to view the change process. And each is important in its own right. Looking at a specific problem, at a particular point in time, may emphasize one view at the expense of another; but in the long run, all are equally valuable. In order to hammer the point home further, [. . .] these three perspectives combine in the following section to give further insights into the process of change.

Table 6.3   A comparison of perspectives on change and innovation

Perspective	House	Bennis et al.	Bolam
Technological	Innovation	Rational-empirical	Innovation
Political	Innovation in context	Power-coercive	Change agent
Cultural	Context	Normative-re-educative	User

The process of change and school improvement

[. . .] There are three further issues from the literature on planned change that are crucial to our formulation of school improvement strategies. They cut across the three perspectives discussed in the previous section, each issue containing elements of the other. These three issues relate to the unfolding of the change process over time, the importance of student outcomes, and the meaning individuals make of the change process.

The first is the way in which the change process *unfolds*. As Miles (1986) and Fullan (1991) have demonstrated, the change process is not linear, but consists of a series of three stages that merge into each other. Although these phases often coexist in practice, there are some advantages in describing them separately; particularly in terms of what happens during them, and what behaviours within each phase make for success. The process is generally considered to consist of three overlapping phases: initiation, implementation, and institutionalization (Figure 6.2).

Although implementation has received the most attention historically, this has most probably been disadvantageous to the process as a whole. Emphasizing initiation and implementation at the expense of institutionalization leads to a short-term view of innovation [. . .]. Consequently, it is probably more helpful to think of the three phases as a series of overlapping circles, as in Figure 6.2, rather than a straight line.

The *initiation* phase is about deciding to embark on innovation, and developing commitment towards the process. The key activities in the initiation phase are the decision to begin the innovation, and a review of the school's current state as regards it. There are, however, a number of factors associated with initiation that will influence whether the change gets started in the first place. [. . .] they are issues such as the existence of and access to innovations, pressures from within and without the school, availability of resources and consultancy support, and the quality of the school's internal conditions and organization. Fullan (1991: 50) describes them in detail and emphasizes that it is not simply the existence of these factors but their combinations that are important.

Matthew Miles (1986) has made an analysis of the various stages of school improvement: here is a summary of his list of factors that make for successful initiation:

- an innovation tied to a *local agenda* and high-profile *local need*;
- a clear, *well-structured* approach to change;
- an active *advocate* or champion who understands the innovation and supports it;
- *active initiation* to start the innovation (top-down is all right under certain conditions);
- *good-quality* innovation.

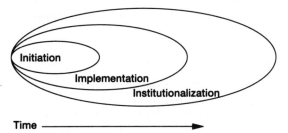

Time ———————————————————▶

Figure 6.2 The three overlapping phases of the change process (Miles *et al.* 1987)

Implementation is, as we have said, the phase of the process which has received the most attention. It is the phase of attempted use of the innovation. [. . .] The factors influencing implementation [include] the characteristics of the change, the internal conditions of the school and the pressure and support from the outside. [. . .] It is during this phase that skills and understanding are being acquired, some success is being achieved, and responsibility is delegated to working groups of teachers. It is often helpful to regard implementation as being of two types: pre-implementation and implementation. Many innovations founder at the pre-implementation stage because not enough initial support has been generated.

The key activities occurring during implementation are the carrying out of action plans, the developing and sustaining of commitment, the checking of progress and the overcoming of problems. The key factors making for success at this stage, according to Miles (1986), are:

- clear responsibility for orchestration/coordination (head, coordinator, external consultant);
- shared control over implementation (top-down is *not* all right); good cross-hierarchical work and relations; empowerment of both individuals and the school;
- a mix of pressure, and insistence on 'doing it right', and support;
- adequate and sustained staff development and inservice support (an external or internal coordinator, or a combination that builds personal and organizational capacity);
- rewards for teachers early in the process (empowerment, collegiality, meeting needs, classroom help, load reduction, supply cover, expenses resources).

Institutionalization is the phase when innovation and change stop being regarded as something new and become part of the school's usual way of doing things. Until recently it was assumed that this happened automatically. This is despite the evidence that innovations associated with many centralized initiatives tend to fade away after the initial wave of enthusiasm, or after a key actor leaves, or when the funding ceases. The move from implementation to institutionalization, however, often involves the transformation of a pilot project to a school-wide initiative, often without the advantage of the previously available funding. It is change of a new order. In these cases there tends to be widespread use of the change by staff, its impact is seen on classroom practice, and by that time the whole process is not regarded as being unusual. [. . .] Key activities at this stage, according to Miles (1986), are:

- an emphasis on *embedding* the change within the school's structures, its organization and resources;
- the elimination of *competing or contradictory practices*;
- strong and purposeful *links to other change efforts*, the curriculum and classroom teaching;
- *widespread use* in the school and local area;
- an adequate *bank of local facilitators* – advisory teachers for skills training.

The failure of many efforts towards change to progress beyond early implementation is partially explained by the lack of realization on the part of those involved that the above activities are necessary. They have also failed to understand that each of these phases has different characteristics that require different strategies if success is to be achieved.

The second and related issue is the importance of *process* leading to *outcomes*. The logic of the approach is as follows: we begin with some educational goal, which leads to some form of innovation. The impact and outcomes of the innovation are dependent on the nature of the initiation decisions (both within and outside the school), the factors affecting implementation, the implementation strategy and the degree to which institutionalization is achieved; all of which are embedded in, and dependent on, the culture of the school. The important point is that all of this effort should have some impact on student learning. Unfortunately many school improvement efforts have neglected this 'bottom line' by underemphasizing the 'end of the chain'.

Despite the evident truth of this point, it is unfortunately one that has been implicitly neglected in many educational change efforts. Michael Huberman (1992: 11) summarizes the issue nicely:

> [We need] to draw on studies that can actually demonstrate the causal relationship between adoption > implementation > enhanced technical capacity > revised institutional arrangements > measurable impacts on pupils in line with the 'thrust' of the innovation. Without that causal chain, we shall have no 'social technology' of implementation. Nor shall we be able to talk of 'school improvement' with a straight face. And by not addressing the impact on pupils, we will have indulged in some magical thinking as before: that adoption meant implementation . . . that implementation meant institutionalization . . . that enhanced teacher capacity means enhanced pupil achievement or development.
>
> . . . if changes in organizational and instructional practices are not followed down to the level of effects on pupils, we will have to admit more openly that we are essentially investing in staff development rather than in the improvement of pupils' abilities.

[. . .]

The third issue relates to the *meaning* that individuals give to their involvement in the change process. This perspective needs to underpin all the rational and political conceptions of change reviewed in this chapter. Fullan (1991: 32) reminds us that real change, 'whether desired or not, represents a serious personal and collective experience characterized by ambivalence and uncertainty' for the individual involved. If the result of this engagement is to be empowerment and fulfilment, then such a judgement can only be made with hindsight. There is no such certainty as one works through the process that meaning will be achieved.

[. . .] The existing internal conditions within the school will make success or failure more or less likely. The reason we need organizational settings in schools which support teachers and students in the process of change is that the experience of change is individually threatening and disconcerting. These settings should be organized around the realization that change is a process whereby individuals alter their ways of thinking and doing. There are a number of implications that stem from this (Fullan 1985: 396):

- change takes place over time;
- change initially involves anxiety and uncertainty;
- technical and psychological support is crucial;
- the learning of new skills is incremental and developmental;

- organizational conditions within and in relation to the school make it more or less likely that school improvement will occur;
- successful change involves pressure and support within a collaborative setting.

Messages

In concluding this chapter, which has contained many different themes and cut across boundaries between rational change strategies and the subjective meaning of change, we need a summary that unites these dichotomous perspectives. The following 'messages about change' attempt to capture some of the ambivalence, ironies, paradoxes and uncertainty of making progress in difficult times. Taken together they provide the basis for creating a 'mind set' about change (see Fullan 1991: 105–7). Individually these suggestions are of little help: even when taken together they do not tell us how to proceed; but they do suggest a way of thinking about change [. . .]. As a whole these assumptions help us to think creatively, proactively and realistically about change and provide us with the essential foundation for [taking action].

- *Change takes place over time.* Assume that effective change takes time. Unrealistic or undefined time-lines fail to recognize that implementation occurs developmentally. Persistence is a critical attribute of successful change. It is helpful to view change as a journey that has the present situation as a starting point, but no clear destination. This having been said, there are still some predictable staging posts along the way and different skills and approaches are needed to ensure success at different times.
- *Embrace multiple perspectives.* Because different perspectives on change are often in conflict they provide complementary forms of understanding and routes for action. Technical approaches are useful for planning, for example, but micro-political views give deeper understanding.
- *Be self-conscious about the process of change.* No amount of research knowledge will ever make it totally clear what to do. But those who do not think about change or attempt to conceptualize it do not do it very well. Teachers know a great deal about change in students, but rarely is this understanding translated to adult or organizational learning. The insights about change that all teachers have are an untapped resource.
- *Assume resistance.* Conflict and disagreement are not only inevitable but fundamental to successful planned change. Rational models of change underestimate resistance or treat it as a problem. Resistance is normal; collaboration is about utilizing conflict.
- *Invest in teachers and schools.* All successful change requires an individual response. Often the experience of change is individually threatening and disconcerting, which is why we need organizational settings in schools which support teachers and students in the process of change. These settings need first to be organized around the realization that change is a process whereby individuals alter their ways of thinking and doing. But teachers and schools are not the same and one needs to pay regard to these differences.

References

Aoki, T. (1984) Towards a reconceptualisation of curriculum implementation, in D. Hopkins and M. Wideen (eds) *Alternative Perspectives on School Improvement*. London: Falmer Press.

Ball, S. J. (1987) *The Micro-politics of the School*. London: Methuen.

Ball, S. J. (1981) *Beachside Comprehensive*. Cambridge: Cambridge University Press.

Bennis, W. E., Benne, K. and Chin, R. (1969) *The Planning of Change*. London: Holt, Rinehart & Winston.

Bolam, R. (1975) The management of educational change: towards a conceptual framework, in A. Harris, M. Lawn and W. Prescott (eds) *Curriculum Innovation*. London: Croom Helm.

Corbett, H. D. and Rossman, G. (1989) Three paths to implementing change, *Curriculum Inquiry*, 19 (2): 163–90.

Fullan, M. (1985) Change processes and strategies at the local level, *The Elementary School Journal*, 85 (3): 391–421.

Fullan, M. (1991) *The New Meaning of Educational Change*. London: Cassell.

Guba, E. and Clark, D. (1965) Examination of political change roles in education, *Strategies for Educational Group Newsletter*, 2 October.

Guba, E. and Clark, D. (1975) The configurational perspective, *Educational Researcher*, 4 (4): 6–9.

Hall, G. and Hord, S. (1987) *Change in Schools*. New York: State University of New York Press.

Hall, G. and Loucks, S. (1977) A developmental model for determining whether the treatment is actually implemented, *American Educational Research Journal*, 14: 236–70.

Hall, G. and Loucks, S. (1978) Teachers' concerns as a basis for facilitating and pesonalising staff development, *Teachers College Record*, 80 (1): 36–53.

Hargreaves, A. (1986) *Two Cultures of Schooling*. London: Falmer Press.

Hargreaves, D. H. (1967) *Social Relations in a Secondary School*. London: Routledge & Kegan Paul.

Havelock, R. (1975) The utilisation of educational change and development, in A. Harris, M. Lawn and W. Prescott (eds) *Curriculum Innovation*. London: Croom Helm.

Hopkins, D. (1984) Change and the organisational character of teacher education, *Studies in Higher Education*, 9 (1): 37–45.

House, E. (1979) Technology and craft: a ten year perspective on innovation, *Journal of Curriculum Studies*, 11 (1): 1–15.

Hoyle, E. (1976) Strategies of Curriculum Change, Unit 23 Open University Course: Curriculum Design and Development. Milton Keynes: Open University Press.

Hoyle, E. (1986) *The Politics of School Management*. London: Hodder & Stoughton.

Huberman, M. (1992) Critical introduction, in M. Fullan, *Successful School Improvement*. Buckingham: Open University Press.

Lippitt, R., Hooyman, G., Sashkin, M. and Kaplan, J. (1978) *Resource Book for Planned Change*. Ann Arbor: Human Resource Development Association.

Loucks-Horsley, S. and Hergert, L. (1985) *An Action Guide to School Improvement*. Alexandria, VA: ASCD/The Network.

Macdonald, B. and Walker, R. (1976) *Changing the Curriculum*. London: Open Books.

Miles, M. (1986) 'Research findings on the stages of school improvement', mimeo. Center for Policy Research, New York.

Miles, M., Ekholm, M. and Vandenberghe, R. (eds) (1987) *Lasting School Improvement: Exploring the Process of Institutionalization*. Leuven, Belgium: ACCO.

Nias, J. (1989) Refining the cultural perspective, *Cambridge Journal of Education*, 19 (2): 143–6.

Nias, J., Southworth, G. and Yeomans, R. (1989) *Staff Relationships in the Primary School*. London: Cassell.

Patterson, J., Purkey, S. and Parker, J. (1986) *Productive School Systems for a Non-rational World*. Alexandria, VA: ASCD.

Rudduck, J. (1991) *Innovation and Change*. Milton Keynes: Open University Press.
Sarason, S. (1982) *The Culture of the School and the Problem of Change*, 2nd edn. Boston: Allyn & Bacon.
Skilbeck, M. (1984) *School Based Curriculum Development*. London: Harper & Row.
Willis, P. (1977) *Learning to Labour*. London: Saxon House.
Woods, P. (1979) *The Divided School*. London: Routledge & Kegan Paul.
Woods, P. (1986) *Inside Schools*. London: Routledge & Kegan Paul.

7 | A framework for curriculum development, policy implementation and monitoring quality

NEVILLE WEST

The purpose of this chapter is to present an over-arching framework derived from working with [primary school] headteachers, assistant heads and coordinators, all of whom wished to explore constructive, manageable and feasible ways of responding to the requirements of the Education Reform Act (ERA). The purpose of the framework is to make the processes of curriculum development, implementation and monitoring more manageable. It is comprised of nine components, each of which is explored in the sections which follow.

[. . .]

The complete framework, comprised of nine components, is presented in Figure 7.1. It is offered as a conceptual framework to assist schools as they undertake the practical but complex and challenging business of improving the quality of teaching and learning. It is based on a few simple but effective management principles:

- wherever possible don't act until you are conceptually clear about what you are trying to do;
- keep things as simple as possible;
- wherever possible make one task do more than one thing;
- empower others;
- keep documentation action-orientated and avoid essay writing;
- make sure that everyone understands how the actions of individuals and the work of groups relate to the whole (hence the value of an over-arching framework);
- make sure that learning within the staff group is at least equal to, or greater than, the changes you are trying to bring about.

Component 1: A generic policy for teaching and learning

The first component in the framework is a policy for teaching and learning. Policy has been defined 'as a course or method of action *selected* (by an institution, a group or an

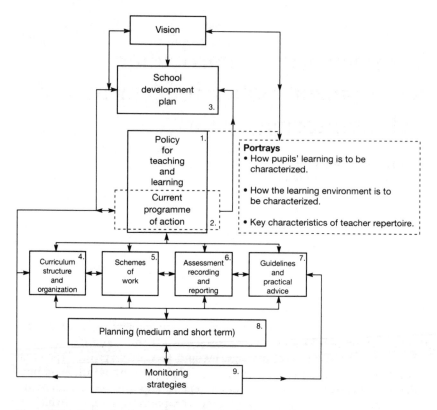

Figure 7.1   Policy implementation and monitoring quality

individual) from among alternatives and in the light of *given conditions* to guide and determine present and future *decisions*' (Webster's dictionary). There are three key words in this definition. First, the word *selected*, which implies that alternatives have been considered and that the policy will be less likely to be regarded as arbitrary. Policies are unique to given situations and we would therefore expect a school's policies to reflect its particular context and *given conditions*. The word *decision* reminds us that the major purpose of policy is to empower others. This definition is the more helpful since it does not trade in words which are sometimes regarded as synonymous with policy such as 'guideline', or 'framework'. This is not a semantic quibble. Within the framework described here specific meanings are attributed to such terms as 'scheme of work', 'guideline' and 'policy'.

Middle managers will be working within the context of a wide range of policies and it is therefore useful to make a distinction between two categories of policy: *generic* policy and *specific* policy. Generic policy focuses on a complex area of concern and in consequence is prone to a range of different interpretations. The central values which underpin the policy are likely to be contested. Examples of generic policies in the school context would be policies for teaching and learning, equal opportunities, staff development, or special needs. Desirable behaviour and principles may be outlined, but in implementing generic policy, staff are called upon to exercise professional judgement. To use a theatrical analogy, the situation is akin to one in which staff share the same script and each is expected to enact a role creatively, but within the terms of the playwright's intentions. The fact that generic policies are susceptible to individual interpretation makes monitoring an essential feature of implementation. This point will be developed further as the framework is explained.

The second category of policy, that of *specific* policy, embraces those policies which focus on much less complex areas of concern and which are much more amenable to codification or converting into protocol. Such policies link procedures to an agreed and intended result. Examples of specific policy in schools would be policies relating to school uniform, school visits, or finance and resource management. Since school governors will be involved in the process of policy formulation it is far preferable, in a situation where they may be unfamiliar with formulating policy, to work first on *specific* policy areas rather than expecting them to cut their teeth on a contested area of generic policy such as teaching and learning.

Policies represent the intentions or the 'oughts' of the institution and to this extent reflect the kind of place the school seeks to become. They represent a response to such questions as, 'Where are we now?', or 'Where do we want to be?' Some schools have responded to the second question by formulating a vision statement backed by policies which are congruent with that vision. Other schools have undertaken a strategic analysis of trends and needs and have formulated their policies in the light of such an analysis. Starrat (1990) recognized this distinction: 'Other educators are better engineers than rhetoricians. They will point to policies, structures and programmes in their school as embodying the vision of the school. To them it is the management arrangements that channel energy and attention towards those values and meanings that lie at the core of the school's vision'. In terms of the framework being offered here, a policy for teaching and learning lies at the heart of a school and is central to all that happens. The formulation of that generic policy will be the biggest investment a school makes on behalf of the pupils the staff seek to serve.

In the pre-ERA publication, *The Curriculum 5 to 16* (DES 1985), HMI identified five characteristics of the curriculum that have gained wide acceptance within schools. The characteristics are as follows:

- *Breadth*: that is to say that the curriculum should bring pupils into contact with the nine areas of learning and experience . . . (the National Curriculum presented these in terms of subjects, but the principle still holds true). To achieve this, HMI pointed out that teachers 'should be able to call on the support of teachers who, as well as having responsibilities for their own classes, act as consultants in particular subjects or areas of the curriculum. This is particularly effective when such consultants help other teachers to identify objectives, to plan the teaching and learning and to evaluate it' (para. 109).
- *Balance*: between the various areas of learning and experience, approaches to teaching and learning and forms of classroom organization.
- *Relevance*: 'in the sense that it is seen by pupils to meet their present and prospective needs . . . that all that pupils learn should be practical, and therefore relevant in ways that enable them to build on it or use it for their own purposes in everyday life' (paras 116 and 118).
- *Differentiation*: 'to allow for differences in the abilities and other characteristics of children, even of the same age . . . If it is to be effective, the curriculum must allow for differences' (para. 121, citing HMSO 1980).

- *Progression and continuity:* in that learning experiences cumulatively lead to learning outcomes so as to 'ensure an orderly advance in their capabilities over a period of time . . . each successive element making appropriate demands and leading to better performance' (para. 121).

The question that these characteristics raise is the $64,000 question which every school must resolve through dialogue with coordinators and other members of staff, namely:

What degree of variation in classroom practice is permissible if such criteria are to remain meaningful?

A constructive answer to this question is to be found in a whole-school policy for teaching and learning. The situation in the context of the National Curriculum may be summarized in terms of Figure 7.2.

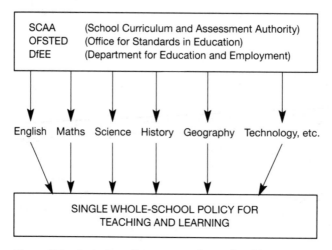

Figure 7.2 A single policy, not one for each subject

Many schools have produced separate policies for each subject in the National Curriculum. Figure 7.2 proposes a *single* policy for teaching and learning which underpins the work in *all* the subjects. This strategy avoids repetition and simplifies the process of policy formulation. Instead of individual middle managers undertaking the same process (who needs nine generic policies?) we have the possibility of solving the problem by means of a task group comprised of the curriculum coordinators/subject managers led by the headteacher.

The rationale for this proposal is not based on organizational expediency: it is grounded in the view that the ways in which pupils acquire their sets of understanding in the different curriculum areas have more similarities than differences. As they participate in learning, pupils engage in investigative work, problem solving, hypothesizing, trialling, testing, exploring, communicating and so on; they acquire new concepts and extend existing conceptual frameworks, and they practise new skills and engage in their work through a mixed economy of individual, group and whole-class activities. The differences between subjects lie in the nature of the evidence that is cited in the different subjects and the tests for truth which are applied in the course of learning.

The learning processes cited earlier are common to science, history, mathematics, drama, geography, art and so on, but the nature of the evidence is different in each case. The tests for truth that are applied in mathematics are peculiar to that subject and different from those which would be cited in, say, history or music. This distinction was well argued by the educational philosopher Paul Hirst (1974) and many would say that the structure of the National Curriculum is largely based on his analysis of the nature of knowledge.

The policy for teaching and learning provides the answer to the question, 'What do we want to *witness* in classrooms', a question which immediately evokes clear images of practice and helps to move us away from generalized principles and broad statements of philosophy which staff may affirm, but whose practice stays the same. The policy becomes the central reference point to guide the carefully sequenced work subsequently undertaken by middle managers. The policy is made up of three *elements*, each of which provides an answer to a specific question:

- *What should characterize the learning experiences offered to pupils?*
  i.e. What is it that we want pupils to do as they engage in the learning process? What is it that we should *witness* if we engaged in systematic observation over a reasonable amount of time? Clearly, not every process would be evident in every lesson.
- *What should characterize the learning environment?*
  i.e. What would we expect to see in the physical environment in terms of the management of teaching and learning resources, the layout and use of space, classroom organization and the ground rules which underpin the learning process? What does the learning milieu tell us about relationships between pupil and pupil, pupil and teacher?
- *What should be the major characteristics of the teacher's repertoire to achieve the high quality of learning experiences outlined in the first two elements above?*

Formulating a policy for teaching and learning

Where coordinators engage in the formulation of individual policies for their subjects, the task has often been undertaken in relative isolation, with some consultation along the way with other members of staff. This approach has a number of problems associated with it. Policy documents written in isolation 'can become a source of mystification and a symbol of the remoteness and unreality of the school and its purposes. Policy is not encompassed simply by the old English art of essay writing' (Bailey 1986). More importantly, a policy produced in isolation denies opportunities for others to learn. A policy for teaching and learning is best approached by a task group comprised of three to five curriculum and/or key stage coordinators with the headteacher acting as chair. Every member of staff will be involved in the process but at different times and with specific purposes in mind. All staff will have the opportunity to comment upon and add to drafts along the way. Governors will be consulted and kept informed.

The work of a policy working group may be outlined as follows. First, the group should analyse existing practice and draw together the ways in which learning is currently characterized in the school, the way learning environments are typified and the range of strategies currently used by the staff to promote learning. The task is one of descriptive analysis, not evaluation.

Second, in the light of the descriptive analysis the group should then identify what *should* be witnessed in respect of the three elements of the policy, and in doing so engage in dialogue with staff. This is likely to mean going beyond current practice and adding features which are essential if high quality provision is to be achieved. The group may wish to invite outsiders with relevant knowledge and experience to help them at this stage. Where appropriate they may find it helpful to refer to the school's Ofsted or LEA inspection report together with published reports on schools similar to their own. Any and every relevant source should be explored. The criteria for inclusion in the policy is whether the point in question will result, in the long term, in benefits to teaching and learning within the school and not whether a particular point will be acceptable to everyone, or deemed too difficult to be attempted. Iconoclasm and the capacity to think divergently should be encouraged within the group.

Third, having identified the content of each of the three elements, the group should then make first drafts of each element and circulate these for comment to all teaching staff and to governors. Current concerns should be shared with governors during the process, not at the end. The purposes of the policy and its role in relation to the implementation of the National Curriculum should be explained and observations from the lay perspective welcomed. When consultations have been completed a first draft should be circulated to staff for comment and in similar fashion to the governing body. A final version should be approved formally by the teaching staff and the governing body.

[. . .]

Definitions of teaching and the concept of teacher repertoire

The third element in a policy for teaching and learning is that of teacher repertoire. The concept of teacher repertoire was first developed by the author in 1986 and has been applied to a number of different contexts since that time (see, for example, West 1992a and 1992b). The term has been found to be much more productive than teaching 'style' which is associated with simplistic dichotomies such as formal-informal; traditional-progressive; teacher centred-pupil centred, and the like. [. . .] Repertoire is [. . .] defined as: the set of skills, devices, methods, strategies, knowledge and understandings which enables a teacher to make effective decisions in the course of promoting learning in the range of curriculum areas which they profess to teach.

Repertoire has proved to be a useful term of reference in the context of monitoring, since it enables us to proceed from a position in which no one has a 'perfect repertoire' and the idea of a preferred teaching style has been dispensed with. It acknowledges that learning is promoted through a wide range of skills and sensitivities such as lucid explanation, higher-order questioning skills, maintaining an effective classroom dynamic, the ability to engage pupils in effective forms of collaborative learning and so on. In this, the third element in a policy for teaching and learning, the characteristics associated with the promotion of high quality learning are identified. These characteristics, like those relating to pupils' learning, or the learning environment, may be used as the focus for a programme of action.

[. . .]

Structuring the policy document

The final document might be structured as follows:

- a short outline of the origins of the policy;
- a statement of the aims of the policy and the needs which it seeks to meet;
- the three elements of the policy, each element being developed separately, and the various characteristics presented in bullet format;
- the resources which will be devoted to implementing the policy;
- review and evaluation, which outlines when and how this will be undertaken;
- appendices which can be attached to the document which outline
  (a) the current action programme, and
  (b) details of staff who are to play significant roles in the implementation/monitoring process.

Component 2: The programme of action

The programme of action is the second feature of the framework presented in Figure 7.1 and is the strategy used to facilitate policy implementation and monitoring. Policy formulation takes a good deal of energy and it is sometimes assumed that since staff have engaged fully in the process that they will, *ipso facto*, own the policy. That assumption confuses affirmation with the more important process of ownership and the latter can only be said to have occurred when the policy has been implemented.

One of the key functions of a subject manager [. . . is] that of 'advice, documentation and support for staff'. One of the elements [is] that of policy implementation. It is not reasonable to assume that individual middle managers can undertake this role across the nine areas of the curriculum concurrently. If each coordinator, however hard working, engages in that process at individual level then what we may finish up with is atomized effort, tired staff, and no impact at whole-school level. Effective management is about working with and through others in order to maximize impact where it most benefits *all* pupils. It is about enabling things to happen, empowering colleagues and helping establish the necessary conditions. [. . .] A mixed economy of task groups for developmental work and individualized roles for maintenance has much to commend it.

Implementing policy and monitoring quality are development tasks. A policy for teaching and learning is a generic policy, and as such it will be prone to a range of interpretations. Such a policy will outline aspects of teaching and learning which may not currently be part of normal practice at whole-school level. The policy represents the *'public map'* of intentions concerning practice. The policy will surface in classrooms where it reflects the *private image* of that policy as perceived by individual teachers. Some of those images will reflect inventive practice which none of the policy constructors envisaged at the outset. The purpose of coordinators engaging in the monitoring process as part of a programme of action at whole-school level is not to *prove*, but to *improve*. One way of doing this is to encourage inventiveness and creativity wherever it is witnessed or, as one HMI with a penchant for mixing his metaphors was heard to say recently, 'If ever you see a spark of creativity, water it!'

Teaching and learning are complex processes and it would be foolish to think that just because we have a written policy it is a simple matter for staff to adopt what it contains. The purpose of the programme of action is to facilitate implementation by taking *one* strand of the policy and making this the focus at whole-school level over a realistic period of time such as half a term. During that time the whole staff will delegate to a *group of coordinators* the joint tasks of implementation and monitoring. [. . .]

Component 3: The school development plan

In Figure 7.1 the link is made between the policy for teaching and learning, the programme of action and the school development plan. The business of implementing the most important policy in the school is of the highest priority. We should therefore expect to find the programmes of action lying at the heart of the school development plan.

Component 4: Curriculum structure and organization

The policy for teaching and learning portrays what it is that we should witness as we observe the processes of teaching and learning. Such processes take place within a curriculum structure. The document on curriculum structure and organization represents the school's response to the [National Curriculum] and should make clear:

- the amount of time which is to be devoted to the different subjects or combinations of subjects. This can only be done by carrying out a careful analysis of the current use of time in the school day, week, term and year, questioning the outcomes and deciding on the best use of time. [. . .] In making decisions about time allocations due regard needs to be paid to the time taken up by registration requirements, collective worship and lunch and break periods and also to time which is taken up in the year on special events, school visits and by Key Stage assessments;
- how the different subjects comprising the curriculum are to be organized and the forms these should take in the various year-groups. It will indicate the subjects which are to comprise cross-curricular work such as topic, project or thematic work and which subjects are to be taught as separate entities. It will reflect due regard for balance within the curriculum. The guidance from SCAA, *Planning the Curriculum at Key Stages 1 and 2* (1995) refers to 'units of work' which fall into two broad categories: 'continuing' and 'blocked', both types drawing, in the first instance, on work from a single subject or aspect of the curriculum. 'Continuing work' is defined as 'a planned sequence of lessons or activities drawn from a single area of the curriculum' (p. 40). 'Blocked' work can be taught within a specific amount of time, not exceeding a term. It should focus on a distinct and cohesive body of knowledge, understanding and skills. Such work can be taught on its own or be linked with units in other subjects or aspects of the curriculum;
- how decisions regarding curriculum structure have been agreed and the extent to which teachers' subject knowledge and resources have been borne in mind.

Awareness of the ground rules relating to curriculum structure and organization will greatly assist coordinators who have responsibility for drawing up the scheme of work in their particular curriculum area in consultation with their colleagues. The time allocations will be *indicative allocations* in the first instance and may need to be revised in the light of subsequent monitoring and evaluation. Component 4 of the framework should have the effect of safeguarding the entitlement curriculum of all pupils and assist coordinators when they make decisions relating to schemes of work. Schemes of work which cannot be fitted into the agreed curriculum structure are recipes for frustration.

Component 5: Schemes of work

Schemes of work are represented by component 5 of the framework and are the outcome of discussions on what is to be taught in the light of decisions made about curriculum structure and organization. Each scheme should reflect the fact that pupils [. . .] should acquire progressive capability in, and understanding of, information systems. Schemes of work are not the same as policy and provide the answer to a different question. Schemes of work answer the basic question posed by teachers who have particular specialisms but who are obliged to teach nine subject areas, namely, 'What do I teach, to my age and stage of pupils, in what sequence, with what degree of choice?' We only need one policy for teaching and learning but we do need nine schemes of work. The task here is that of transposing the [National Curriculum] subject outlines, and statutory and non-statutory guidance into a form which is appropriate to the school in question and which matches the time deployment outlined in the curriculum structure (component 4).

[. . .] For each year-group the schemes of work should:

- outline the content to be taught;
- organize the content in terms of 'continuous work', 'blocked work' and manageable and coherent units of work;
- identify links between different aspects of the curriculum: units can be linked when they contain common or complementary knowledge, understanding and skills; or when the skills acquired in one subject are applied or consolidated in a different context; or where work in one unit provides a stimulus for work in another;
- indicate the notional time to be devoted to teaching and assessing the work;
- sequence the work into three terms;
- clearly indicate where staff are permitted to select between agreed options.

Component 6: Assessment, recording and reporting

Component 6 consists of the whole-school policy for the assessment, recording and reporting of pupil progress. Many schools have assessment coordinators whilst in others this may be one of the aspects of a key stage coordinator's role. Curriculum coordinators need good channels of communication with the assessment coordinator in order that the latter can produce an effective policy document which indicates how assessment will be undertaken in the various areas of the curriculum. It is preferable to have a separate document relating to assessment rather than including assessment in the various schemes of work or the policy for teaching and learning. The assessment policy should assist teachers when they engage in detailed planning and should make clear how learning objectives are to be identified, when and in what ways pupils' progress will be assessed, and how information gained from assessment is to be used to assist staff in matching work to the learning needs of pupils and communicated to parents and other stakeholders.

Component 7: Guidelines

Guidelines are neither policy, nor are they schemes. Their function is to service both in a specific way. Guidelines answer the question, 'How?' If, for example, a teacher has limited knowledge of science and is obliged to introduce pupils to the concept of mass, he or she might seek the help of the science coordinator. The coordinator is likely to respond to such requests informally, explaining what is needed, citing useful resources and so on. Where the same issue persistently recurs then the coordinator's response might be to mount a school-based workshop on the issue in question. But it is not always possible for every inquiry to be dealt with individually or by means of a staff workshop. Written guidelines fill this gap and are intended as a means of providing a first response to questions that have been raised. Over time an archive of such written guidance is established, an archive which may be of great assistance to new members of staff. Other examples of guidelines might be those relating to: collaborative groupwork and its organization; organizing an effective consultation evening for parents; the design of learning tasks; displaying the work of pupils; or the role of non-teaching assistants in the classroom. The inclusion of such detail in a policy document would make it unwieldy. Guidelines are akin to the sort of information which mountaineers might draw upon when planning how a particular feature on their route might be traversed.

Component 8: Medium- and short-term planning

Medium-term planning is frequently undertaken within year-group teams supported by subject-managers or Key Stage coordinators. The planning unit is usually half-termly. Many schools set aside non-contact time for this type of planning. Schemes of work are transposed into detailed plans in which broad learning objectives are defined; resources are identified and allocated; confirmation is made of the way the curriculum is to be organized in terms of the agreed structures of different kinds of work and linkages; and assessment points are agreed. In terms of the overall framework, the role of medium- and short-term planning is absolutely crucial, since it is at this point that staff bear in mind the agreed focus for policy implementation and monitoring. The policy for teaching and learning has equal importance alongside the schemes of work. The planning should therefore make clear those aspects which constitute the developmental aspects of the year-group team. If, for example, it had been agreed that the focus for monitoring during the half-term unit was to be collaborative learning, then it would be expected that each year-group team would provide specific details of this aspect in drawing up their plans. In drawing up their short-term (weekly) plans, each member of staff would outline how they intended to engage their pupils in collaborative groupwork, and what aspects of the latter they were seeking to extend as their contribution to the current programme of action (component 2 of the framework presented in Figure 7.1).

Medium- and short-term planning have to be kept in proportion. Most schools use some form of planning framework which provides a shorthand means of communicating current work across each year-group. What is being proposed here is a balance between shorthand frameworks and more detailed information in relation to the agreed monitoring focus for the half-term in question. [. . .]

Component 9: Monitoring strategies

This is the final component of the framework and outlines the monitoring strategies which will be adopted in the school as the means of implementing the teaching and learning policy and monitoring quality. [. . .]

Monitoring answers the question, 'Do we do what we say that we do?' and is concerned with tracking policy into practice and improving practice in a constructive, supportive and rigorous way. It may be compared to taking a series of 'snapshots' or film clips of the curriculum-in-action and comparing these to the 'film script' of agreed intentions. It is about building quality in at the beginning and during the process, rather than relying on infrequent summative evaluations. Programmes of action provide the vehicle for *sustained* attention to *specific* aspects of teaching and learning. Such programmes recognize that teaching and learning are complex processes. In the course of monitoring we may come to understand a particular facet more profoundly, or even, perhaps, for the first time. To focus, say, on collaborative learning will require us to pose questions, go beneath the surface features of groupwork, analyse findings and explore the implications these may have in terms of current practice. In doing so, we will probably identify further questions along the way. Amongst the outcomes may be a firmer definition of collaborative learning, or an extension of teacher repertoires as a consequence of witnessing illuminative practice, or it may lead us to workshops on the design of collaborative learning tasks.

Monitoring is not something that is 'done' to colleagues: it is essentially a shared endeavour which is effectively managed at whole-school level. [. . .]

We need to monitor so that we may:

- acknowledge the contributions of staff in implementing agreed policy;
- celebrate and share good practice;
- maintain commitment to building quality into the curriculum-in-action;
- engage in informed dialogue on specific aspects of practice;
- extend existing insights into the complexities of teaching and learning and go below the surface of classroom practice;
- generate a common language relating to teaching and learning;
- identify and provide what forms of support and development are needed;
- extend teacher repertoires.

[. . .]

This then is the over-arching framework which seeks to aid clarity and make the task of policy implementation and monitoring more manageable. It provides a map for middle managers to colonize by means of a mixed economy of task groups and designated maintenance/service functions. It is intended to provide the basis for half-termly programmes of action which are linked to the school development plan. Each programme of action is concerned with the implementation of policy in constructive, supportive but rigorous ways in which middle managers play a key role in realistic units of time. [. . .]

References

Bailey, A. J. (1986) 'Policy-making in schools: creating a sense of educational purpose', unpublished mimeo. Brighton: University of Sussex.
DES (1985) *The Curriculum from 5–16*, Curriculum matters no. 2. London: HMSO.
Hirst, P. (1974) *Knowledge and the Curriculum*. London: Routledge & Kegan Paul.
SCAA (1995) *Planning the Curriculum at Key Stages 1 and 2*. London: SCAA Publications.
West, N. F. (1992a) *Classroom Observation in the Context of Appraisal*. Harlow: Longman.
West, N. F. (1992b) *Primary Headship*. Harlow: Longman.

8 | Organising learning*

JOAN DEAN

The National Curriculum and the school's statement of aims are starting points for the process of education. The other starting point is the individual student. Each child comes to school with his or her own unique set of experiences, interests and abilities and these affect the child's ability to take from what the school has to offer. The difficult task of management and of the classroom teacher is to bring together the students and the curriculum in such a way that the students learn.

[. . .]

The management tasks of organisation are as follows:

1 Organise the school effectively for teaching and learning.
2 Ensure that there are equal opportunities for all students.
3 Deploy staff and other resources effectively.

[. . .]

Organise the school effectively for teaching and learning

It is the task of management to organise so that there is optimum learning for students, by deploying people, time and space to the best advantage. This involves grouping students in various ways for learning, sometimes attempting to form homogeneous groups and sometimes deliberately forming mixed groups. There may also be opportunities for students to learn as individuals, using computer-based or other resource materials and this opportunity is likely to increase as more programmes are produced for this purpose. Management must plan the use of time to provide a programme over the school year which uses the skills of staff and the space and other resources available to the best advantage.

* Abridged version.

Grouping for learning

Hargreaves speaks of the importance of the social group as a basis for acquiring common morality. He believes that this development happens as a result of being part of a cohesive group and notes that past secondary schools kept students in their form group with teachers moving rather than students (Hargreaves 1982). The demands of specialist subjects have made this no longer a possibility because most subjects now require a lot of equipment and there are also many advantages in teachers having their own rooms. The result is that students are less part of the form group or tutor group than they were in the past and this needs to be borne in mind and every effort made to foster stable groups, especially at the early stages of secondary education. Later on students may begin to identify with the larger group of the year or the school.

Group learning involves the opportunity to work as a group as well as being organised as a group. Much adult activity involves working in groups and students need to learn the skills of leading, following, sharing and contributing to group goals. Hargreaves notes that individuals need to learn that it is sometimes necessary to abandon one's own interests in the interests of the group or because one's interests encroach upon or negate the rights of others. He stresses the need for schools to prepare young people to be part of several communities as adults by being part of different groups in school (Hargreaves 1982). They are part of various groups in any case because of the need to organise large numbers, but the point he is making is that schools need to be aware of the learning potential of this and to make use of it in a positive way. He also stresses the value of the cooperative project for this kind of learning.

Since there are fewer teachers than students in a school, decisions have to be made about how students will be grouped for learning. There are a number of choices available:

- *Form/tutor group/specialist group* [. . .]
- *Ability/mixed ability grouping* [. . .]
- *Friendship grouping* [. . .]
- *Single sex/mixed groups* [. . .]
- *Grouping by age/mixed age groups* [. . .]
- *Group size* A further point to consider is group size. [. . .]

The use of time

Time is finite and although in prosperous times we can increase it in one sense by increasing the staff of the school or by teaching for more of the time, we cannot produce more time for the students except by pruning non-classroom aspects of the school day. Improvements generally have to come from a better use of existing time. This is particularly important now that the existence of directed time sets definite limits on what teachers can be asked to do, although many teachers are still prepared to give much more than is demanded.

Any study of the use of time needs to start by analysing what is already happening. This means analysing how people are using time and sampling what is happening in different areas of the school. The school day needs examining, looking at the length of the day, assembly time, form time, breaks and lunch time and the time spent in moving between classes.

We really need a more flexible approach to the school day than is now common. Where a community school develops, it becomes natural to have some classes that go on later than the normal school day. This could lead to different ideas about the way the staff of a secondary school and its students work and some teachers and even some older students might prefer to start later or earlier and go on later or earlier on some days.

There is a strong case for a longer school day for older students. Those who go directly into employment often find the working day long and tiring because they have been used to something much shorter, even though it is usually followed by a period of homework. Part of the transition might be gradually to lengthen the day so that by Year 11 students have a similar length of day to that in most places of employment, using the additional time for private study so that homework time is consequently reduced. There are problems about arranging this, particularly where many students come in by school bus, but it can be done, especially where there is a community use of the school. City technology colleges are already running a longer school day and other schools may need to keep pace.

Assembly time has been built into the legal framework of education but assembly does not necessarily have to be an assembly of the whole school. This is impossible in some schools because there is no space which would take everyone at once. Many schools now feel that a change in the law which would allow flexibility about time and place and in particular limit the number of assemblies each week so that they could be properly prepared would be helpful to the cause of profitable assemblies and religious observation as well as to the school more generally. A mixture of assembly on some days and form time on others seems to be a more satisfactory pattern for many purposes. There is also a case, where there is pressure on specialist accommodation, for having assemblies for part of the school at a time, with other groups using hard-pressed accommodation.

The breaks in the school day should also be examined to see whether they are contributing to the optimum use of time. In particular there needs to be a check on whether time is being taken out of the learning period in order to prepare for the breaks. Is what is happening at break times making work more difficult afterwards? Is the fact of having the whole school breaking at the same time creating discipline problems with misbehaviour in corridors and cloakrooms? The organisation of break times should use as little as possible of the time of staff and students.

Another time-consuming activity is changing lessons. While there is much to be said for each department having its own suite of rooms, it nevertheless results in a lot of movement on the part of students. This is lessened if the period length chosen coincides with breaks in the day or if there are a number of double periods.

The most important place to consider the use of time is in the classroom. Each student's time is precious and classroom organisation which holds some students back while others catch up or merely occupies some while others learn, is inefficient. There is much to be learned from following one student or one group of students around the school for a day and seeing what the programme looks like from their angle.

Blocking subjects together in team teaching or blocking subjects with adjoining accommodation can provide a longer space of time for activities where continuity would be valuable, as well as reducing time spent in movement about the school. It may be that subjects are taught on a fortnightly basis or there is a different concentration in each half term in order to make such provision. Field study benefits from this kind of provision and many craft activities are more effective when they are given a continuous period of time.

Time can also be blocked for some subjects without necessarily invoking team teaching. If a department or a faculty is timetabled with the whole year or a half-year group, arrangements about which teacher is responsible for which group of students becomes something for the head of department or head of faculty to decide with his or her colleagues.

Some provision of blocked time can also be made after examinations are over. Another way of providing blocked time is to take an occasional day out of the time-table, perhaps once a term, to devote to activities which benefit from uninterrupted work.

There is also a tendency to assume that everything must be studied all the time. If we think in terms of modules within subjects, based on particular parts of the National Curriculum, students can study a limited number of modules for a period and then move on to others. This allows for more concentrated attention on some subjects or groups of subjects for a period and is a more effective way of using time. There is, of course, the problem that if some subjects are left for half a term, students may forget what they have learned. This may be offset by the more concentrated learning possible when time is blocked. It also says something about what is likely to remain in students' minds when schooling is over!

Students also need training in using time well. This means that there should be a gradual move towards more of the time being planned by students. In practice, the development of coursework as part of examinations has encouraged this, but it needs to be taught and learnt from the beginning of secondary education. Secondary schools also need to consider how much attention has been given to this at the primary stage. Some primary schools do a good deal to train children to plan their time and the secondary school can build on this.

The task of management in all this is partly that of evaluating how time is being used and of making people aware of the importance of good use of time.

The use of space and equipment

A school needs to ensure that space and other resources are being used to the best advantage. The use of space is part of the time-tabling process but there are some general issues:

Provision of suites of rooms for different departments

Secondary education is strongly specialist and in this context it is undoubtedly to the advantage of teachers if all the rooms in which a particular subject is taught are close together. This enables a department to share thinking and materials and equipment. It makes it easy to share aids of various kinds and to provide materials for students which otherwise might have to be carried a long distance. Rooms normally used by a small number of teachers tend to be better cared for and there is more use of display and self-service organisation of materials.

On the other hand, if teachers stay in the same place, students' movement needs careful handling. Subject suites also encourage departments to be separate when there is a good deal to be said for bringing different aspects of the curriculum closer together. The development of faculties may help this but equally may simply enlarge the group which remains separate.

Housing groups of different sizes

Most schools have comparatively few spaces designed for groups which are larger or smaller than the average form. This poses problems for the school which would like to explore team teaching and it also poses problems at the sixth form level where comparatively small groups may be obliged to use a lot of space because no smaller rooms are available. This is basically a timetabling problem but there may be a case for dividing some rooms.

Selecting, storing and maintaining equipment

A school needs systems for ensuring that adequate care is taken in selecting equipment and seeing that it gets optimum use. This means checking that departments have studied the market adequately when selecting large items of equipment or substantial amounts of new material, perhaps arranging for them to visit other schools or talk to teachers elsewhere with experience of using the material or equipment under consideration. Specialist advisers also ought to be able to give good advice on purchasing such material.

The way equipment is stored and the system for accessing it affect its use, since anything which is difficult to obtain or often needing repair is likely to remain unused. The school needs a good system for checking that equipment is in working order and appropriately maintained. Money spent on technicians with responsibility for looking after equipment may be money well spent, since they save the time of teachers and ensure that money spent on equipment is equally well spent. While much of this is the responsibility of individual departments, management must see that it happens.

Ensure that there are equal opportunities for all students

Every school needs to have a whole school policy on equal opportunities for all students. This is not only a matter of equal opportunities for girls and boys and students of different races, important as these issues are. Schools may also discriminate without realising it against students of working-class background, against students with handicaps and against students of different abilities – sometimes the most as well as the least able. Many local authorities have policies and documents about equal opportunities and offer schools a good deal of guidance on these issues. It is necessary to have a whole school policy, emanating from staff discussion in which everyone has been involved. The involvement of the headteacher and senior staff and their support of the policy will be crucial. It will also be important to make the policy clear to parents. The whole issue of equal opportunities needs to be looked at regularly with particular reference to the hidden curriculum. Staff, ancillary as well as teaching, need opportunities to talk about their own prejudices and attitudes if they are to support a whole school policy.

Work on equal opportunities applies not only to work in the classroom but to the way the school runs from day to day. It will be important to see that no aspect of school life poses problems for any particular students because of their race, gender, class, ability or disability. The school's task is to educate all students to take their place in a plural society and to try to produce people who value this pluralism and enjoy its richness.

It is perhaps worth remembering that people generally have fundamental attitudes towards people who are different from them. These attitudes tend to be at a subconscious level and influence behaviour without the person concerned being aware of it. Very often the attitudes people hold towards those who are different from themselves have little to do with their experience and much to do with the attitudes their parents hold and with attitudes absorbed from friends and acquaintances and from the media. These deep-seated attitudes are difficult to change and the most that schools can hope to do is to change conscious attitudes so that they help to govern behaviour.

Gender

[Recent years have] seen considerable changes in the position of women in society and much greater consciousness of the need for girls to be encouraged to aim for careers which were not previously open to them. However, according to Joanna Foster, in a lecture given to the National Association of Inspectors and Educational Advisers, there are still only 11 per cent of women in top jobs and women's earnings are only 74 per cent of men's. Girls still do more chores at home than boys and it should not be forgotten that children's earliest experience in most cases is of mother in the home. It is probably also the case that for many students the example given at home is still of mother dealing with domestic issues, even if she is also in employment. It is also somewhat ironic that legislation designed to give women equal opportunities should have resulted in some schools having an all-male senior management team which makes it difficult to give girls a model of women in top jobs. It is therefore not surprising that girls still see themselves in subsidiary roles aspiring to a more limited range of careers than those aspired to by boys.

It is therefore important for the school to do everything possible to raise the sights of girls, increase their aspirations and encourage broader choices of courses and careers. This is partly a matter of providing models in situations chosen for work experience and in people who come to talk about their work. It may also be a matter of attempting to change attitudes on the part of boys, since some of the attitudes of girls are conditioned by the way boys regard and treat them. It may be valuable to give both sexes the opportunity to talk about this in a single sex group, sometimes with mature teachers of their own sex and sometimes with mature teachers of the opposite sex so that views can be expressed freely and an attempt made to influence the way both sexes think about themselves and about the opposite sex. The way teachers deal with each other and the way they talk about each other may be influential as well. It is also useful to discuss these issues with parents.

There is a tendency to regard gender issues as something concerning girls in particular. Boys have their own problems in accepting their gender, particularly where the local idea of masculinity is *macho*. They may need to be given confidence that it is possible for boys to enjoy the arts, to be gentle, to show emotion and have some of the characteristics which tend to be regarded as feminine, as well as the more masculine characteristics.

Race

A school needs to consider both multicultural education and anti-racist education. Multicultural education will stem naturally from some aspects of the National Curriculum and schools today should be concerned not only with the European dimension of education but with world dimensions for students who are growing up in a world where what happens far away affects what is happening close to us. The celebration of holidays and festivals from different cultures, study of countries from which students of other races come, literature from other cultures and much else may all contribute. Discussion of characteristics of Asian languages as compared with European languages may contribute interestingly to the study of language. Teachers should constantly be looking at the curriculum with the multicultural approach in mind. Schools need to celebrate the diversity of their students and teachers need to show that they value students of different cultures.

It is much more difficult to tackle the question of race more directly. There should be opportunities for discussing human rights issues, items in the news, racial stereotypes, issues such as anti-semitism and much else. Drama offers a particular opportunity for exploring the feelings of others. History and geography both have contributions to make in discussion of situations in which racism has been evident. There are also opportunities to tackle the issues of racism arising out of incidents where there has been conflict between students of different races. There is the possibility that discussion and work on racism may reinforce rather than counteract prejudice, but this is no reason to ignore the problems that exist. There is a constant need to learn about the best way to live in a plural society.

Issues of race are particularly important in all-white schools where it is easy to assume that there is no problem. Children growing up in communities where they seldom meet people of other races have a particular need to consider the effects of racism and to have a multicultural dimension to their curriculum. Schools in such areas may profitably make links with schools which have a more mixed population. Schools in all areas might also make links with schools in third world countries.

Social class

It is very easy to under-estimate working-class students [. . .]. Our low expectations for such students probably have something to do with our poor showing internationally at the lower end of the ability range. This is compounded by the fact that such students often have low expectations for themselves, partly the result of low teacher expectation and partly of parental expectation. There is a cycle of expectation whereby parents, because of their own experience, have written off school learning as something not worth having, and pass this view on to their children whom they consequently do not expect to do well at school. This is in contrast to some other cultures where a much wider range of parents expect success in school from their children.

The task of the school is to try to raise expectations so that such students break the cycle. This again is something which a headteacher can influence by not accepting low expectations from teachers but constantly encouraging both teachers and students to aim high. Praise for teachers who do well with students of working-class background is important. It is also valuable to get across to working-class parents that the school has high expectations of their children and hopes that many will stay on into the sixth form and get better jobs by having more education.

Ability

Discrimination by ability is closely related to discrimination by social class. There is a good deal of evidence from research that we under-estimate students of low ability. It is interesting to compare the achievements of students in special schools for students with moderate learning difficulties with those of students of low ability in secondary schools. The students in special schools often do better although those in the secondary schools may well be rather more able in some cases. The National Curriculum demands that we make the curriculum accessible to all students and this may mean developing steps towards attainment targets for some students rather than aiming at them directly.

There is also a danger that able students will be under-estimated because they have chosen the easy path and do just enough to get by. It is, for this reason, important to see that teachers are aware of those students known to have exceptional ability and vigilant for others who may not have been identified. In a sense equal opportunities for such students means giving them different and more demanding opportunities than those given to others.

Students with disabilities

It is all too easy to assume that a student with a serious physical handicap also has learning difficulties, particularly in cases where the handicap limits speech. A child may have good intelligence but have been unable to develop it because of deafness or a speech problem. He or she may therefore be unable to show the ability which is there. Students with serious physical disabilities may also have difficulties in writing and using tools which may lead to an under-estimation of their abilities. We also tend to treat students according to their appearance and a student who looks extremely young or is extremely small for his or her age is likely to be treated in a more childish way than others, both by teachers and students. Teachers need to be aware of this danger and try to avoid it.

The equal opportunities policy

A whole school policy on equal opportunities would include the following:

1 A statement about the attitudes expected from staff towards all students, together with some comment about the kinds of students to whom it may apply in particular.
2 Information about what teachers should actually do to support the equal opportunities policy.

3 Statements about specific responsibilities for seeing that the policy is implemented.
4 Statements about the resources available to support the equal opportunities policy.
5 Information about the way the implementation of the policy will be assessed.

Assessing the equal opportunities programme

It is not enough to have an equal opportunities policy. There must be regular assessment of how well it is working. The people best placed to make this assessment are the students, although there must also be assessment and discussion by the staff. Questionnaires to selected groups of students may reveal aspects which are not evident otherwise, and these can be followed up by discussions with small groups of students and then with staff. Parents may also have something to say about this.

Deploy staff and other resources effectively

Most headteachers inherit a structure and cannot easily make wholesale changes, partly because people are in post and might not fit a different structure and partly because reorganisation is always costly. However, local management of schools (LMS) gives greater freedom to headteachers to change the staffing structure, even if it is through the negative route of needing to lose staff to meet the overall budget. Although this is unfortunate, it can sometimes create ways of starting to implement desirable change. In any case, a headteacher who is clear about the changes he or she wishes to make can gradually move to a new structure over a period of time as opportunities occur. The important thing is to be aware of the advantages and disadvantages of different structures and to make judgements about how they would work in the particular school, so that a possible future structure gradually becomes clear.

Handy suggests that there are four sets of activities in any organisation:

1 Steady-state: This 'implies all those activities which can be programmed in some way, are routine as opposed to non-routine.'
2 Innovative/developmental: 'All activities directed to changing things the organisation does or the way it does them.'
3 Breakdown/crisis: This is largely self-explanatory but includes the unexpected as well as disasters.
4 Policy/direction: 'The setting of priorities, the establishment of standards, the direction and allocation of resources, the initiation of action, these are activities which form a category of their own, although there is some overlap with other sets.'

(Handy 1976: 198–9)

Handy goes on to suggest that parts of an organisation will probably have some activities falling into each of these categories. However, there is a tendency for some groups of people to have more of one kind of activity than another and to become better at that kind of activity. He concludes from this that there is a case for differentiation of groups with some having more of a particular kind of activity than other kinds (ibid.).

In schools, as in most organisations, all staff have a good deal of work in the steady-state category. Policy and direction are the responsibility of management even in the most democratic of schools, although much decision making may be delegated and there may be many collaborative decisions. The breakdown, crisis, unexpected situation tends to become the responsibility of the more experienced people and often falls to those who happen to be available at the time the crisis occurs. Innovation and development can be anyone's task, however, and many headteachers find that their young and inexperienced staff have much to offer. This suggests that it may be possible to create a structure in which there is an attempt to separate innovation from steady-state activities, perhaps forming a volunteer group with some members known to have innovative potential invited to join to look at possible developments, leaving the tasks of the day-to-day running of the school to the official leaders of the school community.

Beare *et al.* suggest a number of much more radical changes in the school as we know it. They believe that it is possible to restructure schools to involve mastery learning in which students learn 'through their own efforts in dialogue and cooperation with their peers and with each other in peer tutoring'; or they can belong to cross-age groups in which the older students help the younger ones. This ties in with what Beare calls the vertical curriculum in which 'all subject areas [are] divided into developmental units placed on a vertical grid. The students work individually or in small groups and teachers act as counsellors. Students have different rates of progress' (Beare *et al.* 1989).

This does not seem to accord with much of the work on effective schools which finds that a mixture of individual, group and whole class work is the most effective way forward. On the other hand there is something to be learned from it. Many schools do not give enough thought to the possibility of students helping each other and planning their work collaboratively in some areas of the curriculum. It happens in practical subjects but not in the more academic, though this is changing. The idea of dividing the curriculum into developmental units is also one which the National Curriculum would make comparatively easy and would enable students who are slower or those who have missed work to catch up.

Beare *et al.* also have ideas about the structure of the school. Like Handy they suggest four domains: routine operational management; planning and developmental; professional; political (Beare *et al.* 1989).

Each of these requires a different form of behaviour. Some people will take part in several domains and will need to act differently in each. They suggest that it is in the operational domain that the sorts of structures we now have operate most effectively. The planning domain will require temporary structures using task forces and project teams, each with their own leaders. In this context the organisation could involve people who have abilities in this direction. This is very like the innovatory role which Handy identifies.

Beare *et al.* then suggest that there should be a domain which is concerned with the delivery of a professional service to clients. They see the 'professionals' – the teachers cooperating to pool their ideas and skills to ensure that there is the best possible analysis, that collective wisdom is accumulated for the person receiving the service and the most competent operation carried out. While this in one sense is no different from the way schools normally operate, an emphasis on 'clients' might well produce rather a different feeling and approach, particularly in relation to parents, where legislation and government propaganda are combining to create a different relationship between school and the parents they serve.

The final domain is the political. Here the writers suggest that the headteacher in particular has an important role in dealing with the various interest groups outside the school. They stress the need to work with power coalitions and lobby groups and, in effect, to manage the political scene as it affects the school (Beare *et al.* 1989).

These four domains have implications for the structure a school adopts. Their suggestion is for a situation which allows project teams to be formed which cut across other structures and for much decision making to be collegial.

The staffing structure a headteacher eventually develops is a means of achieving various aspects of the tasks of management. These can be distributed in a variety of ways and the distribution of tasks must be reflected to some extent in the money available for salaries. The staffing structure is also part of the communication system, since a headteacher may use it both to inform and to consult. It is closely related to the way the school is divided into units for learning and pastoral care.

[. . .]

References

Beare, H., Caldwell, B. J. and Millikan, R. H. (1989) *Creating an Excellent School*. London: Routledge.

Handy, C. (1976) *Understanding Organisations* 2nd edn. London: Penguin Books.

Hargreaves, D. H. (1982) *The Challenge for the Comprehensive School*. London: Routledge.

Balancing school and individual approaches to pupil behaviour*

PENNY HOLLAND AND PHIL HAMERTON

This chapter has been written by two members of the Nottinghamshire Elton project team, a psychologist and a teacher. It is based on our experiences, before and during the project, as individuals and as members of the team. [. . .] Our experiences have shown us that there are opportunities in some schools to improve the support offered to pupils who, otherwise, may be excluded.

The title of this chapter suggests that there may be some tension between meeting the needs of individual pupils, those whom teachers regard as the 'most difficult to teach' because of their behaviour, and the needs of the whole-school community. We shall argue that the tension can be resolved by careful balancing of resources *within a whole-school approach*. By a 'whole-school approach' we mean an approach to matters to do with behaviour and discipline that maximises involvement and consistency and minimises confusion and isolation. Such an approach is essentially preventive, rather than reactive, forming part of the normal, planned provision of the school. We recognise that there is also a need for reactive procedures, but we believe that these are not the essential approach that the school should adopt and upon which it should rely.

[. . .]

The report of the Elton Committee (DES 1989) was not altogether welcomed by teachers. This report argued strongly that teachers and the schools in which they work can dramatically affect the behaviour of their young people. [. . .] The objectives of the Nottinghamshire Elton project were to:

- improve the provision generally made within schools for the most difficult pupils, including intervention at pre-exclusion stages and support for reintegration;
- support schools in managing their most difficult pupils and in developing effective approaches and policies that highlight both staff and pupil needs;

* This material has been abridged.

- make more effective use of existing mechanisms for managing difficult pupils and improve the coordination and delivery of a range of support from Support Services;
- to enlist positive cooperation and mutual understanding between schools and parents to form an effective response to the needs of pupils with difficult behaviour.

[. . .]

In order to help schools identify their development objectives, and in negotiation with them, we agreed to examine aspects of their existing practice. [. . .] The data gained [. . .] were not encouraging. All of our schools had policies for the management of pupils' behaviour. All regarded themselves as meeting the needs of the majority of their pupils. Most of the teachers expressed what we would see as desirable, child-centred, positive teaching attitudes, preferring to see pupils in mainstream rather than segregated education wherever possible. Nevertheless many of the schools appeared unable to limit sufficiently the numbers of pupils considered difficult to teach, and their resources were not adequate to meet the needs of the many identified. [. . .] We were led to conclude that support for the difficult to teach can be provided most effectively in schools where whole-school provision ensures that the needs of the overwhelming majority of pupils are met through sound curricular, disciplinary and pastoral provision.

[. . .]

Definition

We [found] that schools often have highly complex policies that are sometimes not operating effectively. This may be because those required to perform specific tasks are not given the necessary resources, which usually means time, or because the policies simply do not have the support and understanding of the staff. We have found that what is required is a clarity of roles and the provision of the resources necessary for their performance.

We believe that effective school policies for promoting good behaviour should make clear the normal expectations of all members of the school community. These expectations, possibly expressed in the form of a code of conduct, might also indicate the possible rewards and sanctions that should result from desirable or undesirable behaviour. Within the constraints of the school policy, it should be made clear where individual members of the community are free to adopt their own rules. For example, in a school where there is a stated policy of not chewing, a teacher who condones chewing will be undermining the whole-school approach. If, however, no school policy exists regarding chewing, each teacher will need to establish his or her own rules/expectations and should then be internally consistent.

Where a pupil frequently fails to meet the normal expectations, there may be a need to offer support and possibly guidance in addition to any discipline. We believe that it is essential, if both are to be effective, to distinguish clearly between the disciplinary structures in the school and the support structures. If it is to be the responsibility of the subject teacher, supported by the head of department, to maintain discipline, this should be clearly stated. If the form tutor is to be informed of difficulties, it should be clear that this passage of information is to enable an overall picture to be built up so that coordinated action and effective support is possible, and that it is not intended

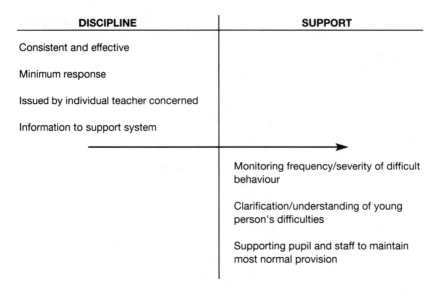

DISCIPLINE	SUPPORT
Consistent and effective	
Minimum response	
Issued by individual teacher concerned	
Information to support system	
	Monitoring frequency/severity of difficult behaviour
	Clarification/understanding of young person's difficulties
	Supporting pupil and staff to maintain most normal provision

Figure 9.1 A clear distinction must be drawn between support and discipline

to involve the tutor in delivering the sanctions. We believe that the links between the disciplinary and the support structure need to be strong but should not confuse the roles (Figure 9.1). Having defined the roles of the various teams within the school, there should be equal clarity regarding the allocation of necessary resources.

If the role requires liaison with external agencies, home visiting and consultation with other teachers, consideration should be given regarding time and skills. It may be necessary to consider who should offer support and what time-allocation and skills they will require.

When all the details have been worked out, the school should have laid the foundations of a whole-school approach to behaviour, affecting all, involving all and owned by all.

Meeting the needs of individual pupils

In the ordinary routine of a school, when a pupil does not meet the normal expectations in some respect, discipline may be considered appropriate. Alongside discipline there is usually some support, perhaps in the form of guidance or simply listening, though this may not be formally arranged. We have suggested that the performance of these tasks should be separate but operating in concert within a whole-school policy for promoting good behaviour.

Every whole-school system will fail some pupils

While the vast majority of pupils routinely get adequate motivation, reward and support through normal classroom interaction with their teachers and parents/carers, so the normal pastoral provision should meet the predictable needs of pupils undergoing the stresses of normal life: growing up, moving house, failing in lessons, etc.

We believe that no pastoral system will be adequate to meet the needs of all the pupils who come to its attention if subject teachers are unable to meet the needs of many. Likewise, the pastoral system must respond effectively to meet the needs of most of the pupils coming to its attention, otherwise the more intensive support on offer will be overwhelmed and consequently will meet the needs of none.

No matter how effectively the school policies have been developed, how clearly defined the responsibilities or how generously resourced the preventive arm of the school support, some pupils and their teachers will need further support. Such support will depend upon a coherent system for the identification of those in need and the adequate provision of necessary resources.

Identifying those in greatest need

One of the most surprising discoveries we made was that schools are not very effective in the interpretation of the mass of data available to them. This might be partly because of the allocation of time to the people who have access to the data, but we believe that it may reflect assumptions which teachers seem to make about who the most difficult pupils are. It seems to us, and to the teachers when they observed lessons, that the pupils they expected to see causing the most disruption were often not the ones observed doing so. This general finding suggests that school systems are not very sensitive to feedback about what is *actually* happening in lessons. Detailed questioning of teachers in schools and examination of their policy documents show that responsibility for the collation of concern forms, if specifically anyone's responsibility, is often the responsibility of someone without sufficient time to do it effectively. We found that time is not usually provided for teachers to share their concerns, even if a teacher, whether tutor or head of year, is well-informed. In some cases, it seems, information about domestic difficulties, which some believe to be vital for all teachers, is limited to those in the pastoral system furthest removed from teaching the pupil.

In a few cases we found schools where there is an established pattern of 'concern meetings' in which those directly involved in teaching a pupil can share their concerns in non-directed time outside the teaching day. In one case a school has developed a within-the-day meeting opportunity for form tutors and year heads to discuss individuals and to develop, with outside agencies if necessary, a specific action plan. In another school a weekly meeting is held involving: pastoral deputy, learning support co-ordinator, EWO, EPS, [educational welfare officer and educational psychology service] special needs support service personnel and heads of year/tutors as appropriate. These meetings are supported by a regular programme of pastoral team meetings. In another geographical area of the county there is a practice of regular multi-agency meetings involving, in addition, police and social services; this is considered highly effective.

It is our view that, unless specific responsibility and time is given for the identification of the pupils in greatest need of intensive support, this process is unlikely to be effective. We believe that the process of identification is the most important step towards describing needs. Learning support co-ordinators and their colleagues from the internal and external support services are usually then able, in a positive school environment, to find problem-solving approaches that suit them and help them suggest hypotheses and develop action plans accordingly.

Making special provision within the mainstream school

Identification alone is not enough. The school system should aim, not only to identify those pupils successfully and recognise their needs, but also to meet those needs *from within the available resources.*

Within the project schools, it quickly became clear that decisions are made about allocation of resources – staff time, class sizes and rooms, for example – often without the conscious knowledge of the majority of the staff. While overall teacher:pupil ratios are fairly constant within the county (approximately 15.5:1 in Nottinghamshire secondary schools), average class sizes vary widely, from as small as eighteen to as large as twenty-five; and *actual* class sizes vary even more widely. These variations sometimes seem not to reflect the apparent needs.

The provision of support made by schools for pupils who have special needs can vary, in terms of staff time, from none to more than the equivalent of four full-time teachers (4 FTEs) in a school of 700 pupils. Schools allocate rooms to specific subjects or functions according to criteria that are not always made clear. So, a suite of rooms might be allocated to TVEI and another to commerce, while there are no rooms for the support coordinator or heads of year to provide a space for calm intervention when a classroom crisis occurs.

The distinction between pupils 'with learning difficulties' and those 'with behavioural difficulties' is strengthened in some schools where the role of the support co-ordinator is seen as being concerned with remedial educational functions and curriculum differentiation *for* departments rather than *with* departments. The responsibility for support in cases where behaviour is perceived to be the problem is here given to the form tutors, who, as we found in some schools, may do no more than punish again!

Schools have the freedom to decide how they attempt to meet the needs of their most demanding pupils. We believe that, as the level of difficulty increases, it becomes more and more important that the functions of discipline and support are constructed separately. It is difficult for both parties, in cases of complex or long-term difficulties over behaviour, when the form tutor, for example, takes on the role of befriender and disciplinarian simultaneously. Further, the role of supporter should be defined (Figure 9.2) and the supporters themselves should be supported. Support for the supportive tutor is unlikely to be provided by a system which escalates pupils into the exclusion system by involving the senior management team unless it is in a containing, problem-solving role (Figure 9.3).

To perform the role of a supportive tutor, a certain allocation of time is required. Time will also be required for the senior pastoral staff to support the tutors and so on. Alternatively, support might be viewed as the job of the support coordinator and the allocation of time might be made through that person. Before crying, '*But we haven't enough time now!*', let us look at the present ways in which time may be used in schools.

SUPPORT IS . . .

A Collecting and collating information
    (a) receiving teacher concerns
    (b) pupil interview
    (c) classroom observation
    (d) parent/carer information
    (e) curriculum access

B Interventions

    Pupil –
    (a) befriending
    (b) parent/carer involvement
    (c) guidance/counselling
    (d) behavioural strategies
    (e) planned timetable alterations

    Teacher –
    (a) peer support
    (b) problem-solving strategies
    (c) curriculum differentiation
    (d) classroom management skills

    External agency liaison –
    (a) involvement
    (b) coordination

C Review

Figure 9.2 The role of the supporter is defined

A model of school staffing

As our work took us into a large number of schools we quickly realised that there are enormous variations in the ways in which schools of similar sizes and serving similar catchment areas are organised. We found that, when encouraged to examine critically the way in which classes, timetables and responsibilities are organised, highly imaginative approaches can develop to meet the needs of specific institutions. This section explores the potential for development in a typical secondary school. Two different approaches will be described. The initial position and both developments are based on project schools and work actually undertaken, with rolls and staffing equalised for numbers and slightly simplified to give a basic arithmetical model.

Let us take a typical secondary school of seven hundred and fifty pupils with a pupil:teacher ratio of 17:1. In this model the teaching week comprises twenty-five periods. Staffing establishment is forty-four, with a head and three deputies. What follows is a very crude staffing model, used to demonstrate the effect of certain choices.

The senior management team's teaching load is fairly typical, teaching fifty-five periods per week between them (2.2 FTE). (We found that wide variations exist in the extent of timetabled teaching done by senior management teams, with the four most senior teachers contributing anywhere between less than 2 FTEs and over

Code of Conduct Rewards and Sanctions Policy

Role of (Class) Teacher

1   Maintenance of (classroom) discipline: ensuring pupils' awareness of school code of conduct.
2   Maintenance of discipline: use of agreed rewards and sanctions.
3   Ensuring pupil/curriculum match.
4   Ensuring prompt passage of information to tutor concerning individual pupil's behaviour.
5   Commitment to work with tutor as peer supporter/critical friend.

Role of Head of Department

1   Supports class teacher re curriculum, etc.
2   Supports operation of necessary classroom-level rewards and sanctions.
3   Oversees department timetabling.
4   Allocates resources with Special Needs Coordinator.

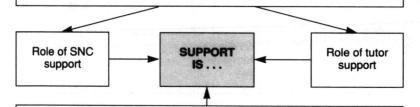

Role of SNC support → **SUPPORT IS . . .** ← Role of tutor support

Role of Head of Year/House

1   Supports tutor to maintain links with home and continue with positive strategies.
2   Major aim is to return pupil down tariff system, ensuring that sanctions are not escalating.

Role of Deputy Head/Head Teacher

1   Major role to feed pupils back down the system and not make exclusions easy.
2   Oversees the use of fixed-term and indefinite exclusions.
3   Ensures that the tutor and head of year have adequate time to perform duties.

Figure 9.3   The supporter is supported

3 FTEs to the timetable.) Minimum non-contact time is set at three periods each week, thirteen other staff have additional non-contact time as heads of department (one or two periods weekly) or heads of year (two periods weekly).

At the beginning of the development the school's policy is to keep class sizes as low as possible in order to meet the needs of all pupils most efficiently. Average class size is twenty-one and this allows just 1 FTE (the support coordinator) to be released from the timetable for other duties, such as learning support. There is no further flexibility and nobody has really got time to follow up the pastoral support needs of pupils when things go wrong, except for the senior management team, who have fewer options as we have seen. Heads of all departments are also tutors.

After some staff discussions, average teaching groups might be increased to twenty-five. One of the project schools made just such a decision after prolonged whole-staff consultation in the early days of the project. In our model school this releases a further one hundred and forty-three teacher-periods for learning support, pastoral support, etc. Now the school has some flexibility in staffing, a total of one hundred and sixty-five teacher-periods weekly, and has also freed five additional classrooms at any time. Only three heads of departments need now be tutors.

It is now possible to make arrangements for extensive support provision. This support may be channelled through the support coordinator, through the pastoral system, through curriculum departments, or through a combination.

Organising support to come through the pastoral system (Figure 9.4, Model A) tutors could be allocated a further five periods each week for tutorial duties: three periods of curricular support through department heads and two periods of pastoral support. In negotiation between heads of department and the 0.5 special needs coordinator, the ninety periods of learning support can be allocated according to need. Where possible it might be hoped to use tutors to support their own classes. The pastoral support now would have two periods weekly from each tutor, in addition to the contact during form times and PSE sessions. Heads of year could release tutors from these duties in exceptional circumstances for further pastoral work. Such a system should provide very effective support for the vast majority of pupils and their teachers. There would have been an increase in group size, but there would now be time to undertake the important duties necessary to offer effective support when behaviour causes problems, and there would be significant support available within the classroom when learning becomes difficult. The role of the tutor would have been considerably enhanced and all become teachers of pupils with special needs. In one of the project schools just such a reorganisation took place.

Alternatively, our typical school might channel most support through an expanded Support Centre provision (Figure 9.5, Model B). Here the distinctions between learning and pastoral support would become blurred. In addition to the, now full-time, support coordinator, there could be two more full-time staff working from the Centre and a further 2 FTEs released for liaison and preparation with staff from the Support Centre. Another project school had established such a provision shortly before the project began. In our model school tutors might be given one extra non-contact period for their pastoral work, in particular to liaise with the Support Centre. Fifteen periods not allocated could, for example, be timetabled to Science for year 7 classes to help with practical work. Now individual pupils can be supported intensively and the pupils with the greatest need can be allocated full-time 1:1 support if needed. The Support Centre staff would have time to coordinate external support

Allocation of teachers' time (A)

Average teaching group = 25   Week = 25 periods

Learning support

3 periods per week from all tutors
Allocation to 0.5 support coordinator and head of department for flexible usage
Most effectively, tutor supports own tutor group by:

(a) Team teaching
(b) In-class support to pupil
(c) Small group withdrawal
(d) Individual withdrawal

Pastoral support

30 mins. daily (tutor period) + 2 periods per week
Allocated by tutor to:

(a) Individual pupil/group observation
(b) Learning support
(c) Individual guidance/counselling/target-setting, etc.
(d) Parent/carer contact
(e) External agency liaison
(f) Support from head of year

PSE

1 period per week with tutor group

Non-contact time

3 periods per week

Figure 9.4   Organising support (Model A)

staff, liaise with pastoral staff and even undertake home visits. The role of the tutor is reduced and the skills required are fewer. Expertise is seen to be located, however, in *others*, potentially de-skilling the class teacher, who is also a tutor.

Balancing whole-school and individual approaches

Schools allocate resources according to their own priorities. The descriptions above show how schools can vary those allocations. It is clear that the tutor-led support provision allows less intensive support for individuals but should enhance the whole-school provision dramatically. The Support Centre model allows very intensive support for individuals, as well as a range of departmental support approaches; but it does emphasise the separate nature of support and, if the normal provision of the school is not good, is liable to be overwhelmed (Figure 9.6).

A balance has to be found – an effective system that enables the maximum number of pupils to maximise their achievement will need to offer different levels of support,

---

Allocation of teachers' time (B)

Average teaching group = 25   Week = 25 periods

Learning support

Full-time support coordinator +
2 full-time staff, based in Support Centre +
44 periods per week (selected staff) allocated to head of lower school and heads of departments for
   flexible usage, e.g.:

(a) Team teaching
(b) In-class support to pupil
(c) Small group withdrawal
(d) Individual withdrawal
(e) Programmed materials preparation

Pastoral support

20 mins. daily (tutor period) + 1 period per week
Allocated by tutor to:

(a) Individual pupil/group observation
(b) Learning support
(c) Individual guidance/counselling/target-setting, etc.
(d) Parent/carer contact
(e) External agency liaison
(f) Support from head of year

PSE

1 period per week with tutor group

Non-contact time

3 periods per week

Figure 9.5   Organising support (Model B)

from the normal support of caring classroom teachers and tutors within their routine contact with pupils, to the intensive, full-time 1:1 support, delivered on-site to a pupil in the moment of crisis that makes normal classroom provision impossible. The balance appropriate to one school will be different in another and it will change as the school's and pupils' needs change.

Conclusion

We have not advocated a right way to support pupils in school. We have not indicated a correct balance between school and individual approaches. We have suggested an approach to development and we have suggested a range of options that schools

MODEL A	MODEL B
Advantages	
Support for all pupils	Support for the most difficult pupils
Early identification of problems	Teachers teach own specialism
Tutor maintains ownership	Breathing space for teachers
More home contact possible	Effective coordination of external agencies
Pupil kept down tariff system	Increase in work differentiation
Tutor skills developed	Calm environment for pupils
Roles and expectations defined	Teachers feel supported
Reduction in class teaching	Allows flexible response
Peer support	
Proper time allocation	
Disadvantages	
No full-time withdrawal	Teachers disown problems
Potential increase in exclusions	Lack of tutor involvement
No 'expertise' in learning support	Home/school liaison difficult
Time delay in tutor skill acquisition	Less support for most pupils
Difficulty in coordinating external support	Skills stay with few people
Larger teaching/tutor groups	Early response less likely

Figure 9.6 Each model has its merits and problems

might consider. It is our view that schools can satisfactorily meet the needs of the most difficult to teach for much more of the time than many now do. What is needed is a strong commitment to maintaining these young people in mainstream schools, rather than resorting to offloading and looking for alternatives outside school. Our experience has shown that, with the firm commitment of the senior management and within an effective whole-school supportive approach, it is possible to improve significantly the support available for the most difficult to teach. Where effective support *is* available within mainstream schools, the need to expand off-site provision should be significantly reduced. Experience in project schools has shown us that in such schools the teaching and learning experience is improved for all.

Reference

Department of Education and Science (1989) *Discipline in Schools*, The Report of the Elton Committee. London: HMSO.

10 | Curriculum evaluation as review and development: the curriculum leader's role in creating a community of enquiry

MARTIN COLES

Evaluation, in various forms, has been working its way to the top of the educational agenda for some time now. Political reality and the climate of opinion about education means that external evaluation, via inspections by the Office for Standards in Education (Ofsted) and, less explicitly, via general perceptions of the success of a school on the part of parents, LEA advisers, teachers in other schools etc, will continue to be part of educational life. It appears at the present time at least, that external evaluation is the kind that has credibility outside the profession. National Curriculum testing has external accountability as at least part of its rationale. Yet this is all the more reason why schools should, in this climate, prove themselves capable of conducting self-evaluation and acting on the results. I consider that self-evaluation is an integral part of good teaching and should continue to be at the heart of all forms of evaluation. The concept of professionalism implies a responsibility to continuously update knowledge and skills in a striving for improvement. Teachers who view themselves as professionals will want to improve their professional practice through processes of monitoring and review. Curriculum leaders, coordinators in primary schools and heads of department in secondary schools, will be expected to take a lead in this process.

Central to evaluation procedures is curriculum review and development. In practice it is impossible to separate out review and development of the curriculum from consideration of other aspects of school life such as relationships between teachers and children, teachers' professional competence and attitudes, school ethos, and importantly, children's progress and achievements. However, the discussion in this chapter aims specifically to consider the curriculum as the starting point for a school's self-evaluation.

Curriculum evaluation has to take place against the background of the National Curriculum. Contrary to popular opinion the National Curriculum does not make curriculum planning and evaluation on an individual school basis redundant. For instance the English Statutory Orders and non-statutory guidance do not provide any detailed policies in respect to reading. Should your school continue to use reading schemes? At what point in their reading development should children be encouraged to make sensible choices about their own reading materials? What should a school be doing to develop a pupil's study skills? Individual schools will have to continue to work out policies in these as in many other areas. So even if we accept that the National Curriculum places some restraints on the freedom of teachers to choose materials and objectives, as does the exam syllabus in secondary schools, there is still a considerable latitude within which they can make independent judgements with regard to the learning experiences they offer the children in their classroom and the ways in which these are evaluated.

Participatory evaluation: towards a synthesis of individual and school development

In considering curriculum review it is important always to recognize the crucial role of collegiality and the management 'climate' of a school. Curriculum leaders can act most effectively as catalysts in relation to curriculum evaluation and development if there is this sense of collegiality. Both theory and practice suggest that the style of leadership and management from the headteacher will be crucial in any school both for the form any evaluation takes and for the commitment of the staff to it. Participatory self-evaluation inevitably requires a participatory management style. In other words, if self-evaluation is going to work properly it has to be done by, and for, members of staff, rather than to them.

Let me try to be more precise about exactly what I mean by the notion of internal, participatory curriculum review and development. Holly and Southworth (1989) offer a description which could apply to the business of curriculum review and development. They say that it is, at best, 'a learning journey based on staff involvement and focusing on classroom processes'. They suggest it is a matter of 'orchestrating and managing the change process, providing a framework for development' and 'establishing a collaborative support partnership'.

Every teacher probably carries out curriculum review as a regular but informal appraisal of the success of her own work. This process is, however, likely to be unsystematic and usually based on impressions and personal experiences without taking explicit account of information from, for instance, colleagues or pupils. Evaluation of the sort defined by Holly and Southworth implies that teachers should be prepared to think about their own practice in such a way as to enable them to make detailed judgements about that practice to themselves, but also that teachers who are moving through the change process must be supported by an institutional framework rather than working on their own. In other words curriculum review, development and evaluation of the sort I would wish to recommend is neither classroom self-evaluation (which sometimes includes action research), nor school self-evaluation (which has in the past normally been to do with institutional review according to a LEA 'booklet' or 'guidelines'), nor school-based review following process guidelines such as those developed by the GRIDS – Guidelines for Review and Internal Development in Schools – project (1984), nor even review that must follow an Ofsted inspection. Rather it is a synthesis of these activities. The whole staff look at the whole school so that everyone feels equally involved and committed to the review, but the focus is on the curriculum in individual classrooms. The aim is to combine staff ownership of the programme of review and development with a commitment to the improvement of classroom practices throughout the whole school.

The kinds of activities that might be undertaken include such things as:

- 'open house' classrooms where teachers can openly visit each other as basis for later discussion;
- staff workshops which concentrate on the practicalities of organizing learning in the classroom;
- paired observation with a 'critical friend' leading to the formation of relevant issues which are fed into staff discussions.

Asking staff to observe in each others' classrooms may at first appear impractical and idealistic, but as Little (1981) points out there *are* schools where 'classroom observation is so frequent, so intellectually lively and intense, so thoroughly integrated into the daily work, and so associated with accomplishments for all who participate that it is difficult to see how the practices could fail to improve teaching'.

One other point needs to be made. Resources and time are obviously inhibiting factors in any attempt at curriculum review. It is important that the workload of the review matches the availability of people to take it on and a timetable is drawn up which involves minimum disruption. In a primary school it is almost inevitable for example that meetings between staff will have to take place outside 'teaching time', but it is most important that the suggestions that follow are not seen simply as 'bolt-on' activities. By combining various approaches to the review process, it ought to be possible to provide a framework which becomes integrated into the on-going work of the school rather than an extra burden. The general principle is that for curriculum review and development to work it must be absorbed into current practice, integral to the organization of learning, not an optional extra. In other words, if curriculum review and development is to become important in any school it must take root in the institution itself, rather than be seen as just one more administrative feature of school life, or a 'one-off' in response to a single event, such as an inspection.

Curriculum review and development: planning for action

Although school-based curriculum review starts with the needs within the school, this does not mean that external demands and advice can be ignored. At the start of any internal review it is important to find out about recent research and other developments relevant to the aspect of the curriculum under review and to try to draw together a picture of what is generally regarded as good practice. This picture will necessarily have to take account of the National Curriculum programmes of study. And it will often have to take account of the findings of an Ofsted inspection.

Thinking about change and external accountability

Ofsted's corporate aim is 'improvement through inspection' (Ofsted 1994a) and, despite the scepticism with which many teachers undoubtedly view the inspection process, there is mounting evidence that preparation for inspection, and action planning after it, is having an impact on school improvement (Ofsted 1994b). Having regard to what is said in the rest of this chapter, it is important that within the life and culture of a school, self-review and inspection are not seen as two mutually separate processes. Of course it is possible to view the Ofsted inspection process negatively, to see it as

> a process where judgements and measures are introduced in ways and forms that do not occur in daily practice and in the form and style which can represent a threat to the professionalism and autonomy of the teacher and the school.
>
> (Moon 1995)

But it is possible also to take a professionally confident attitude to external inspection. Indeed, integrating external review into the school's internal review process is the only way forward if teachers want to promote a culture of professional autonomy. Ofsted itself recommends that 'schools should seek to assimilate inspection and action planning into the ongoing process of forward planning and self-review' (Ofsted, 1995).

Ofsted inspections have to recognize the strengths as well as the weaknesses of a school, and they have to collect a wide range of evidence. This evidence base includes information from the parent body, from pupils' opinions, from the scrutiny of pupil work, and evidence gathered from consistent procedures for observing work in classrooms. Certainly these are elements which could become part of any school's internal review process, as could the criteria defined within the Ofsted handbook. But the developmental remit of Ofsted is limited to identification of 'key issues for action'. The school staff and governors have to respond to these findings and implement the action planning which will lead to developmental change.

Bringing about such change demands changes of attitude as well as changes of teaching practice. This is a sensitive area and it is essential to select strategies for change that will suit both the curriculum leader and the rest of the staff. There is a range of strategies that might be used to support curriculum review and development. There are those which involve work in school. These might include for instance:

- staff/curriculum meetings
- INSET days
- INSET packs and videos
- observation of pupils working
- sharing pupil's work
- questionnaires and other forms of information gathering
- workshops
- sharing with colleagues the planning of project work
- working alongside or team-teaching with colleagues

This last is important. Teachers rarely see other teachers at work and therefore have only hazy notions against which to judge their own teaching. Working in another classroom inevitably involves observation and perhaps consequent nervousness, but if a teacher 'under observation' today is 'observer' in another classroom tomorrow a collaborative atmosphere should be engendered where all value visiting each others' classrooms and accept its consequences. In particular 'paired teaching' can be a good way of influencing others and implementing curriculum policies.

A large part of the task of a curriculum leader then is about influencing colleagues. This is an activity fraught with difficulties, but enlisting a colleague's support in a joint venture of some kind avoids accusations of exceeding authority and engenders a commitment to the proposal. In any case two 'points of procedure' in any joint venture would have to be friendship and voluntaryism.

Making a plan

The model below suggests one possible approach to developing a review and development plan, but it is by no means definitive. Although the model is systematic, any school will need to adapt the approach to its particular circumstances. Any review will reflect previous work done in the area, the level of knowledge and expertise amongst the staff, the requirements of the National Curriculum, the findings of any inspection, and the opinions of parents and governors, amongst other factors. This procedure is based on a model developed by Coles and Banks (1990) which in turn is freely adapted from a model for developing a school assessment policy produced by the Primary School Assessment Project (Hants LEA with Southampton University, 1989). That project's procedures have been redesigned so that the model has six elements which together form the acronym ADRENALIN.

1 Analyse
2 Decide and
  Review
3 Establish what you are going to do and
  Note your action plan
4 Advise colleagues and
  Let people know what is happening
5 Implement
6 Now evaluate

Each element involves asking a question, agreeing a task and engaging in a number of activities with a specific result in mind.

1 Analyse

Question: What is the school's current practice?
Task: To review and analyse existing practice.
Activities: If any review is to be rigorous it must have some degree of objectivity, and objectivity requires the use of evidence. It does not though necessarily mean 'from the outside'. Below are brief summary statements of the type of activity it would be useful to undertake in order to collect evidence.

- Ask each teacher to summarize on one side of A4 paper her practice in the area under consideration. Circulate these sheets among the staff prior to a whole staff discussion.
- Send out a brief questionnaire to all staff asking relevant questions about existing practice. Again, circulate responses in preparation for a staff discussion. Questionnaires are economic in terms of time but they are not as easy to design as might first appear. Keep it short, make it easy to respond to, make it easy to return the form.

- Collect relevant examples of pupils' work which demonstrates current practice, and bring them to the staff meeting.
- Collect relevant books and other teaching materials which demonstrate current practice and bring them to a staff meeting.
- Organize a simple questionnaire for the pupils, to gather information about their understanding of current practice.
- In groups, brainstorm the various approaches taken in different classrooms.
- Organize 'paired teaching' sessions when the curriculum area under review is being concentrated on in the classroom.
- Hold interviews with staff about their current practice. This might be threatening but can be most fruitful if findings are shared, since interviews have the advantage of allowing for follow up and clarification of response. Be aware also though that interviewing can be expensive in terms of time; for example in a primary school of ordinary size, all staff would have to be interviewed to gain a fair picture. A sheet can be constructed with a set of prepared questions to assist information gathering and reporting back.

Result: A common understanding of the range of curriculum activities practised within the school.

2 Decide and Review

Question: What shall we do to improve existing practice?
Task: To review existing practice and to agree principles related to the area under review.
Activities: Using information gathered during the previous stage, as well as ideas formed as a result of other INSET activities, identify and agree the principles and purposes which will influence your school's policy by asking teachers to ask themselves certain questions. Your school will already have a curriculum statement which might be used as a focus for this activity. Questions that could be asked include:

- What needs changing?
- Identify some differences and similarities in the approaches taken by various teachers. Do the differences matter?
- Looking at your school's current curriculum statement(s), National Curriculum programmes of study and Statements of Attainment, is the curriculum you offer falling short in any area? Remember that the root of any decisions lies in what each child is doing in the classroom. Formally note decisions taken and provide each member of staff with a copy of those decisions.

Result: The establishment of some firm principles for developing existing practice which have the agreement of the whole staff.

3 Establish and Note your action plan

Question: What approach shall we take to make any changes necessary?
Task: To produce an action plan for introducing new practice or revising existing practice.
Activities: Through discussion:

- Consider what the policy decisions mean for classroom practice.
- Agree a time scale for all innovations.
- Find out what costs and resources are involved, if any.
- Decide what monitoring procedures will be adopted.
- Determine how any changes will be evaluated.
- Identify people responsible for carrying out particular tasks.

Result: The establishment of a plan of action for carrying through some curriculum development.

4 Advise and Let people know

Question: Who needs to know about the review and resulting proposed developments?
Task: To make formal and informal reports on the review and any changes in practice to governors, parents, and receiving or feeder schools.
Activities: Discuss the review and proposed developments with other professional colleagues, such as other local curriculum coordinators and heads of department, LEA advisers, and the relevant teachers in receiving or feeder schools.

- Prepare a document detailing the agreed changes in practice for circulation amongst staff (these documents can eventually build into a file of agreed practice across the curriculum for new appointees to the school).
- Summarize the review and developments which led to the new practice in a concise statement for parents and governors. Then perhaps hold a meeting to discuss the change and explain it to parents and governors.

Result: The change is approved and agreed, perhaps with modifications. It is stated in a precise written form and made available for consultation by interested parties.

5 Implement

Question: How do we manage the implementation of the development stage?
Task: To support and monitor changes in practice.
Activities:

- Prepare a series of stages, identifying specific activities, and communicate this to all concerned.
- Introduce monitoring meetings which involve either 'paired' staff, or small teams or the whole staff.
- Identify one person who will note and document the implementation process, especially staff reactions, implications for resources, the responses of children and parents, and any emerging difficulties that become apparent.
- Continue with 'paired observation' and 'team teaching' activities, this time perhaps asking these questions:
    What did the pupils actually do?
    How worthwhile was it?
- Decide when the implementation stage is complete, and agree upon what evidence this decision will be based.

Result: The full introduction into the school of some new or revised classroom practice in a particular curriculum area.

6 *Now evaluate:*

Question: How well is the curriculum working in practice?
Task: To evaluate the new or revised practice.
Activities: The activities in this section take for granted a willingness not only to plan and enact worthwhile developments in the curriculum in your school, but also to evaluate those developments and use that evaluation for future planning in the cyclical model of curriculum review and development.

- Review the notes and documentation that were gathered as part of the implementation process.
- Hold a single item staff meeting to discuss the new policy or practice focussed on the question 'How well are we doing?'

Result: An awareness of the success or failure of the change, and an opportunity to consider adjustments.

It is important to understand that evaluation is an integral part of the review and development process. For instance, if you assess, evaluate and carefully observe children as part of a pupil profiling procedure, some of the information you gather will help evaluate the curriculum in action. Similarly, if you have an appraisal system for staff, this gives teachers a chance to contribute to the evaluation, and to air views about change in the curriculum. So within the cycle of curriculum development it is best to see implementation and evaluation as occurring in the same phase, otherwise evaluation may occur so long after the planning and enactment of the new practice that it cannot suggest ways of improving implementation. The School Development Plans Project (DES 1989) links implementation with evaluation, suggesting some necessary elements for a successful implementation of the innovations which follow from curriculum review (see Figure 10.1).

Checks on implementation and success mean continually asking the question 'How well are we doing?'. Curriculum review and development is rather like painting the Forth Bridge – never completed. Having discussed and agreed change and attempted to put that change into practice, evaluation of that practice will more often than not reveal other aspects of practice that require attention. The following list of questions and activities are suggestions for ways to keep this cyclic process as effective and smooth as possible.

Are the staff as a team continuing to offer each other collegial support? For instance:

- Headteachers could make themselves available to discuss progress and problems with staff on a one-to-one basis.
- Teachers might find a way of letting each other know that their work in the change process is appreciated.
- Team meetings could be held to discuss progress and deal with problems. Ensuring that everyone receives regular feedback and summaries of progress can help keep up commitment and motivation.

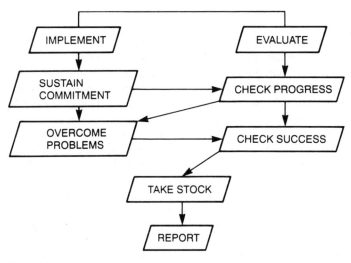

Figure 10.1

- The school might organize informal lunchtime chats amongst staff on curriculum matters.

What checks on implementation and progress are being made? For instance:

- Each staff meeting could have a brief time set aside for reviewing progress, reflecting on the developments, noting changes that have taken place and working out the implications for future work.
- The curriculum leader might want to collect evidence of changes and record that evidence, and the lessons drawn from it, so that the information can be used as necessary in future developments.
- Feedback from parents might be fed into the process, either through informal discussions, or more formally via curriculum evenings, or simply noted in an incidental way through comments of parents to individual members of staff.
- Pupils' reactions might become part of the evaluation process, both through observation of their work in the classroom and through explicit discussion which lets them express a point of view about the curriculum.

How are you taking stock and overcoming problems? This means for instance:

- Looking again at priorities for review and development that were decided earlier.
- Taking account of curriculum initiatives/policy changes at national or local level.
- Remembering that the particular needs of a school change with time and taking this into account by readjustments or major rethinking.
- Renegotiating the review timetable as priorities change, or if it takes longer than you expected to do things.

Finally, this section has emphasized that planning for continuing curriculum review should be part of a development policy and that a structured way of doing that is needed.

The role of the curriculum leader

So what is the role of the curriculum leader in all of this? Well, since any curriculum review may lead to proposals for major changes, skills of leadership are of the greatest importance. It has been suggested that the type of school leader needed for effective evaluation to be carried through is 'able to diffuse professional threat, engender openness and honesty, ensure participation, and carry forward reforms' (Clift *et al.* 1987), and that the staff climate most conducive to successful review is characterized by 'openness, trust, a preparedness to face risk and ambiguity, a positive attitude to curriculum' (Holly and Southworth 1989). So what factors can foster these qualities? Perhaps the major factor is to do with who retains ownership of the exercise. Is there a management style of reciprocity that fosters commitment to the review?

If staff work as a team then all should feel involved and committed to the enterprise and all should feel to some extent under review. And collaboration should also lessen the personal anxiety which any review will engender. So curriculum review and development by collaborative enquiry offers a solution to the apparently intractable situation in many schools where teachers remain isolated from one another behind classroom doors, where schools have an ethos that promotes isolation, so that though in most schools, school-wide problems are solved together, teachers still do not discuss in any detail what they do in the classroom, or seek collegial solutions to significant classroom problems, or ensure through such discussion that pupils are getting a genuinely consistent experience through the school.

The concept of 'critical friendship' is important here. Part of a curriculum leader's role in a staff team will be to observe and facilitate, to act as a sounding board in their area of expertise, to question practice in a way which poses no threat to other individuals, or indeed to the whole school ethos. This implies a central role for the curriculum postholder which carries genuine professional leadership tasks. The curriculum leader is the individual who has prime responsibility for developing the curriculum in a particular area, and working to maintain good practice in that area. So now curriculum leaders, in order that they are able to provide the impetus for curriculum review and development, must keep up to date in their area of curriculum responsibility, know its conceptual structure, be able to make professional judgements about methodologies, resources and materials, represent their area of responsibility to outsiders, as well as perhaps teach alongside colleagues, lead discussions, and advise probationary teachers.

The ambiguities and complexities of engaging in these kinds of activities inevitably bring potential problems. For instance, some tension might be created if the particular area of responsibility of one teacher is seen to be operating inadequately; but this is one more reason for staff relations to be such that the overarching feeling, regardless of day to day pressures and 'hassles', is one of mutual support, sharing and professional growth. Another potential problem may be a tension between the role of the curriculum leader in curriculum review and development, the headteacher's curriculum role, and some teachers' desire for autonomy in the classroom. Suffice it to say here that possible areas of conflict might be anticipated and avoided to a large extent if members of staff have agreed amongst themselves the areas of a curriculum leader's responsibilities (through job descriptions for example) and have themselves, by sharing experience and expertise, fashioned the curriculum policy decisions which might act as a yardstick against which practice is measured.

Some time ago Skilbeck (1982) anticipated some of the expertise and social skills that might be required: 'The task is complex and difficult for all concerned. It requires cognitive skills, strong motivation . . . constructive interactions in planning groups and emotional maturity.'

So the school's expectations of the curriculum leader and her role in curriculum review are crucial. Effectiveness will be increased if the headteacher and curriculum leader have spent time clarifying the role and responsibilities. How the curriculum leader views her role in the review and development exercise will depend on various factors, such as how recently she has taken the role on, how long she has worked at the school, and how the school is organized. The following are some of the activities and roles that may be considered, perhaps as a basis for negotiating a job description.

- Providing colleagues with information on research and developments in curriculum.
- Developing and demonstrating your own good practice.
- Sorting out resources and ordering new stock.
- Setting up displays and coordinating specific school activities related to your area.
- Leading discussions about the curriculum.
- Coordinating record-keeping and assessment.
- Providing support and advice to colleagues.
- Acting as a 'critical friend'.
- Coordinating liaison with other schools.
- Looking at ways of involving parents and keeping them informed of developments.
- Spreading enthusiasm for the area of your expertise amongst other staff.
- Paired observation projects.
- Keeping in touch with local and national developments in your particular curriculum area.

I have emphasized, in this chapter, how important it is that curriculum leaders see one of their prime tasks as the creation of an atmosphere of mutual trust and support, so that curriculum planning and renewal is done within a community of enquiry. I want also to repeat the other main theme of this chapter. The processes of monitoring and review are integral to good teaching, and this is as true at institutional level as it is at the level of the individual teacher. If a school is to be successful in terms of the quality of the learning experiences it offers its children, curriculum evaluation and development have to be integral to its work. It is a commitment to the improvement of classroom practices throughout the whole school.

References

Clift, P., Nuttall, R. and McCormick, R. (1987) *Studies in School Self-evaluation*. Basingstoke: Falmer Press.

Coles, M. and Banks, H. (1990) *School INSET: English*. Leamington Spa: Scholastic.

Department of Education (1989) *Planning for School Development*, the School Development Plans Project. London: HMSO.

Hampshire LEA with Southampton University (1989) *The Primary School Pupil Assessment Project: Topics in Assessment 3*. Southampton: Southampton University School of Education Assessment and Evaluation Unit.

Holly, P. and Southworth, G. (1989) *The Developing School*. Lewes: Falmer Press.

Little, A. (1981) *Contemporary Issues in Education: Block 4, Educational Standards*. Milton Keynes: The Open University.

Moon, B. (1995) Judgement and evidence: redefining professionality in a new era of school accountability, in Brighouse, T. and Moon, B. *School Inspection*. London: Pitman Publishing.

National Curriculum Council (1990) *Curriculum Guidance Three: The Whole Curriculum*. York: NCC.

Office for Standards in Education (1994a) *Corporate Plan 1994–1997*. London: HMSO.

Office for Standards in Education (1994b) *Standards and Quality in Education*. London: HMSO.

Office for Standards in Education (1995) *Planning Improvement: Schools' Post-Inspection Action Plans*. London: HMSO.

Schools Curriculum Development Committee (1984) *Guidelines for Review and Internal Development in Schools*. York: Longman.

Skilbeck, M. (1982) *A Core Curriculum for the Common School*. London: University of London Institute of Education.

Stenhouse, L. (1975) *An Introduction to Curriculum Research and Development*. London: Heinemann.

PART 2

Managing resources

11 | Managing resources in educational institutions: an open systems approach

ROSALIND LEVAČIĆ

This chapter is concerned with developing an understanding of the role of resource management in relation to the functioning of the educational organization as a whole. The discussion relates to schools and colleges which have responsibility for managing their own budgets covering most of their expenditures and where these budgets depend largely on the number of students recruited. I will refer to such schools and colleges as 'self-managing' so as to encompass locally managed, grant maintained and independent schools and incorporated colleges and as well as other forms of budget devolution or delegation to be found outside England.

In the UK at least, the government's justification for creating 'self-managing' schools and colleges is that this makes for greater efficiency and improvements in the quality of teaching and learning compared with the previous system of administrative allocation of resources to schools and colleges by LEAs. However, the validity of this claim was neither theoretically nor empirically well established prior to these policies being introduced. Much of the justifying argument was based on generalizations from the business sector. In order to assess the claim that delegated budgeting is a vital ingredient for improving efficiency and educational effectiveness and to understand how schools and colleges need to manage their resources in order to achieve these ends, a better appreciation is required of the causal chain which potentially links budget decisions to the achievement of greater efficiency and educational effectiveness.

The open systems model

A helpful conceptual tool for this undertaking is the open systems model. This depicts the organization as a complex living organism which interacts with its environment (Morgan 1986, Hanna 1997). Understood as an organism, the organization is depicted as distinct and separate from its external environment but with permeable and often ill-defined boundaries. It is a purposeful entity producing outputs which it exchanges with stakeholders in its external environment in return for resources and support and so is dependent upon its environment. The model also focuses on how relationships between resource inputs and outputs are mediated by internal processes. Certain key elements, such as the technology of the organization's productive processes and the culture of its human relations, are singled out for study. These elements have important and interdependent effects on the processes which relate inputs to outputs and which connect the organization with its environment. Appropriate feedback mechanisms between the organization and its environment and within the system itself are required for the organization to be responsive and adaptive.

An open systems input–output model of the educational organization enables one to trace out the possible linkages between increased flexibility in deploying resources and the intended desirable effects on educational processes and outcomes. The model indicates therefore how self-management of finances and resources might improve efficiency and effectiveness. It also assists in understanding why the necessary linkages between greater flexibility in resource allocation within the organization and the desired effects on educational outputs may not get established.

Before examining the linkages in the model in detail, it is useful to consider the problem of lack of agreement on the aims of education and their relative importance and the difficulty of specifying the outputs and outcomes of schooling.

Educational outcomes and outputs

If giving educational organizations greater choice in how they use resources is to result in improvements in teaching and learning then logically there must be a link between the resource inputs and the resulting educational outputs and outcomes for students. There are however, well known problems in defining educational outputs and outcomes because many of them are intangible and there are considerable disagreements, often ideologically founded, about what are desirable educational aims and objectives.

The aims of education refer to its broad purposes and usually include a productive labour force, transmission of knowledge and culture, socialization and enhanced ability to participate in democratic politics. The outcomes of formal education are the broad effects which it actually has on individuals – knowledge, ability to appreciate and enjoy cultural activities, behave with social responsibility, participate in democratic politics and be productive members of the labour force. It is usual to distinguish the broad outcomes of formal education from its narrower and more specific outputs, some of which are measurable and some of which are not. Outputs are the immediate effects of the organization on its students, whereas outcomes are the longer term effects both for the individuals who attended the organization and the consequences of these effects for society in general. So examination results are an organizational *output*, and the students' income earning capacity in later life is an *outcome*. Examples of measurable outputs are examination results and qualifications, rates of participation in higher and further education and training, and subsequent employment. Certain process variables are also used to measure school and college performance such as attendance. Outputs which are much more difficult to measure are the effects of school on pupils' attitudes, beliefs and behaviour.

A major problem in using unadjusted indicators of school and college output, such as raw examination results, is that they are measures of gross output i.e. the equivalent of measuring company performance by the monetary value of sales. In order to assess net educational output, account has to be taken of students' social background and cognitive ability, since these are the primary determinants of measured educational attainment. Statistical estimates of value added measures of school and college effectiveness separate out the effect of the educational organization on test and examination scores from the effects of social background, cognitive ability and prior attainment (MacPherson 1997).

The problem that bedevils all attempts to relate inputs to the resulting outputs and outcomes of education is that they are multiple, many are intangible, and there is no agreement on their relative social value. Measuring school and college effectiveness in terms of quantifiable output indicators of educational attainment in relation to given student characteristics assumes that these measured attainments are important, even if it is recognized that there are other desirable outputs and outcomes which have not been or cannot be measured. Emphasizing measurable outputs is likely to bias organizations towards concentrating on these at the expense of the less measurable; but making no attempt to measure output encourages concentration on short term processes at the expense of longer term attainment and fails to produce transferable knowledge of the links between teaching methods and consequent educational outputs.

The educational organization as an input–output system

The criteria of efficiency and effectiveness against which schools and colleges in the UK are now being held accountable are crucially dependent on those making the judgement being able to assess the value of the educational output of the organization. In public sector management and accountancy 'effectiveness' is defined as the extent to which an organization's actual output matches the output desired from it and efficiency is assessed by comparing output to inputs. Thus, if financial and resource management are being judged against the criteria of efficiency and effectiveness, educational organizations need to understand the linkages between their inputs of human and material resources and the subsequent educational outputs. From this perspective the educational organization is an input–output system. The open systems model is an elaboration of a simple input–output system which focuses on three key constituent elements of the organization (e.g. Butler 1991):

- the external environment from which the organization acquires its resources and to which it supplies its outputs;
- the production technology through which inputs are transformed into outputs;
- human relations system which mediates between the external environment and the organization and affects how production is undertaken.

Figure 11.1 depicts such an open systems model of a school or college in which resource inputs are transformed into educational outputs through a sequence of stages in a production process.

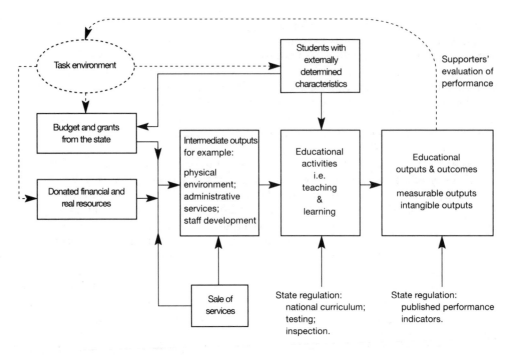

Figure 11.1   An input–output open systems model of the educational organization

The task environment

The external environment in which schools and colleges operate can be subdivided into the general environment which is influenced by the major technological, social, political and economic forces operating in society and the specific environment made up of parents, the local community, local business, the local education authority, other educational organizations and central government and its agencies. This immediate external environment is also referred to as the task environment (Butler 1991) in order to emphasize that in order to survive the organization needs to pursue ends that sufficiently satisfy the needs of its stakeholders. The organization exchanges its outputs broadly defined for resources and support.

Schools and colleges obtain resources in the form of students, finance and donations in kind in return for the educational services it provides. The success with which an organization obtains resources from its task environment depends on norms which its supporters – actual and potential – use to evaluate the organization's performance and the supporters' perceptions of the quality of the organization's performance relative to alternative suppliers. In the general model organizations jostle with rival organizations to attract support and hence resources and face different degrees of uncertainty in their task environment. Self-management is intended to enhance the importance of the organization's own actions in securing support from its task environment by improving its performance as perceived by its supporters.

An important dimension of the external environment is the regulatory regime in which the organization operates. In the case of schools the government has tightened up the specification of the tasks expected of schools and promoted the dissemination of information outside the school about its performance in undertaking these tasks. Further education colleges have also been subject to increased accountability through inspection, publication of comparative performance data and oversight by the Further Education Funding Council.

Transforming inputs into outputs: the production technology

Inputs acquired from the task environment are transformed through educational processes into outputs and outcomes which are exported back to the environment. The stages this transformation goes through are depicted in Figure 11.1 as a flow of intermediate transformations preceding from left to right. Under self-management the school or college obtains most of its resources as a lump sum budget dependent on student numbers, with additional specific grants for stated purposes. The organization may also sell services directly and receive various donations from non-state supporters in the form of finance or real inputs, such as the time of volunteers. A state funded organization may also get a direct allocation of capital assets such as buildings.

The flexibility of self-management comes from tying schools and colleges into the market economy through the medium of money, which gives them the ability to decide for themselves the mix of real resources to purchase. The school or college uses its allocation of financial resources to purchase real resources in the form of staff, materials, energy, water, and other services. This first intermediate transformation is planned and recorded through budgets and involves preparing and monitoring budgets for all or most of the resources used.

The real resources acquired and financed through the budget are used in conjunction with other real resources, such as existing buildings, plant and equipment, to produce what can be called 'intermediate outputs' or 'operating services' which support teaching and learning indirectly. An appropriate physical environment has to be created and maintained in which learning can occur, administrative services must be provided to support learning, and investment must take place in maintaining and developing the staff.

The next stage in the educational organization's productive process is the utilization of its physical and human resources – the intermediate outputs – to produce educational activities. This, unlike the operational services, is the core technology of the school or college. The ways in which real resources are combined in order to produce educational activities, outputs and outcomes are subsumed in the term the 'production technology'. The core technology embraces a wide range of issues such as teaching method, group size and organization, the ratio of support staff in the classroom to qualified teachers/lecturers, quality of teaching materials and the organization of the teaching day. The organization of time, a resource which cannot be stored for future use, is the key to effective learning. School and teacher effectiveness studies have shown that the amount of student time on task achieved by teachers is a significant variable in explaining differential effectiveness. There is a wide range of alternative resource mixes which can be employed in producing a distinct educational activity, such as specific skills in English. The problem is establishing criteria which would enable teachers (and inspectors) to judge the relative efficiency of the different ways of combining resources to produce educational activities. The cost of producing a specific activity, such as an English lesson, is not an adequate guide to cost-effectiveness, because the organization's output is not the activities themselves, such as two periods of English a week for a particular class, but the learning objectives thereby achieved. The educational activities are not the final outputs of the college or school: these are the improvements in students' knowledge, understanding, skills and attitudes achieved as a result of experiencing the educational activities.

Self-management gives schools and colleges some additional flexibility in how they deploy resources and therefore change the core technology. More support staff can be used in classes with lecturers and teachers, or more administrative staff can be employed to reduce the time teaching staff spend on clerical tasks. Alternatively flexible learning approaches can be developed, which need more learning materials and different arrangements of study space. This kind of flexibility is restricted by state legislation, such as the national curriculum or health and safety regulations.

The input–output model is useful for analysing the potential effects of budget self-management because it shows that this affects the educational organization from only two directions. At the very beginning of the input–output process organizations' range of choice over inputs is increased compared to direct administrative allocation of resources by a funding agency. The second point of influence is through stimulating greater institutional responsiveness to the external environment because the inflow of resources is linked to stakeholders' reactions to perceived organizational performance. An important and complex set of internal processes mediate between budget setting and the production of educational output. These processes are not directly altered by delegated budget management, though they may be indirectly affected through changes in culture.

In Figure 11.1 these three sets of sequenced decision processes are distinguished.

1 The translation of the financial resources via the budget into real resources (i.e. human and material).
2 The management of real resources so as to create and maintain the learning environment. This can be subdivided into (a) operational expenses for example on premises and administration and (b) expenditure on resources to be directly used in learning, for example books, materials and equipment, payment of staff salaries and expenditure on recruiting and developing staff.
3 The deployment of the resources acquired at stage 2(b) to support teaching and learning. At this point the decisions are no longer directly concerned with the budget. A given amount of expenditure on human and material resources can be used more or less effectively for promoting student learning depending on the quality of the professional judgements exercised by teachers and lecturers.

Delegated budgets impact on the first two processes: budgeting and real resource management. Much of what concerns educational organizations in operating delegated budgets does not directly impinge on improving learning unless the college or school makes a conscious effort to do this.

Efficiency, productivity and effectiveness

If self-management can improve the efficiency and effectiveness with which resources are used in education, then it must do so via affecting the processes that determine the way financial and real inputs are converted into educational activities and thus into educational outputs. Using the input–output model of the educational organization it is now possible to re-examine and further clarify the concepts of efficiency and effectiveness in order to establish the ways in which self-management of resources might achieve its intended effects.

Efficiency and productivity are distinct but related concepts. Productivity is the relationship between the amounts of output produced and the amount of inputs used. The average product of a single input or factor of production is simply the physical amount of output produced divided by the physical quantity of the input used. So, for example, the measure of the average product of teachers at a school in these terms would be the total value added GCSE examination scores of all students divided by the full time equivalent number of teachers. Productivity increases over time when the average product of the factor of production rises. The average product of one factor of production (say labour) can usually be increased by raising the quantity of other factors of production (e.g. capital) with which the labour input works. Higher output per head of the labour force, and with this, higher living standards have been achieved over the centuries by increasing the quantity and quality of capital per unit of labour. Education has not been able as yet to raise teacher productivity significantly with the use of capital. The only exception is probably distance education, while the use of information technology may in the future increase teacher productivity. However, because of the difficulty of comparing educational standards over time, it is extremely difficult to ascertain whether productivity has improved. In the absence of easily available output measures in education, it is common practice, particularly of government agencies, to suppose that productivity has risen in education when the number of students per teacher or lecturer increases. This is only an increase in productivity if the total educational output (e.g. total examination grade scores or other measures of learning) per teacher time on the job rises.

The increase in the productivity of a single input may not mean an overall rise in productivity if it is due to a substantial increase in other inputs. Total factor productivity is a better measure of overall productivity as it is the value of output divided by the value of all inputs used in production. The causes of increases in total factor productivity over time are improvements in technical knowledge, which is then embodied in more productive capital and production processes, and improvements in the organization of production. Hence improvements in teaching methods and in the organization of learning could increase total factor productivity.

I have elaborated the concept of productivity in order to distinguish productivity from efficiency. Efficiency is achieved when a given quantity of output is produced at minimum cost. Economists separate efficiency into two components. The first component is *technical efficiency*: this is the relationship between the volume of physical inputs used and the resulting quantity of output. If there are two inputs (say capital and labour) needed to produce a particular good and there are several production methods each using different quantities of the two inputs to produce a given quantity of output, then any method which uses the minimum quantity of one input for a given quantity of the other input is technically efficient. Technical efficiency thus exists if it is impossible to reduce the amount of one input and keep output from falling without using more of some other type of input. If there are a number of different technically efficient methods of production then it is possible to use less of one input and substitute it for more of the other input and still produce the same quantity of output. The production function is the name given to all the combinations of the different types of inputs which are technically efficient.

But which of all the technically efficient production methods are the cheapest to use depends on the relative price of the inputs. A *cost efficient production* method is one which produces a given quantity of output at least cost. (Alternatively it is a production method which produces the most output for a given total monetary cost.) For example a number of different combinations of learning materials per student and teacher time per student could produce equivalent amounts of learning. The cost efficient method is the one which costs least given the price of learning materials and the salaries of teachers. If relative factor prices change, even though the available production methods remain unchanged, the cost efficient combination of inputs will change. Efficiency is always judged relative to a standard. If production is cost efficient then it is not possible – with the current state of technical knowledge – to reduce the cost per unit produced by decreasing amount of one input and replacing it by more of some other input. An inefficient organization is one which could reduce unit costs by cutting down on some of its inputs or by changing its method of production (i.e. using inputs in a different combination) and still produce the same amount of output. For example, if a college reduces its costs by running larger classes with lecturers each working the same number of hours but supported by more clerical backup and students' learning remains the same as before, then the college becomes more cost-efficient. However, if the larger classes mean that lecturers are working longer hours for the same pay because of the extra preparation and assessment done at home, then lecturer productivity per hour worked can fall, even though output per pound spent on staff salaries has risen. In this example the college may appear to have become more cost effective when the costs taken into account are restricted by those which are financial, but this is not so when the actual quantity of resources used to produce to output is assessed.

Ultimately the issue of efficiency cannot be separated from the distribution of costs and benefits amongst different people. Making working practices more productive or more efficient often implies increasing work effort or changing working practices. The factors contributing to organizations not using the most efficient production techniques and quantities of input are all labelled under the term 'x-inefficiency'. These factors include employees slacking or using their time to pursue other objectives than the ones desired by the organization's owners or chief stakeholders (parents, tax payers and politicians in the case of state education). Since making the organization more efficient by reducing slack or redirecting energies may diminish employees' job satisfaction, the pursuit of increased productivity and efficiency is not a value free activity and attitudes to such efficiency drives depend on personal values and interests.

Self-management provides schools and colleges with incentives and opportunities to improve efficiency and productivity in a number of ways. An example of a technical source of efficiency is maintaining a given room temperature through substituting insulation for energy consumption. This is cost efficient if the reduction in expenditure on heating over a number of years is greater than the cost of the insulation and alternative rate of interest which the money invested in insulation could have earned if invested in financial assets. Inefficiency due to slack can be eliminated by more careful monitoring in order, say, to stop heating an empty building. These are both examples of more efficient use of resources in producing operating services. Moving further along the input–output process, educational organizations can make choices between different input mixes to produce a given set of educational activities. For example, the history department could decide to shift spending from books to videos. However, an efficient combination of resources is not one that produces the cheapest teaching periods, since this is an intermediate educational activity: it is one which produces the highest learning output for a given expenditure of money.

As well as finding the most efficient mix of resources for producing a given educational activity, schools and colleges also have some choice over the mix of educational activities they produce. Different mixes may be more or less effective in achieving specific educational objectives. For instance, if an increase in the amount of time spent on English or on a course on problem solving improves examination results across a range of subjects, then this output/input measure indicates that efficiency is improved through changing the mix of activities.

If a change in the mix of activities leads to a demonstrable improvement in educational outputs without an increase in physical quantity of resources then educational productivity has unambiguously increased. Provided educational output increases by more than total costs then efficiency has also increased. If more efficient ways of producing operating services are found, there is only an increase in total educational output if the resources thus 'saved' on operational services are used to improve educational activities, which in turn increase educational output. Assuming a given amount of expenditure, the institution's total educational output could increase either by finding a more productive mix of activities or by producing more educational activities using resources saved from the more efficient management of operating services. A school or college could increase its operating services' efficiency, but not end up spending the money thus saved in ways which raised the total educational output. In this case overall educational productivity would not have increased. Alternatively, a college or school which responded to a budget cut by managing its operating services more efficiently and used the money saved in this way to sustain its previous level of educational output would be more efficient overall, more productive and provide better value for money, but it would not have increased its total educational output.

The problem facing teachers and school managers in making resource allocation decisions, especially those concerning the most efficient and productive mix of learning resources and educational activities, is the absence of a well specified technical knowledge base which gives a 'blue print' of efficient methods. Knowledge about what are efficient production methods in education has been particularly elusive and there appears to be no strong or systematic relationship between educational expenditure per student and student performance. Hanushek (1986: 1162) in a comprehensive survey of the literature concluded:

> The results are startlingly consistent in finding no strong evidence that teacher–student ratios, teacher education, or teacher experience have an expected positive effect on student achievement.

However, Hanushek also points out that the evidence does show that individual schools and teachers have a significant impact on student performance, a finding supported by the effective schools literature where much greater attention is paid to school processes than in education production function studies.

The nature of educational organizations' production technology is central to understanding how self-management might affect educational productivity and efficiency. If it is the case that the search for a clearly specified input–output relationship is doomed to failure because of the essentially ambiguous and subjective nature of the educative process, as depicted by writers such as Weick (1976) and Greenfield and Ribbins (1993), then there are two lines of argument which can be pursued. One is that self-management of resources will not impinge on these processes because they are not amenable to improvement through manipulating inputs in relation to specified outputs. The other is that the education production function is still meaningful as a relationship between inputs and resulting outputs but that its exact form is specific to the local context. It is discovered by practitioners through personal experience and by the application of individual specific skills. The search for efficiency and effectiveness then depends on teachers' professional skill in making appropriate selections from a repertoire of possibilities. If knowledge about efficient and effective means–ends relationships has to be discovered by teachers in their specific contexts rather than be given to them by some generalizable technical blue print, then self-management may still work by providing greater stimulus to discover and apply professional knowledge about input–output relationships. An example of this is Hughes' demonstration of the greater effectiveness of flexible learning over traditional methods for teaching GCSE geography (O'Connor 1993). In these ways teachers can build up and disseminate their own knowledge of efficient means-end relationships through formal evaluation of their own practice.

References

Butler, R. J. (1991) *Designing Organisations: A Decision Making Perspective*. London: Routledge.

Greenfield, T. and Ribbins, P. (1993) *Greenfield on Educational Administration*. London: Routledge.

Hanna, D. (1997) Open systems model in A. Harris, N. Bennett and M. Preedy (eds) *Organizational Effectiveness and Improvement in Education*. Buckingham: Open University Press.

Hanushek, E. (1986) The economics of schooling: production and efficiency in public schools, *Journal of Economic Literature*, 24: 1141–77.

MacPherson, A. (1997) Measuring Added Value in Schools, in A. Harris, N. Bennett and M. Preedy (eds) *Organizational Effectiveness and Improvements in Education*. Buckingham: Open University Press.

Morgan, G. (1986) *Images of Organisation*. London: Sage.

Mortimore, P., Sammons, P., Stoll, L., Lewis, D. and Ecob, R. (1988) *School Matters: The Junior Years*. Wells: Open Books.

O'Connor, M. (1993) The Balcarras experiment, *Times Educational Supplement*, May 14.

Reynolds, D. (1992) School Effectiveness and School Improvement: An Updated Review of the British Literature, in D. Reynolds and P. Cuttance (eds) *School Effectiveness, Research, Policy and Practice*. London: Cassell.

Weick, K. E. (1976) Educational organisations as loosely coupled systems, *Administrative Science Quarterly*, 21: 1–19.

Willms, J. D. (1992) *Monitoring School Performance: A Guide for Educators*. London: Falmer Press.

12 | Resourcing education: linking budgeting to educational objectives

DEREK GLOVER

Background

The achievement of the stated aims of a school or college or of the sub-units within the organization depends primarily on the quality of teaching and learning. These are facilitated by the way in which staff are deployed to teaching groups, the availability of professional development support, the use of accommodation and other facilities, and the availability of what many LEA budget systems formerly called 'materials of instruction'. As schools and colleges endeavour to secure improvement in their educational effectiveness, more attention is being paid to the link between good teaching and learning, and good management of resources. To secure an improvement in student attainment in a subject area, or in a group of subjects at a particular stage, requires consideration of the way in which teaching and material resources are to be used in combination to secure the desired outcome. In other words, there is need for a link between the educational objectives and the resourcing patterns to achieve those objectives. This chapter brings together the issues connected with planning processes within an organization and the formulation, implementation and evaluation of the budget that makes possible the achievement of aims.

In times of generous public spending it is more likely that, providing the case is sufficiently well argued, the inputs, as unit resource levels, are likely to be maintained or increased, but in periods of retrenchment attention shifts to the process within the system as a means of using the same resources more efficiently and effectively to attain different outputs. Institutional development planning as the means of linking the budget with the objectives of the organization has been particularly stressed, both in advice to schools (e.g. Hargreaves *et al.* 1989) and in the Office for Standards in Education (Ofsted) (1995) framework.

Much of the material upon which this chapter is based has been drawn from the Managing for Efficiency and Effectiveness (MEES) research project which has examined the way in which schools link resource management and planning. The most readily available source of information which combines comment on the organization and effectiveness of schools is provided by reports written according to the Ofsted inspection framework. During the first stage of the research (Levačić and Glover, 1995) 66 reports were objectively analysed and it became clear that those schools which were considered to be attaining good standards of teaching and learning, tended also to be using a planning and management process which established aims, was costed in both human and resource terms and was evaluated against previously defined success criteria. This prompted further investigation of the link between planning processes and outcomes in a further 125 schools. No school could be identified which was producing good outcomes in teaching and learning and examination results but was openly criticized for its planning. Rather, all 'good' schools were either commended for the quality of their planning or minor modifications to existing procedures were suggested. To understand the way in which planning was evolved and used within schools detailed case study investigation of perceptions of decision making was undertaken in four schools. Two of these had been commended in their Ofsted inspection for the quality of their rational planning, and two of which had been asked to consider a tightening of their planning system. The quotations used come from this research work (Glover *et al.* 1996).

The movement towards more efficient and effective school and college development planning predates the Education Act 1988 but these attempts tended to be rather piecemeal and reactive and lacking in strategic vision. However, the need for schools and colleges to adapt to existence in a market-oriented, and more accountable, public service has imposed a stronger discipline and made strategic adaptation more crucial for organizational survival. The use of resources to meet both immediate and strategic aims is thus fundamental, and budgeting is the process by which this occurs.

Rational approaches to resource management

A 'rational' planning process is sequential. Objectives are agreed, and then information is obtained on all the alternative means by which the objectives might be attained. The selection of the most appropriate course of action, e.g. the use of resources for information technology or building repairs, then depends upon knowledge of the costs of introducing the action balanced against the benefits which might accrue. Thus ends and means are clearly linked. The budgetary planning process, because it identifies costs and possible benefits, is thus part of rational planning. The establishment of systems which ensure decision making based upon the perceived priorities of the organization stems from this rationality.

Rational planning, although variously presented, follows a common theme with a cyclic process of

- audit – establishing the present situation;
- planning – considering alternative tactics and strategies to meet aims;
- linking – matching component plans to the development plan;
- prioritizing – establishing which plans are logistically and financially possible;
- implementing – putting the selected plans into operation;
- evaluating – measuring progress towards aims as a result of implemented plans;

and then repeating the process so that development is a continuous activity.

Examples of the guidance given to schools include that of the School Development Plans Project (Hargreaves *et al.* 1989) which establishes ground rules for the participation of all elements of school management in an openly discussed and developed system and stresses the importance of identifying criteria for success as a feature of all planning. Hargreaves and Hopkins (1991) follow these processes in detail with consideration of the way in which development planning, as the establishment of the strategy, requires action planning which is concerned with the detailed implementation of parts of the plan and costs involved at classroom level. After several years of observation of planning, Hargreaves (1995) has stressed the importance of focused development on a more limited front with frequent feedback and readjustment of the plans.

The budget imperative is even more evident in the guidance to action planning given by Sheffield Education Department (1991) who suggest that plans are of an hierarchical and interdependent nature. To cope with this, it is argued that schools need to plan their developments at whole school and departmental or sub-unit level across a period of time because a single budget cycle is too constraining for a school wishing to achieve its aims. During the year of implementation of a plan, the school or college will also be concerned with evaluating the completed plan for the past year and using this evidence for strategic review and planning for the year to come.

Davies and Ellison (1995) differentiate between the strategic plan, giving medium-term aims, and a development plan based upon action to achieve short-term objectives, targets and tasks with indicators of success and resources implications. In their view, decisions on implementation involve consideration of resource costs in assessing the suitability, acceptability and feasibility of any proposal. The national Audit Office (1994) in their advice to grant-maintained primary and secondary schools, contends that rational planning processes geared to strategic development offer advantages because they focus attention on the aims and objectives of the organization, and require detailed plans with financial implications to be available before decisions are taken on the priority action to achieve objectives. In organization terms, the advantages of this approach lie in the need to maintain communication with all concerned in the planning and decision-making, and with the establishment of criteria for continuing evaluation. Ofsted (1995) suggests, in paragraph 6.3 of the revised Framework, that effectiveness is promoted through careful financial planning, effective use of resources, and efficient financial control and administration. None of these is possible without clear aims and the existence of a system which supports development towards the achievement of these aims.

The Ofsted model of rational planning underpins the judgements of efficiency and effectiveness made by inspectors in reports. In a detailed analysis of the comments made by inspectors in the reports on 120 schools, good practice was characterized by the following elements:

Setting strategic aims and objectives through:
• involvement of governors and senior staff
• statement of aims related to the SDP
• whole-hearted commitment of the staff
Development planning through the work of working parties and task groups to ensure involvement through:
• strategic planning as a framework with forward budget use plans
• identification of alternatives

- identified in terms of programme costs, with
  - known allocation systems with clear criteria for cost centre
  - related to criteria for success and anticipated outcomes
  - nominated responsible staff

Budget processes to give:

- alternative possibilities costed and benefit related prioritization criteria
- relation to departmental allocation procedures
- awareness of percentages spent on staff, accommodation and resources

Monitoring:

- role of senior staff in attaining whole school objectives
- financial control

Evaluation:

- related to efficiency, effectiveness and value for money
- feedback into planning cycles
- clear understanding of accountability structures.

Whilst not all Ofsted inspection reports mentioned all these elements, summary comments show that assessment has been based on this integrative model. This process contrasts with the loose coupling which occurs when two aspects of an organization which have elements in common co-exist separately. For example, ambiguity exists when organizational ends (objectives) and means (resources) are not well linked together. However, the degree of ends–means coupling required by the rational approach may also vary in its 'tightness'. The 'tight' model, characterized by formality, shows some or all of the following characteristics:

- clear and unambiguous goals, acknowledged and shared by all employees;
- a clear hierarchy of office, with clear job descriptions for every office-holder within it, showing unambiguous reporting and accountability relationships;
- a substantial degree of centralization, so that individuals with delegated responsibility exercise it within clear guidelines and with relatively little autonomy and discretion;
- a clear linking of budgetary decisions to wider planning decisions;
- a rigorous procedure for assessing decision options against the organization's goals;
- effective and comprehensive vertical communication between levels within the hierarchy.

The 'loose' model offers many of the characteristics of collegial management with:

- a broad view of management in the hands of the staff as a whole;
- aims and objectives directed towards broad principles and shared values;
- decision-making based, as far as possible, on negotiation and consensus;
- structured but flexible budget decision-making and mid-term changes of plan;
- widespread open discussion and evaluation of plans.

The degree of tightness is also affected by two human factors – the nature of leadership, and the interaction of people which results in the culture of the school. This can be seen in the contrast between Runnymede and Uplands Schools, two of the MEES case study schools. Runnymede is a systems based school where the head was appointed to take the school through a phase of development in a highly competitive environment. He has a clear view of the direction in which the school is going and is determined to take the staff with him but manages them through highly structured job descriptions in a strongly organized school with clearly stated objectives, criteria for success and evaluative data. The headteacher at Uplands was appointed to maintain existing strong community ties and sustains the management upon consensus as far as possible by using an integrative approach so that senior and middle managers work within less rigorous systems drawing their conclusions from much more qualitative 'hunch' data. Both, however, link planning to the aims which have been set for the school.

Runnymede School has an inclusive planning document but it is vision driven and is seen as the headteacher's means of guidance for the development of all sections of the school. The process of development planning is based on sound rational principles. Planning is undertaken at both whole-school and sub-unit levels, with the former influencing but not totally constraining the latter. Every activity in the plan is now linked to an element in the Ofsted framework, and will be linked to a time scale, a statement of what will be counted as success, and of the evidence which will be used to assess this, the anticipated cost, and named individuals or groups who will be responsible for the work. The head says: 'I regard myself as the leader, we know where we're heading, we know where we want to be, what size of school, what kind of ethos we want to project within the school, so working along that line the school development plan is actually putting flesh upon that skeleton.' The school development plan is not formally discussed with the rest of the staff and most middle managers and other non-managerial staff did not see any formal consultation: rather, they viewed the plan as a top–down, senior-management generated guide to departmental heads as they begin their own process of preparing departmental development plans.

At Uplands School the process is both all-embracing and on-going. The headteacher's views on school development planning drive the process and the documentation but not the content which comes from the extensive consultation process operative in the school. Hers is not the Hargreaves–Hopkins (1991) model in which maintenance and development activities are clearly separated, with developmental planning being solely focused on the latter. In their model the development plan for each year singles out a few priorities, some of which may be carried into a second year but then become embedded and institutionalized in maintenance activities. At Uplands the development plan is quite different. It is a comprehensive planning and monitoring structure for the entire range of management activities, both maintenance and development. The school development plan occupies two very large ring binders which contain all the policies, action plans and any subsequent evaluation documents for every aspect of the school. The plan represents the entire management of the school: it is a comprehensive map. Only the senior management team, and the headteacher most of all, have an overview and understanding of the development plan in its entirety.

There is evidence that budgetary planning is most difficult in those organizations which lack rationality. Sometimes the allocation system is not known to the staff of the school either because it is pragmatic or used in an ambiguous way. In other schools there is tension between differing interest groups and the eventual allocation of resources reflects the interplay of power and control. Decision-making is affected by the pressures which these groups can engender and planning lacks cohesion and evaluation. Simkins (1989) has compared the rational and the political models of financial management and demonstrates that, where the political system dominates, the sense of overall growth is lost and developments are dependent upon the power exercised by groups or individuals in the negotiation of resources. Unclear structures with random planning and resource allocation appear to favour micro-political power groups and to result in what Fullan (1991) sees as the 'Balkanisation' of the organization with a loss of strategic direction.

The practical issues

The practice of rational planning has highlighted certain practical issues. These are mainly concerned with the way in which both the strategic and development plans and the associated action plans with their budget implications feed into the resource allocation system.

- There is need for a calendar for the *cycle of activities* which must be met if the review of activities and their outcomes in the previous year is to affect decisions for the subsequent year's planning. Budgetary decisions are consequent upon acceptance of programmes of activity which, once planned in outline, have to be broken into component parts such as books, equipment, and computer access for ordering in accordance with the schedules of the administrative framework in order that the materials are available when needed. Unless all class, group, or other cost centre spending plans which contribute to the overall development plan are subject to careful management, there is a risk of crisis allocation of resources and the discipline of the plan is lost. Runnymede, one of our case study schools, has moved its development planning processes to operate alongside the financial year to ensure that the link between planning and resource allocation is maintained.
- The ability of those responsible for cost centres to calculate accurate costs at the level required for *informed decision-making* affects the possibility of successful planning. The 'level required' may vary between organizations. Wong (1995) argues that accurate information is essential for accurate planning and review. To avoid incomplete and inaccurate information, he suggests that computerized data collection can offer a management decision support system. Much of the comment made by Ofsted inspectors suggests that schools are making decisions on an inadequate information base and that there is a need for management information to be collected to inform decision-making and evaluation. Schools and colleges following the tighter approach may require details of accommodation, staffing and educational resources based on a per student or per teaching group apportionment. To produce accurate figures for the cost of activities involves agreement on basic cost accounting principles so that proper apportioning of costs can be implemented. Many college departments which may have to re-charge the actual costs of courses to outside agencies rely on this level of detail but few schools are costing the staff or accommodation used in maintaining their basic programme except to yield data which can be used for comparative purposes. Some schools operate upon an agreed cost for all items including staffing, accommodation, overhead costs and student related book and equipment needs. It is possible to cost alternatives which might meet the desired objectives so that informed budgetary decision-making is possible. Limited planning (Knight, Chapter 13), accepts the argument that staffing

and accommodation costs do not enter the equation because a fundamental student–teacher–room relationship is necessary simply to maintain basic curriculum delivery. In this situation, the additional costs of operating a course such as teacher development and training, computer requirements, and consumable materials become fundamental to cost structures. In the research investigations, Uplands School costed amendments to the previously offered programme but Runnymede required all departments to cost basic provision, development work and staff training for the planned activities annually.

- Whilst staff may be fully involved in rational planning, our evidence suggests that they are less involved in *budget-making* which is more frequently a senior staff function. This may be founded on three assertions. These are: that the work of the school or college is constrained by the national curriculum and examination requirements and that there is little room for change of programmes; that the time taken in planning and negotiation is out of proportion to the funding saved; and that good quality teaching is not necessarily related to the quality of planning. At the same time, those schools which have a full involvement of staff in both planning and budget-making seem to gain from the existence of shared understanding. At Uplands, for example, staff are aware of the priorities and why they have been established, but feel that the inherent fairness of decision-making after discussion has led to commonly supported choices. The Ofsted report for one school was critical of a budget system which perpetuated allocations on an historic basis because 'whilst departments know how much money they are likely to get year on year the needs of the school are not recognized in budget planning'.

- The existence of a structure for *monitoring and evaluation* which has procedures for assessing efficiency, effectiveness, equity, and value for money is considered essential if future decisions are to be based upon reliable data, but it appears that the processes of evaluation are often poorly understood. The extent to which evaluation does take place but essentially 'on the hoof' and in an unstructured way is demonstrated by the fact that of the 117 school reports examined only 54 per cent had some structured system whilst 72 per cent held annual reviews with staff. One head of a school judged by Ofsted to be successful, commented that 'much of the evaluation is based upon hunch . . . either things worked or they didn't' but Law (1995) has shown that senior staff in schools and colleges are anxious to develop their own understanding of budgetary techniques so that their audit procedures are more reliable. The availability of management information has already been identified as fundamental to evaluation but the data have to be usable both in terms of understanding and in its availability. Whilst it is possible for a budget to be set out and agreed, there is need for monitoring during the financial period so that the plans are implemented, or if not, the reasons are known and explained. The existence of virement between budgetary headings or programmes as a means of allowing flexibility so that spending plans can be altered to meet contingencies is not inhibited by such control. The need to explain what has happened does however, impose a discipline which pragmatic spending might negate. The guidance to schools offered in by the Audit Commission (1993) offers schools a framework which is assessed by auditors in an objective way and Ofsted evidence suggests that this element of management is most frequently maintained.

- Frequent inspection comments identify the need for the establishment of *success criteria* for planned programmes – often 'departments lack clear goals and have no means of knowing whether these are being achieved'. The league table approach to the publication of results offers one form of evaluation and many schools and colleges are now pursuing a value-added approach to the analysis of this measurable outcome using objective data. Within further and higher education, success rates in examinations and completion rates for course members offer similarly basic statistics. However, the concentration on outcomes may oversimplify the real purposes of the educational process and whilst the subjectivity of much of the evidence for this inhibits its use there is evidence (West-Burnham 1992) that process indicators are as significant as those for outcomes in productive evaluation, i.e. that which will lead to change. Where plans are written in such a way that both the process and the outcome indicators are established, it is possible to monitor as progress is made towards goals, and evaluate when the activity is completed.

- The *dynamic nature* of the school or college environment has implications for long-term planning. The management of an ongoing programme may affect the success of budgetary planning. Where the annual cycle allows for a review of both the strategic and the development plan in the light of progress towards aims, the extension into the future is automatic. However, longer term planning may be affected by events which precipitate a change of direction and planning is disrupted. This was evident as colleges of further education became incorporated and the consequent change of culture has been detailed for one college where much tighter planning and accountability were established (Rigby 1995). The effect of a change in the long-term view has been particularly evident where schools have faced an Ofsted inspection or where colleges have been subject to scrutiny by the Further Education Funding Council. In the words of one head, 'the inspection was the target and we built up to that making sure that all was in order . . . the aftermath has been characterized by the need to push people so that they maintain their momentum for improvement'.

Whilst strategic management is based on ideas for some three to five years ahead, a revised building programme in the locality, a sudden loss of students because of adverse local publicity, or a change in staff turnover so that the basis of costing changes, can all affect the inputs upon which the system is based. Most schools and colleges maintain their long-term plans without detailed costs and give global figures based upon average present costs extended to allow for inflation. This gives a sufficient guide for planning purposes but the need for review and re-costing of programmes remains as an annual task. Mintzberg (1994) has suggested that development planning needs to be flexible, usually through frequent revision, so that 'emergent strategy' may condition all resource decisions. He stresses the need for analysis to see why and how an organization can see where it is in a changing world, and synthesis to enable coherent planning within each foreseeable planning period. This was shown at Uplands School where budget decision-making was essentially short term so that the impact of changing pupil numbers and local funding could be taken into account in maintaining an essential programme.

Conclusion

Rational planning appears to be a factor in securing the effectiveness of school as judged by the measurable outcomes. The approach to development and resource management gives a framework for discussion and decision making. Appreciation of the culture of the organization by the headteacher and the use of appropriate leadership style and management techniques may result in 'hard', or directive, and 'soft' or emergent forms of planning. Two juxtaposed comments from contrasted Ofsted reports highlight the differing interpretation of rational approaches. As with all schools mentioned in this chapter the names are fictitious!

Marsh High

The leadership of the school has outstanding features with corporate professional trust amongst all staff, appropriate and effective structures, genuine empowerment of staff, firm leadership offered where needed and appropriate acceptance of the consequences of decisions taken. The school development planning process involves a wide range of consultation. It is clearly related to the educational needs of the pupils which in turn drive the school's budget . . .

The governors' finance sub-committee takes direct responsibility for the school's financial affairs. Its work is excellent with the budget efficiency set after considerable consultation with staff. Heads of faculties judiciously use their powers to set faculty budgets and vire funds within the school development plan boundaries and within strict guidelines . . . Each faculty has a named person whose responsibilities include monitoring resources and related expenditure.

Lea Green

Although the school's financial planning is thorough it has been difficult for it to be strategic in the difficult and changing financial circumstances imposed upon it . . . The senior management team and senior staff are fully involved in the financial planning of the school. Financial planning is thorough and although most contingencies are considered, the recent changes to the budget have presented a particular challenge . . .

The headteacher has shown very effective leadership, accomplishing significant improvements in school and maintaining positive staff morale in difficult times of staff reductions. She is clear about the main developments needed and has devised appropriate strategies to address the key issues for action . . .

The development plans were produced after appropriate consultation between governors, senior staff and LEA officers. There is still need to refine the planning even further to include; resource and financial implications; more focused medium and longer term targets; and scheduled cycles for reviewing and evaluating all aspects of school development.

Whilst both these schools use some form of open consultation, the latter is more top–down in its approach and shows that the presentation of a budget which will fulfil the aims of the organization does not necessarily have to rely on open discussion and decision-making. There have been several examples of school improvement being achieved following a period of more autocratic management by a new head appointed to 'turn the school round'. Where this requires firm and centralized financial decision-making, this may be an appropriate course of action. Whilst hard systems more generally ensure a disciplined approach and may be appropriate in securing major change, there are situations where softer approaches can be equally effective and where they may sustain a collegial approach in school management. Rational planning sets the framework but it is not a simple model and has to be managed according to the culture and direction of the organization.

From the research evidence, it appears that the rational approach to planning is an essential for educational effectiveness because it establishes the aims of the school, and transmits these as part of the shared values of staff, students and community. The way in which the budget is allocated to fulfil those aims relies upon decisions made to achieve the aims of the organization and this is usually dependent upon the complex tasks of the leader working within the internal and external cultural environment. Whether the approach is used in a formalized or a more intuitive way, rationality does have advantages compared with systems in which ambiguity and micropolitical pressures operate unchecked. It provides a framework and discipline, thus reducing ambiguity, and enhances the development of decision-making systems which inhibit the impact of pressure groups. When planning procedures are too firmly structured, responsiveness and flexibility to meet rapidly changing situations are impaired, but frequent reviews building upon evaluation and feedback are a possible solution and actually foster staff involvement. Evidence from the Managing for Efficiency and Effectiveness in Schools project shows that schools which follow rational processes are more likely to be judged to be effective but that this is likely to be a reflection of the way in which people work. Staff who plan effectively in curriculum and teaching matters will also be likely to do so in relation to financial and resource management.

References

Audit Commission (1993) *Keeping Your Balance*. London: Ofsted.

Davies, B. and Ellison, L. (1995) Taking the long view. *Managing Schools Today*, October.

Fullan, M. (1991) *The New Meaning of Educational Change*. London: Cassell.

Glover, D., Levačić, R., Bennett, N. and Earley, P. (1996) Leadership, planning and resource management in very effective schools, *School Organisation*, 16(2): 135–48 and 16(3).

Hargreaves, D. (1995) Self-managing schools and development planning – chaos or control?, *School Organisation*, 15 (3).

Hargreaves, D. and Hopkins, D. (1991) *The Empowered School*. London: Cassell.

Hargreaves, D., Hopkins, D., Leask, M., Connolly, J. and Robinson, P. (1989) *Planning for School Development*, School Development Plans Project. London: Department of Education and Science.

Law, S. (1995) *Primary and Secondary Professional Development Survey Reports*. Keele: University In-service and Education Management Unit.

Levačić, R. and Glover, D. (1995) The relationship between efficient resource management and school effectiveness: evidence from Ofsted secondary school inspections. European Conference on Educational Research, Bath University, September.

Mintzberg, H. (1994) *The Rise and Fall of Strategic Planning*. London: Prentice Hall.

National Audit Office (1994) *Value for Money at Grant-maintained Schools: a review of performance*. London: HMSO.

Office for Standards in Education (Ofsted) (1995) *The OFSTED Handbook: Guidance on the inspection of secondary schools*. London: HMSO.

Rigby, H. (1995) Through teamwork to autocracy. *Management in Education*, 9 (1), February.

Sheffield Education Department (1991) *School Development Planning Under LMS*, Sheffield, City Council.

Simkins, T. (1989) Budgeting as a political and organisational process, in R. Levačić (ed.) *Financial Management in Education*. Milton Keynes: Open University Press.

West-Burnham, J. (1992) *Managing Quality in Schools*. Harlow: Longman.

Wong, S. (1995) Management decision support systems: From theory to practice. *Education Management and Administration*, 23 (2), April.

13 | Budget analysis and construction

BRIAN KNIGHT

The budget process normally lasts for nearly two years, with four main phases:

1 Preliminary analysis	Strategic	Before financial year
2 Budget construction	Operational	Before financial year
3 Control and monitoring of expenditure	Operational	During financial year
4 Evaluation	Strategic	After financial year

The first two phases are discussed in this chapter.

Inevitably there are linkage problems between the phases. As Figure 13.1 suggests, phases 1 and 2 have to be completed for year 2 before phase 3 is complete for year 1; whereas phase 4 for year 1 can only affect phase 1 of year 3.

There are other linkage problems, particularly with the school development plan and its longer time scales, and also with information on student numbers, level of funding, prices etc. Schools in those unhappy systems where academic and financial years do not coincide have further problems.

It is not surprising that schools find the budget process troublesome. Most seem to cope reasonably well with operational aspects such as control and monitoring, but deal much less effectively with preliminary analysis, strategic budget planning and final evaluation. Indeed these processes are often quite superficial, sometimes invisible.

This chapter therefore stresses the importance of school managers clarifying the *purpose* of the budget process, choosing the best *strategy*, and improving the budget *format*. However, there is a marked difference in the needs of schools. Primary school budgets are simpler and more easily related to school objectives as a whole, but less easily focused on delivery of aspects of the curriculum. Secondary school budgets are the opposite, dispersed across departments and timetable subject allocations. Small primary schools should find the principles of this chapter relevant though they may need to prune away the detail.

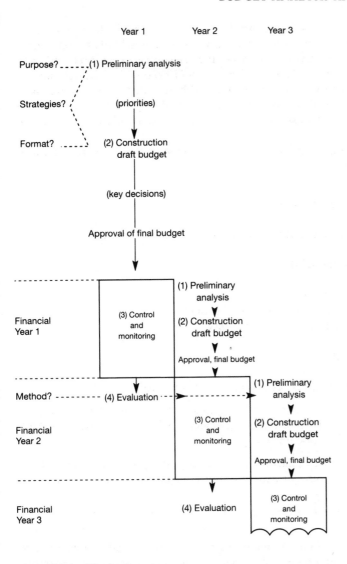

Figure 13.1 The budget process

Preliminary analysis

The purpose of a budget

A budget is not a balance sheet, or even a financial statement of projected expenditure. It is, or should be, a management tool for planning, implementing and evaluating. A workaday definition would be: 'A plan for the allocation and expenditure of resources to achieve the objectives of the school'. This definition emphasises the focus on planning, and the need to relate expenditure to the achievement of objectives, rather than the more familiar instrumental function of authorising and controlling expenditure.

A budget has two faces – income and expenditure. In state schools the former tends to be taken for granted, almost as an act of God. However, as schools become more entrepreneurial we can expect them to identify their resource needs first and then seek the funds for them. So the budget's supply side will become increasingly important. A budget does not necessarily involve finance, although that is our interest here – it can equally take the form of a manpower or time budget. But it always needs a time-scale – usually a year, but possibly longer or shorter, particularly for a special project.

Writers on financial management have identified a range of functions for a budget:

Planning
Forecasting
Matching income and expenditure
Establishing priorities
Comparing diverse activities through common financial denominators
Implementing plans
Coordinating activities of the school
Allocating resources
Authorising expenditure and activities
Communicating objectives and priorities to personnel
Motivating personnel by delegating responsibility
Controlling and monitoring expenditure
Strengthening accountability
Obtaining value for money, economy
Matching outcomes against inputs, assessing cost effectiveness.

Given such a diverse range of functions, it is unrealistic to expect that all or most can be executed from just one type of budget statement. Schools really need to think of three different sets of budget documents:

1 Preliminary analysis – discursive, narrative, speculative and presenting alternatives.
2 The budget statement, for both construction and control phases, quantitative and systematised.
3 The evaluation process, largely qualitative, linked to objectives, criteria and indicators.

At each stage we need to ask: 'What are we trying to do? What exactly do we hope to achieve with this document or process? And who is the audience?' So, for example, the format of any financial statement for stage 2 may need to be completely modified for stages 1 or 3.

Alternatives and priorities

Any initial analysis will have two starting points: the school's current objectives, ideally derived from a development plan; and an early prognosis for the coming financial year about the likely level of funding, student numbers, prices and any major financial commitments. Such an analysis should begin early, long before final funding figures are known. It will obviously be very tentative at the beginning. But the problem is not so much clarity as creativity. Many schools are locked into a narrow and blinkered view of the alternatives open to them.

Example

A school identifies, as a major objective, improvement of the writing and reading of the weakest 20 per cent of its intake. The alternatives examined are:

Increased teacher staffing for extra in-class support.
Ditto, for withdrawal of students from classes in small groups.
Ditto, to improve the teacher/student ratio.
Provision of an incentive allowance and special funds for a teacher to improve the choice of books and materials for these students in all subjects.
Improved funding for the school library.
Funds for extra computers and other learning aids.
INSET for all the school's staff on more effective learning for such children.

At first sight this seems a broad range of alternatives. But consider what else might have been included:

Payment of an incentive allowance and expenses for a teacher to improve home–school liaison.
An extended day programme; e.g. an after-school or twilight clinic.
Regular individual coaching, out of school.
An adult literacy type programme; i.e. informal and with activity and timing determined by the client.
An 'intensive burst' holiday scheme.
Extra support for at-risk students in feeder schools.
Peer tutoring from older students.
Peer tutoring provided by under-performing students to at-risk students in feeder schools.
Personal counselling to improve self-image.
Financial incentives, to reward individual students for progress.

Whatever the reasons, schools do not generally relish fundamental re-examination of the relationship of the budget to their objectives. Just look at strategies such as improved home–school liaison, parental involvement in reading, improvement of self-image through coaching or counselling, peer-tutoring – all with strong evidence of cost-effectiveness, but with marginal or non-existent funding in most school budgets.

So if your school wishes to consider a wide range of alternatives, what should you do? Somehow you have to create a brainstorming environment where wild ideas float free and are tolerated. You can then assess each for probability of likely effectiveness, and come up with a guesstimate of likely cost. It is also possible – though certainly not essential – to use a technique to sharpen such decision-making:

1 Decide criteria to assess the alternatives.
2 Give a weight to each criterion for its importance.
3 Grade the alternatives against the criteria.
4 Adjust the gradings in step 3 for the weighting, and aggregate these.

Table 13.1 illustrates this, using some of the alternatives from the earlier example. This method is not very time-consuming. It is quite difficult to decide on grading and weighting – very subjective – but the process does help you to think more rigorously and objectively. Notice that there are two stages: determining the weighted criteria,

Table 13.1   Example of multi-criterion budgetary decision-making (figures are mainly for illustration)

	Grading for criteria			Weighted grading			Total	Likely cost
	A*	B*	C*	A†	B†	C†		£
Increased in-class support	6	7	5	36	70	40	146	6 000
Improved choice of books/ materials	3	5	3	18	50	24	92	3 000
Home–school liaison	8	6	4	48	60	32	140	7 000
Computers/learning aids	4	6	3	24	60	24	108	12 000
INSET	3	4	4	18	40	32	90	1 500
Peer tutoring	7	7	3	42	70	24	136	500
Financial incentives	5	7	5	30	70	40	140	1 200

* Criterion A: Improvement to self image and confidence
 Criterion B: Improvement to reading skills
 Criterion C: Improvement to writing skills

†Weighting for criterion A: 6
 Weighting for criterion B: 10
 Weighting for criterion C: 8

and then choosing the best alternatives. These can then be matched against likely costs. In Table 13.1 the last two alternatives seem to be the 'best buy'.

Once you have narrowed the choice you can refine the costing and model the effect on the budget. In fact computer modelling, using some of the friendly programs now available, is important in the later stages of analysis. Also at these later stages it is important to use comparative data (unit cost, percentages, comparisons with past years or between schools) as discussed later in this chapter. By the end of this preliminary analysis you should have produced a clear set of priorities.

Budget construction

There are several different ways of approaching this.

Budget strategies

Incremental

This involves adjusting the previous year's budget with increments for any changes in volume (or in the case of decrease, with decrements). It is difficult to justify because it involves no thinking analysis, planning or linking of the budget to objectives and priorities. But it still lurks more commonly than is acknowledged.

Pragmatic

This is a down-to-earth approach, particularly useful when schools first take responsibility for their budget. It firmly bases the new budget upon the old one, and so is

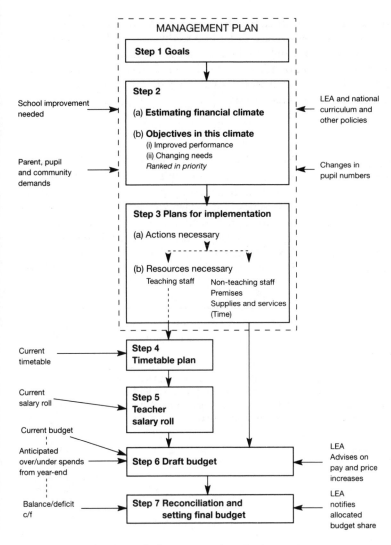

Figure 13.2 The 'limited plan' approach to budget making
Source: B. Knight (1989)

low-risk and economical in time and effort. But it does attempt to improve the previous budget and make savings that can be redeployed elsewhere. These savings may be treated as a windfall, to be shared out at the year's end, or planned for and so re-allocated during budget construction. [. . .]

Limited plan

Like the pragmatic approach, this is rooted in the previous year's budget and uses the timetable plan (i.e. allocation of teachers and their time) as a major instrument of resource allocation. However, it also includes a more overt but limited planning element, drawn pragmatically from changes that seem necessary or desirable but within the parameters of what seems likely to be financially practicable. There is no attempt to produce a grand design if only limited resources are likely to be available. Such an approach is set out in Figure 13.2 [. . .]. This kind of strategy is still low-risk and relatively uncomplicated, but it does not encourage long-term planning or consideration of a broader range of alternatives.

Base budget

This has been strongly advocated by the UK Audit Commission in *Management Within Primary Schools* (1991: 23–6), though the principle is equally applicable to secondary schools. It advocates a school plan as a starting point. However, it accepts that the major part of most schools' budgets will be irrevocably committed to on-going commitments or core activities, and so not available for alternative uses. But this budget core is seen as a strict minimum, not a comfortable optimum – if you like, the lowest minimum that would be tolerable in a desperate cuts situation. In the Audit Commission example below, 84 per cent is shown as base budget and 16 per cent as discretionary.

The starting point of the budgetary process is the unavoidable expenditure facing the school. Once this first call on funds or *base budget* has been identified, the school can then explore options because resources in excess of the base budget are available for alignment with the school's aims. The guiding principle of the base budget is that it prejudges as few ways of meeting the particular needs of the pupils as possible.

. . . Vincent Square School is situated in a metropolitan district and has 220 pupils on roll; its total funding allocation is £232 300 . . . The largely unavoidable expenditure for the operation of Vincent Square School, excluding classroom staff, is:

	£
Repairs and maintenance	1 500
Energy	2 500
Rates	8 000
Water	1 000
Cleaning	6 500
Caretaking	9 000
Refuse collection	300
Equipment	200
Recruitment advertising	100
Adult free school meals	2 000
Support to governing body	300
Administrative supplies and equipment	2 000
Total	33 400

These items include the running costs of the school premises because, although there will be some scope for efficiency savings, these costs are largely fixed.

The real flexibility in resourcing revolves around staffing decisions. The teacher staffing element of the base budget can be determined by reference to the organisation of the school into classes. A reasonable starting point would be the number of teachers (including the head) required to form groups of not more than 30 pupils, together with a part-time element sufficient to release the headteacher for $1\frac{1}{2}$ days a week for administration and for seeing parents. The base should also include other unavoidable staffing costs, such as midday supervision.

Applying this approach to Vincent Square implies a need for the 220 pupils to be formed into eight groups. If there were only seven groups, the maximum of 30 pupils would have to breached in at least some of the groups but with eight groups all can be contained within the maximum. To enable the head to be released from teaching the number of teachers would be 8.3. . . . The estimated base staffing budget is:

	£
Headteacher (Group 2 point 10)	24 200
Deputy Headteacher (Group 2 point 2)	21 400
6.3 other teachers	105 100
	150 700
Add: premises etc. [above]	33 400
Midday supervision	5 500
Total base budget costs	189 600
Budget remaining	42 700

It is important to stress that neither Vincent Square nor any other school can be expected to operate successfully on its base budget – it is simply a budgeting approach to identify the maximum sum of money available for deployment by the governing body to meet its school development plan.

This approach has much to commend it. Like the earlier strategies it works from the given and so avoids time-consuming re-creation of the base budget. It does adopt a clean-slate attitude to the remainder of the budget, and so opens up more possibility of a thorough examination of alternatives linked to the school's plans and objectives; but by doing so it may of course create more internal concern and conflict.

Programme budgeting

Programme budgeting [relates expenditure to objectives . . .]

The line-item budget, disaggregating expenditure by categories like salaries and not by activities or programmes, is uncoupled from objectives, difficult to evaluate against performance, and driven by history as much as by identification of actual needs. The programme approach in education has been encouraged by recent trends – the move towards school self-management; the increased concern with effectiveness and efficiency; the borrowing of methods from the business sector; the demand for greater accountability; and the desire to increase team-working and collaboration with schools and with their communities.

[. . .]

Programme budgeting has developed extensively in the Australian state of Victoria, largely following the original model set out by Brian Caldwell and Jim Spinks in *The Self Managing School*, and more recently in New Zealand. The original Caldwell/ Spinks management model [. . .] separates policy-making, from policy implementation – i.e. strategy from operations. It bridges the gap between objectives and budget provision with two stages: formulating policies and deriving programmes and plans from them. It builds up the budget by aggregating the individual budget proposals for each programme and reconciling the total against funds available. [. . .]

Programme budgeting seems to be taking root in Australia, although it is too early to say whether this is permanent or whether it will die back. Its logic is powerful. But there are several reservations. First, it is undoubtedly more time-consuming than the strategies discussed earlier. The process is more elaborate, and collaboration is always more time-consuming. Also, its bottom-up budget building ignores the Audit Commission argument for a reserved base budget. Second, it has found it hard to break out of conventional 'subject' compartments. It is difficult to translate an objective such as 'Improve student cooperative working and problem-solving' into the budget. (In fairness this is equally true of other strategies.) Third, its collaborative character enhances the role of teachers in decision-making, and while this may enhance short-term efficiency and even effectiveness, it is not clear that it will encourage bolder long-term innovation.

Probably the real value of programme budgeting lies less in the technique than in the frame of mind. *Programme thinking* is what matters.

[. . .]

Zero budgeting

Zero budgeting was introduced by President Jimmy Carter into US government. It proved very greedy for information and died back quickly. The author does not know of any school currently operating it. But as a concept – as opposed to a system – it is attractive. It involves wiping the slate clean and requiring each activity to justify its claims for any funds *at all*. It is particularly useful for questioning the status quo, reducing expenditures for which priorities have fallen, and making space for new needs.

Apart from being very time-consuming, it is also threatening: no one starts with any claim to anything! It is not realistic for annual operation, but it could be very useful for cleansing the stables periodically – say every five years, ideally linked with whole-school review. Alternatively, it could be used to scrutinise different areas of expenditure each year. A simple form of zero budgeting would use questions such as:

Should this function or activity be performed at all?
If so, on what scale? And at what quality level?
Should it be performed in this way?
Or are there better, or cheaper, alternatives?
How much should it cost?

The best strategy?

Tim Simkins and David Lancaster in *Budgeting and Resource Allocation in Educational Institutions* examined various approaches to budgetary construction. They suggested that each school needs to adopt a system that fits its own needs, and saw a wide range of possible criteria (pp. 105–8):

- Respond equitably to needs of different subject areas.
- Take account of priorities.
- Promote achievement of the school's objectives.
- Encourage innovation.
- Facilitate long-term planning.

- React rapidly to environmental change.
- Facilitate evaluation of 'sub-units' (departments etc.).
- Take account of patterns of power and influence.
- Take account of differences in ability to spend wisely.
- Avoid incurring substantial time or other costs.
- Be easily understood and widely accepted.

Budget format and presentation of information

Your budget format is not preordained. You can design it for your own needs, just as for any other planning document. Of course you may be required to keep accounts in a specified form by an LEA, school board or government department, but that is only required for that specified purpose. With modern spreadsheets there is no reason why financial information should not be shaken up, like a kaleidoscope, into different patterns. Indeed a main argument of this chapter is that this is essential for intelligent management: different information formats are needed for different purposes.

Budget layout

There are three main types in use.

Subjective or line-item (Figure 13.3)   This is the familiar layout by categories of expenditure; e.g. employees' salaries, premises, supplies and services, establishment

Line-item	Function
Employees	Instruction
Full time/PT teachers	Full time/PT teachers
Supply teachers	Supply teachers
Supply teachers (INSET)	Technical
Administrative/clerical	Books and equipment
Technical	Administration
Caretakers	Full-time teachers
Premises	Administrative, clerical
Electricity	Postage and telephone
Water	Premises
Cleaning materials	Caretakers
Refuse collection	Electricity
Maintenance	Water
Supplies and services	Insurance
Books and equipment	Teacher support services
Postage and telephone	INSET
Establishment	Supply teachers (INSET)
Advertising	Clerical support
Staff travel/subsistence	Student support and services
Insurance	Transportation
Miscellaneous	Catering

Figure 13.3   Alternative budget formats (abbreviated examples)

expenses, miscellaneous, transport, catering. It is well-tried and effective for control-ling and monitoring expenditure, because it collates similar expenditures together and allows comparison of like with like. But it is of limited use for strategic planning or relating expenditure to objectives, and it does not aid evaluation beyond the purely financial.

Function (Figure 13.3)   This classifies information by the function for which funds are spent; e.g., instruction, administration, premises, teacher support services, student support and services, transportation, catering. It is easier to see how money is being used and to question priorities, and so makes planning and evaluation somewhat easier. But it is less suitable for control – a category like non-teaching salaries may be spread over several functions. And it is still not closely related to objectives or activities.

Programme [. . .]   Here expenditures for each programme or activity are grouped, as discussed above under programme budgeting. In *The Self Managing School* Caldwell and Spinks list 41 programmes for Rosebery District High School (all-age) in Tas-mania. Nineteen of them are subjects, but there are also programme areas like pastoral care, support services, special needs, administration, public relations, cleaning, grounds and some complementary areas such as extra-curricular activities, gifted children, drama festival, school magazine and council. An alternative to subject programmes could be broader groupings (e.g. creative and performing arts) or programmes for groups of students or by skill development (communication, numeracy, problem-solving etc.) – but these are difficult to create.

   This programme format links expenditure more closely to objectives, though still largely on a subject, or function-centred, basis. It could recharge an element like pre-mises to each programme unless this is retained as a function. But while it is the best of the three formats for strategic planning and evaluation, it is the weakest for control. Teaching or non-teaching salaries, for example, will be spread across many budget heads.
   [. . .]

The best format?   It seems clear that some kind of function or programme format is to be preferred for analysis and evaluation, but the traditional line-item format for control. There is no reason why schools should not use different formats for the differ-ent purposes. In fact both can be used together, and linked through a matrix, with programmes on one axis and a subjective format on the other. This then allows teacher salaries for various programmes, for example, to be aggregated into a total.
   [. . .]

Raw totals . . . or comparative figures?

It is very difficult to make sense of any single figure in a budget estimate or out-turn statement, just as it is difficult to make sense of your own domestic electricity bill unless you can compare it with previous similar bills and with neighbours' bills.
   [. . .]
As a general rule any budget *estimate* document should set out last year's figures against this year's, and should convert both to unit costs to allow easier comparison.

A budget *out-turn* document for evaluation should ideally include a series of unit costs over three or four years or so, plus data from peer schools, to allow broader comparisons and detection of trends. But the final budget estimates, used for control and monitoring, do not need previous year's figures or unit cost data.

What are the best format arrangements:

The ideal situation would be:

Budget analysis	Budget control and monitoring	Budget evaluation
Programme*	Line-item	Programme*
Disaggregated	Aggregated	Disaggregated
New year and previous years	Current year only	Out-turn and previous years
Totals and unit costs	Totals	Series of unit costs, unit costs for peer schools

* Aggregated into line-item totals by a matrix.

[. . .]

This chapter has stressed the need for a thoughtful approach to the budget, particularly over budget analysis, choice of a budgetary strategy and selection of improved formats.

References

Audit Commission (1991) *Management Within Primary Schools*. London: HMSO.

Caldwell, B. and Spinks, J. (1988) *The Self-Managing School*. Lewes: Falmer Press.

Knight, B. (1989) *Managing School Time*. Harlow: Longman.

Simkins, T. and Lancaster, D. (1987) Budgeting and Resource Allocation in Educational Institutions., *Education Management*, 35. Sheffield: Sheffield City Polytechnic (Sheffield Hallam University).

14 | Allocating budgets for curriculum support

MARK SUTTON

Introduction

Alongside the development of delegated budgeting to schools there has been a parallel movement towards greater delegation of financial responsibility within schools. The pressures that have led to this movement have come from many directions. Alongside Local Management of Schools in England and Wales, the plethora of legislation since the late 1980s aimed at making schools more accountable has enormously increased the managerial and administrative burden upon senior management; and headteachers have had no option but to delegate. Theories gleaned from business management have long promoted delegation as a motivational force. More enlightened middle managers in schools have increasingly demanded more flexibility and more command over the resources available to them. In response, headteachers have sought ways in which to allocate finance to an increasing number of cost centres or budget holders on their staff.

Organizational perspectives on resource allocation

Internal systems of resource allocation can be usefully analysed from a number of organizational perspectives, in particular rational decision-making, bureaucracy, micropolitics and collegiality. Each provides a particular purpose to be served by the resource allocation systems and an associated set of processes.

The rational model of decision-making is characterized by the articulation of a single set of clear organizational objectives, the assessment of all the alternative courses of action against these objectives and the choice of the one which best achieves them. In order to make rational judgements about the wisdom and desirability of internal delegation and its form and extent, senior managers must first consider the objectives of their institution. Schools' statements of aims and objectives will inevitably and quite properly concentrate upon the experiences and opportunities offered to students. Terms such as 'high standards' and 'quality' will typically feature prominently. Ensuring that what the school does is 'effective' is often explicitly stated, while the increased financial responsibility placed upon schools has carried with it an expectation of 'efficiency' and 'value for money'.

'Efficiency' and 'effectiveness' have accepted definitions in public sector accountancy, although both are used much more loosely and as if they were synonymous in everyday parlance. By efficiency we mean that a given quantity of output is produced at the least possible cost or, perhaps more appropriately in the educational environment, that the maximum output is achieved for a given set of scarce resources. How one measures the quantity of output of a school is obviously a matter of debate, undoubtedly a heated one on the issue of value added, but not the subject of this chapter.

The term effectiveness carried an additional meaning and an assumption of the social value of that output and the quality of the process, i.e. how well does a particular activity achieve its objectives. It can be argued that the oft quoted term 'value for money' requires not just efficiency (doing things right) but also effectiveness (doing the right things). Resources will always be scarce in education, so to what extent can the process of internal delegation promote an efficient and effective use of limited resources?

In the bureaucratic model, schools are viewed as having hierarchical authority structures with formal chains of command between the different levels. Schools pursue those goals determined by their official leaders at the apex of the pyramid. Decision-making is still deemed to be rational, based on a careful evaluation of alternatives and a considered choice of the most appropriate option. A bureaucratic system of internal resource allocation will not only be rational, but will also re-inforce the hierarchical structure and the authority of the appointed leaders of the institution.

In contrast, the micro-political model sees schools as collections of sectional interests, each of which has its own objectives. It is these sectional interests which press for decisions in their favour. In this model, there are either no clear organizational objectives or they are far less important than the objective of containing the conflicts of interests within workable coalitions. This may be achieved by negotiating compromises with curriculum leaders and sustaining harmony between them all. An alternative strategy would be to keep power by dividing and thereby ruling them.

In the collegial model, the emphasis is on staff consultation and participation in decision-making. The quality of the processes of human interaction is valued over and above the organization's performance in terms of the results achieved by students. Here the organizational purpose of a system of internal resource allocation will be dominated by the desire to motivate staff and maximize their contribution to the functioning of the institution.

Finally, schools in England and Wales are subject to inspections by Ofsted, whose criteria for the efficiency of the school expect a close and explicit link between the aims, objectives and priorities set in the school development plan and the budget. These external expectations serve to underpin the rational and bureaucratic models.

Different models of cost-centre budget allocation

Before considering how budgets may be allocated, one should consider which areas of expenditure, if any, should be included. Consumable classroom materials, text books etc. are commonly considered to be the foundation of delegation, but what about resources for minor equipment, reprographics, classroom furniture and training? Some schools may even wish to consider delegating an element of staffing decisions.

Another crucial issue to be addressed is that of to whom to delegate, i.e. what are the cost-centres to be? In a sense, in a hierarchical structure the responsibilities of middle managers will identify them as budget holders, for example heads of faculties or departments. But what about cross-curricular areas, or delegation within a department? Should some areas of expenditure be delegated to groupings of budget holders?

There are a number of different decision methods for deciding allocations, some based on a centralized approach, others based on delegation. Each must be evaluated in terms of how well it allows the various objectives appropriate to the relevant organizational model to be met. Moreover, the appropriate model (or combination of models) for a school to adopt depends on the particular individual school context, its organizational culture and management philosophy and style.

Centralized model

In a centralized system, decisions are made by a single body. Such a system can operate either through, at the one extreme, the headteacher acting as the all powerful autocrat, in Knight (1983) the 'benevolent despot', or through varying degrees of collective decision-making by committees of staff. These committees could be made up of governors, the senior management team, curriculum leaders, an elected group of staff making up a Staff Finance Committee or even all staff in the case of small schools.

However narrow or wide the consultation, schools should consider carefully that decision makers need to possess, assimilate and evaluate all the relevant information in order to make effective decisions on how to use resources to meet their objectives. The decision-making hub at the centre of the organization needs to pool all the information gleaned from the peripheries and communicate its vision back, so that all the sub-units are integrated and can co-ordinate their activities to pull in the same direction to meet the school's aims.

The wider the consultation, the greater the need for thorough preparation and dissemination of financial data so that informed decisions can be made. There is an administrative burden in this, and it is time-consuming, but it does ensure that resources are more likely to be allocated effectively between the competing demands for them.

A centralized system where teachers are involved on committees to participate in financial decision-making may motivate staff and meet the collegial model objectives. Most large schools will typically operate with a pyramid-shaped hierarchical organizational structure, consistent with the bureaucratic model. Any delegation will therefore be down the chain of command. In the collegial model, however, there is a much flatter structure. This may be more appropriate to a smaller school with fewer staff in which the objectives of working through people are better achieved not by delegation of financial resources but by retaining them centrally whilst consulting widely about their disposal.

Any system of delegation depends upon the ability of middle managers to deal with that greater responsibility and to get value for money for the education of students from what are clearly limited resources. This in itself has resource implications: staff need training, other forms of support and the time for making effective decisions.

If curriculum leaders are either not interested, or not capable of financial management, or not motivated by or properly informed about whole school objectives, by handing over the purse-strings, schools lose an element of control and may not be able to secure the most effective use of scarce resources. In contrast, the headteacher and/or senior management team may have more expertise and experience in financial decision-making.

In the case of a school where decisions are made autocratically by the headteacher (or occasionally by a deputy or bursar) he or she could simply take last year's allocations and uprate them in line with inflation or revise them in proportion to changes in the global budget. This 'creeping incrementalist' approach described in Knight (1983) is simple, time-saving and low on conflict, but never challenges the status quo. It mitigates against institutional development and cannot realistically meet the needs of departments faced with fluctuating student numbers and changes in their curriculum. It is more than likely that different subject areas will need larger injections of finance at different times over a number of years as new initiatives, curriculum changes etc. are implemented. Changes in needs like these are more easily dealt with centrally and it would seem prudent for the headteacher of a school to withhold some of its budget to support such developments.

A more enlightened headteacher will seek representations from curriculum leaders and assess priorities for expenditure. This can vary from formal bids, or very informal discussions. Done badly, the outcome could be an arbitrary allocation based on bias and pressure, and not necessarily even published. However, if done well, the headteacher will be evaluating a range of well-costed departmental plans and prioritizing them within the framework of the school development plan. It is entirely possible that the omniscient despot could achieve efficiency, effectiveness and value for money.

In a bidding system, formal, costed plans can of course be submitted to committees for consideration, in which case the system is much more akin to an auction or, in the typology of Knight (1983), an 'open market', although it must still be classified as centralized. If a bidding system is employed, it does put pressure on curriculum leaders to justify and cost their requests for spending in terms of current achievements and how the proposed developments will affect the quality of learning and contribute to the school development plan. Demands for additional resources have more authority and impact if they are linked to clear priorities and planning and are far more likely to achieve value for money. There is an element of democracy and collective accountability if each bid is subject to a process of professional review by peers. It can also lead to a closer examination and questioning of the status quo.

However, in the micro-political model, decision makers do require a degree of skill in identifying both the optimists and the pessimists, those who shout the loudest but have weak cases, against those whose departments have real need but who are weaker characters lacking the skill, confidence, experience to make forceful, well argued bids. Invariably the bids outweigh the funds available and the tendency is to inflate bids in the perceived view that budget holders will receive a proportion of what they have requested. One way round this is to adopt the pendulum arbitration approach, i.e. departments are awarded all or nothing, and this will usually moderate the size of bids.

There are a number of permutations to the awarding of grants in response to successful bids. The resources allocated may depend on the outcomes expected, expressed in terms of performance criteria. Budget holders may be allowed to retain any savings they make on the specified project which may encourage efficiency. Allowances may be earmarked for general areas of expenditure, such as differentiated learning, or only for a specific project that is costed and deemed to be effective. Awards may be for the whole sum requested, or on a matched funding basis. Alternatively the centrally held budget may pump prime an initiative, and gradually reduce its contribution to the total cost of the project.

Centralized decision-making does have a number of other advantages. Whole school priorities are better understood and dealt with and all decisions can be made within the schools' global aims and objectives. Consequently, it encourages whole school consistency and the pursuit of sectional interests is avoided. It is also possible to make decisions much more quickly when fewer people are involved in the process, and therefore meets one of the criteria of the rational model.

Lastly, it has to be acknowledged that centralized decision-making is more appropriate to an autocratic style of management, as autocrats who delegate frequently interfere and undermine those to whom they have delegated, de-motivating rather than motivating them.

Decentralized model

In a decentralized system, decisions are made by individual teachers acting as budget holders. When capitation (i.e. an amount per pupil for stationery and materials) marked the limit of financial delegation to schools, many headteachers put in place a formula for the allocation of some of this money to curriculum leaders. If a formula is used, the process of allocating resources is very much simpler, quicker, open, and perceived to be objective and fair. Commonly such a formula is based upon the number of pupils and the number of periods taught in a week. More sophisticated formulae use a system of weights dependent upon the age of the pupils and/or the nature of the subject, as described by Boulton (1986).

There are many advantages to this approach: it is transparent and can be seen to be fair; changes in need caused by increasing numbers of pupils are easily accommodated; having a formula as its basis, it mirrors the system of delegating finance to schools.

However, it has its shortfalls. It does not deal adequately with developmental needs and having no lump sum element it fails to recognize that there may well be a fixed cost element to curriculum delivery, e.g. the provision of a teacher's handbook. Once the money is delegated it is usually without strings attached. The school could in effect have lost control of it if there is no requirement to evaluate, no accountability or expectation that its disposal should be solely related to departmental or whole school objectives. Even if the resources are allocated with recommendations, there is a danger that such recommendations are ignored.

Moreover, using a formula begs as many questions as it answers. How should a school fund cross-curricular work and areas such as Information Technology, the Library, Special Needs and Careers which do not easily fit into such a formula? How much more should Design and Technology receive per pupil than English? How much extra funding should a 16-year-old be allocated than a 12-year-old?

Notwithstanding these questions, by delegating to curriculum leaders, the greater authority and responsibility invested in them may be a motivating force, leading to greater job satisfaction. Theorists such as Maslow (1970), Herzberg (1966) and

McGregor (1960) suggest that staff will be better motivated in their work if given greater responsibility and the status and recognition that go with it. By being actively involved in financial decision-making about their own curriculum area, rather than just rubber-stamping senior management decisions, budget holders will be motivated to secure a more efficient and effective use of scarce resources. In the context of the collegial model, the motivational advantages of delegation will enhance the staff's perception of their own value to the institution. This decentralized approach also means that the school is developing its middle managers and preparing them for promotion. This is totally consistent with the objectives of a collegial model, but could considerably strengthen the hands of sectional interests in a micro-political model. Political harmony may be harder to achieve unless this development is balanced.

Compared with senior managers and administrators, departments and individual teachers have a much better idea of what their needs are and will be able to target their spending more accurately to improve the learning experiences of their students. Moreover, they will be able to implement those spending decisions much more quickly and be more flexible in their purchasing strategies.

Another advantage of the decentralization of financial decision-making is that there is less stress and burden on an overstretched senior management team, which should enable its members to carry out their functions more efficiently and effectively.

Hybrid model

Of course, these systems are not mutually exclusive and most schools will undoubtedly mix and match to suit their own organizational models, managerial styles, educational objectives and developmental needs. Hybrid strategies may delegate maintenance expenditure according to a formula, but retain resources for developmental purposes centrally. Some centralized decision-making may be made by the headteacher alone, whilst other decisions about formal bids may be put to a staff committee or alternatively to governors.

Empirical evidence from secondary and middle schools

A survey of 49 secondary and middle schools carried out by Sutton (1995), gave an interesting insight into the actual practice of allocating budgets for curriculum support. Encouragingly, a significant number of schools commented that they were increasingly linking their delegation to development plans, both whole school and departmental. In all cases financial resources were delegated to curriculum leaders, but in all but one some funds were retained centrally. Not surprisingly, the variation was very large in the sample. At one extreme, seven schools retained nothing for development, whilst one school kept back 55 per cent. The average however across the sample was 14.3 per cent.

The survey used the typologies outlined by Knight (1983) and asked respondents to state which of four alternative (though not mutually exclusive) allocation strategies they employed to delegate funds within schools. Twenty-two per cent of the sample admitted to 'benevolent despotism' in which, with varying degrees of consultation, the headteacher (or deputy) was the arbiter, deciding how much each budget holder should receive. A similar proportion of schools have adopted an 'open market' approach in which a committee of staff adjudicates on bids for funds. Only 14 per cent of the sample used 'incrementalism' whereby the previous year's allocations were merely updated in line with the size of the global school budget.

By far the biggest proportion – in fact 65 per cent of schools in the survey – used a formula based upon weighted student periods to allocate finance for educational resources. Although there were understandably considerable differences between schools, a clear pattern did emerge. Those schools which did use a formula distributed anything from 36.7 per cent to 100 per cent of educational resources to academic budget holders by means of the formula, although the average was 73.2 per cent.

Ninety-six per cent of these schools used a system of weightings to reflect differences in unit costs of teaching different subjects, whilst a slightly smaller number (85 per cent) used weights according to the age of students taught. Less than half (43 per cent) of those schools which used an age-weighted formula employed the weights used by their LEA for determining their global budget. The remaining schools which used a different system of age weighting tended to have a much simpler system and distinguish only between key stages. Fifteen per cent of schools using a formula did not differentiate explicitly between students of different ages at all, one school funded its sixth form 40 per cent more than its KS3 students, whilst another gave a weight 400 per cent more. Excluding these outliers and taking KS3 as the base weight, the average weightings used by these schools were 1.43 for KS4 and 1.75 for Post-16.

Table 14.1 shows the average subject weightings used by the 26 schools that were able to provide data. Normal classroom subjects provided the base weighting, although Humanities subjects were relatively better funded than languages, English and maths. PE and drama were then further favourably treated. IT was marginally better funded as schools perhaps make a token gesture through the formula to the enormous capital costs of delivering that part of the curriculum. Music was better funded still, in recognition of the cost of sheet music and of providing new technology.

Table 14.1   Average subject weightings for formula allocation

Subject area	(a) Average weights	(b) (a) divided by 1.11	(c) (b) to 1 dec. place
Personal & Social Education	1.06	0.95	1.0
Modern Languages	1.09	0.98	1.0
Mathematics	1.11	1.00	1.0
English	1.11	1.00	1.0
Religious Education	1.12	1.01	1.0
History	1.15	1.04	1.0
Geography	1.16	1.05	1.0
Physical Education	1.20	1.08	1.1
Drama	1.21	1.09	1.1
Information Technology	1.31	1.18	1.2
Music	1.38	1.24	1.2
Art	1.83	1.65	1.6
Science	2.01	1.81	1.8
Design & Technology	2.27	2.05	2.0

The big leap came with the practical subjects. In recognition of the cost of consumable materials, art had an average weighting that was 65 per cent higher than the base subjects. Science came next, a reflection of the higher cost of purchasing consumables and equipment. Most favourably treated was design and technology with an average weighting which was more than twice that of the base subjects. Clearly the experience of schools was that this area of the curriculum was the most costly to deliver.

The survey also sought from respondents an indication of how they came to their decisions about the weightings used in their formulae. The recurring theme throughout the survey was that schools did what was felt to be right what seemed to reflect the cost of consumable items, what did not upset too many people too much. An encouraging number of schools did employ the collective wisdom of a finance committee. If they had been able to, they had asked colleagues from other schools and found ways of discovering what went on elsewhere. One respondent summed up the practice very succinctly: 'Previous experience. Other schools. Adjustments. General acceptance'. A different school spoke of the 'fiddle factor' and another of 'trial and error'.

The survey also enquired of schools as to which additional areas of expenditure were being delegated to internal budget holders and what else was being actively considered.

Table 14.2 ranks those areas according to the potential for delegation in the near future, i.e. combining those items of schools budgets which were already being delegated internally and those which were being considered. Resources for minor equipment were already delegated in 82 per cent of the schools surveyed and being considered in a further 8 per cent. A slightly higher number of schools had delegated reprographics.

One of the areas of expenditure most likely to be a candidate for internal delegation in the future appeared to be training. Classroom furniture was being considered by the same number of schools, putting a greater onus on curriculum leaders to be responsible for the upkeep of the fabric of their teaching environment.

Table 14.2   Other budget headings for delegation

Budget heading	% of schools		
	Already delegating	Considering delegating in the future	Total
Minor equipment (up to £100)	82	8	90
Reprographics	84	4	88
Major equipment (over £100)	55	8	63
GEST resources	39	6	45
GEST training	31	12	43
Educational visits	37	4	41
Furniture	20	12	32
Non-teaching support staff	2	8	10
Teachers' salaries	4	4	8
Maintenance of premises	6	2	8
Energy	4	2	6
Supply cover	6	0	6

Most interestingly, was the evidence that even a small number of schools had handed over some financial responsibility for staffing to academic budget holders (or were considering doing so). Comments from those schools indicated that this was at the margin only, for example giving curriculum leaders some power over the employment of part-time teachers' extra hours, support staff and additional temporary pay points.

The experience of primary schools

By their very nature, primary schools are much smaller than secondary schools, and the scope for internal delegation is therefore nowhere near as great. Budgets are smaller, as are the numbers of staff to whom delegation can be given. Nevertheless, even at the margins, possibilities do exist. The case studies below contrast the different approaches adopted by two primary schools. In the first a hybrid model is employed with a fair degree of decentralized decision-making. In the second, smaller school, the system of resource allocation is very much more centralized.

Case study 1

Primary school A has 235 pupils and 10 teaching staff including the headteacher. Its catchment area contains an army barracks and therefore it suffers from a high pupil turnover rate.

Of the entire budget, 2 per cent is allocated for educational materials, and that is split:

Classroom materials (consumables)	40%
Curriculum resources (e.g. reading scheme)	40%
Administration consumables	15%
Miscellaneous (for TV programme support material)	5%

Finance for classroom stationery and materials is delegated on a fixed sum basis.

The arguments put forward for delegation of this area of the budget are very practical. By giving the responsibility for ordering materials to staff, the headteacher is released from the administrative burdens of this chore. He has witnessed a greater cooperation between teachers who have shown willingness to share materials, and there is a view that this financial responsibility has led to more economical use.

The disadvantages identified are the increase in administrative costs – a loss of administrative economies of scale – as 30 orders have to be processed, sometimes incurring small order charges. Clearly this decision would not in itself meet the criterion of efficiency.

In terms of the motivation of staff, it was observed that teachers have welcomed the authority given to them to take decisions over the resourcing of their areas of school, although it has to be said that teachers in primary schools have much less non-contact time in which to carry out these additional responsibilities.

For that part of the budget which is delegated, a simple formula had been tried:

$$\frac{\text{Allocated sum} \times \text{No. of pupils in each class} \times \text{age weight}}{\text{No. of pupils in school}}$$

However, this had been abandoned in the face of intense unpopularity with the staff, and because it failed to reflect the turnover of pupils. Rather than try to refine a formula, it was decided to allocate this sum of money to class teachers as budget holders on a straightforward lump sum basis, i.e.

$$\frac{\text{Allocated sum}}{\text{No. of classes} (+2)}$$

The additional 2 covers contingency and the activities of a 'withdrawal' group for art.

In the area of curriculum resources, the allocated budget is delegated first to curriculum coordinators for maths and English. After they have spent what they deem necessary, the balance is available for distribution to other curriculum coordinators on a paper bid system. Each bid must be costed and decisions are then made by the senior management team, consisting of the headteacher, deputy head and the two key stage coordinators with reference to the school development plan.

For larger items of educational equipment, an informal bid system operates in which the headteacher acts very much as a benevolent despot. Additionally, the training budget is delegated to the deputy head.

Case study 2

Primary school B has 189 pupils, 7 staff plus the headteacher. With a very small budget, the curriculum support budget is determined by what is left over after what are viewed as the fixed costs of teachers' salaries, premises and contracted services have been calculated. As a result, this figure fluctuates annually and is heavily influenced by small changes in numbers on roll. On average this figure is 2.5 per cent of the total school budget.

With such a small amount available for distribution, the headteacher retains the role of 'benevolent despot'. There is a strongly held view that delegation of very small amounts would lead to staff spending up to their limit, purchasing small amounts of non-essentials which would have a limited impact on the quality of learning. If those sums were pooled and available centrally, they could finance a major purchase which would have a more significant impact. In this case, the perception is that value for money will be best achieved through a centralized approach.

The system operated instead, effectively allows all staff to bid for consumable classroom materials at the beginning of each year. The headteacher, acting again as 'benevolent despot' will make the final decision of what to purchase, but once the materials have been purchased, there is no limit on what each member of staff may make use of.

As far as larger items of expenditure are concerned, decisions are made in full staff meetings, where alternative proposals are discussed, with reference to the school development plan, the staff effectively acting as a committee to decide on open market bids. There is invariably a consensus of opinion, the logic of this being quite understandable, in that small school primary teachers are more likely to be non-specialist teachers of children across the curriculum as opposed to secondary school specialists who will have a corner to fight for their own sectional interests.

Conclusions

The experiences of primary schools confirm that the costs of delegation are likely to outweigh the benefits the smaller the school, the smaller the budget and the smaller the number of staff. Also there is much less scope for delegation in smaller schools. Experienced staff who have been in post long before delegated budgeting are much more likely to focus their job on the teaching of children, notwithstanding their responsibilities for different curriculum areas, and resent the burden of financial responsibility. However, in a larger school, the pool of staff from which to pick a proportion of budget holders who have the skill and motivation to take on financial responsibility is that much larger.

When deciding upon the extent of and the mechanisms for allocating budgets to curriculum leaders, senior managers need to go back to the objectives of the school, for that is the context in which all financial decisions need to be made.

The twin benchmarks of efficiency and effectiveness should be applied to the allocative decisions of what, how much, to whom and how. No single system has a monopoly over ensuring value for money, and each individual school will make its own choices along the continuum from centralization to decentralization, striking its own balance between control, consistency, flexibility and motivation.

References

Boulton, A. (1986) A developed formula for the distribution of capitation allowances, in *Educational Management and Administration*, 14(1): 31–8.

Herzberg, F. (1966) *Work and the Nature of Man*. New York: Staple Press.

Knight, B. (1983) *Managing School Finance*. London: Heinemann Educational Books.

Maslow, A. (1970) *Motivation and Personality*. New York: Harper & Row.

McGregor, D. (1960) *The Human Side of Enterprise*. Maidenhead: McGraw-Hill.

Sutton, M. (1995) Sharing the purse-strings, in *Managing Schools Today*, 4(7): 14–16.

15 | Unit costing in colleges

J. G. CARR

Why unit costs?

Unit costing seeks to measure the cost of the outputs of an organisation or function. Outputs are related to objectives or purpose and are typically described in terms of products or services. Unit costing defines output in terms of the cost of production or the cost of the provision of a service (or for colleges, the delivery of education and training).

Unit cost data is essential for pricing products and services, measuring the relative profitability of products and services and establishing measures of efficiency. In a college environment unit costs give college management information to assist activities such as:

- relating the unit of resource for a course/student to the cost of delivery;
- evaluating alternative delivery methods;
- choosing to run, expand or drop courses;
- developing a case for additional funding;
- identifying the marginal costs of additional students for bidding purposes;
- developing output as opposed to input cost based budgets;
- setting targets and monitoring performance based on the cost of delivery.

This chapter reviews the design approach to unit costing in colleges; examines the main issues raised in systems development and outlines the potential of more advanced methods adopting an activity based approach to unit costs. A small case example is included to demonstrate aspects of the calculation of unit costs.

The move to unit costing

[. . .] It is clear that changes in funding patterns provides the key motivator for unit costing. By attaching elements of funding directly to students using different fee rates for different course categories, the funding bodies create a market focus by attaching a price/value to each student taken. When funding becomes attached to outputs and is differentiated between different types of outputs then unit costs become essential information for college management. [. . .]

Similar changes to information needs have taken place in Further Education Funding Council colleges as a result of the introduction of bidding elements in funding and the need to establish the cost of marginally priced students. [. . .]

Calculating unit costs

Which college outputs are measured as unit costs is determined by management information needs. Typical and obvious examples would be the cost per:

- teacher or researcher or technician hour;
- facility provided; lecture room, laboratory, computer access;
- course or programme;
- course student (course cost divided by enrolled students, completed students or successful students).

Some classes of output such as courses or programmes are ambiguous and may relate to a tutorial group, class, year of a course, full course programme or a group of inter-related courses. [. . .]

Unit costing methodology requires the restatement of input costs as output costs, using a total absorption costing approach. [. . .]

Total absorption costing systems utilise all or part of a three stage approach covering cost allocation, cost apportionment and cost absorption. In outline:

1 The allocation of costs as direct costs to academic and support cost centres and courses.
2 The apportionment of support centre costs to courses and academic cost centres.
3 The absorption of academic cost centre aggregate direct and apportioned indirect costs to courses using an absorption formula (invariably based on teaching staff hours).

Totally absorbed unit costs are calculated at the commencement of the academic or budget year using planned student numbers, planned hours loading for course delivery and budgeted levels of expenditure for cost centres (staff, premises, supplies etc). The resulting unit costs are therefore target figures which are available for bidding, course pricing, budget development and target setting. The calculation of actual unit costs can only be carried out *ex post* and provides information for reporting to funding bodies and internal control.

The application of course unit costing is illustrated in this section by reference to the Birbridge case problem. The case study presents a simplified illustration of a cost and resource profile for a college which can be used to demonstrate the principles and issues involved. The resource and cost data of the college is reproduced in Table 15.1.

Table 15.1

	Support centres			Academic centres			
	Premises	Adminis-tration	Central services	Business faculty	Engineering faculty	Science faculty	Total
Space (metres)	300	2500	3000	7000	10 000	9000	31 800
Staff FTE	25	50	60	150	130	110	525
FTE students				1800	1200	1000	4000
Taught hours				76500	58500	52800	187800
Direct costs £,000	1850	1250	1650	3850	3650	3150	15400

Resource profile at Birbridge College

Birbridge College has created a responsibility accounting structure based on six cost centres. Three of these are support centres and three academic centres. The support centres comprise Administration, Central Services which covers both computing and library services and Premises. Academic centres comprise three large teaching faculties namely, Business Studies, Engineering and Science. A resource profile and direct cost budget for each of the six cost centres is as follows:

Cost allocation

Cost allocation is a process by which input costs are allocated to areas of budget responsibility. Costs are allocated to expense or account codes prescribed by the college chart of accounts. The chart of accounts establishes the basic structure of the college general ledger system which, with its combination of revenue, expense, asset and liability codes, provides the basis for the preparation of college financial reports. The chart of accounts can also act as a basis for financial control by setting budget targets for expense codes and reporting actual spending to target spending on a code by code basis.

Account codes are designed to group expenses under main and sub-codes which relate to the structure of budget responsibility. For example, code 2500 may be the generic code for the library with sub-codes of 2510 for library salaries, 2520 for journal subscriptions and so on. The level of detail built into each code is determined by reporting needs. For example, code 2520 could be split into sub-codes for journals in different subject areas.

Allocated costs should be direct expenditure of the cost centre account code to which they are charged. In other words the expenditure should be wholly and exclusively attributed to that cost centre. Direct cost allocation can be to:

- support centres such as premises, library, central computing services;
- academic centres such as schools, departments, faculties;
- courses and programmes.

Direct allocation to course based expense codes would be used to attribute expense items such as validation and franchise fees, field trips, visits and student registration fees for external examinations.

General ledger systems are not appropriate nor would be fully capable of restating costs for unit cost purposes. Most general ledger packages have add-in job costing modules which can be adapted for unit costing purposes but could not provide the simulation capability necessary to undertake resource modelling. Unit cost resource modelling permits academic management to test out the impact of planning assumptions such as student numbers, group sizes, taught hours, course mix, different delivery approaches and so on. A spreadsheet package should be adequate for most resource modelling applications although modelling systems may be selected for very large scale costing models.

Cost apportionment

The cost apportionment process re-allocates the budgeted cost of each support centre between the academic cost centres using pre-determined apportionment rates. The choice of a base for establishing an apportionment rate is somewhat arbitrary in industrial cost accounting and the same is true for colleges, since there is no single correct method of allocating costs to courses. [. . .] In practice, there is always conflict in unit costing systems between accuracy and materiality. The final choice must be based on the cost of providing information set against the potential benefit arising from its use. The cost to benefit decision represents a dynamic relationship in the sense that what was a satisfactory balance yesterday may not be so today. In management accounting systems there is no longer-term stability in either the cost of providing information or the cost of being wrong. It follows that college management must keep under continual review the effort applied to such systems [. . .]. The incorporation of colleges has resulted in a major shift in the cost to benefit relationship of management systems by increasing substantially the consequences of being wrong.

The apportionment base should be selected by choosing a resource relationship between support and academic centre which most closely reflects the linkage between the two. In other words how does the activity level of an academic centre change the activity level of the support centre – for example, enrolled students to library usage. The term cost driver can be used to describe this relationship. Identification and selection of the most appropriate cost driver is crucial for accurate unit costing. By selecting an unsuitable apportionment rate a college runs a risk of cross-subsidisation across courses and academic areas. The extent to which cross-subsidisation is material can only be established by testing unit costs against a range of apportionment rates to isolate the extent of any variation. Generally, absorption rates and hence, unit costs, are recalculated each financial year although some colleges have adopted the practice of establishing absorption rates which apply for a number of financial years subject only to an annual cost inflation adjustment [. . .]. Some methods of rate calculation are relatively self-evident, such as floor area occupied for premises cost centres, while for other cost centres, such as administration, the calculations are more problematic. The most common cost apportionment methods include:

Administration   FTE staff (to departments)
                 FTE students (to course)
                 Department direct cost
                 Top slicing

Premises	Space occupied (to department)
	Room hourly rate (to course)
Library	FTE staff (to departments)
	FTE students (to course)
	Staff/student weighted
	Actual user profile
	Weighted student
Computing	FTE staff (to departments)
	FTE students (to course)
	Staff/student weighted
	Actual user profile
	Weighted student

FTE (full time equivalent) staff (to departments)

Here the planned cost of the support centre is divided by the number of full-time equivalent staff in the college to give a cost per FTE staff member.
[. . .] The apportionment to an individual department is calculated by multiplying the FTE staff associated with the department by the apportionment rate per FTE staff member. Using the Birbridge case as an example, one possible apportionment rate for administration could be calculated as £1.25 million (direct cost of administration) divided by 390 (FTE staff in faculties) giving a rate of £3,205 per FTE staff member. The resulting cost apportionment to the business faculty would be £480,750 (150 staff times £3,205). The selection of the all college staff category for cost apportionment can give rise to a problem of reciprocal services between inter-dependent support centres. [. . .]

FTE students (to course)

Here the planned cost of the support centre is divided by the full time equivalent student numbers of the college to give a cost per FTE student. Taking the Birbridge example, the central services cost per FTE student would be £412.50 (£1.65 million divided by 4,000 FTE students) and a charge to a course with twenty five students would be £10,312.50 (25 × £412.50). The FTE student figure will be calculated using a weighting factor, for example, a full-time student as 1.0, part-time day student 0.4, evening student 0.2 and so on. [. . .]

Department direct costs

Here the cost apportionment rate would reflect not only staff numbers but salary levels, additional payments and faculty supplies budgets. At Birbridge this would give a rate for administration centre costs of £0.117 per £ of direct costs (£1.25 million divided by £10.65 million faculty direct costs). Using this approach the business faculty would be apportioned £450,450 (£3.850 million × £0.117). Note that this figure is £30,000 less than when using a FTE staff rate. The difference may be a reflection of the relatively lower direct supplies costs of business, as opposed to engineering or science faculties.

Top slicing

[This] is not strictly an apportionment method but has been adopted by some colleges as a means of dealing with difficult to apportion cost areas such as administration (Jones and Scholes, 1992). In effect a percentage deduction is made from the income of each academic department to cover some or all of central costs. The method has the merits of simplicity but denies the college the opportunity to calculate accurate unit costs and thereby leaves college management in the dark as to the degree of cross-subsidisation across courses.

Space occupied or room-based rates

Where academic departments have full control over their own premises, space such as faculty offices, laboratories, dedicated teaching rooms, then the premises costs would be apportioned to the faculty using a cost per metre rate. The rate would be calculated by dividing the planned premises budget by the total usable college space specified in square metres. Non-usable space would include corridors, toilets, stairways etc. Where teaching rooms are held centrally and booked out by faculties, then premises costs can be apportioned direct to a course using a room based hourly rate. The rate would be based on the room area times the premises cost per metre and then divided by the planned annual occupancy hours (maximum annual hours availability times the % planned room utilisation factor). Both methods underline the opportunity cost associated with under utilised space. A typical positive effect of the former method is to encourage faculties to release space which is under-utilised, thus allowing its re-allocation to other use.

Staff/student weighted

[This] is a combined rate useful where there are two or more distinct cost drivers for a support department. For example, a college library or central computing facility would typically be used by academic staff, research staff and students. To reflect this use the support centre costs may be apportioned on the basis of estimates of demand. For example, if twenty per cent of library usage is thought to derive from research activity then this proportion of library costs may be apportioned to faculties or research contracts/groups on the basis of FTE research staff. To ascertain the basis for such splits the support centre must be in a position to provide statistical data on user profiles and usage patterns. If such data is available then colleges may consider the apportionment of costs *ex ante* based on actual usage data for the period. While this method has the merit of accuracy it cannot be used for providing planned or target unit costs other than by adopting the current year usage data as the basis of apportionment.

Weighted student methods

[These] aim to improve the accuracy of support centre apportionment by seeking to reflect the different usage patterns of different student groups. For example, a central computing facility may divide its student users into three groups; heavy users, medium users and intermittent users. Courses would be assigned to one of the three user groups based on discussions between computer centre and academic staff. Typical example outcomes could be to categorise a course in software engineering as band A, a business studies course as band B and an arts course as band C. Each user band is given a weighting which reflects perceived usage patterns. For example, a band A weighting of 1.0, a band B of 0.6 and a band C of 0.2. A planned weighted student FTE is calculated for the college using the assigned weightings and, by dividing the support centre cost by the weighted FTE, a cost per weighted FTE is derived.

An important factor for consideration in apportionment decisions is the behavioural dimension of cost chargeout. The method used to apportion costs sends a message to recipients about the charge or consequence resulting from the use of central resources. College management must pay particular attention to ensuring that the message given out by the apportionment method is consistent with overall college strategy. As an example, apportioning administration costs on the basis of student numbers would penalise faculties which taught using large group sizes, while apportioning by staff FTE would benefit such faculties. If a college plans to move toward large group teaching and wishes to encourage adoption, then the apportionment policy must be aligned to the college curriculum strategy by choosing the latter rather than the former method.

It should be noted that while total apportioned costs are necessary for unit costing, for the purpose of management control, only those costs which are directly controllable by responsibility centre managers should form a part of the control system. In other words financial control reports to academic centre managers should focus on actual direct and controllable costs, not on apportioned and hence non-controllable costs. The control focus of apportioned costs is at the cost centre where such costs are direct.

[. . .]

Cost absorption

Cost absorption transfers the total cost of academic and in some cases support centres to the cost unit using an absorption rate. Typically, an absorption rate for an academic centre will be calculated using planned taught hours. The budgeted direct costs of the academic centre plus the apportioned costs from support centres is divided by the programmed teaching hours for the academic year. This calculation provides an hourly teaching rate which, if applied to the courses or units to be measured, will result in the absorption of the total cost of the centre. The teaching rate for the business faculty at Birbridge is thus £4.727 million divided by 76,500 planned hours or £61.79 per hour.

Data on planned teaching hours is derived from the curriculum budgets established by course teaching teams prior to the start of the academic year. Each course or programme has target student numbers, group sizes and class contact hours which determines the required taught hours for the course and, for all courses, the aggregate taught hours for each faculty. The planned hours should be net of non-chargeable activity such as sickness cover, research, administration and staff development allowances. [. . .]

There are a number of factors to be considered in deciding how specific the hourly rate calculation should be. The most simple approach is to use a college-wide rate while the most complex is to calculate an individual rate for each teaching staff member. Although easy to calculate, a college-wide rate produces course unit cost which can be distorted by cross-subsidisation between high and low cost faculties. A rate calculated for each academic faculty provides the best balance between simplicity and materiality. It may however be advisable to calculate rates for divisions or sections within large faculties particularly where there is significant difference in work patterns. For example, a section carrying out mainly advanced work as against a section which is predominantly non-advanced. It is difficult to construct an argument for individual teacher rates not simply because of the complexity of computation but also on the basis of equity. Typically teaching will be provided to courses from a teaching team on the basis of specialism and expertise. Different teachers from the team will have different direct costs due to such factors as grade, length of service, seniority etc. In most cases these differences are not a factor in timetabling and so an individual hourly rate for each teacher would benefit and penalise courses in a fairly random manner.

Where staff teach across faculties then colleges must determine a transfer price for serviced taught hours. The simple approach is to use the hourly rate of the servicing faculty, however problems can arise where high cost faculties service lower cost faculties. A common problem in transfer pricing situations is for the 'buying in' cost centre to seek to reduce costs by looking for the cheapest provider which may not be the in-company or in-college 'selling out' cost centre. To avoid the potential disruption and sub-optimisation created by what is in effect an internal market, college management must establish rules of conduct. The most common college approach is to identify subject-specific areas of academic leadership and require the recipient faculty to 'buy in' servicing from the faculty designated as holding the subject expertise. Where there are major cost variations between faculties, then the transfer price for servicing work can be set at the hourly rate of the buyer faculty if this is less than the rate of the selling faculty. This approach has a two-fold advantage; firstly, by encouraging the servicing faculty to reduce its staff costs closer to the college norm and secondly, by reflecting the fact that servicing is frequently not core academic work for faculties and should be priced closer to marginal cost rather than the full cost used to calculate a faculties own course costs.

Costing a course at Birbridge

The requirement is to calculate a course and student unit cost for a one year full-time course. The resource profile of the course is:

Number of students	25	
Annual taught hours	480	Business faculty
	240	Engineering faculty
Course direct costs	£5500	[Examination fees, visits, direct materials etc.]

and the unit cost would be built up as follows:

	£
Course direct costs	5500
Teaching costs:	
Business Faculty 480 hours × £61.79	29 659
Engineering Faculty 240 hours × £79.33	19 039
[£4.64 million divided by 58 500 hours]	
Central Services 25 students × £503	12 575
[£2.012 million divided by 4000 FTE students]	
Total	66 773

giving a unit cost per student of £2671 (£66 773 divided by 25 students).

The unit cost calculation naturally gives rise to the question as to what is a 'good' unit cost. The figure of £2671 given by the example needs a benchmark for comparison before judgement can be made. Benchmark data may be derived from a number of sources:

- *Inter-college comparison.* Available published data is generally too aggregated to allow meaningful comparisons. Potential distortions to data include subject mix, staff–student ratios, geographic location and resource profiles. [. . .] The move by the funding bodies to require colleges to provide a financial record which identifies the full cost and hence unit cost of provision across a number of different subject areas should improve the quality of data in this area.
- *Standard unit costs calculated by reference to standard delivery profiles.* A college can establish standard costs based on target staff–student ratios, staff costs and direct course costs.
- *The revenue or unit of resource* attaching to students in specific subject areas may be deemed to have been set by funding bodies at a value which reflects a view of what the unit cost of provision should be. Given the current approach of the funding bodies to set units of resource at values which are designed to influence college recruitment behaviour then the cost message contained in funding values is very problematical.

It cannot be overstressed that unit costs do not measure the quality of provision but simply the efficiency of provision. It requires no great feat for college management to reduce student unit costs whether by increasing group sizes, reducing taught hours, cutting spending on library provision and so on. The difficult management task is to meet unit cost targets while holding or improving quality targets. It follows that any college system of unit costing must be aligned with a system of quality performance measures so that trends and changes in both can be measured on a course by course basis.

Activity based costing

As colleges achieve expertise in unit costing and become accustomed to its benefits, they are likely to wish to assess the potential of an activity based approach to some cost centre apportionment. Activity Based Costing (ABC) is a response of the accounting community to the question of the relevance of existing management accounting systems when faced with the need to cope with the structure and technology of the organisation of the 1990s (see Cooper and Kaplan 1988, [. . .]). Although initially viewed as being relevant to manufacturing environments, the general consensus now is that ABC is equally applicable to service as to manufacturing operations whether organised for or not-for-profit (Cooper and Kaplan 1991).

ABC seeks to link indirect costs, such as support centre costs to the cost unit, through the use of activity relationships. In other words educational processes are viewed as giving rise to support activities such as enrolling a student, paying an invoice, issuing a library book etc. while the activities themselves give rise to indirect costs (admissions, finance, library). Once the nature of the activity relationship is identified, then costs are apportioned on the basis of a cost per activity, such as cost per enrolled student, cost per accounting transaction, cost per library request, and so on. This is a fundamental shift away from a generalised apportionment model using FTE staff or FTE student and can assist in identifying cross subsidisation across course areas. Cross-subsidisation is particularly likely to be found in cases where a college has an extensive mix of different types of courses with different delivery methods, levels of technology, resource usage patterns and academic levels.

Attaching a cost to an activity raises the awareness level of users as to the price and value of that activity. This in turn changes users' behaviour leading to a better use of the resource or better design of courses so that they minimise the use of the activity related resource. Some early research is being carried out in the university sector on the potential of using activity costs in priority based budgeting and activity based management (McCann and Donnelly 1992).

[. . .]

Activity based costing raises the profile of activities and processes by identifying their cost and leads naturally to questions being raised as to the justification for the activity, alternative ways of carrying out the activity, the extent to which the cost of the activity is seen as reasonable and in some cases whether the activity be carried out at all. ABC provides a good example of management accounting systems moving from a reactive to a proactive role.

[. . .]

References

Cooper, R. (1989) You need a new costing system when . . . , *Harvard Business Review*, January/February.

Cooper, R. and Kaplan, R. S. (1988) Measure costs right: make the right decisions, *Harvard Business Review*, September/October.

Cooper, R. and Kaplan, R. S. (1991) Activity Based Systems in service organisations and service functions, *The Design of Cost Management Systems*, Prentice Hall International, pp. 466–74.

McCann, P. and Donnelly, P. (1992) *Activity Based Management in Higher Education*. CIMA Research Foundation.

PART 3

Strategic management

16 | How strategies develop in organisations*

ANDY BAILEY AND GERRY JOHNSON

Introduction

This chapter reports on a major research project being undertaken at Cranfield School of Management which explores the nature of strategy formulation. The aim of this research project is both to discover the general patterns of strategy development within organisations and also to explore the managerial implications of strategy formulation. The chapter presents a number of explanations of strategy development. [. . .]

The early works of writers such as Ansoff[1] and Andrews[2] and the books of the 1970s, in particular on corporate planning, have both emphasised the importance of strategy and have guided thinking in the area; thinking which has been dominated by the view that strategies are formulated through a particularly analytical and intentional process. The basic framework which this 'rational' planned view offers indicates that through the application of appropriate analytical and systematic techniques and checklists organisations are able to secure their own success. Moreover such an approach allows assumptions to be made about the future, assists in the reduction of uncertainty and facilitates the systematic development of strategy. This view and its associated frameworks have become deeply entrenched within strategic thinking, while the prescriptive and normative modes so generated have substantially influenced the approach to strategy formulation in practice, in education, and in research.

To view strategy development in this logical and rational manner is appealing and as such it is not surprising that this view has enjoyed such prominence. In management education strategic texts have traditionally emphasised the rationality of analysis, planning and implementation as a step by step process. Within organisations this school of thought suggests that formal strategic planning processes and mechanisms can operate in a rational and objective manner to allow the comprehensive analysis

---

* This material has been abridged.

of the internal and external environments, the development of alternative strategies, the selection of the best strategy, and the production of objectives, goals, budgets, and targets to guide implementation. In short this rational planning approach is often what is regarded as 'good practice'.

However this view is not without its problems. In particular it fails to account for the social, cultural, political and cognitive aspects of the process of strategy development. Indeed, its dominance has detracted from the equally valid consideration of less 'objective' aspects of the organisation and their critical influence on strategy development.

The emergence of strategies

A natural assumption of this rational planned view of strategy formulation is that strategies are developed and implemented in this linear manner and that an organisation's *intended* strategy will be implemented in its entirety to become realised as *actual* strategy. However this may not always be the case. Unexpected shifts in the environment, unforeseen problems in implementation or limitations in the process can operate to restrict the efficiency of strategy formulation and its realisation. The result of this may mean that an organisation's intended strategy is not realised as actual strategy.[3,4] Indeed even within organisations with effective planning systems intended strategies do not always become realised.

The fact that a planned, intended strategy is not realised does not mean that an organisation has no strategy at all. Indeed the strategies an organisation pursues are not necessarily what is espoused by the organisation or its senior figures and as such they may more accurately be perceived as the direction an organisation is actually pursuing, planned or otherwise. However, the distinction between what is intended and what is realised may not be so defined and the two may interact. A strategy which starts as intended may change and become more emergent as it is implemented, while an emergent strategy may become formalised and more deliberate as it enters the accepted wisdom of the organisation and is encapsulated within its longer-term strategies.

If strategies are defined in terms of future position and consistency of direction or 'the direction an organisation is pursuing', then they may be seen to develop continually in an adaptive or incremental manner. As such, strategies may develop as much from the adaptive processes of the organisation or the actions of management as from deliberate and intended action. In this way strategies emerge gradually as actions are altered to cope with, and adapt to, the environment in a never-ending series of small steps. These small continual changes aggregate,[5] and so reduce the need for large or major change in strategy.

In stable environments strategies may not need to change in a major way. Any change required will, typically, be incremental and enable the organisation to operate in a gradually changing environment. While an organisation is doing well there will be a strong tendency not to change existing successful strategies. As an organisation's strategy develops 'momentum', any changes which occur will generally develop incrementally in a direction consistent with existing strategy and past experience rather than involving large-scale changes in direction.[6] Generally this pattern of strategy development is gradual and continuous, although more dramatic change may occur if the relationship between the environment and organisation alters more substantially. Indeed periods of strategy formulation have been seen to range from those typified by 'continuity', where strategies remain unchanged, to those which are 'continuous' or incremental, to those involving more substantial dramatic frame breaking or 'discontinuous' change, which occur infrequently.[7,8]

In situations where an organisation and its environment are increasingly mismatched, incremental refinements of strategy may not keep pace with environmental changes. As this situation develops and becomes more acute, either through large environmental change or strategic drift (the organisation becoming out of line with the environment), minor or piecemeal change may not easily remedy the situation. Here more global strategic change, incorporating significant and simultaneous reversals in strategy,[9] and involving discontinuous changes, may be required to realign the organisation and its environment.

The research

This chapter reports on a study of how managers make sense of the different ways in which strategy develops. Given the complexity of this process it is not surprising that various explanations of strategy formulation have been advanced. Through a detailed review of such explanations[10] six perspectives on the process have been defined. While these explanations are not novel or indeed definitive, they do represent meaningful classifications of the process which both make intuitive sense to managers and are understandable.

These alternative explanations or views of strategy formulation were deconstructed to identify characteristics singularly attributable to each of them. Based on these characteristics, statements were developed for use in a questionnaire, which was then administered to senior managers, from a cross section of industries, who indicated the degree to which the statements were characteristic of their organisation. Through the analysis of their responses, managerial perceptions of the organisation's process of strategy formulation were revealed. The numerical representation of these perceptions were subsequently plotted to develop strategic decision-making profiles for separate organisations or sub-units. [. . .]

Alternative explanations of strategic decision-making

This section reviews in more detail different explanations as to how strategies develop. However, it is important to stress that it is most unlikely that any one of the explanations given accounts entirely for the processes at work in an organisation: strategy formulation needs to be understood in terms of a *mix* of processes.

The planning perspective

Strategic planning is perhaps the most traditional view of how strategic decisions are made in organisations. The perspective indicates that strategy formulation is a distinctly intentional process involving a logical, rational, planned approach to the organisation and its environment. Further it implies that through the application of appropriate analytical and systematic techniques the 'right' decision can be taken.

The strategies which develop are the outcome of sequential, planned and deliberate procedures and are often the responsibility of specialised departments. Clear and well defined strategic goals and objectives are set by the senior members of an organisation.[11] [. . .] As a goal or strategic issue is defined, the organisation and its environment (both internal and external to the organisation) are systematically analysed in terms of (for example) strategic position, the position of competitors, organisational strengths and weaknesses, and resource availability. The information collected is assessed and strategic options capable of attaining the goal or resolving the strategic issue are generated.

These strategic options, or courses of action, are systematically assessed against the criteria of the strategic goals and objectives to be achieved. This evaluation incorporates an assessment of both the estimated consequences of the alternative courses of action, for example in terms of risk versus return, and the value of these consequences. Similarly the long-term potential of the options are estimated. The option which simultaneously is perceived to maximise the value of outcomes, best fits the selection criterion and presents competitive advantage is chosen. The selected option is subsequently detailed in the form of precise plans and programmes and is passed from the top downwards within the organisation. Throughout this process strategies are determined and guided by those decision-makers in senior management positions and are implemented by those below[12] who act on but are unlikely to decide on strategy.[13]

In line with the systematic development of the strategy, the resources required for implementation are determined and appropriately allocated, and similarly the systems for monitoring and controlling the new strategy are determined. It is argued that strategies developed through this planned, sequential routine should be implemented fully and in a 'surprise free' manner. This formalisation of strategic planning, though appealing, is problematic, and indeed has inherent dangers. In particular it lacks consideration of the less 'objective' aspects of the organisation and their critical influence on strategy development. However, regardless of the problems, the discipline and techniques of planning approaches can be useful because they may provide a framework for strategic thinking; and if managers also address the problems of managing strategy within the social, cultural and political world of organisations, then such thinking can be very helpful. [. . .]

The logical incremental perspective

In the late 1950s Lindblom[14] suggested that managing strategies through logical, sequential planning mechanisms was unrealistic. He argued that, given the complexity of organisations and the environments in which they operate, managers cannot consider all possible options in terms of all possible futures and evaluate these against preset, unambiguous objectives. This is particularly so in an organisational context in which there are likely to be conflicting views, values and power bases. Rather, strategic choice takes place by comparing options against each other and considering which would give the best outcome and be possible to implement. Lindblom called this strategy building through 'successive limited comparisons', but argued that it took place in the everyday world of managing, not through planning systems.

It is a position in many respects similar to that argued by Quinn.[15] His study of nine major multinational businesses concluded that the management process could best be described as *logical incrementalism*. By this he meant that managers have a view of where they want the organisation to be in years to come but try to move towards this position in an evolutionary way. They do this by attempting to ensure the success and development of a strong, secure but flexible core business, but also by continually experimenting with 'side bet' ventures. This mode of strategy formulation is not seen as the sole responsibility of top management and the corporate centre: those in the lower levels of the organisation and the organisation's 'strategic subsystems' are actively involved. [. . .] Here managers accept the uncertainty of their environment because they realise that they cannot do away with this uncertainty by trying to 'know' factually about how the environment will change. Rather they seek to become highly sensitive to environmental signals through constant environmental scanning and by testing and developing strategies in a step by step process of experimentation and limited exposure to the business environment.

The logical incrementalist view does not, then, see strategic management in terms of a neat sequential model: rather the system is seen to be cyclical. It encompasses feedback loops to previous phases where the problem and solution may be redefined or reformulated.[16] Similarly commitment to strategic options may be tentative and subject to review in the early stages of its development. There is also a reluctance to specify precise objectives too early as this might stifle ideas and prevent the sort of experimentation which is desired. Objectives are therefore likely to be fairly general in nature.

Through ongoing analysis, assessment and incremental refinement, changes in the environment are matched with changes in procedure.[17] This iterative process ensures the strengths of an organisation are retained as experimentation and learning are undertaken without excessive risk to the organisation. Throughout the process potential options are eliminated or encouraged in accordance with their assessed appropriateness; the process does not operate to identify the best or optimal solution.[18]

Quinn[19] also suggests that different decisions should not be seen as entirely separate. Because the different organisational subsystems are in a continual state of interplay, the managers of each know what the others are doing, and can interpret each other's actions and requirements. They are, in effect, learning from each other about the feasibility of a course of action in terms of resource management and its internal political acceptability. Moreover, this constant readjustment and limited commitment allows the long-term direction of the organisation to be monitored and the organisational mix of resources and skills altered in reaction to environmental changes. The process broadens the information base available, builds organisational awareness and increases the active search for opportunities and threats not previously defined. Further, the formulation of strategy in this way means that the implications of the strategy are continually being tested out. This continual readjustment does, of course, make a lot of sense if the environment is considered to be a continually changing influence on the organisation.

[. . .]

The political perspective

The formulation of strategy can also be explained in political terms. Organisations are political entities and, as such, powerful internal and external interest groups influence the inputs into decisions. These interest groups, each of which have different concerns,[20] may be in conflict; there may be differences between groups of managers, between managers and shareholders, or between powerful individuals. These differences are likely to be resolved through processes of bargaining, negotiation or perhaps edict; with the result that goals and objectives, strategic issues and even strategies are derived from this political process and not from an analytical neutral assessment and choice.

This political process and the strategies followed by an organisation are susceptible to both internal and external influences[21] by stakeholders ('any group or individual who can affect or is affected by the achievement of the organisation's objectives'[22]), which could include customers and clients, banks, trade associations, shareholders, supplier firms, government departments and agencies, competitors, trade unions and organisational members. The level of influence these stakeholders are able to exercise differs[23] and is often conditional upon the organisation's dependency upon these groups for a resource[24] and the potential difficulty in replacing the present stakeholder as the source of that resource.[25] Similarly the influence of a stakeholder is not constant from decision to decision. The decision situation determines the level of stakeholder involvement and both their level of influence and the dynamics of that influence throughout the process. For example, the influence of top level decision-makers decreases as a strategy enters the implementation stage, while the influence of lower level managers increases.

The power and influence of stakeholders can also be used and acquired by other groups. For example, those internal groups or 'boundary spanners' who deal with the external environment tend to attain greater levels of influence and power over strategy[26] by virtue of the organisation's dependency on the external group with which they deal.

Powerful individuals or groups may also influence decision through the provision of information. Information is not politically neutral, but rather a source of power, particularly for those who control that which is seen to be important; so the withholding of information, or the influences of one manager over another because that manager controls sources of information, can be important. Alternatively the organisation's systems may be restricted to reduce information flow and so legitimise the demands of particular interest groups.[27] Strategic decisions, then, are taken based on information distorted by the preferences of the information providers rather than on information which is politically neutral.

It would be wrong to assume that the identification of key issues and even the strategies eventually selected emerge in a political neutral environment. Differing views will be fought for, not only on the basis of the extent to which they reflect environmental or competitive pressures, for example; but also because they have implications for the status or influence of different stakeholders. Through compromise and mutual adjustment a commonly acceptable strategy will emerge.[28] This strategy will finally be adopted because it is acceptable to both those interest groups influencing the decision-making process and those who must implement the strategy, and not solely because it fulfils any objective criteria.[29] [. . .]

The cultural perspective

Traditionally, strategy has been viewed as the planned response of the organisation to its environment. However, the strategies an organisation follows can also be attributed to cultural factors. Organisations faced with similar environments will respond differently. The strategies they choose to pursue will not result solely from a precise planned approach to the environment, but under influence from the attitudes, values, and perceptions which are common among the members and stakeholders of that organisation. Further, management cannot be conceived of simply in terms of the manipulation of techniques or tools of analysis. Management is also about the application of managerial experience built up over many years; and often within the same organisation or industry. Nor do managers typically work in isolation; they interact with others. Their experience is not only rooted in individual experience, but on group and organisational experience built up over time. It is important therefore to recognise the significance of cultural aspects of management.

By 'organisational culture' is meant the 'deeper level of basic *assumptions and beliefs* that are shared by members of an organisation, that operate unconsciously and define in a basic "taken for granted" fashion an organisation's view of its self and its environment'.[30] A cultural perspective suggests, then, that managerial experience is likely to be based on 'taken-for-granted' frames of reference which are brought to bear by a manager – or group of managers – and which will affect how a given situation is perceived and how it is responded to. Over time this taken for grantedness is likely to be handed on – or 'inherited' – within a group. That group might be, for example, a managerial function such as marketing or finance; a professional grouping, such as accountants; an organisation as a whole; and more widely an industry sector, or even a national culture. Just as these frames exist at the organisational and sub-unit level they also exist on an industry wide basis,[31] or indeed at a national level. Managers, then, are influenced by many cultural frames when making a decision. However, especially important for the strategic management of most organisations is the organisational frame of reference, which we call the '*organisational paradigm*'.

The paradigm is likely to contain within it the beliefs which managers talk about in their day to day lives: but it is also likely that it will contain assumptions which are rarely talked about, are not considered problematic, and about which managers are unlikely to be consciously explicit. Examples might include the deep rooted assumption that banks are about *secure* lending; local newspapers about purveying *news* (i.e. as more their *raison d'être* than advertising); that universities are about doing research and so on. As such, these deep rooted assumptions can play an important part in strategy development.

An organisation's paradigm is, then, built up from different influences such as history and past experience (both personal and organisational) and may also reflect the desires of particular stakeholders.[32] The strength of these influences will depend on a number of factors. For example an organisation with a relatively stable management and a long-term momentum of strategy is likely to have a more homogeneous paradigm than one in which there has been rapid turnover of management and significant change forced upon it. [. . .]

Of course for any organisation to operate efficiently it must, to some extent, have a generally accepted set of beliefs and assumptions. These may not be a static set of beliefs, although it is quite likely that they will evolve gradually rather than change suddenly. What this represents is a collective experience without which managers would have to 'reinvent their world' afresh for all circumstances they face or decisions they need to take; as such it enables new situations to be perceived in a way which is not unique.[33] The paradigm allows the experience gathered over years to be applied to a given situation so that managers can decide upon relevant information by which to assess the need for change, a likely course of action, and the likelihood of success of that course of action.

An organisation's strategies, then, develop in accord and within the confines of its culture and dominant paradigm. The cognitive and perceptual processes operate to orientate the definition and solution of a strategic problem internally ensuring a strategic response is based within the domain of the organisation[34] and the history of its members.[35]

[. . .]

The visionary perspective

The strategy an organisation follows can also be seen as emerging from a vision which represents the desired future state of the organisation,[36] and which is initially and primarily associated with an individual (for example its leader or a past leader). This might be especially so if the organisation is dominated by a leader: such leaders may exist, particularly in organisations which they have founded, or in situations where an organisation has reached a crisis point. Less commonly, perhaps, a vision could be associated with a small group of individuals, rather than one individual.

One explanation for the source of this vision is that it results from the intuition and innovation of its originator. Here the vision is based both on intuition and a rational understanding of the organisation's strategic problems. This understanding is developed through exposure to, and experience of, the important strategic issues of an organisation and enables innovation to be made through the adding of new, to the well understood, and certainty of the old. The vision generated is often based on radical ideas and may challenge accepted norms, contradict established principles and paradigms,[37,38] and go beyond familiar experience and knowledge.[39]

However, visionary management might also be seen as the capacity of managers more generally to *envisage*, rather than plan, the future of their organisation. It can be argued that some market environments are so turbulent that trying to forecast, predict or plan what they will be like is futile. On the other hand experienced managers 'have a feel' for what makes sense in these markets (again there are links here with the notion of the paradigm) and can make decisions about the future on this basis. In this case, the notion of visionary capacity is not limited to the leadership role of the organisation, but is seen as a more general aspect of management.

[. . .]

Regardless of how it emerges, for a vision – however appropriate to the organisation – to develop into strategy it must be effectively articulated and communicated. The transformation of a vision into strategy is not unidirectional: a vision must be shared and receive assistance if it is to be realised. The authorisation for a vision's pursuit comes from its acceptance by the organisation's members[40] who 'contract in' to a vision, and so provide the authority for its realisation, concentrating resources to facilitate the vision's enactment.[41] A visionary alone cannot turn a vision into strategy.

While an individual may gain visionary status for himself [or herself] within the organisation, an organisation's structure and history may be such that it endows an individual with this power, position and authority. Whether the position is achieved through the generation of an idea and vision, the syntheses of existing visions, the communication of a vision, or through the organisation's history, it inevitably places enormous control and power in the hands of the visionary who gains the 'capacity to translate intention into reality and sustain it'.[42] [. . .]

The natural selection perspective

Some writers on management argue that organisations have little or no control over the choice of strategies they follow. Factors in the environment impinge on the organisation in such a way as to select and encourage the adoption of organisational structures and activities which best fit that environment.[43] These external constraints operate to prescribe strategies and sharply limit the role organisational members play in their selection.[44] Equally the strategies an organisation can follow tend to be common to all organisations within their industrial sector or market; their ability to make strategic decisions outside these are restricted. In short, the success of an organisation is due to a fit between strategy, structure and environment produced via a process bearing more similarities to natural selection rather than any rational and intentional choice.

While intentional strategic choice may be restricted, strategic change *does* occur. Initially changes occur within an organisation through variations in its processes, structures and systems. While the process of organisational innovation and variation may come about as a rational intentional response to the environment, they may occur equally unintentionally, through conflict over control of resources; ambiguity of organisational reality; accident; errors; tactical moves; and luck.[45] It is these variations, however they occur, which produce the potentially advantageous or dangerous innovations for an organisation. Those variations which positively fit the environment and which are appropriate and beneficial to the organisation are selected and retained, while those which do not, fail and die or are altered to match the environment.[46] It is these successful variations, which match changes in the environment, which produce advantage and so contribute to the likelihood of an organisation's or subunit's survival.[47] These successful variations are retained and subsequently disseminated throughout the organisation and across its generations through culture, symbols, socialisation, administration and training.

The view taken in this chapter is that for some organisations the impact of the environment is, indeed, very large; and that degrees of managerial latitude are severely reduced: however, this is not so in all environments and even where those pressures are severe, it is the job of managers to develop the skills and strategies to cope with the situation.

[. . .]

Managerial implications

The previous sections demonstrate, to a greater or lesser extent, that each of the perspectives can describe or explain some aspects of the process of strategic decision-making. The very complexity of these decisions makes it unlikely that any one of the perspectives in isolation would adequately capture the complexity of the process operating in all organisations, in every situation, and at any point in time. While the above examples have presented the process in isolation, in many organisations this is not the case: the processes occur in combination. Indeed these different views about how strategies develop are not mutually exclusive and in most organisations managers see strategies developing through a mix of such processes.

[. . .]

Conclusions

This chapter has dealt with the processes of strategic management as they are to be found in organisations: it is therefore *descriptive* not *prescriptive*. There is no suggestion here that, because such processes exist, this is how strategy *should* be managed. However, it is important to understand the reality of strategy making in organisations, not least because those who seek to influence the strategy of organisations must do so within that reality. There is little point in formulating strategies which may be elegant analytically without having an understanding of the processes which are actually at work.

[. . .]

References

1 Ansoff, H. I. (1965) *Corporate Strategy*. London: McGraw-Hill.
2 Andrews, K. R. (1980) *The Concept of Corporate Strategy*, revised edition. Georgetown, Ontario: R. D. Irwin.
3 Mintzberg, H. (1978) Patterns of strategy formation, *Management Science*, 24(9): 934–48.
4 Mintzberg, H. and Waters, J. A. (1985) Of strategies, deliberate and emergent, *Strategic Management Journal*, 6: 257–72.
5 Lindblom, C. E. (1959) The science of 'muddling through', *Public Administration Review*, 19: 79–88, Spring.
6 Miller, D. and Friesen, P. H. (1984) *Organisations: A Quantum View*. Englewood Cliffs, NJ: Prentice-Hall.
7 Mintzberg, H. and Waters, J. A. (1985) *op. cit.*
8 Nadler, D. A. and Tushman, M. L. (1989) Organisational framebending: Principles for managing re-organisation, *Academy of Management Executive*, 3: 194–202.
9 Miller, D. and Friesen, P. H. (1984) *op. cit.*
10 Bailey, A. and Johnson, G. (1991) *Perspectives on the Process of Strategic Decision-Making*, Cranfield School of Management Working Papers Series, SWP 66/91.
11 Chaffee, E. E. (1985) Three models of strategy, *Academy of Management Review*, 10(1): 89–98.
12 Mintzberg, H. (1978) *op. cit.*
13 Mintzberg, H. and Water, J. A. (1985) *op. cit.*
14 Lindblom, C. E. (1959) *op. cit.*
15 Quinn, J. B. (1980) *Strategies for Change – Logical Incrementalism*. Georgetown, Ontario: R. D. Irwin.
16 Lyles, M. A. (1981) Formulating strategic problems: Empirical analysis and model development, *Strategic Management Journal*, 2: 61–75.
17 Schwenk, C. R. (1988) *The Essence of Strategic Decision-making*. D. C. Heath & Co.

18 Mintzberg, H., Raisinghani, D. and Theoret, A. (1976) The structure of 'unstructured' decision processes, *Administrative Science Quarterly*, 21: 246–75.
19 Quinn, J. B. (1980) *op. cit.*
20 Pfeffer, J. and Salancik, G. R. (1978) *The External Control of Organisations*. New York: Harper & Row.
21 Hickson, D. J., Butler, R. J., Gray, D., Mallory, G. R. and Wilson, D. C. (1986) *Top Decisions – Strategic Decision-making in Organisations*. Oxford: Basil Blackwell.
22 Freeman, R. (1984) *Strategic Management: A Stakeholder Approach*. Boston, MA: Pitman.
23 Heller, F., Drenth, P., Koopman, P. and Rus, V. (1988) *Decisions in Organisations: A Three Country Comparative Study*. London: Sage Publications.
24 Pfeffer, J. and Salancik, G. R. (1978) *op. cit.*
25 Hickson, D. J. *et al.* (1986) *op. cit.*
26 Jemison, D. B. (1981) Organisational versus environmental sources of influence in strategic decision-making, *Strategic Management Journal*, 2: 77–89.
27 Pfeffer, J. and Salancik, G. R. (1978) *op. cit.*
28 Mintzberg, H. and Waters, J. A. (1985) *op. cit.*
29 Johnson, G. (1987) *Strategic Change and the Management Process*. Oxford: Blackwell Publishers.
30 Schein, E. H. (1985) *Organisational Culture and Leadership*. San Francisco, CA: Jossey-Bass.
31 Spender, J.-C. (1989) *Industry Recipes: The Nature and Source of Managerial Judgement*. Oxford: Blackwell Publishers.
32 Mason, R. O. and Mitroff, I. I. (1981) *Challenging Strategic Planning Assumptions*. New York: Wiley.
33 Schön, D. A. (1983) *The Reflective Practitioner: How Professionals Think in Action*. London: Temple Smith.
34 Schwenk, C. R. (1988) *op. cit.*
35 Nutt, P. (1984) Types of organisational decision processes, *Administrative Science Quarterly*, 29: 414–50.
36 Rowe, A. J., Dickel, K. E., Mason, R. O. and Snyder, N. H. (1989) *Strategic Management: A Methodological Approach*, 3rd edition. New York: Addison-Wesley.
37 Trice, H. M. and Beyer, J. M. (1986) The concept of charisma, in B. M. Staw and L. L. Cummings (eds) *Research in Organisational Behavior*, vol. 8, pp. 118–64. London: JAI Press.
38 Conger, J. A. and Kanungo, R. N. (1987) Towards a behavioural theory of charismatic leadership in organisational settings, *Academy of Management Review*, 12(4): 637–47.
39 Trice, H. M. and Beyer, J. M. (1986) *op. cit.*
40 Rowe, A. J. *et al.* (1989) *op. cit.*
41 Conger, J. A. and Kanungo, R. N. (1987) *op. cit.*
42 Bennis, W. and Nanus, B. (1985) *Leaders: The Strategies for Taking Charge*. New York: Harper & Row.
43 Hannan, M. T. and Freeman, J. H. (1974) Environment and the structure of organisations: A population ecology perspective. Paper presented at the American Sociology Association, Montreal, Canada, August.
44 Aldrich, H. E. (1979) *Organisations and Environments*. Englewood Cliffs, NJ: Prentice-Hall.
45 Aldrich, H. E. and Mueller, S. (1982) The evolution of organisational form: Technology coordination and control in B. M. Staw and L. L. Cummings (eds) *Research in Organisational Behavior*, vol. 4, pp. 33–89. London: JAI Press.
46 Aldrich, H. E. (1979) *op. cit.*
47 Aldrich, H. E. and Mueller, S. (1982) *op. cit.*

17 | Linking strategic planning with the budgetary process

NATIONAL AUDIT OFFICE

Why plan strategically?

There is a clear expectation that schools will plan strategically. The Funding Authorities' guidance to grant-maintained schools contained in the Rainbow Pack (Guidelines on Financial Systems and Controls, Paragraph 9.1) is that operating budgets should be prepared within the context of a long term (three to five year) plan which should specify the objectives of the school over several years.

When applying for Special Purpose Grant (Development) schools are expected to link their planned expenditure to the School Development Plan. Through seminars, the Department for Education's Architects and Buildings Branch also emphasise to grant-maintained schools the wisdom of developing long term plans both for maintenance, and for the provision of resources to support educational requirements. The Welsh Office have written to schools in Wales asking for a costed development plan which should include performance measures.

As part of their criteria for effective practice in financial management at all maintained schools, Ofsted expect their inspectors to look for a corporate school development plan covering at least three years and updated annually (Handbook for the Inspection of Schools Technical Paper 6). They expect the planning process to be allied to budget planning. They state that, in the efficient school, the costs of major programmes and activities will be known and that priorities will be identified for development and for areas where savings can be made.

Although these external factors provide an impetus to plan strategically, it is important that schools appreciate how they can benefit from the process by channelling the schools' activities and resources towards their longer term objectives. Good strategic planning is essential if schools are to make effective use of their available resources, and avoid financial difficulties.

Of particular importance is the linkage between strategic planning and the budgetary process. At many schools this linkage is not clearly articulated, although it is often apparent that it exists in the mind of the headteacher. It is a good discipline for it to be set down in writing, not least to demonstrate to governors and staff how budgetary decisions contribute to the longer term strategy.

Many schools argue that effective planning of this kind is hampered by uncertainty about external factors beyond their control, particularly funding and the curriculum. Whilst there are inevitably some uncertainties, the planning process should help schools to anticipate potential problems and identify solutions. They should be able to react more effectively to externally imposed changes by reference to a strategic plan which can show the full implications of the change. Longer term decisions will be needed regardless of whether there is a strategic plan, and it is better that these are taken in the context of a plan, even if it is not entirely accurate, than in isolation.

The specific benefits to a [. . .] school of planning strategically are:

- The exercise provides an important focus for determining the school's overall aims and objectives;
- plans to improve the school's educational provision can be identified, options examined and tasks prioritised;
- the financial implications of these plans can be identified, options assessed, and resources directed appropriately;
- the process provides a school with the means to communicate objectives to all concerned, and can develop understanding and involvement, leading to greater commitment to outcomes;
- the resultant plan forms a framework for financial decision-making during the year; and
- the plan allocates prioritised tasks across the school and sets clear criteria for the evaluation of achievements at the end of the year.

The following example shows how the strategic planning process could assist a (hypothetical) school to achieve a particular long term objective.

Example 1

In setting its long term objectives, a primary school decides that it wishes to improve reading standards. It has measured the standards against national criteria, and feels that they could be improved. Options for achieving improvement are discussed with 8 staff in the first instance, and include:

1 Reducing class sizes, enabling each teacher to spend more time hearing children read.
2 Investing in a new set of reading materials, training teachers in its use, and improving the library stock.
3 Finding sufficient resources to have a floating teacher who would be deployed across classes to work with individual children.

Each of the options is evaluated in terms of its cost, its likely effectiveness, and its ease of implementation. The staff decide that Option 3 would be the most effective in the short term, but should be followed by Option 2. Only when both have been achieved should Option 1 be implemented in order to sustain the improvement.

After discussion by the Governing body, it is decided that additional resources would be found for a new teacher by increasing pupil intake. The school recognises that the resulting temporary increase in class sizes, running counter to the reductions proposed in Option 1, is unlikely to be popular. Parents are therefore consulted by means of a questionnaire and through meetings, to ensure that they appreciate the likely benefit of and can accept increased class sizes.

The school proposes to monitor the improvement in the reading standards of children, and to publish these regularly to parents. The arrangement would be tried for three years initially, and if standards improve sufficiently in that time the school would then reduce its staffing by one and no longer have a floating teacher. The salary of that teacher would be used in the next year to fund the new reading scheme, and in the following year the school could begin to reduce its intake to re-establish the optimum class size.

The term 'School Development Planning' is a familiar one, as many schools had to produce plans for their curriculum and staff development under the Local Management in Schools initiative. Many schools have also established less formal procedures for planning for other elements of their activity. However, the National Audit Office consider that good strategic planning requires plans for all aspects of the school's activities to be brought together into one document, to ensure a co-ordinated approach. To differentiate this document from the more traditional school development plan, this is referred to below as the strategic plan.

Content of the strategic plan

There can be no standard format for a strategic plan. It should be drawn up to suit a school's particular circumstances. However, the strategic planning process should include consideration of all aspects of a school's activity. Typically, the main themes covered in good plans are:

- *Context* – external influences and impact of changes in national policies, coupled with a review of the school's strengths and weaknesses to date.
- *Vision* – a view on how governors and staff see the school developing in the long term.
- *Aims and objectives* – what a school aims to provide for its pupils, and how it will achieve this.
- *Curriculum* – breadth, balance, development priorities, assessment and record keeping.
- *Staffing* – costs, age profile, competences and development needs.
- *Pupils* – forecasts of numbers, age balance, diversity of background and ability, welfare, discipline and special needs.
- *Community* – links with other sectors of education, the local community and employers.
- *Physical resources* – plans for capital development, premises maintenance and equipment replacement, linked to pupil numbers and curriculum.
- *Finances* – actual and provisional budgets, funding projections.
- *Implementation* – identification of tasks and timetables, allocation of responsibilities and performance targets.
- *Monitoring and evaluation* – criteria for evaluating performance, and review mechanisms.

Example 2 below illustrates how a school might consider a number of these themes whilst planning to achieve a particular aim.

Example 2

Aim: To improve the quality of the school's physical environment over the next three years, and maintain these standards through a rolling programme of refurbishment and re-decoration.

Objectives:
- to meet priorities identified in a health and safety survey;
- to develop the reception area and school approach, including improved signposting; and
- to re-decorate all classrooms.

Resources:
- enhanced role for caretaker (skills, training, new contract terms);
- use of external contractors (cost comparison with in-house provision, quality); and
- materials (most cost effective source of supply).

Implementation:
- identify tasks;
- set a timetable, including consideration of term-time restrictions;
- allocate responsibility for tasks; and
- establish mechanism for review of progress, and evaluation of results.

Evaluation:
- further independent professional health and safety survey;
- incidence of accidents;
- visitor survey; and
- feedback from governors and staff.

Whilst the main themes should be incorporated into one document, the National Audit Office found that schools often considered discrete themes such as the curriculum and maintenance of premises in separate, more detailed plans. Although responsibility for production of these plans was devolved to different members of staff, those schools with effective planning processes achieved a clear linkage with the whole school strategy.

The planning process

The best plans seen by the National Audit Office had been derived from an annual strategic planning cycle, such as illustrated at Figure 17.1. In this way the plan came to be seen as a live document, to be reviewed and updated regularly.

The timing of the planning cycle is important, as decisions must be made ahead of the financial year. Some schools therefore review progress during the summer term, and produce the main body of the strategic plan in the autumn term. The plan can then be finalised, and budgets set, during the spring term [see Figure 17.2].

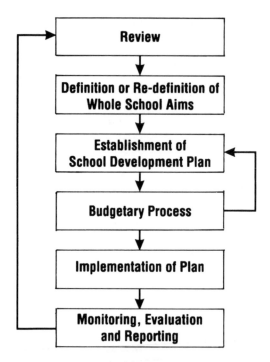

Figure 17.1
Source: Adapted from Davies and Ellison (1992) *School Development Planning*, Figure 2.1,
p. 12

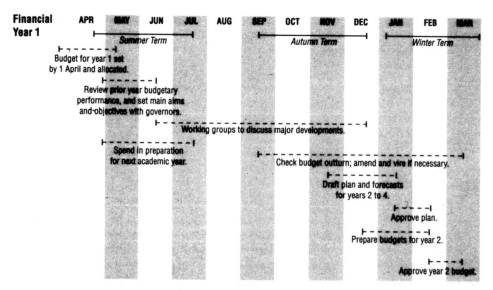

Figure 17.2   Financial and academic year planning

The planning process can involve not only the headteacher and senior management team, but also governors and other staff, and possibly parents and pupils. Schools should seek to allocate clear responsibilities in advance for those involved in preparing the plan, and each part of it, for each stage involved, within a target timetable. The stages which this might involve are outlined below, although their exact format may vary according to a school's particular circumstances:

- Review past performance
- Agree or revise long-term objectives
- Forecast pupil roll
- Curriculum development decisions
- Human resource requirements
- Physical resources planning
- Costing the plan
- Estimating income
- Options analysis
- Finalisation
- Communicate the plan to staff
- Review and renewal

Review past performance

For schools producing their first strategic plan, it is essential to establish the present position with respect to the themes identified [earlier p. 196] including strengths and areas where improvement is needed. Where schools already have an established planning cycle, this review can be carried out against pre-determined criteria. A review of the previous year's budgetary performance and outturn will form part of this process.

Agree or revise long-term objectives

It may not be necessary to revise the overall vision for a school's development each year, but it is beneficial to consult widely and review the more detailed objectives, amending them where appropriate. Major changes ought to be discussed with the governing body at an early stage.

Forecast pupil roll

Accurate forecasting of the future pupil roll, including the likely age profile and diversity of ability, is a vital part of the planning process. These statistics will inform decisions on matters such as curriculum delivery, staffing requirements and accommodation development and will influence the level of a school's income. The forecast pupil roll will also inform decisions on the extent and type of marketing. Sources of information on pupil numbers can include the [. . .] local education authority, local feeder schools, and census information. Many schools are able to predict their pupil rolls quite accurately. Where there is significant uncertainty, the plan may need to consider 'best' and 'worst' case options. [. . .]

Curriculum development decisions

These tend to be heavily influenced by the projected impact of national policies and legislation. However, the school's overall aims and objectives will determine the exact nature of the curriculum and its delivery. Responsibility for curriculum planning commonly lies with the senior management team, taking account of any broad priorities identified by governors and consideration of cross-curricular themes. In larger schools, each department or curriculum co-ordinator may contribute a detailed plan within this framework, including staffing, resource and accommodation requirements.

Human resource requirements

In general, decisions on staffing needs will be informed by the forecast pupil roll, and curriculum requirements. In reviewing these requirements, schools should consider the resource and development implications of the age profile of staff and salary structure, and take decisions as to the need for changes. A school may also have an objective such as improving the pupil:teacher ratio, which will influence staffing decisions. It is valuable for schools to consider whether to change the staff mix by assessing the relationship between full-time and part-time staff, temporary and permanent staff, and teaching and non-teaching staff. Appraisal and staff development are important aspects of planning for human resource requirements. In larger schools a member of the senior management team commonly co-ordinates these requirements after discussion with colleagues.

Physical resources planning

Effective planning requires consideration of equipment replacement and enhancement (driven by the curriculum needs identified in departmental plans, and cross-curricular themes such as information technology); improvement or replacement of furniture and fittings (influenced by feedback from teachers and caretaking staff); maintenance and refurbishment (drawing on an independent survey, and including health and safety issues); and capital development (including major projects requiring external funding).

Costing the plan

An estimate of the costs of each element of the overall plan is needed, over a timescale of at least three years. Costings should take account of changes in school running costs, pay rises and increments and inflation. From these estimates, baseline budgets can be constructed, and any proposed developments costed. If a number of options are costed, this will facilitate decisions on priorities. Once the initial decisions on main priorities have been taken, a three year expenditure forecast can be produced. This could separately identify core commitments, and items of discretionary expenditure if funds permit.

Estimating income

The next stage is to estimate the revenue which is likely to be available to the school from different sources and see whether there is a surplus or shortfall in the funding needed to meet the objectives of the strategic plan. Uncertainty about funding is inevitable, and assumptions need to be made about the future allocation to the school, and an assessment undertaken of the various factors which could influence it.

Options analysis

Once it is known whether there is likely to be enough or a shortfall in funding, the school should revise the plan in accordance with identified priorities, and incorporate pre-determined options for generating further income or making savings. Any surplus should be directed to those needs already highlighted in the strategic plan.

Finalisation

Once the process of considering options, which may involve several iterations, is complete, the plan, including financial forecasts for the period covered, can be finalised. It should invariably be submitted to the governing body for approval at this stage, although there is some advantage if the governors are involved earlier in the process. The final plan should contain details of evaluative criteria, task allocations, targets and a timetable.

Communicate the plan to staff

All staff should be fully aware of the aims and objectives of the whole school, and understand how they can contribute to their implementation and achievement. To an extent this should occur naturally where the plan is built up by staff and through consultation, but staff need still to see the results of this process. Some schools translate corporate targets into more easily measurable lower level targets set within plans for each part of the school. Other schools may wish to consider whether this model would be appropriate to their circumstances.

Review and renewal

The plan should be seen as a working document, and schools may find it more manageable to review it throughout the year. At some schools different aspects of the plan are considered by small working groups of staff and/or governors, or are allocated to individual staff members or governors. Evaluation of performance against pre-determined criteria is an important part of this review process, and may involve consideration of data, and feedback from parents and pupils.

Deriving budgets from the plan

Educational purposes cannot be achieved unless appropriate resources are made available at the right time. Therefore, budgetary decisions have important educational as well as accounting and administrative implications. A good budget-setting process will seek to align financial considerations with the priorities outlined in a school's strategic plan. However, the National Audit Office have found this to be the weakest part of the planning process in many schools.

The importance of this link is illustrated by the following points:

- planning for three years helps predict the implications of current decisions on future costs (such as staff recruitment);
- a fundamental review of activities each year will mean that budgets are not simply incremental;
- the process provides governors with insight into the association between educational aims and budgetary decisions; and
- the allocation of resources to departments can be made consistent with the school's aims and objectives.

The financial projections contained in the strategic plan should be used as a basis for compilation of the annual budget. The plan should be revised, and priorities agreed, before the annual budget is set.

The financial projections will be firmed up as details of areas of expenditure such as staff costs become known. [. . .] Budgets will need to be amended if the final allocation is significantly different. In this case, it is particularly important that priorities are identified in the strategic plan, together with options for savings [. . .].

The difference between academic and financial years makes it harder to achieve a strong link between the strategic plan and budget. Each financial year perforce covers parts of two academic years, and vice versa. At some schools this problem is resolved by aligning the plan with the financial year, but it is more common for schools to plan on an academic year basis. In that case, a school needs to think two years ahead in each cycle in order to ensure that any single year's plan or budget can be effectively implemented. Figure 17.2 shows one possible approach to linking the planning process to the financial year.

The National Audit Office found that secondary schools invariably delegate educational supplies budgets to departmental heads. Some delegate other budgets as well, although only one school was delegating staff cost budgets. Primary schools often delegated educational supplies budgets to curriculum co-ordinators. The allocation process varies between a formula approach, based on weighted pupil numbers, and a bidding system. Whilst the former can be easier to administer, it may not be so responsive to strategic objectives. A good compromise operated by at least one school was to allocate part of the budget by means of a formula to cover core requirements, and the rest in line with bids from budget holders which reflect development needs linked to strategic plan objectives.

In setting the overall budget, it is usual for schools to include a contingency figure to help fund unexpected expenditure or reductions in income. This can more readily be controlled where it is included as a single explicit figure, rather than being spread across a number of budgets. Contingencies represent funding which is not being used to meet its intended objectives and should be kept to a minimum, unless funds are being built up for a specific purpose identified in the strategic plan, such as funding a building project or evening out identified variations in annual funding. Schools which keep a good grip on their budgets are often able to reduce the size of contingencies as they became more experienced at budgeting.

Managing the budget

In order to manage their budget effectively, schools need to be able to provide finance staff, governors and any budget holders with reliable and up to date financial information, commonly monthly during term-time. The level of detail provided to each of the users is best determined in consultation with them, within the limitations of the accounting system used. It is good practice to report commitments incurred as well as cash spent and the value of invoices awaiting payment. This gives staff a clearer idea of what remains in each budget and gives governors a better view of the school's financial position.

For financial monitoring purposes, finance staff and governors also need to be able to compare expenditure (and commitments) against budget headings, to enable them to identify and investigate variances, so as to enable timely action to be taken on over-spends and under-spends. For accurate budget monitoring, the budget should be profiled according to a best estimate of the likely timing of expenditure. [. . .] The National Audit Office found that many schools were not profiling their budgets in line with likely expenditure trends (as opposed to an even spread) or using profile information for in-year monitoring.

In practice, schools have found that the accuracy of profiling, like that of budgeting, improves with experience as they establish patterns of income and expenditure. Some schools therefore revise profiles on a regular basis during the year. This process also facilitates forecasting of the position at the year-end. The National Audit Office found that the schools with good budgetary control undertake such a forecast periodically during the year to indicate whether action should be taken to reduce (or increase) expenditure. The forecast is also an important source of information for the governors.

Where monitoring reveals likely over- or under-spends on certain budget headings, the school may transfer money between budgets or from contingency to maintain a balanced budget. This process is known as 'virement' and enables budget revisions to occur during the year. It is important that the virement process is closely controlled in order that proper accountability relationships are maintained between staff and governors. There should be a clear policy for such decision-making, with governors being involved where the amount exceeds a pre-determined level. In approving virement, governors should ensure that changes are consistent with the strategic plan and that any budgetary problems disclosed are acted upon. Similar arrangements should exist to allocate unspent contingency, towards the year-end, to projects identified in the strategic plan.

[. . .]

Audit checklist

The following checklist summarises the content of this chapter and reiterates the main criteria for effective planning and budgeting.

The main criteria for a good plan and planning process are as follows:

- the school has allocated clear roles and responsibilities for the drawing up, implementing and review of the plan;

- it considers the school's development over at least three years;
- it includes details of the school's present context, its strengths and weaknesses, aims and present values;
- there is a clear vision of where the school should be in the future;
- it takes account of the future context, including pupil numbers, likely resource availability, and relevant legislation;
- it includes the whole of a school's activity;
- it incorporates the financial implications, including the current budget and financial projections for the following years;
- there is appropriate consultation with staff, governors and other interested parties;
- it includes the delivery methodology, with specific targets and a timescale for implementation; and
- achievement can be, and is, measured against pre-determined criteria.

The main criteria for effective budgeting [. . .] are as follows:

- the budget-setting process is closely aligned to those priorities contained in the strategic plan;
- amendments to the budget and the use of contingencies reflect predetermined priorities and options for savings outlined in the strategic plan;
- performance against the budget is closely monitored, with a regular review of outturn income and expenditure against that profiled, and with effective control over delegated budgets.

[. . .]

18 | Strategy and management in the further education sector

STEPHEN DRODGE AND NEVILLE COOPER

Introduction

This chapter derives from a small-scale research project undertaken in late 1994 and early 1995 which investigated how a number of newly independent colleges managed strategic planning. At the centre of the investigation were interviews with senior managers and other staff at three colleges of further education. These appear below as 'Easton', 'Norbury' and 'Southam'. These are fictitious names.

In conducting the research, we were interested in finding out how college managers plan in a situation where:

- they now have the responsibility to plan, rather than to inform and operationalize local education authority (LEA) planning;
- the environment is changing rapidly, and perhaps very differently from college to college; and
- the Further Education Funding Council (FEFC) has established a common national framework for planning.

The British further education (FE) system of post-16, largely vocational provision has undergone major changes in recent years. The most dramatic development, following the Further and Higher Education Act 1992, has been the generation in England and Wales of a new sector, outside LEA control. On 1 April 1993, colleges became independent bodies responsible for managing their own finance, preparing audited accounting reports and exercising proper control of the funds they were to receive from the new Funding Councils.

The Funding Councils themselves, to be able to fulfil their duties under the Act to secure sufficient and adequate provision for post-16 students, required information about the *intentions* of institutions, focusing attention on the need for more formal strategic planning. Following a period of consultation with the FE sector, a strategic planning framework was established (FEFC 1992a,b) which is shown in Figure 18.1.

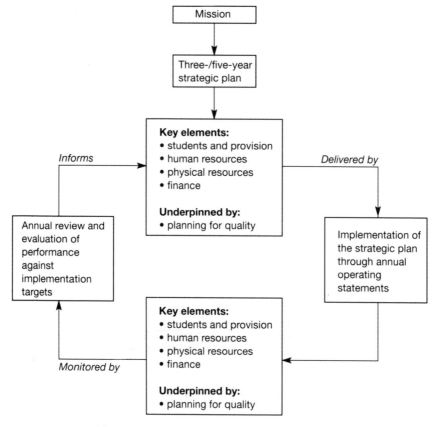

Figure 18.1   The FEFC framework for strategic planning
Source: FEFC 1992b

Whilst forward planning was nothing new to most colleges, an explicit framework for planning had not existed before incorporation. Nor indeed was there such an explicitly formulated rationale for planning as the FEFC now articulated:

> The strategic plan has a pivotal role in the management of a college. It is the route map which guides the college in its short and long term planning and provides the setting for the college's operating plans. Most importantly, the plan is the culmination of a process, within the college, of analysis, testing, discussion, negotiation, persuasion and finally, agreement on the fundamental purpose and direction of the college.
>
> (FEFC 1992b)

Our investigation sought to examine the reality of these planning processes with the following particular questions in mind:

- has the appearance of the planning framework led to a uniformity in college strategic planning or are there adaptations and interpretations?
- How does the process of strategic planning affect the management of colleges?

- What relationship exists between the planning process and college development?
- Is there a relationship between strategic planning and organizational culture?

The colleges studied

The three colleges were chosen to enable a snapshot of actual strategic planning practice to be gained. The colleges illustrate different aspects of the FE sector, although they are not claimed, or intended to be, a representative sample.

Southam and Norbury colleges were chosen on the basis of the published views of their chief executives on managing change in their institutions. These were seen as representing different styles of management which it was felt might impact on the process of strategic planning in different ways. Since both of these colleges were small to medium in size, Easton, a significantly larger college, was selected in order to observe strategic planning in a larger organization.

All three colleges are located in urban areas, although two of them are close to rural hinterlands. Each, therefore, has access to large urban populations although, in the case of Norbury, this is accompanied by the pressures of a highly competitive environment, with a number of other colleges in the vicinity.

All three colleges have a broad range of vocational provision including a small percentage of work with higher education partners (a substantial provision in the case of the larger college). By current FE standards, two of the chief executives are longserving. The third had joined the college about a year before the interviews took place.

Methodology

The primary intention of the survey was to gain a comparative perspective on strategic planning across three differing FE institutions. A series of structured interviews provided the main means of investigation.

Preliminary research drew on current FEFC publications in relation to college strategic planning and general management theory on strategy and planning. This helped in determining an investigative method and establishing criteria for the analysis of findings.

The interview process followed three stages:

Stage 1
Pilot structured interviews with two college senior managers. The interview questions were adapted in the light of interviewees' comments and analysis of the range of responses elicited.

Stage 2
Interviews with the chief executives of two colleges and the representative (the senior manager with designated responsibility for planning) of the chief executive of the third college.

Stage 3
Interviews with three other members of staff of differing status and responsibilities at each of the participating colleges.

Key issues

What became clear very early in the process of investigation was that, despite the identical nature of the planning framework given by the FEFC, each college worked with this framework in distinctively different ways. All the colleges in the study showed a structured approach to planning and were clearly formulating the 'route map' for short- and long-term decisions which the FEFC sees as a function of strategic planning. It was in the *management* of the process of strategic planning, however, that essential differences emerged and three key themes are of particular significance:

- the role of mission, vision and leadership in the planning process;
- directive or participative approaches to strategic planning in a context of environmental change;
- the relationship between strategic planning, values and organizational culture.

The role of mission, vision and leadership in the planning process

Southam

The rhetoric of the college is that there is a shared vision, and that from this all staff have the opportunity to participate in decision-making through working groups, open staff development sessions, and the negotiation of sectional and personal action plans. It is clear, and accepted in the college, that not everyone is 'on board', but our interviews showed that the rhetoric is not too far removed from reality at Southam.

This reality manifests itself in several ways. The chief executive sees the production and maintenance of the college mission as a key function of his role, this vision being the starting point for the college's planning process. In setting out the strategic vision, the chief executive defines the college as a learning organization, in which all can participate fully. This introduces an element of ambiguity, as the participative nature of the organization is, in a sense, imposed from above. So far as we could tell, this was largely accepted, and the opportunity to participate, perceived as genuine, outweighed any reservations about the origin of the initial vision. At the same time, nobody claimed that everyone in the college was happy with the arrangement, and several interviewees referred to colleagues who did not feel at home with it.

If the mission derived in this way was largely acceptable, that does not mean that it is totally unproblematic. Whilst the nature of a mission is that it will set broad and ambitious aims, there is a sense in which it can pose too much of a challenge and become a daunting prospect or a millstone, according to one's view. Especially if day-to-day pressures lead to practice diverging from the aspirations of the mission, the feeling can arise – and was expressed to us – that, 'we may have overstated what we can do' or, more bluntly, that the mission may be 'unachievable' and lead to institutional and individual conflict.

Norbury

At Norbury, as at Southam, the mission has come from the top, with the senior management team developing a statement based on a vision provided essentially by the chief executive. A middle manager described the mission as the 'focusing pinnacle' and felt that the planning process as a whole had resulted in a much greater focus in the college's activities.

It was very clear that the mission and the way in which this translated into more detailed planning and into action, formed an essentially top–down process (though this does not necessarily mean non-participative). One manager emphasized that it was crucial for the chief executive to be 'showing leadership' in the current environment, and that the development of the college had to be subject to 'clear steers' from above. It appeared that both the overall mission, and the framework within which more detailed planning would take place were largely non-negotiable, although many staff were heavily involved in the development of the detailed action planning.

Easton

In Easton College, a mission was originally developed through a consultative process, involving a series of staff workshops. A change of chief executive since incorporation and a review of the current mission have led to a need, as perceived by senior management, to rewrite the mission. An interim set of general objectives, arguably below 'mission level', but clearly indicating some changes in direction, has been generated from within the senior management team. Consultations are now in progress with the staff at large, through a series of marketing workshops facilitated by an internal consultant, about the direction for the college. A new mission statement will be produced by the chief executive – informed, but not necessarily determined, by the consultation. In this instance, therefore, we have been able to observe a shift towards a more top–down approach. Nevertheless, the participative element in mission development is substantial and seemed perceived as such by the staff to whom we spoke.

Discussion

The importance of mission in giving an overarching set of values and purpose to the strategic planning process is recognised in the FEFC planning framework and it is hard to envisage an effective plan which is uninformed by at least some sense of general purpose. The interviews revealed evidence of the way in which mission formation contributed to the strategic planning process, but, as we have seen, this varied between institutions. Just as importantly, the way in which interviewees saw the process also varied within institutions.

Peeke (1994) has identified some of the issues associated with introducing mission concepts into FE and we found evidence to support this in each of the colleges we visited. These are:

- the difficulty of establishing a single, meaningful, common mission for an organization of professionals;
- suspicion of the process of developing a mission statement;
- difficulty of acceptance of a centrally led mission.

In the interviews with managers at all three colleges we heard comments about the benefits deriving from the process of mission formulation coupled with the expression of doubt as to how far these were appreciated by staff. This may well relate to Peeke's reference to the suspicion which attends a centrally led, or top–down process of mission development.

The colleges share a broadly top–down approach to the development of mission. There are important differences about the degree of consultation involved in the process, but it is clear that decisions about the declared mission of each college lie at senior management or even chief executive level and that mission or vision plays a significant part in shaping strategic planning. Indeed, for vision to develop into strategy, it must be effectively articulated, communicated and shared, and the role of the chief executive in providing vision and leadership to the strategic planning process as a whole was of significance in all the colleges. In some cases, however, the chief executive's vision is almost as much about the nature of the process as about the end result. This means that, in the context of a handed-down initial concept, there can still be major contributions and real decision-making at lower levels of the organization.

Directive or participative approaches to strategic planning in a context of environmental change

Southam

Southam College sets out to operate avowedly as a learning organization, a key characteristic of which is that all organization members are essentially involved in learning, growth and transformation. The college encourages staff not only to participate in the annual review process, but also to develop working groups to explore and build upon issues raised at the open, voluntary staff development seminars which are one of its defining features. In this process, space is being made for staff to engage in discussion and creative work which will, inevitably, result in operational decisions being taken. This style of planning was very much at the stimulus of, and associated with, the chief executive whose role in promoting the values of the learning organization, both in principle and practice, was acknowledged by colleagues.

A main grade lecturer at this college commented that the nature of the planning process was such that, 'if you want to be, you can be involved, and *make it part of your working life*' (italics added). Inevitably, it is particularly at the level of the section or programme team, where policy is being interpreted into action, that this involvement, internalization and commitment is most likely to occur.

Easton

At Easton College, the opportunities for staff to take local decisions are less clear cut, but there was a clear desire to generate an open, communicative, 'dynamic' process which both stimulated debate about planning and involved a wide range of college staff. The recently appointed chief executive sought to create the conditions for people to make significant contributions and shape direction: to allow good ideas to surface ('creating some energy' as the chief executive put it). Creating smaller, cross-college teams was seen as a crucial tactic here. The chief executive also sought to communicate strategic goals more widely, this being manifested in open meetings with staff in each sector. These so-called 'roadshows' were referred to by one respondent as 'symbols of openness', conveying both the potential of the process and the suspicion which may simultaneously attend it.

One interviewee welcomed the feeling of being 'more consulted', though there were also some suggestions of a wait-and-see attitude on the part of some staff. A key test, one interviewee suggested, would be whether you found your proposals included in the plans.

The use of an internal consultant as a change agent is significant here. It both assists all concerned to understand the implications and possible outcomes of what they are discussing, and distances the process, to some extent at least, from the chief executive and senior management. The independence of such a person from senior management may be seen as of great importance. Dependent on this, the process may be viewed as either manipulative or liberating, empowering or directing.

Norbury

Norbury College has introduced its planning process as part of a conscious attempt to alter the overall direction of the college in response to changes in its competitive environment. In so doing, it has adopted a much more managerial model than the other colleges.

Senior management set the major planning objectives, although there was, both in principle and practice, the opportunity for staff as a whole to put forward proposals which could influence college planning objectives. Middle managers were significantly involved in, and had the ability to influence, the planning process. This was linked to increased levels of responsibility and accountability. This group also acted as the link between the planning process at management level and the wider college community. There was a perception, however, that main grade lecturers felt a degree of 'remoteness' from the planning process and that the scope for staff to develop ideas existed, but only if they were aligned with strategic objectives.

Once actions have been agreed, a very detailed structure of targets forms the basis of monitoring, and this element of control is central to the process. This is expressed in varying ways: There is 'a feeling of needing to achieve' a middle manager commented, and the monitoring and performance management processes have 'sharpened up people's understanding of where they are in the system and what is expected of them by the system', in the view of a senior manager. On the other hand, a middle manager expresses doubt as to how far main grade staff are aware of the possibilities to participate which exist. At a lower level in the college, interviewees placed more emphasis on the pressures of the system, and on its remoteness from day-to-day concerns: 'we've all got to do more, work harder', the details of the plan are 'fairly unintelligible'.

Discussion

All the colleges studied show both the importance of management decision-making in the strategic planning process and evidence of devolved and participative methods of managing the planning process. However, the degree of devolution and participation in planning varied between institutions.

At Southam and Easton, decision-making is devolved at least to some extent, within an overall agreed vision, to those people who are faced with day-to-day choices. The approach at Norbury seems to have more in common with directive approaches to management. The senior manager's role is more central, envisaging a consultation process which is, in essence, designed to win over staff and to gain their commitment to a pre-ordained plan. Leadership here is essentially defined as giving emphasis to key objectives and setting the frameworks for accountability within the strategic planning process.

The approaches of both Easton and Southam have manifest links with Mintzberg's (1978) concept of emergent strategy. The college's deliberate strategy (i.e. long-term, essentially rational, foreseen and foreseeable view) is set out in its plan. It is accepted, however, that other strategies will develop at different points throughout the organization in order to meet particular requirements. More than this, the intentional creation of space and provision of stimuli to creativity and personal growth seem to encourage alternative or additional strategies. We characterize this as 'strategic opportunism', a model of development created and sustained by conditions which:

- allow flexible decision-making; and
- create an ambience in which staff feel sufficiently empowered to take advantage of this possibility.

For staff to do this, they must be secure in the knowledge that their decisions will take effect, and that, at least within limits, no blame will accrue in the event of an error being made. The chief executive of Southam refers to the importance of a 'no blame culture'. Easton College is described by an interviewee as having a 'reasonably tolerant culture'.

The creation of this space for local decision-making may be an aspect of 'logical incrementalism' in an organization, referred to by Quinn (1978) and Bailey and Johnson (1992). According to these commentators, organizations may make a series of small decisions to change, reacting to the pressures confronting them day by day. This can lead to a growing divergence between the organization's perception of its purpose and the demands of the environment. Whilst we have no evidence that such divergence has taken place at either Easton or Southam, it is a possible consequence of this form of devolved decision-making.

Strategic planning, values and organizational culture

Southam

At Southam College there is a very public emphasis on key values which are seen to guide individual and organizational practice. Of particular importance in this expression of guiding principles is the desire to create a culture which fosters openness and the conditions for individual learning and growth. Such a cultural climate is then seen as providing the essential dynamic for personal and organizational development in the emerging 'learning organization'. The chief executive is acknowledged as being the prime mover in this creation of values and principles.

There was clear evidence that this ethos had affected both staff attitudes and the planning process. The extent to which these values were shared was evident in staff perceptions of the openness of the planning process, the opportunities to become involved and the relationship between the planning process and the fulfilment of college mission. Values 'are remarkably alive here' one interviewee said and this, in his opinion, had allowed the college to deal more effectively with some of the challenges posed following incorporation.

Planning was seen as providing a framework for decision-making in which accountability and responsibility were encouraged as a characteristic of this learning culture.

There was also the perception, however, that the values and principles underpinning college practice might be restrictive in placing expectations which individuals may find it difficult to embrace or live up to. 'We may have overstated what can be done', one interviewee commented. There was also the sense that external pressures to increase numbers might compromise college mission.

Norbury

At Norbury College we found a more directive, managerialist, planning process, the major responsibility for which lay with senior managers.

A business ethic was seen as emerging, the characteristics of which were a raised awareness of the need for efficiency in meeting targets and increasing college effectiveness to do so. Although this ethic had currency, interviewees also perceived a tension between the achievability of targets and sustained effectiveness in the quality of their delivery in terms of curriculum practice. One view expressed related particularly to a concern that measures of 'achievement' might fail to take full account of student satisfaction.

Alongside the targets set within the planning documentation, the performance management system in operation at the college set clear frameworks for accountability and underpinned the perception that managers 'are tested and have to prove their competence'. This accountability was reinforced at management level through peer pressure to achieve standards of performance. There was also the perception that the 'feeling of a need to achieve' existed for staff at all levels.

Easton

At Easton College, as noted above, the recent change of chief executive has been significant in triggering change in approaches to college planning processes, through promoting wider staff involvement, more explicit communication of planning goals and a greater cross-college planning focus. Those working in smaller cross-college teams were able to see their part in the whole and put forward ideas which could influence the planning process. The chief executive saw these changes as 'bringing people closer to what is happening'.

Comments from interviewees showed that such approaches were having an impact on both thinking and practice. They had, in the words of one interviewee, 'engendered a more open style of communication and a more participative approach'. Explicit mention was also made of the change in 'atmosphere' which had been created, this being seen as 'supportive of risk taking' and 'reasonably tolerant'.

The change to a more 'whole college' planning approach, bringing together cross-college teams, had to some degree, however, challenged the influence, sense of priorities and planning methods of existing and long-standing sectional interests. There was also the perception that the change in customer focus, brought about by new planning priorities, was beginning, for some, to challenge long established perceptions of who the college's clients were, who the college should be serving and what the values which govern college purpose should be (when commercial pressures were perceived as gaining ground).

Discussion

The impact of planning is not only manifested as a single, total activity resulting in perceivable outcomes, but also as a series of decisions, behaviours and actions. The way in which staff experience these various events, together with their participation in and consultation about planning, appears to shape their perceptions about both planning and college culture. This experience is influenced by the particular style of leadership adopted by the chief executive.

Both Southam and Norbury College have adopted approaches which reflect the view that the task of strategic management is to create and maintain systems of shared meaning that facilitate organized action (Smircich and Stubbart 1985). There must, in other words, be a common understanding of what the college is about. Different approaches have been adopted in the fulfilment of this aim. These reflect, on the one hand, an approach which sees strategic management realising the mission by fostering individual and collective learning, and, on the other, a managerial, directive approach in which the role of strategic management is to define college purpose and direction and then secure commitment to it.

At Easton College, the range of perceptions evident in the study draws attention to a culture in which the values and sense of purpose emerging are not fully shared in the college community and have yet to be tested over time. The change to a more participative planning process was acknowledged and welcomed, although one interviewee perceived a degree of cynicism among staff about attempts to engage a wider participation in the planning process.

Conclusion

All three of our colleges have planning processes in place, and these have points of both similarity and dissimilarity. Expressed broadly, the similarities cluster around the mechanics of planning, whereas the dissimilarities relate primarily to ethos and management style – to the way in which the process is enacted.

In terms of the detail of planning, the principle resemblances among the strategic planning processes of the colleges studied are:

- a structured approach;
- clear corporate objectives;
- commitment at senior management level to a central mission;
- production of whole college goals in line with the mission;
- production of sector targets to support college goals;
- a monitoring process through one year and towards the next;
- stress on the role of the chief executive as a leader in the process.

The essential differences were seen in:

- the nature of consultation;
- the degree of freedom allowed to staff in devising sector targets;
- the commitment to personal growth;
- the approach to 'growing' or 'imposing' commitment/compliance.

In all colleges, it was acknowledged that the strategic planning processes adopted had increased awareness of, and the level of consultation and participation in planning. This is in line with the outline process expected by the FEFC, as are the detailed activities which are common to the colleges.

Within this commonality, however, there was scope for wide variations in the reality of the experience. We believe that these differences are critically related to two issues: the management ethos of the college and college management's perception of planning. The first of these is about style, the second about the concept of strategy.

Style

We see the three colleges as falling into three broad areas of management style. We have characterized these as: Southam – essentially humanist; Easton – pragmatist; and Norbury – managerialist (Cooper and Drodge 1995). These are accepted as the broadest of brush strokes.

We have seen how, at Southam College, personal and organizational development were perceived as intimately connected and of central importance. Together they underlie the concept of the learning organization. This humanistic appreciation of the value of individual learning and growth to the success of the organization meant that it became natural for management to encourage openness and participation throughout the planning process.

Easton College's pragmatic style had features in common with the humanistic approach of Southam. Staff were encouraged to participate in decision-making processes with the expectation that this would result in outcomes in the final plans. This significant involvement, however, took place in the context of a management agenda for specific actions. The intention was to stimulate and deploy individual creativity in the service of a whole-college concept.

At Norbury College we found a more controlled, managerialist planning process, conceived, directed and monitored by senior managers in line with their perception of college priorities. It was not that staff views were not sought or utilized within the planning process, but that the major emphasis of strategic planning lay with senior managers. The role of leadership was to identify the changes demanded by the environment, provide a clear direction and purpose for the college in response to these, and to create the conditions in which staff could align themselves with college priorities.

The concept of strategy

Traditional strategic planning has involved the precise specification of targets and of the actions and resources required to achieve them. This assumes that relatively accurate projection is possible from current data. The validity of this type of 'rational–analytical' approach in a time of unpredictable change has increasingly been questioned. In particular, there is debate about the clarity of goals within sectors such as education, where there may, additionally, be a considerable divergence of view about both method and purpose. Peeke (1994) raises this problem in relation to mission-setting.

Cohen and March (1983) argue that the reality of education management is that the linkage between many decisions and their practical outcomes is problematic. This subverts the idea of a rigidly structured planning and decision-making process and leads to more flexible, responsive and permissive approaches.

Of the three colleges, only Norbury appears to have a process operating largely within the traditional model, based on target-setting and quantitative monitoring. To a greater or lesser extent, both Southam and Easton appear to accept the need for planning to include space for devolved decision-making in response to unforeseen circumstances.

It is conceivable that these divergences are not as real or significant as they might at first appear. We have seen that the planning frameworks of the colleges are not dissimilar, influenced, of course, by the FEFC and its requirements. It is possible to interpret the major differences in style as reflecting the colleges' different positions in the organizational life cycle. Tushman *et al.* (1986) show periods of incremental change in organizations being interspersed with short periods of large upheaval and discontinuous change, arising from a variety of possible internally driven or externally imposed causes. It might be argued that, in the three colleges, we merely observe the results of one college (Southam) being secure within a period of incremental change; one (Easton) possibly just leaving such a period and about to change rapidly; and the third (Norbury) in the process of implementing discontinuous change through swift action.

However, within a culture of participation it is perfectly possible for major change to take place. The space to take decisions at many levels includes the opportunity to instigate major change, as well as to develop ideas on a small scale and incrementally. It may also increase the likelihood, through encouraging debate and creativity, that proposals for, and acceptance of, major change, which may indeed be necessary, will develop at various levels of the organization, rather than only within the senior management team.

Acknowledgements

Our greatest debt is, of course, to colleagues at 'Easton', 'Norbury' and 'Southam' colleges, and a Training and Enterprise Council, who kindly expended time and thought in assisting us in this investigation, but whom we cannot identify by name for reasons of confidentiality. We are, however, grateful to them for their help and openness.

We can name and thank our two 'pilot' interviewees, C. A. Herd, Principal of Tamworth College, and Kim Punshon, Deputy Principal of Tile Hill College. Their views helped us to design our subsequent interview strategy, but none of the comments in this chapter should be taken as representing their opinions or referring to their colleges.

Our thanks, finally, to Professor Ron Glatter of the Open University, who has kept an eye on us, and offered valuable support, at all stages of the research.

References

Bailey, A. and Johnson, G. (1992) How strategies develop in organisations, in D. Faulkner and G. Johnson (eds) *Challenge of Strategic Management*. London: Kogan Page.

Cohen, M. and March, J. (1983) Leadership and ambiguity, in O. Boyd-Barrett *et al.* (eds) *Approaches to Post-school Management*. London: Harper and Row.

Cooper, N. and Drodge, S. (1995) Strategic management in action. *FE Now*, 20 October, 33.

FEFC (1992a) *Circular 92/18*. Coventry: FEFC.

FEFC (1992b) *Funding learning*. Coventry: FEFC.

Mintzberg, H. (1978) Patterns in strategy formation. *Management Science*, 24 (9): May, 934–48.

Peeke, G. (1994) *Mission and Change: Institutional mission and its application to the management of further and higher education*. Buckingham: SRHE/Open University Press.

Quinn, J. (1978) Strategic change: 'logical incrementalism'. *Sloan Management Review*, I (20): Fall, 7–21.

Smircich, L. and Stubbart, C. (1985) Strategic management in an enacted world. *Academy of Management Review*, 10 (4): 724–36.

Tushman, M., Newman, W. and Romanelli, E. (1986) Convergence and upheaval: managing the unsteady pace of organizational evolution. *California Management Review*, 29 (1): Fall, 29–44.

19 | Strategic planning in schools: some practical techniques

DICK WEINDLING

Introduction

This chapter discusses the concept of strategic planning and provides a model for education which can be integrated into the school development plan. The intention is to provide practical guidance to help schools in the use of strategic planning as a means of coping with multiple change.

Planning has always been one of the key management functions for an organization and schools have undertaken planning at various levels for many years, but with the recent reforms, such as the National Curriculum and local management of schools (LMS), longer range planning has become even more important for effective management. The problem is that schools are experiencing a very turbulent environment and like the most successful companies, they have to learn how to 'thrive on chaos' (Peters 1987).

Kaufman (1992) argues that most educational reforms concentrate on means without a close examination of ends, and that strategic planning offers a way of integrating the two. Although he is discussing US education, his points apply equally powerfully to the situation in the UK.

> Caring is not enough. Changing is not enough. Spending more money is not enough. Raising standards is not enough. In fact, each of the single-issue, quick fixes imposed upon education might be failing for the wrong reasons. . . . We have been selecting means (hows) before agreeing upon the ends. It is now time to get ends and means related. Being strategic is knowing what to achieve, being able to justify the direction, and then finding the best ways to get there.
>
> (Kaufman 1992: 10–11)

Most schools now have School Development Plans (SDPs), sometimes called institutional development plans, and indeed, these are expected as part of the Office for Standards in Education (Ofsted) inspection. A school development plan should integrate curriculum development, staff development, management development and finance. The situation is further confused as there are now also Ofsted Action Plans which all schools are required to produce following an inspection to address the 'key issues' identified by the inspectors.

In this chapter, it is suggested that there are three interconnected levels of planning which move from the long-term overview of strategic planning, through the school development plan, to the more detailed action plan. Strategic planning has as its key the notion of strategic thinking which considers the vision and values of the organization as well as the anticipated external forces and trends which affect the school, to produce what can be called the 'helicopter view'. While schools have made considerable progress with SDPs as a means of long-range planning, and are coming to terms with the requirements of Ofsted, the use of strategic planning can further improve their effectiveness.

What is strategic planning?

Education, like many other fields, is going through a period of unprecedented change and it has become very difficult to anticipate the future – as the science fiction writer Arthur C. Clarke said, 'the future ain't what it used to be!' Strategic planning is a means for establishing and maintaining a sense of direction when the future has become more and more difficult to predict. It is a continuous process by which the organization is kept on course, through making adjustments as both the internal and external contexts change. Planning, of course, is not finished when the written plan is produced – this is a record of the process as seen at a particular point in time – the difficult part is to implement the plan. In strategic planning, the emphasis is on evolutionary or rolling planning where the plan itself is changed to adapt to changing circumstances.

The *Concise Oxford Dictionary* definition of strategy is 'generalship, the art of war' and the early work reflected this by focusing on the military use during campaigns and battles. Much later the notion of strategy was used to improve business planning.

> Strategy became popular in the 1950s and 1960s when large numbers of firms and expanding business opportunities necessitated looking more systematically at the future. This took the form of long-range planning, the purpose of which was to first define the firm's objectives, then establish some plans in order to achieve those objectives, and finally to allocate resources through capital budgeting. . . . Such long-range planning, as a way of formulating strategy, lost its appeal when it became evident that forecasting existing trends into the future did not produce accurate results. Consequently, long-range planning was replaced by strategic planning, which incorporated accepting possible changes in trends and was not based on the assumption that adequate growth could be assured.
>
> (King and Cleland 1987, quoted in Valentine 1991: 17)

Today, strategic planning can be seen as a technique which assists leaders and managers in dealing with the increasingly turbulent environment and the challenges which confront organizations. The business literature uses a variety of terms such as 'strategic management', 'strategic planning' and 'strategic thinking', but in essence, strategy is the process by which members of the organization envision its future and develop the necessary procedures to achieve that future.

Differences between long-range and strategic planning

Confusion between long-range planning and strategic planning is very common, but an understanding of the differences is crucial in developing an approach for schools. The long-range planning approach, shown in Table 19.1, has dominated thinking about how organizations work for most of this century, and in fact, continues largely to do so. Its prevalence is probably because this is how many people feel schools and other organizations should run. In fact, as observational studies show, the real world of organizations is messy and non-rational (see Paterson *et al.* 1986, for a discussion on the non-rational world and the implications for schools). The features of strategic planning listed in Table 19.1 provide better working assumptions and a closer approximation of how schools actually operate, than the traditional model.

A useful analogy for considering the differences is to think first about firing an arrow at a target. If the situation is relatively stable, that is, the target is stationary, you are stationary and there is little wind, it is fairly easy to hit the target. If, however, the situation is unpredictable and the target is moving and you are moving, a guided missile is a more useful means of hitting the target. The missile does not fly in a straight line, but uses a feedback system to constantly check on the relative position between the target and the missile and then adjusts its direction accordingly. It is argued that in a situation where the targets are moving and the school is moving, strategic planning is a more useful model. But this means that the school has to monitor its progress and adjust course as the circumstances change.

Table 19.1 Differences between long-range and strategic planning

Long-range planning	*Strategic planning*
Assumes a closed system within which reasonably accurate 3–5-year blueprints can be constructed	Assumes an open system in which organizations are dynamic and constantly changing as they integrate information from the shifting environmental factors
Planning is seen as a separate function	Planning is an integral part of running the organization
The focus tends to be on the final plan and the 3–5-year future organizational goals and objectives	The focus is on the process
Mainly just an internal analysis	Uses both internal and external analysis to move toward the shared vision
Decisions about the future are based on present data	Current and future trends are used to make current, not future, decisions

Source: Adapted from Valentine 1991: 16

If the advantages of strategic planning are so obvious why have so few schools used it? Bowman (1990: 9) provides a summary of why some business organizations have not adopted strategic planning and this is adapted for the educational context below:

- There is a lack of awareness by the head and senior management team (SMT) of the school's true situation.
- The SMT are collectively deluding themselves about the position of the school. This can come about, paradoxically, where they consider themselves to be a tightly knit group and develop 'group think' – a shared stereotypic view of the staff, the school and its relationship with the outside world. They reinterpret, or ignore, unpleasant information that does not fit in with their preferred way of looking at the world.
- There are some powerful people in the school with vested interests in maintaining the status quo. Their position and status depend on the continuation of the existing strategy and they discourage staff from asking challenging questions.
- Schools are having to deal with externally imposed change and this tends to promote reactive, incremental responses rather than a strategic approach.
- A common problem often related to the above, results from the head and senior management being too locked into everyday problems. This gives the SMT no time to consider longer-term issues, nor does it prepare them to take a strategic perspective on the school.
- The past success of the school can make people blind to the current situation. It also encourages management to stick with the tried and tested strategies which may be inappropriate to present and future circumstances.
- Clinging to past glories can also make managers reluctant to see the school move in a different direction. Moreover, changing direction can be seen as an admission that what was done before was a mistake.

As Proctor (1993) points out, organizations can become 'entrapped' with ineffective old strategies. He suggests that they need to be alert and capitalize on any appropriate 'strategic windows' which are only open for limited periods.

The origin of strategic planning and its relevance for education

The idea of strategic planning originated in the business world in the early 1970s and has now become a standard part of management thinking in many organizations. The Harvard Business School model (Andrews 1980, 1987) is the most dominant. The main purpose of the model is to help a company develop the best fit between itself and the environment, that is to develop the best strategy for the firm. Not everyone accepts the dominant model and Mintzberg (1994), in particular, has mounted a powerful critique in his book, *The Rise and Fall of Strategic Planning*. After describing the origins of strategic planning, he illustrates the confusion over terminology and points out a number of the pitfalls and fallacies of strategic planning. He also distinguishes between 'deliberate' strategies, where the planners' intentions are fully realized, and 'emergent' strategies which arise as a pattern over time, but which were not expressly intended.

But if the model was designed for business, to give companies a strategic advantage and improve their profits, how can it be relevant to non-profit organizations such as schools? Although used in the business world for a number of years, it is only recently that strategic planning has been considered by the non-profit sector. There are both similarities and differences between the two sectors and the business model has to be adapted for use in schools. Some of the problems in using strategic planning for education are outlined by Bowman (1990) who points out the wide range of stakeholders and the lack of a single, simple bottom line measure in schools.

> The absence of a 'bottom line' (like profits) means that the management of a school cannot act with clarity and certainty in making decisions. Good strategic managers in these circumstances tend to be able to combine acute political and interpersonal skills (to manage the disparate interest groups) with a clear set of values, or a 'vision'. Armed with this clarity of purpose they are then able to set a direction and make judgements between conflicting requirements. So in this sense, the strategic managers of not-for-profit organisations are more in need of well developed 'strategies' or 'missions' (if they are going to inspire others, give them a sense of direction and a feeling of confidence) than managers in firms.
>
> (Bowman 1990: 12)

Schools need to be wary of using private sector approaches that assume clear goals, profit measures, considerable freedom to act, limited responsibility for actions, and oversight of the financial market. For schools many of these assumptions are simply not valid.

It is important to realize that strategic planning is not a single concept, procedure or tool, but embraces a range of approaches that vary in their applicability to the public and non-profit sectors. Arguably, some of the models, such as the portfolio approach and competitive analysis, are less useful for schools, although it is possible to examine the curriculum and courses on offer as the school's portfolio, and with open enrolment and LMS, schools have had to consider their competitors to a greater extent than in the past.

Despite the difficulties, various authors have developed strategic planning models that can be applied to non-profit organizations (e.g. Bryson 1988; Nutt and Backoff 1992) and specifically for education and schools (e.g. McCune 1986; Muriel 1989; Cook 1990; Valentine 1991). However, all of these are of American origin and need to be further modified to fit the local context.

Strategic planning and school development plans

In the UK, one of the earliest writers on the use of strategic planning in education was Fidler (1989) who said: 'There is almost nothing in the literature on school management about strategic management. The closest topic is that concerned with the aims and objectives of the school or perhaps goals.' Since then considerable work has been done on school development planning. Hargreaves and Hopkins were commissioned by the then Department of Education and Science (DES) to provide a series of short documents which offered advice on school development planning (DES 1989, 1991). They stressed the link between planning and school improvement and said that, 'the purpose of development planning is to improve the quality of teaching and learning in a school through the successful management of innovation and change'.

It provides an overall plan which brings together: national and local policies and initiatives, the school's aims and values, existing achievements and development needs. The SDP must not be seen as another initiative, but as a means of managing and coping with innovation overload.

The Hargreaves and Hopkins model has four main processes in the developmental planning cycle:

- *Audit:* the school reviews its strengths and weaknesses.
- *Construction:* priorities for development are selected and then turned into specific targets.
- *Implementation:* the planned priorities and targets are implemented.
- *Evaluation:* the success of the implementation is checked.

As the DES documents were sent to every school, this stimulated interest in development planning and a number of schools and LEAs began work in this area.

Davies and Ellison (1992) provide another variation on the model and offer a number of examples of SDPs. The case studies by Wallace and McMahon (1994) show how primary schools have used development planning as they struggled to cope with the complexity of change. MacGilchrist *et al.* (1995) describe the results of a major three-year study, and the collection of papers edited by Hargreaves and Hopkins (1994) demonstrate some of the later approaches used in a number of different countries. A book by Fidler *et al.* (1996) illustrates the use of strategic planning for schools in the UK.

The process of strategic planning

Although the Hargreaves and Hopkins' model is a very good starting point, it can be developed further by integrating elements from strategic planning. The following sections demonstrate the practical application of strategic planning for schools. Each of the techniques has been used with several hundred heads and teachers in workshop sessions and with the whole staff in about a dozen schools. Figure 19.1 indicates the main stages in the process. Although drawn as such to illustrate the stages, this should not be taken as a simple linear model with a fixed order. Schools need to adapt the sequence, depending on their current position and it may be necessary to circle back to earlier stages. Not all the stages should be repeated each year. If the school has a high staff turnover, it is important periodically to reappraise events and trends, thereby helping new members of staff to understand the past, while also giving them the opportunity to question some of the taken for granted values.

Readiness and the need for a strategic planning group

For this first stage you need to answer questions such as:

- How much commitment to the planning process is present?
- Who should be involved?
- How long will the process take?
- What information is needed to assist the process?

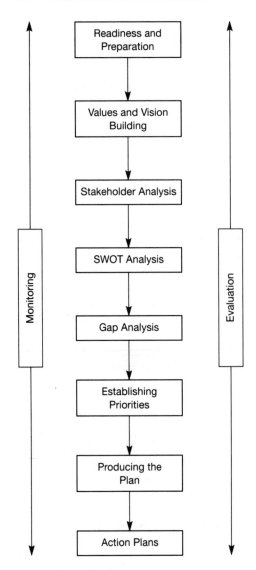

Figure 19.1   The strategic planning process

A person, or small group should initiate, champion and sustain the process, because strategic planning does not just happen. The process requires full recognition and agreement of the head and governors. Their sponsorship gives the process legitimacy.

There are some differences in approach between primary and secondary schools due to size and organizational structure. In a small school it is best to involve all members of staff and the non-teaching staff if the anticipated changes are likely to affect them as well. In larger schools decisions have to be made about the composition of the strategic planning group (SPG). It is essential that the key decision-makers are committed and involved from the beginning, therefore the head and senior management team should form the core of the group. A good cross-section of staff is required in secondary schools and it may be possible to select representatives from existing groups. Clearly governors have a key role to play in decision-making and some members of the governing body should be invited to join the group. It may be productive to have representatives from various other stakeholder groups such as parents, students, employers, the LEA etc., in the group. However, thought should be given to the size of the group and it must not become too unwieldy.

A good way of starting the process is to use a residential weekend when the strategic planning group map out the process and undertake some of the initial stages. Members of the group should be told how they were selected and what they are expected to do. Other members of staff need to be kept informed throughout the process. The recall and examination of the school's recent past is a valuable stage in helping the SPG to establish their values and project forward to the vision of the desired future. By recalling history, the group can set objectives that are both realistic and clear. Considerable progress can be made by using an external consultant to facilitate the group work and to provide an orientation and overview of the strategic planning process.

Values audit

This stage involves an analysis of the values of staff and other key stakeholders. The strategic plan must be in congruence with the organization's values. Strategic planning which does not take account of values will almost certainly fail. Early in the strategic planning process any differences in values of individuals need to be clarified and (where possible) resolved. Values are reflected in the culture and the way the organization approaches its work, and lie at the heart of almost all key organizational decisions. Some of these values may already exist in written form in the school's prospectus or staff handbook, but all the values should be re-assessed during the audit. This is an important, but difficult, exercise which requires in-depth discussion of the fundamental beliefs that underlie the way the school works and resolution of any conflicting values. Without such efforts, differences in values, philosophies and assumptions will constantly surface and block the SPG's progress.

Pfeiffer *et al.* (1988) point out that values exist at individual, group and organizational levels. They recommend that the values audit should start at the individual level and then move to the organizational levels.

Several techniques can be used for a values audit in a school:

- Interviews (either with individuals or groups) are a very useful means of exploring values. Some typical questions are:
    'What are your personal beliefs about how this school should be run?'
    'What do you like, and don't like, about this school?'
    'What are your personal beliefs about teaching and learning?'
- Questionnaires
    For example, staff could be asked to rank order, or rate their agreement to a list of values on a 5-point scale.
- Projective techniques
    For example, ask staff to write an imaginary diary for a typical working day five years in the future, beginning with waking up in the morning and ending with

going to bed. This method should cause a number of issues to surface, including values around work style, and growth and change of the organization.

The values audit is useful in helping the SPG to understand the relationship between teachers' personal goals and organizational planning.

Vision

In all the recent literature, vision has been stressed as a major element in leadership and strategic planning in both the business and school context (e.g. Bennis and Nanus 1985; Nias *et al.* 1989). Some of the business literature assumes that it is the leader's task to produce the vision. However, it is not necessarily the job of the head to have a vision and then tell everybody. As Senge (1990), points out, the task of the leader is to generate a shared vision:

> Today, vision is a familiar concept in corporate leadership. But when you look carefully you find that most visions are one person's (or one group's) vision imposed on an organisation. Such visions, at best, command compliance – not commitment. A shared vision is a vision that many people are truly committed to, because it reflects their own personal vision.
>
> (Senge 1990: 206)

In their research on US high schools, Louis and Miles (1992) discussed the relationship of vision and school improvement. They found that, in reality, the process differed somewhat from that offered by most of the theoretical writers:

- First, visions are not fully articulated (or even articulated at all) at the beginning of the change process. Instead, visions develop over the course of the evolutionary planning process.
- Second, visions are not generated solely by the principal (the head) or another individual in a leadership position but, even where the principal is strong, are developed collectively, through action and reflection, by all those who play active roles in the change effort.
- Third, visions are not a simple, unified view of 'what this school can be', but are a complex braid of the evolving themes of the change program. 'Visioning' is a dynamic process, [not] a one-time event that has a beginning and an end . . . Visions are developed and reinforced from the action . . . Vision provides a shared meaning: people talk about it, use the same language to describe it, and believe that they are engaged in a common task.
- Fourth, although themes and the resulting vision tend to be generated with a small group of people, the principal plays a significant role in spreading the vision to a broader group in the school.

(Louis and Miles 1992: 236–7)

When discussing successful companies which had a 'bias for action', Peters and Waterman (1982) used the notion of 'ready, fire, aim', instead of 'ready, aim, fire', when they quoted a Cadbury executive. This idea was picked up by Fullan (1993) who said:

> Ready, fire, aim, is the more fruitful sequence if we want to take a linear snapshot of an organisation undergoing major reform. Ready is important, there has to be some notion of direction, but it is killing to bog down the process

with vision, mission, and strategic planning, before you know enough about dynamic reality. Fire is action and inquiry where skills, clarity, and learning are fostered. Aim is crystallising new beliefs, formulating mission and vision statements and focusing strategic planning. Vision and strategic planning come later: if anything they come at step 3, not step 1.

(Fullan 1993: 31)

Mintzberg (1994) extends and clarifies this point:

Ready, fire, aim makes a great deal of sense, as long as one gets to fire more than once, which is normally the case. Extend the phrase, and you have strategy formation as a learning process: 'Ready–fire–aim–fire–aim–fire–aim', etc. Just as structure must always follow strategy, . . . so too must firing always follow aiming, and precede it too, in order to make the necessary corrections. Action and thought must interact. Planners may be rightfully concerned about Rambo-type behaviour in management – 'fire–fire–fire' in every direction, with no aiming. But managers must be equally wary of planning behaviour that amounts to 'Ready. Aim. Aim'.

(Mintzberg 1994: 292)

This notion fits in with the analogy of the guided missile made earlier – the path rarely follows a straight line and corrections have to be made during implementation.

It is important for staff and governors to really try to envisage how they would like the school to be in, say, three years time. But unlike some writers who suggest that this should be an 'ideal', it is more useful to *picture a future that could actually be achieved*, bearing in mind current levels of resourcing and the present staff. It is futile to assume an unlimited budget, totally new buildings and a perfect staff!

The author has successfully used a vision-building exercise with the whole staff (and some governors) in a number of schools. People are asked to first think about the school as it is now and, individually, to write down what they like about it and would want to keep, under three broad headings: physical, curricular and inter-relationships. Then they are asked to think about how they would like the school to be in three years time – remembering to make it an achievable vision! They are asked to imagine that they can see the school and that their vision had been achieved. Looking down from above and seeing into the classrooms, the hall, the staffroom, the offices, the playground, etc. what would the school look like? They write down what would have changed under the same three headings as before. Each person's vision is then discussed in mixed groups and a summary of the points is produced to form a shared picture of the future of the school. Experience has shown that this exercise usually generates a considerable amount of agreement among the staff.

Stakeholder analysis

Who are the various groups who have a 'stake' in the school and are able to affect or be affected by what happens in the school? What do each of these groups require or demand from the school? To what extent is the school meeting their concerns? The strategic planning group should undertake a stakeholder analysis of the various groups, both inside and outside the school, as their perceptions and demands need to be taken into account when formulating the strategic plan. This type of analysis is an

Stakeholder Analysis Worksheet

Stakeholder Groups	Importance (Hi/Med/Lo)	Involvement (Hi/Med/Lo)	What criteria do the stakeholders use to assess the performance of the school?	My/our judgement of the current performance of the school Poor (1) – Very good (5)
1.				
2.				
3.				
4.				
5.				
6.				

Figure 19.2   Stakeholder analysis worksheet

important part of strategic planning as it sensitizes the SPG to the concerns of a wide range of people whose views may not always be given adequate consideration.

Figure 19.2 provides a format for analysing your views on a number of stakeholder groups which are entered in the first column. Use Hi/Med/Lo to indicate how important you think each group is to the running of the school. In the third column you should show the current level of involvement of the stakeholders with the school. Now you need to consider the criteria which you think the groups use to assess the performance of the school. (Each stakeholder group will probably have several criteria.) Finally, you must judge how well you think the school is currently doing on each of the criteria and indicate this with a number from 1–5 in the last column. The whole staff should complete a stakeholder analysis, first on an individual basis and then combining the views of each member to produce a group composite. Other groups such as governors, parents and students could also complete a stakeholder sheet. This technique provides a powerful stimulus for discussion and clarification of views.

The purpose of this exercise is not to demonstrate that a school could or should attempt to satisfy every wish of every group, but to enable values and expectations to be taken into account more systematically. It is also useful to know more clearly where there are overlaps in expectations among different groups, as well as where there are contradictory expectations! Obviously, the more individuals and groups are satisfied with the school, the better. A limitation of the exercise, however, is the way it treats groups in a stereotypical manner, without allowing for the differences in values and expectations between individual members of a group. So long as this limitation is borne in mind, the exercise can still provide valuable insights.

Internal and external scanning and review (SWOT analysis)

A key facet of strategic planning is to examine both internal and external factors, and the SWOT technique, which considers Strengths, Weaknesses, Opportunities and Threats, is widely used. The analysis looks internally to determine the school's areas of strength and weakness, and also at external trends – possible changes which could affect the school – under the headings: Political, Economic, Social, Technological and Educational (PESTE) and asks, what opportunities and threats do these pose for the school?

This activity can be undertaken either individually or with a group using brainstorming techniques, to produce a list of what you see as the internal strengths and weaknesses of your school. Then look ahead and list the possible external trends which you think are likely to affect the school during the next three to five years. You can think about these under the PESTE headings although some of the headings may overlap. Consider these trends as either opportunities or threats to the current running of the school and list them accordingly. A further refinement is to examine each of the opportunities and threats on your lists and consider, both how likely it is to occur and how powerful an effect it would have on the school, and to mark these as HIGH or LOW. This would focus particular attention on those trends which are seen as HIGH–HIGH, e.g. very likely to occur and cause a very powerful effect. Staff could use 'Post-Its', writing one issue on each and posting it on the appropriate SWOT sheet. 'Post-its are useful as they allow the items to be moved and regrouped. Having completed the analysis, you need to think about building on your strengths, overcoming weaknesses, exploiting the opportunities and blunting the threats.

This is a very simple but powerful technique. It has considerable potential for discussion, particularly if used with colleagues in school, or with groups including a variety of stakeholders, e.g. governors, parents, students, employers, etc.

Mission statements

The formulation of a mission statement is often recommended as one of the stages in strategic planning. A mission statement is a declaration of organizational purpose, designed to inspire and focus the efforts of all the members of the organization. They are usually short, no more than a page in length, and often simply a punchy slogan. The statement is generated from a discussion of the following six questions:

- Who are we – what is our identity?
- What are the basic needs we exist to fulfil?
- What do we want to do to recognize and respond to these needs?
- How should we respond to our key stakeholders?
- What is our philosophy and what are our core values?
- What makes us distinctive or unique?

(It is worth noting that it may not be possible, at this early stage, to say what qualities or attributes set the particular school aside from its neighbours.)

Developing answers to these questions is a valuable but very demanding process and the SPG may need several hours of discussion to reach a consensus. The group should carry out exercises such as the stakeholder analysis, the values audit and vision building, before completing a draft mission statement. The statement needs to be kept in front of the SPG, to act as a guide and reference point, as they move through the process, and the draft version may need to be revised. The final mission statement should be widely used with people both inside and outside the school as a basic reference point.

Gap analysis and prioritizing

At this stage, a careful analysis is needed to determine what are the gaps between the future vision and the current reality? A small number of priorities must be selected as it is not possible to do everything! What are the main priorities which emerge from a comparison between the shared vision, the stakeholder and SWOT analyses? Priorities should be established and the feasibility of the goals considered in terms of the availability of the necessary resources, time, money and people, etc. A number of prioritizing techniques exist to help schools, but ultimately, the priorities should be based on the values and vision identified earlier.

If the gaps between the current state and the desired future seem too large to bridge, then one of two actions is necessary:

1 Solutions for closing the gap must be developed.
2 The desired future must be redefined, with a focus on those aspects that are most likely to be accomplished and that will have the most significant impact.

Gap analysis is a time for candour and honesty. Can the gaps really be closed, given all the other things that you are trying to do? The SPG need to consider each gap, one at a time, and also look at their interaction. The answers may necessitate cycling back to some of the earlier stages and a reconsideration of the goals.

The school development plan and action plans

The production of the school development plan should provide a summary of the outcomes of the above process. More detailed action plans needs to be developed for each of the selected priorities. Hargreaves and Hopkins (1991) provide a very useful discussion of how this can be done.

As mentioned at the beginning of this chapter, schools have to produce an Ofsted action plan following the four-yearly inspection. The format is similar, though not exactly the same as that suggested by Hargreaves and Hopkins. A report was produced by Ofsted following HMI visits to a representative sample of 85 schools from the almost 1000 who had inspections in 1993–94. HMI found that most action plans had addressed the key issues identified by the inspectors, set out a clear timetable and person responsible for each aspect, and made some early progress in taking measures to improve teaching, raise expectations and address underachievement. But they found a lack of systematic evaluation. Only 4 per cent of the schools had set specific targets for improvement of achievement, 8 per cent had developed success criteria to evaluate the effectiveness of the proposed action and 6 per cent had assessed the full costs of resources. Those schools which required special measures received substantial and effective help from their LEAs in drawing up their action plans. Schools with serious weaknesses, but not formally identified as requiring special measures, did not receive sufficient support to produce an effective action plan (Ofsted 1995: 3–4).

Figure 19.3 shows a version of a planning sheet which has been developed by the author and used with schools. The action plan, ideally using one side of A4 paper for each of the priorities, or focus areas, contains a series of objectives, a list of tasks and activities, a time line showing dates when each activity should occur, any resources (money, equipment, Inset, etc.) which are needed, the key people responsible, any anticipated constraints, and a set of success criteria by which progress can be judged. Although not perfect, this format seems to provide staff with a very effective planning tool.

Monitoring and evaluation

It is important that evaluation is not something which is simply tacked onto the end of the cycle, as it seems to be in many models. On the main strategic planning diagram it is indicated that monitoring and evaluation should occur periodically throughout the whole cycle as a means of feedback. A distinction needs to be made between monitoring and evaluation, although in reality they often merge into each other.

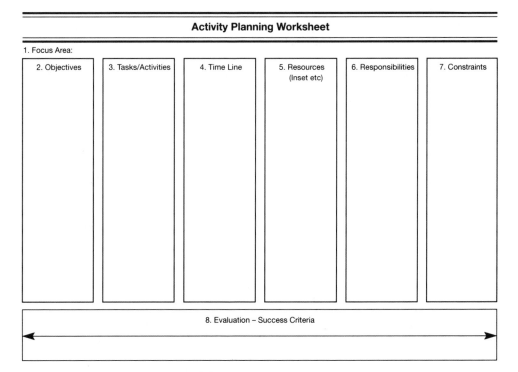

Figure 19.3 Activity planning worksheet

- 'Monitoring', like the everyday use of the term, is the checking that things are going as planned.
- 'Evaluation' is the deeper study of the impact and outcomes of the programme.

Critical success factors or performance indicators should be established at an early stage. As HMI reported, and the author's experience confirms, teachers tend to find producing the success criteria the most difficult part of the action plan. The staff directly involved need to decide, *what evidence can we produce that we are succeeding, and how do we get this evidence?* Success criteria can take the form of either quantitative or qualitative data depending on the issue. Some success criteria may be formative (occurring during the process) and others may be summative (at the end of a period); both types are usually needed.

Evaluation and monitoring play a key role in strategic planning as they provide the essential feedback needed throughout the process to make the necessary adjustments to the constantly changing situation. (Recall the guided missile analogy at the beginning of the chapter.)

Implementation

Having produced an agreed SDP and a set of action plans for each major topic, the difficult phase of implementation is now required. This is a crucial stage: even the best designed plans on paper fail if they are not carefully implemented. The lessons learned from the management of change are applicable to the implementation phase, and the reader is referred to Louis and Miles (1992), Fullan and Stieglebauer (1991), Fullan (1993), Wallace and McMahon (1994) and MacGilchrist *et al.* (1995) for useful guidance.

Most schools are now fairly well advanced with school development planning and it is hoped that this chapter has provided an introduction to strategic planning and sufficient practical assistance to help schools improve the process further. Trying to plan in times of tremendous change has been a difficult learning experience for most schools, but the majority have coped very well and managed to implement reforms such as the National Curriculum and other aspects of the Education Reform Act. We are now in a period of 'School Improvement', when all schools need to focus on the complex task of improving teaching and learning. The clarion call from people like Senge (1990) and others, is to become a learning organization, which if achieved in schools, means an improvement in both teachers' and children's learning. Strategic planning is a tool which can be used to help schools to become better learning organizations.

References

Andrews, K. (1980, 1987) *The Concept of Corporate Strategy*, 1st and 2nd editions respectively. Homewood, IL: Irwin.

Bennis, W. and Nanus, B. (1985) *Leaders*. New York: Harper and Row.

Bowman, C. (1990) *The Essence of Strategic Management*. New York and London: Prentice Hall.

Bryson, J. (1988) *Strategic Planning for Public and Non-profit Organisations*. San Francisco: Jossey Bass.

Cook, B. (1990) *Strategic Planning for America's Schools*. Arlington, VA: American Association of School Administrators.

Davies, B. and Ellison, L. (1992) *School Development Planning*. Harlow: Longman.

DES (1989) *Planning for School Development 1*. London: Department of Education and Science.

DES (1991) *Development Planning 2*. London: Department of Education and Science.

Fidler, B. (1989) Strategic Management: where is the school going?: A guide to strategic thinking, in B. Fidler and G. Bowles, *Effective Local Management of Schools*. Harlow: Longman/BEMAS.

Fidler, B. with Edwards, M., Evans, B., Mann, P. and Thomas, P. (1996) *Strategic Planning for School Improvement*. London: Pitman.

Fullan, M. with Stieglebauer, S. (1991) *The New Meaning of Educational Change*. London: Cassell.

Fullan, M. (1993) *Change Forces*. London: Falmer Press.

Hargreaves, D. and Hopkins, D. (1991) *The Empowered School*. London: Cassell.

Hargreaves, D. and Hopkins, D. (eds) (1994) *Development Planning for School Improvement*. London: Cassell.

Kaufman, R. (1992) *Mapping Educational Success: strategic thinking and planning for school administrators*. Newbury Park, CA: Corwin Press.

Louis, K. S. and Miles, M. (1992) *Improving the Urban High School*. London: Cassell.

MacGilchrist, B., Mortimore, P., Savage, J. and Beresford, C. (1995) *Planning Matters*. London: Paul Chapman.

McCune, S. D. (1986) *Guide to Strategic Planning for Educators*. Alexandria, VA: Association for Supervision and Curriculum Development.

Mintzberg, H. (1994) *The Rise and Fall of Strategic Planning*. London: Prentice Hall.

Muriel, J. L. (1989) *Strategic Leadership for Schools*. San Francisco: Jossey Bass.

Nias, J., Southworth, G. and Yeomans, R. (1989) *Staff Relationships in the Primary School*. London: Cassell.

Nutt, P. C. and Backoff, R. W. (1992) *Strategic Management of Public and Third Sector Organizations*. San Francisco: Jossey Bass.

Office for Standards in Education (OFSTED) (1995) *Planning Improvements: schools post-inspection action plans*. London: HMSO.

Paterson, J. L., Purkey, S. C. and Parker, J. V. (1986) *Productive Schools Systems for a Non-rational World*. Alexandria, VA: Association for Supervision and Curriculum Development.

Peters, T. (1987) *Thriving on Chaos*. London: Macmillan.

Peters, T. and Waterman, R. (1982) *In Search of Excellence*. New York: Harper and Row.

Pfeiffer, J. W., Goodstein, L. D. and Nolan, T. M. (1988) *Shaping Strategic Planning*. San Diego, University Associates.

Proctor, R. A. (1993) Strategic windows and entrapment, *Management Decision*, 31(5): 55–9.

Senge, P. (1990) *The Fifth Discipline*. New York: Doubleday.

Valentine, E. (1991) *Strategic Management in Education*. Boston: Allyn and Bacon.

Wallace, M. and McMahon, A. (1994) *Planning for Change in Turbulent Times*. London: Cassell.

20 | The impact of development planning in primary schools*

BARBARA MacGILCHRIST, PETER MORTIMORE,
JANE SAVAGE AND CHARLES BERESFORD

[. . .] Through a systematic analysis of the headteachers' and classteachers' accounts and a comparison of these with other sources of data, considerable evidence has been found to substantiate the hypothesis that four different types of development plans were in use across the nine schools [in our study] and that it was possible to identify the type of plan in use in each school.

Some key findings emerged in relation to this typology. It was found that school development plans (SDPs) did make a difference and that they had the potential to make a very significant impact on the school. The nature of that impact, however, was determined by the type of plan. The consequence of this was that some plans were found to be more effective than others in respect of identifiable improvements for the school as a whole, for teachers in classrooms and for pupils. The rhetorical plan was found to be the least effective; the corporate plan the most.

The effectiveness of the plan was associated with a set of characteristics which delineated each type of plan. The characteristics represented a number of key factors that appeared to be generic across the plans. They were factors which concerned a combination of the use of the process itself, that was determined by the degree of shared ownership, purpose, leadership and management of the plan, and the focus of the plan. It was the combination of these two factors which proved to be critical. The focus of the plan, not just the quality of leadership and management of the process, marks out the difference between the plans.

The main characteristics of the four types of SDPs derived from the empirical data

[. . .] The considerable differences between the four types [of SDP] are a reflection of

---

* This material has been abridged.

the different characteristics of each plan. What follows is a description of those characteristics.

The rhetorical plan

The rhetorical plan was characterised by a lack of a shared sense of ownership and purpose by both the headteacher and the classteachers. The written plan was not a working document and the leadership and management of the process was weak. This resulted in a limited sense of control over the process and a lack of confidence that benefits would ensue. Neither financial resources nor INSET were linked with the plan and monitoring and evaluation strategies were weak. The impact of the plan was a negative one. Teachers became frustrated and disillusioned and the headteacher was distanced from the staff.

The singular plan

The singular plan was characterised by a sense of ownership and purpose by the headteacher alone. The purpose of the plan was singular in nature. It was used as a tool to improve the efficiency of the management and organisation of the school and provided a means whereby the headteacher could be accountable to governors. It instilled a degree of confidence in the headteacher but the sense of control over the process was minimal. The written plan was not a working document and the leadership and management of the process was limited; the headteacher assumed the main responsibility for both. There was little or no financial and professional development to support the implementation of the plan, and monitoring and evaluation procedures were weak. The plan had a limited impact. It resulted in improved efficiency in relation to the overall management and organisation of the school, but there was no evidence of any impact on teachers and pupils.

The co-operative plan

The co-operative plan was characterised by a co-operative effort to improve. Whilst there was only partial shared ownership by the teaching staff of the content of the plan, there was a general willingness to participate in the process. The plan was perceived as multipurpose in nature. There was a dual emphasis on improving both the efficiency and effectiveness of the school with a noticeable focus on school-wide improvements and the professional development of teachers. The leadership of the plan was vested in the headteacher. However, the management of the process was shared among some key staff, many of whom were members of the senior management team. The written plan tended to be a working document. The implementation of the plan was supported by financial resources and a linked programme of professional development. Teachers' learning was seen to be important. There was a sense of growing confidence and control over the process, although involvement in the implementation of the plan tended to be confined to the teaching staff. The process was perceived as a complex and continuous one, although monitoring and evaluation procedures lacked rigour. The impact of the plan was a positive one. It resulted in improvements in whole-school management and organisation, professional relationships and teachers' effectiveness in the classroom. There was limited evidence, however, of improvements for pupils.

The corporate plan

The corporate plan was characterised by a united effort to improve. There was a strong sense of shared ownership and involvement by the teaching staff and an attempt was made to include others in the process. The plan was seen to be multi-purpose in nature and there was a sense of control over the process and confidence that it would lead to improvements in efficiency and effectiveness. The focus on teaching and learning, especially on improvements in the quality of pupils' learning, was a particular characteristic. The written plan was an open, working document and the leadership of the plan was shared among the senior management team. The complexity and continuous nature of the process were recognised and the management of the process was shared by all the staff. Financial resources and staff development were linked to the implementation of the plan and monitoring and evaluation strategies were sound. Teachers had a definite sense of responsibility for the outcome of the plan. The impact of the plan was significant across the school as a whole, for teachers in classrooms and for pupils' learning. A link could be discerned among school development, teacher development and pupils' development. There was evidence of a learning community within the school with headteachers and classteachers exhibiting the characteristics of reflective practitioners, continuously seeking to develop and improve their practice.

An analysis of the typology

The characteristics of each plan represent a continuum from the least to the most effective type of plan: a continuum in respect of the nature of the impact of the plan, from one that is negative to one that is very positive. However, the typology does not represent a linear, developmental process. It is not a stage theory of development planning. It was schools with co-operative and corporate plans that revealed this finding, in particular, Schools G and H. These two schools were engaged in co-operative and corporate planning respectively, although they had had little or no previous experience of planning in this way. The schools involved in co-operative planning were also on a continuum themselves and demonstrated how schools can change from one type of plan to another. School D was new to this type of plan, having previously had a rhetorical one, whereas Schools F and G were already beginning to demonstrate some of the characteristics of corporate planning.

The characteristics of the typology indicate a differential awareness of the complexity of development planning, with the rhetorical plan the simplest, the corporate plan the most sophisticated. What was particularly surprising was the finding that the more effective the plan, the more complex the characteristics appeared to be. Whilst this contradicts the message of much of the guidance which has been published on school development planning [. . .], it confirms what is known from the literature about the complexity of schools. It was interesting that the actual number of components and priorities in the plan were not a determining factor. What was more important was the main focus of the plan and therefore the nature of the priorities and the integrated nature of the planning process, especially the extent to which financial resources and the professional development programme were linked with the implementation of the plan.

The characteristics revealed a link between the extent to which there was a shared sense of agreement between the staff and the headteacher about the purposes and priorities of the plan and the effectiveness of the plan. Not unrelated was the fact that the two schools with the most effective plans had both established a policy statement about the aims and practices of development planning. In these policy statements a link had been made between the school's overall aims and the role of development planning in fulfilling these. In these schools development planning had become embedded into the culture of the school.

Shared ownership and involvement and shared leadership and management were noticeable characteristics of the most effective plan. The corporate plan was characterised by the degree to which all the teaching staff were engaged in the process. [. . .]

The implications of the findings for the headteacher and staff

A key finding of this study is that SDPs make a difference, but the nature of that difference is determined by the type of plan in use. Development planning can be used as a school improvement strategy but not all development plans lead to school improvement. There is one type of plan that, because of its particular characteristics, can improve learning opportunities for pupils. This is the type of plan which seeks to develop strong links among pupil learning, teacher development and school-wide improvements. For secondary schools, the latter are more than likely to incorporate departmental and interdepartmental improvements, as well as whole-school conditions. The key characteristics of this type of plan [. . .] concern issues to do with the extent to which there is a shared sense of purpose and ownership of the plan; the quality of leadership and management of the planning process; and the focus of the plan. These findings have considerable implications for headteachers, those with senior and middle management responsibilities and all classteachers. They also have implications for others who work in the school. These will be considered in respect of how plans are formulated, implemented, evaluated and reported.

The formulation of plans

One of the implications of our findings is that the formulation of a development plan is much more complex than the guidance available [. . .] suggests. Issues of particular importance concern the process of identifying priorities for development; who should be involved; the nature of the priorities for development chosen; the identification of success criteria; and the kind of document produced.

The audit

The identification of priorities for development is called, in the published guidance (DES 1989), the 'audit' stage. Our study has revealed that the content of that audit needs to be broadened. Headteachers and the senior management team need to ensure that the audit includes the following aspects:

- A review of the extent to which there is a shared sense of understanding about the purposes of development planning and an understanding that, although development planning is multipurpose in nature, the central purpose is to improve pupil progress and achievement.
- A review of the overall aims of the school and the relationship between these and the development plan. The review needs to ask the question, 'To what extent have the priorities in the plan which has just been implemented help to further the aims of the school?'
- An identification of the type of plan currently in use, using the characteristics of the corporate plan [. . .] to guide the analysis. For a new headteacher, it will be necessary to ascertain the type of plan used in the past. The action required as a result of this aspect of the audit will be determined by the type of plan identified. If it is a corporate plan, for example, it will be important to sustain and continue to improve the implementation and evaluation of the plan. If it is not a corporate type of plan, then this in itself should become a priority for change. The culture of the school in respect of professional relationships, organisational arrangements and opportunities for learning for teachers and pupils [. . .] will need to become the focus for improvement.
- An improved database for deciding priorities. To achieve and maintain a focus on pupil learning, evidence about the quality of teaching and learning in the classroom and the levels of achievement of the pupils, including differential levels of achievement across subjects and the school as a whole, needs to be gathered to enable future priorities for development to be identified and agreed by all. The study has revealed that during the implementation phase of the planning process, monitoring and evaluation strategies were weak in a number of the schools. This in turn means that limited information is available to feed back into the audit phase of the next planning cycle. Without sufficient information it is difficult for a headteacher or governing body to decide what needs to be developed next and what needs to be done to sustain the improvements achieved so far, so that the process really does become a continuous one.

Involvement in the audit

Included in the broadening of the audit process needs to be a reconsideration of who is involved in the process and the nature of that involvement. The study has shown that it is essential for teachers to have a shared sense of ownership of the plan. Without this, the plan is likely to have little or no positive impact and could result in a negative outcome, as was the case with the rhetorical plan. The study has also revealed that the definition of involvement varies depending on the type of plan, as exemplified, for example, by the singular type of plan. To achieve a united effort to improve, requires the kinds of strategies adopted by the schools engaged in corporate planning; strategies which enable teachers to play an active role in establishing priorities for development. We found that the involvement of teachers in the leadership and management of this aspect of the planning process was an important factor.

It is essential, however, that teachers do not perceive the plan as a threat to their professional autonomy. Rather, they need to be helped to understand and experience the benefits of taking a 'classroom exceeding perspective' (Hopkins 1989) and collaborating with, and learning from, others across a year group, a department and the school as a whole, as described by teachers engaged in co-operative and corporate plans. These should be the kinds of benefits which concern teachers' own learning and that of their pupils. [. . .] This should not be seen as a one-way process. At the same time, there is a need for headteachers and senior and middle management teams to have a *classroom perceiving perspective*. It is important for them to be able to focus on classrooms as part of the process of gathering evidence about aspects of teaching and learning which need to be improved further. Headteachers and their management teams need to develop strategies for knowing more about what goes on in classrooms. In this way, the identification of priorities for development can become a shared two-way process across the teaching staff as a whole.

Strategies for involving others are needed if the school is to achieve a more corporate approach to development planning. The study has revealed that the content of the plans are determined, on the whole, by the headteacher and, depending on the type of plan, by the teaching staff. There was evidence, however, from schools engaged in co-operative planning, and in corporate planning in particular, that they were opening up to include and take account of the views of others, such as support or associate staff as they have been called (Mortimore *et al.* 1994), pupils, parents and governors. [. . .] By engaging others in the audit and taking account of their views this should strengthen their sense of ownership, involvement and commitment to the plan.

The type of priorities for development chosen

One of the major findings of our study is that it is not the number of components and priorities in the plan but the focus for development chosen which appears to have an important bearing on the impact of the plan. This implies that when choosing priorities for development headteachers and teachers need to be clear about the distinction between *means and ends* in development planning. For example, whilst teacher development is, in one respect, an end in itself, it also needs to be seen as a means to improving pupil learning. Similarly, whilst improving organisational arrangements and professional relationships across the school as a whole and across departments are important priorities, the rationale for choosing these needs to reflect the extent to which such changes are likely ultimately to improve learning opportunities for pupils. The study has shown that the priorities chosen can enable the link between school-wide and departmental development, teacher development and pupils' own development to be strengthened and that this principle should guide the selection of priorities. Related to this, the study has also shown that when teachers recognise that there are priorities in the plan which will serve their own purposes in the classroom, they are more likely to be committed to their implementation.

The identification of success criteria

For the schools engaged in rhetorical, singular or co-operative types of plans, the identification of success criteria in respect of the priorities for development chosen is a weakness, despite its importance. It is the schools engaged in corporate planning which recognise the need to be more rigorous in deciding, at the outset, how the improvements sought are likely to be demonstrated in practice. They understand the necessity to select ways of assessing the subsequent effectiveness of the plan. Schools need to ask the question, therefore, 'How will we know we have made a difference?' The answer to this question will, in turn, indicate the nature of the evidence which needs to be gathered to monitor the implementation of the priorities for development and evaluate the outcomes of the plan.

The written plan

The evidence from our study is that the written plan needs to be formulated in such a way that it is an open, working document: a document which, rather than being a published finite statement of intent, is practical and flexible in nature and can be amended if necessary. We found that if this is the case it will be regularly referred to and progress and achievements will be recorded. It will thus be more likely to lead to the implementation of the chosen priorities for development. In several of the schools not only did individual members of staff have a copy of the plan but also a synopsis which was regularly amended and updated was on display for all to see. There also needs to be a shared understanding about who else needs to have a copy of the plan. The audience for the written plan and the purpose for providing it should determine its format and content. For example, agreement needs to be reached with governors as to whether or not they should receive the detailed operational plan or a synopsis. Similarly, the requirements of others, such as support staff, parents, the LEA or an inspection team, will also determine the nature of the written document they receive.

The implementation of the plan

The importance of the quality of the leadership and management of the implementation of the plan, and the extent to which this was shared by all the staff and others, proved to be one of our key findings. Practical issues of particular importance concern the establishment of an action plan; the identification of roles and responsibilities; the provision of financial support for the implementation of the plan; the provision of a programme of professional development for teachers; and the systematic monitoring of the process as well as the progress in implementing the priorities for development.

The action plan

All the schools recognised the need to establish an action plan which would enable the identified priorities for improvement to be realised in practice. However, it was only the schools engaged in co-operative and corporate types of plans which were able to draw up action plans in such a way that they led to improvements in the effectiveness of the school. An action plan, therefore, needs to include the identification of targets; tasks; roles and responsibilities; timescales; an effective communication system; and a system for regular review and monitoring. This has important implications in respect of the requirement to establish an action plan following an Ofsted inspection. Schools need to be clear about the relationship between this kind of action plan and action planning as part of the continuous development planning process. In practice the two should be combined and this will have considerable implications for the way the plan is led and managed.

Roles and responsibilities

Those engaged in co-operative and corporate types of plans recognised that integral to the success of the action plan is the identification and clarification of specific roles and responsibilities. These concern both the leadership and management of the process and a combination of shared and individual responsibility by all the teaching staff and, in some cases, other groups. This has important implications for the approach to leadership and management adopted by senior management and middle management teams and the extent to which this enables individual teachers to have delegated, personal responsibility for implementing an aspect of the development plan. The approach to leadership and management adopted by the headteachers engaged in corporate planning engendered in all those involved a sense of confidence and control over the process. For this to happen, there is a need for headteachers to delegate responsibility in such a way that those concerned not only have a remit to act and make decisions but also will be held accountable for the outcomes.

A problem common to all the schools is the limited time available for implementing the plan. All important, therefore, is the efficient management of the use of time. Those headteachers that had confidence in, and control over, the process, were constantly seeking ways of creating sufficient time for classteachers, and teams of teachers, to fulfil their roles and responsibilities in respect of the plan.

Financial support

Financial support directly linked to the implementation of the plan was found to be a characteristic only of the most effective types of plans. Schools need to decide not only how much money to spend on development activities but also the type of support needed. Supply cover will be necessary, not just for teacher release to work with and alongside others and to attend inservice training sessions but also to enable individual and teams of teachers to fulfil their leadership and management responsibilities in relation to the implementation of the plan. In addition, depending on the priorities in the plan, both in connection with sustaining past developments and introducing new ones, money will be needed to augment classroom resources and support departmental activities as well as school-wide improvements.

Staff development

In common with the previous issue, a programme of professional development directly linked to the implementation of the plan was found to be a characteristic of the most effective types of plans. The inservice training programme needs to serve at least two purposes and to take a variety of forms. The development of knowledge and skills in relation to the priorities for improvement is important and will require attendance at school-based and offsite workshops and courses; opportunities for teachers to learn with and from one another through, for example, paired work and teams of teachers working together; and the use of consultants and advisory support both from colleagues and from those bought in from outside. At the same time, there will be those members of staff who, because of their particular roles and responsibilities in relation to the implementation of the plan and oversight of the planning process, will require management development opportunities including attendance at appropriate offsite courses.

Our finding that the more complex and sophisticated the plan, the more effective it is, also has important implications for the professional development of headteachers. They need to ensure that the professional development programme for the school includes opportunities for them to develop and extend their own approaches to leadership and management and to learn more about the characteristics of the most effective types of SDPs.

Monitoring the implementation of the plan

A number of weaknesses emerged in relation to this aspect of the planning process. There was an absence of monitoring in those schools engaged in rhetorical and singular types of plans. Although monitoring was recognised as important by the schools involved in co-operative plans, in the main it was only the headteachers who fulfilled this responsibility. By way of contrast, for those involved in corporate plans, be they headteachers, senior staff or classteachers, monitoring was seen to be a shared responsibility requiring a range of strategies to reflect the different roles and responsibilities individuals held.

The implication of this finding is that strategies for monitoring the planning process itself, as well as progress in implementing the specific priorities for developments, need to be built into the action plan at the outset. A systematic set of procedures for regularly reviewing progress is essential. This emerged as an important lesson learned by those engaged in the more effective types of plans. The procedures need to include opportunities for different groups to meet on a regular basis. The size of the school, the management structure and the way responsibility for implementing the plan has been designated to different groups, as well as the number and range of priorities for development in the plan, will determine the frequency with which these groups will need to meet. The groups are likely to include the whole staff, the whole, or a subgroup of, the governing body, senior and middle management teams and task groups which may involve teaching staff and others, for example, associate staff, governors and pupils. These different groups need to have a clear monitoring role supported by an agreed system for communication and decision-making, to enable any problems to be overcome and any necessary changes to be made. The corporate plan demonstrates that the procedures also need to include opportunities for the exercise of individual responsibility in respect of monitoring a specific aspect of the plan. In this way, teachers' sense of ownership and involvement can be strengthened. Through such procedures regular feedback on progress is possible; the kind of feedback that not only identifies problems to be solved but also tasks successfully achieved. The latter should provide an important source of motivation for those involved.

The evaluation of the plan

[. . .] Monitoring and evaluation need to occur simultaneously throughout the implementation of the plan. The reason for creating a separate heading for evaluation here is that, like monitoring, this aspect of the planning process was a noticeable weakness in some of the schools. [. . .] It was found that self-management does not necessarily lead to improvements in the effectiveness of the school. For those involved in rhetorical and singular plans, little or no evaluation took place. The only evidence alluded to by respondents concerned the achievement of tasks identified in the plan, not their evaluation. Evaluation appeared to be equated with monitoring the implementation of the action plan itself. For the schools engaged in co-operative and corporate plans, however, there is a clear recognition of the importance of gathering a range of quantitative and qualitative evidence to enable the impact of the plan to be evaluated. [. . .] It was only those engaged in corporate plans who had a strong emphasis on the collection of data directly related to the work of teachers and pupils in the classroom.

These findings have important implications for practice. Integral to the action plan, and closely linked with the success criteria identified at the formulation stage, needs to be the systematic collection of evidence to enable the impact of the plan and the planning process to be evaluated. The lessons learned, particularly by those involved in co-operative and corporate plans, provide useful indicators as to the different aspects of development planning which need to be incorporated within the evaluation process. The impact of the agreed priorities for development must be assessed. Also important is an assessment of the strategies used in the planning process itself and the extent to which any of these can be improved upon. A third dimension of the evaluation should concern the culture of the school. This study has revealed that development planning can have a positive impact on those aspects which are an observable demonstration of the culture, namely, professional relationships, organisational arrangements and opportunities for learning.

The evidence gathered in relation to these different kinds of evaluation needs to include a range of quantitative and qualitative data in order to enable a comprehensive evaluation to be achieved. The priorities for development will determine the nature of the information needed for the evaluation. The kinds of quantitative data should be a combination of documentary evidence such as policy documents, inspection reports, schemes of work and teachers' plans; evidence of pupil progress, such as samples of work and records of achievements; and statistical data including, for example, pupils' academic attainment, progress and attendance. Qualitative data also need to combine observable evidence, such as environmental changes, new classroom resources and organisation and the quality of pupils' work in books and on display, with data related to the priorities for development which concern the attitudes and expectations of, for example, pupils, teachers, governors, parents and external visitors to the school. As revealed in our study, the focus of data collection is a particularly important issue. It is essential to ensure that improvements in the quality of teaching and learning in the classroom are central to the evaluation. It is the outcomes of these data analyses which need to feed back into the audit phase as the next cycle of development is formulated. At the same time, the process of evaluation should be continuous throughout the implementation of the plan. This will enable changes deemed appropriate to be made and unexpected new demands to be addressed.

Reporting the outcomes

[. . . There are] a number of issues concerned with who was informed about the outcomes of the development plan. At the end of the planning cycle all the headteachers said they communicated outcomes to governors. Beyond this, there is no unanimous agreement about other groups, although the LEA and parents were mentioned by at least two-thirds of the headteachers. By way of contrast, the teachers were noticeably unclear about this aspect of the process and there was considerable disagreement among them as to who, if anybody, was or needs to be informed.

Arising from this are two practical implications. The first concerns the need for a decision by the headteacher and senior management team about who should be involved in development planning and the nature of that involvement. The strong professional base of the plans has already been identified. As more groups become involved, such as associate staff, pupils, governors and parents, then communication about the progress and outcomes of the plan needs to be thought through and made clear.

The second implication concerns the multipurpose nature of development planning. Our study has confirmed that it can be used as a school improvement strategy. It has also confirmed that all the headteachers recognised that one of the purposes of development planning is to enable the school to become more accountable for its work. This was one of the reasons why all the headteachers reported outcomes to the governors despite the fact that not all the governing bodies required them to do so. The government-initiated national inspection programme heightens the importance of the accountability aspect of development planning, not least because it forms part of the inspection procedures. More attention needs to be given as to how, and to whom, outcomes are reported. The governors, in particular, need to pay closer attention to this issue as it relates to their role in development planning.

The implications of the findings for governors

The implications of this study are that governors find it difficult to become involved in, and informed about, school development planning, not least because of the lack of clarity in general about their role and responsibility in respect of the leadership and management of the school. There needs to be a shared understanding among governors, the headteacher and the senior management team about the purposes of development planning and the characteristics of the type of plan most likely to improve the effectiveness of the school. Governors should have a role in the formulation of the plan, not least to enable them to exercise their responsibility in respect of the curriculum, special educational needs and budgetary decisions linked with the priorities for development chosen. Ways need to be found to include governors in the auditing process if a more corporate approach to planning is to be achieved and if governors are to fulfil their responsibilities in relation to the action plan which they are required to establish following an Ofsted inspection.

The involvement of governors in the implementation and evaluation of the plan was found to be problematical. There is a tension in the findings. On the one hand, governors were content for the headteacher and staff to exercise the day-to-day leadership and management of the plan. On the other hand, governors wanted a role in monitoring the plan. Linked with this was their limited ability to evaluate the impact of the plan and their heavy reliance on the headteacher's report of the outcomes. Ways need to be found to enable governors to be better informed about the impact of the plan. [. . .]

The implications of the findings for LEAs

Our national survey revealed four types of LEA involvement in development planning. However, despite the initial surge of activity and interest in relation to SDPs, which was indicated in the LEA survey, there is little evidence from our subsequent study of this being sustained. During the time of the data collection the role of LEAs was changing considerably as a result of the 1988 legislation about local management and the devolution of financial responsibility to schools. The subsequent legislation about school inspections was also beginning to have an impact. The interviews with the personnel in the three LEAs in our study reveal a change in the nature of LEA involvement in development planning with a noticeable shift from support to monitoring. It would appear that the local authorities in our study are no longer able to provide a coherent infrastructure of support for the schools in respect of advice and inservice training. The practical implications of this, given the findings of the study, are a cause for concern. Our research has revealed the differential impact of SDPs and the need for 'stuck' schools with, for example, rhetorical or singular plans, to have external support to enable them to change from the current type of plan to a more effective one.

Our study indicates that what is required is an external infrastructure of support which:

- enables those advising and inspecting a school locally to do their own audit of the type of development plan in use and the school's collective understanding of the complex nature of the development planning process. This, in turn, will determine the kinds of support and intervention required;
- complements, as well as helps to develop, a school's own self-evaluation procedures through the external evaluation of the planning process and its impact;
- provides opportunities for headteachers and teachers to engage in school development planning moderation whereby they can share and learn from one another; and
- provides an inservice education programme which meets three specific needs related to school development planning. Advisory support and professional development opportunities for teachers and others will be needed in respect of the specific focuses for development. Similarly, management development opportunities for staff assuming specific management responsibilities in relation to the plan will be required. For headteachers and those seeking headship, a professional development programme is needed which enables them to understand the complexity of development planning and to develop and strengthen their approach to the leadership and management of the plan.

[. . .]

Concluding comments

The history of school development planning is relatively short. Since the recommendation by the Thomas Committee in 1985 that 'every school should have a plan for development . . . and the central purpose should be expressed in terms of the improvements sought in children's learning' (ILEA 1985: para. 3.94), [our] LEA survey has revealed that school development planning has become part of the practice of schools in almost every LEA throughout the UK. International studies reveal their introduction and use in a number of other countries.

Underlying this rapid expansion of development planning is an assumption, made particularly by policy-makers, that SDPs will improve schools; they are the answer to self-management and as such will make schools more effective. The findings of this study challenge these assumptions.

Our study has revealed that development planning is much more complex than many of those advocating its use have recognised. Its complexity is, in many respects, a reflection of the complexity of schools and the change process itself. Hargreaves and Hopkins (1993: 239) argue that 'the advantage of school development planning . . . is that it provides a means whereby knowledge about school improvement strategies can be put to the test of practice'. This study, through its focus on the process and impact of development planning in nine primary schools, has endeavoured to put that knowledge to the test. It has shown that school development planning can be used as a school improvement strategy, but that the extent to which this becomes a reality in practice is dependent upon the type of development plan in use. Of the four types identified, only one was found to have a positive impact on student, teacher and school-wide improvements. The main contribution of this study has been to identify the characteristics of this type of plan; characteristics which have implications for both the theory and practice of school improvement.

References

DES (1989) *Planning for School Development: advice for governors, headteachers and teachers.* London: HMSO.
Hargreaves, D. and Hopkins, D. (1993) School effectiveness, school improvement and development planning, in Preedy, M. (ed.) *Managing the Effective School.* London: Paul Chapman.
Hopkins, D. (1989) *Evaluation for School Development.* Milton Keynes: Open University Press.
ILEA (1985) *Improving Primary Schools.* London: ILEA.
Mortimore, P. *et al.* (1994) School development planning in primary schools, in D. Hargreaves and D. Hopkins (eds) *Development Planning for School Improvement.* London: Cassell.

21 | Leading projects*

TREVOR L. YOUNG

What is a project?

A simple definition [of a project] is just a 'special task'. This suggests it is something that is outside normal day to day operating activities. [. . .] It is when the organisation realises a new approach is needed that the magic words 'special task' pop up. The new approach is separated from the day to day activities if only for the reason that the team are too busy to devote time to coming up with a solution. [. . .] The 'special task' starts to take on a new appearance. It is suddenly something unique and special and it is realised that there is a definite need to carry out this task in a different manner from normal day to day operations.

So everything that happens during the execution of the 'special task' is regarded as part of a temporary group of activities, unique to the task and set apart from operations. The 'special task' has been born as a PROJECT.

The project therefore has defined constraints and specified results required by the organisation.

A project can be defined as:

A group of activities which are carried out within a clearly defined time and cost to reach a set of specific objectives.

A project has particular characteristics:

- has a specific purpose;
- it is usually not routine;
- comprises interdependent activities;
- has defined time constraints;
- often complex;
- has defined cost constraints;

---

* This material has been abridged.

- subject to cancellation;
- flexible to respond to further change;
- involves many unknowns;
- involves risk.

Projects are traditionally perceived as highly technical activities carried out by engineers and technologists. [. . .] In most organisations managers have projects that are smaller in size and duration. They are not necessarily very technical in engineering or scientific content, but retain most of the characteristics of a project.

The tools, techniques and methods employed to manage all projects are the same and only differ in their selection and application depending on the duration and complexity of the work. Complex analytical planning and monitoring tools are not usually selected for use on short projects that involve only a few people. Other simpler methods and procedures are applicable with such projects.

Projects can be divided into two broad categories:

- Hard
- Soft

There is no clear definition of each type because many 'soft' projects eventually become 'hard' in the latter stages of the project. A project may start [. . .] at the conceptual stage with vague boundaries and limits. This allows flexibility and a creative climate to prevail. As the work of the project progresses the soft edges of the project boundaries start to take a more defined shape. The objectives become clearer and specific, and realistic deadlines for achieving results are agreed. The initial softness of the project disappears and a 'hard' project develops. [. . .]

Table 21.1 gives some common properties for each category of project.

Table 21.1   Properties of projects

Hard projects	Soft projects
Clearly defined objectives	Objectives broadly stated
Scope identified	Scope wide open intentionally
Constraints generally known	Many constraints unknown at start
Specifications established at start	Specifications part of project
Planning based on past experience	Planning limited at start – little experience
Skills required known at start	Skills required assessed continually
Resources readily identified	Resources not easily identified at start
Base plan fixed at start	Base plan difficult to establish
Control process usually in place	Control process custom designed
Quality standards exist	Quality standards written during project
Performance standards fixed at start	Performance standards flexible
Team structuring during planning	Team structuring flexible
Organisation for projects established	Organisation for projects missing
Risk limited and predictable	Risk unpredictable
Success criteria agreed at start	Success criteria change with time
Project cost defined at start	Project cost difficult to define
Project duration fixed at start	Project duration flexible
Constant leadership	Leadership moves during project

The role of the project leader

As a project comprises a unique set of activities combined to achieve specific objectives, your role as the project leader is often complex. It probably only occupies part of your daily routine. It is outside the traditionally accepted line hierarchy in the organisation and requires links to your colleagues and managers at all levels. These links are specifically only for the work of the project during its life and create a large number of short term relationships which form part of a matrix.

This matrix embraces the small team assigned to the project. They are dedicated to spend a part of their time on the project. This is in contrast to many other people at all levels in various functional areas who have inputs to make, who are not operating with similar priorities to the project team. The co-ordination of the efforts of all these people and the project team is an essential part of your role as the project leader.

For the project to progress you have to respond to changing needs and demands in ways which are not always clearly defined within established procedures or accepted practices. These usually do not exist either formally or informally. In practice you will probably need to adopt methods, in the interests of the project, which break across accepted boundaries and confront the traditions and culture of the organisation. At times you will feel left outside the normal hierarchy in the role, vulnerable to opposition from people at all levels whom you previously regarded as your colleagues and friends. [. . .]

As the project leader you are:

- responsible for achieving project objectives;
- clearly in charge and in a position of high risk;
- limited in authority to get resources internally and externally;
- expected to get results, cutting across established customs;
- operating in unknown and unpredictable areas;
- susceptible to low credibility with other managers;
- regarded with distrust by those not involved.

As the leader you are obliged to operate in an environment where you must:

- examine self performance continually;
- ensure team leadership stays positive;
- manage the client, end users and all those with an interest;
- manage project integration and interfaces;
- ensure the expectations of all those involved are satisfied;
- monitor progress and track project targets and deadlines;
- ensure plans are accurate;
- keep resource levels in line with plans;
- maintain senior management commitment;
- attend to teamworking to maintain high performance.

So you have a difficult role to fulfil with many operating areas and activities that rarely, if ever, are of major concern in hierarchical line management. A priority for you is to 'manage' all those people who have an interest in the project at any stage of the project life cycle, regardless of their level of involvement. If success is to be achieved then the effective management of performance is essential at all stages of the project life.

There are three functional areas to your new role:

- managing all those with an interest in the project;
- managing each phase of the project effectively;
- managing performance of the people.

[. . .]

Getting the project in context

[. . .] When you start, the project data available are limited, often just a general description or 'terms of reference' which may be supported by a feasibility study carried out much earlier. The project specification is probably vague – 'to allow flexibility'. Little planning has been carried out and no one has any real idea what is involved.

The project will certainly have some objectives, although these are not always immediately obvious to you. The stated objectives are often unclear and sometimes even misguided. Availability of resources has probably received little attention but there could be a budget limit set. The information available to you is constrained by personal and organisational influences of those involved at the conceptual stage of the project. You will have many distractions at this point, principally day to day operational activities. These have to continue and the project role is an additional burden for you which can lead to additional stress.

If the project is to get a good start, [. . .] at an early stage you will consider the resources available and start to assemble the core team for the project. This may comprise people from your own team or close associates.

The next major leap forward is the key to the success of the whole project. It is made up of two giant steps:

- getting the project in context;
- identifying all those with an interest in the project. [. . .]

Both you and the core team need to be clear on the context of the project in the overall organisation. You need answers to questions such as:

- How does this fit into [the organisation's] strategy?
- Why is it necessary?
- What has been done before?
- What is the real purpose of this project?
- Why are we selected for the project?
- What will we gain from the project if it succeeds?
- What happens if we fail?
- What will the organisation gain from the project?
- What are the expectations of the senior management?

Getting answers to these and many other similar fact finding questions creates a vision for the project and removes some of the [uncertainty]. The core team will become 'involved' with the project, gaining acceptance of the need for their future efforts. They will understand the reasons behind the project and the risks to be faced in the process of change that the project is to achieve. This is the first great step you take to build commitment in the project team.

Identifying the stakeholders

The stakeholders comprise a group of people who have an interest in the project. This starts with you and the core team since your interest is obvious. In every project the interest in the results is not limited to this group. There are always many others with a vested interest in all or parts of the project life-cycle as well as the results achieved finally.

Every project will have a sponsor, a senior manager who is directly sponsoring the project and is often accountable at senior level. [. . .]

Each project has its own group of stakeholders and it is clearly important to try to identify them all at this early stage. All of them have an input to make and they will all have a different perception of the needs, purpose and objectives of the project. [. . .]

The stakeholders have their own individual strategy, mission and strengths and weaknesses. Each has their own hidden agenda, in the same way as you and your team members, who as individuals, have aspirations to personal gain from their involvement. [. . .]

The stakeholders fall into two groups:

- Internal
- External

You have first to secure the support and commitment of the internal stakeholders. Since they all work for the same organisation this is theoretically preset by the decision to proceed with the project.

In practice this is not so simple. There is always a political dimension to be considered that influences the degree of co-operation across functional barriers at all levels. You often have to work hard to secure the support and commitment the project needs for success. The project has to compete with other projects as well as day to day operations to acquire the essential resources. Other colleague managers may believe they should have the project responsibility because they believe they could do a better job. [This] can create difficult relationships and conflict for you.

The external stakeholders cover a wide range of possibilities from the end user and client (who may not be the same), to the local community, external institutions, suppliers, consultants and contractors. Their influence may be central or on the fringes, at the start or much later in the project life cycle.

You have limited authority over many of these stakeholders and will often have difficulty influencing them to advantage. It is a formidable challenge to manage them effectively and ensure they remain positive in supporting you to achieve the project objectives.

The effective project leader

As the project leader you are working to get results with and through other people – the project team. One key element to success is your ability to energise and direct this diverse group to give high performance, willingly, throughout the project life.

The individuals in the team come from different parts of the organisation and have different priorities, experiences, skills and interests. In many organisations different departments have their own departmental culture. Inter-departmental barriers exist as departments protect their interests. You have to overcome these barriers and create a climate of co-operation and co-ordinate the team's efforts successfully. You must *lead* and also *motivate* the members of the project team often with minimal legitimate line authority over their actions.

To be seen as an effective project leader you have to orchestrate the work, manage the numerous inter-departmental interfaces, seek and co-ordinate all the skills necessary to achieve results. You have to manage *the process* aspects of project management as well as the people involved. The process is dependent on identifying the right skills necessary for the project at any particular time and ensuring they are used effectively in accordance with the plans and schedules. [. . .]

Everyone is an individual in the way the job is done. Everyone has a particular behaviour pattern which is influenced by many factors, both intrinsic and extrinsic. Although most people display a range of behaviour patterns it is common to examine such behaviour at two extremes of a spectrum. [. . .]

[Leadership] style theories are usually based on the range of behaviours perceived between total autocracy and democracy. The style adopted in any situation has an important impact on the members of the project team. The extremes of style can be summarised as:

- *Autocratic leader*
  You *dictate* what should be done, how and when. Beyond that you expect things to be done and avoid being involved in problem solving or external influences on the progress of the work. You are only really interested to know that the tasks are complete on time.
- *Democratic leader*
  If autocratic leadership is the traditional style then the democratic style is the contemporary approach to maximum participation. You *involve* everybody in all aspects of the team's activities. There is more discussion and consultation in decision making and taking. Team member skills and creativity are actively encouraged by you creating a climate to help everybody achieve project, team and personal goals.
- *Laissez-faire leader*
  It is worth mentioning this style which is often found to exist in practice. This leadership style describes you when you have effectively *abdicated* into the team. All the team members work on their own as independent units, including you. The team is no longer a team but becomes a *work group* with only personal objectives dominant. Team spirit and project objectives are lost in a fog of indecision, poor planning and inadequate co-ordination of effort. Project success is unlikely with the group members behaving in sometimes unpredictable ways to protect themselves.

It is widely recognised that a participative style is preferred in most organisations because it allows the employees to feel involved in their work. This is a major element of motivation at work. In project work a participative style is certain to yield better results, if only because of the wide range of skills employed at each stage of the project process. Participative leaders are not afraid to get their hands soiled by doing some of the work with the team. When the need arises, you adopt a high enough profile and position to make your power and influence felt to the benefit of the project and the team.

The key challenge for you as the project leader today is to anticipate changing situations and respond appropriately, using available skills in the team to keep the project momentum towards its objectives. You can only respond to this challenge with actions in all parts of the project process to get results. This *functional approach* is essential to project leadership. The action-centred leadership developed by John Adair (*Effective Leadership*, Gower Press, 1983) identifies the functions of an effective leader with a balance between the needs of the team, the individuals and the tasks they are performing. [. . .]

The project leader is in a position to ensure that the project objectives are kept in high profile at all times and keep the project process going in the right direction. In this process you are constantly monitoring that:

- scheduled work is carried out;
- deadlines are met on time;
- the team is working well together;
- all individuals are equipped with the skills needed.

You are always moving between the three functional areas co-ordinating the work, making sure the team has sufficient resources and is clear about its purpose and responsibilities. Any individual having problems will need guidance or assistance to meet the deadlines and complete the current tasks. Throughout these activities you are concerned to stand back and take an overview from the centre, to see that everything is going to plan.

If you are confined to these areas of activity then the project process is likely to be effectively under control. But you are operating in a confined situation – the inner working of the project process – and are therefore *inner directed*.

Earlier it was concluded that you also have to manage all those with an interest in the project throughout its life. These stakeholders are on the outer fringes of the project process as most are probably not involved in the day to day operating activities of the project team. Yet they can influence the project directly and indirectly and must be brought into your sphere of operating control. [. . .] So apart from concern for the inner working of the project process, you must expand your sphere of influence. All the stakeholders must be brought into the operating area and your efforts must also become *outer directed*.

As the project leader you are therefore faced with the holistic role of managing and controlling the project process, the team, the team members and all the stakeholders to achieve the objectives. This is achieved in practice by your continual migration between the two positions of being inner and outer directed, balancing the needs and expectations of each area to reach the objectives. This is shown on the leadership model in Figure 21.1.

This wide ranging role brings additional pressures on you to have good influencing and negotiating skills to keep all the elements in balance. The potential for conflicts arising is fairly high as the individual agendas of everybody involved surface over particular issues, problems and projected plans. You need tact and diplomacy but good communication skills are clearly essential for this balancing process to succeed.

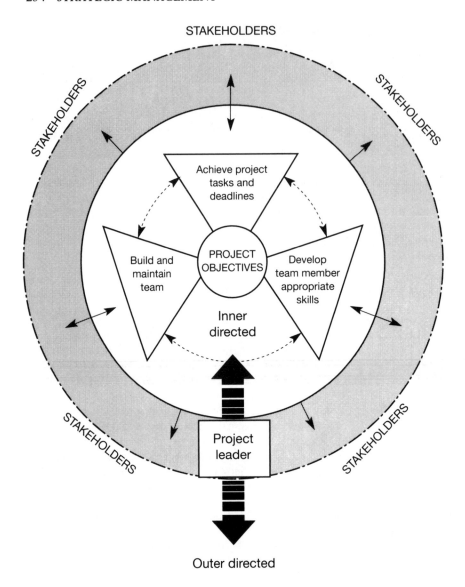

Figure 21.1 The objective-centred project leader

The leader's action cycle

At every stage of the project you will follow a process which has five basic steps. This process is applicable to the project as a whole through the four basic phases of the project life. It is equally applicable to any individual part of the project plan such as one key task to be completed.

Step 1: Defining the objectives and deadlines

You need to define the overall project and task objectives, at the same time making sure that the team understands these in context. You must take particular care at this point to ensure that everyone can accept their involvement in the work ahead as this is essential to building commitment. Deadlines form an integral part of these short, medium or long term objectives with clearly identified results and the benefits expected. The scope of the project is specified and you demonstrate your own commitment and enthusiasm for the project.

Step 2: Preparing the plan and schedules

With clear objectives established the planning process usually follows two stages – fact finding and decision taking. In each you will involve the team members as a team building activity. This helps you to create the right climate for generating acceptance and commitment to the work to be carried out.

- *Fact finding* is an information gathering process to ensure that all relevant data are collected together for the planning process. You encourage ideas and suggestions to be tabled and consult with team members, colleagues and others to generate all available relevant data on any particular aspect of the project. This will comprise a mixture of historical experience, facts, opinions and legend which has to be sorted and filtered to provide really useful data.
- *Decision taking* is the process of drawing conclusions for action from the alternatives and options generated in the consultative stage. This signals the termination of gathering data and using the data to generate the plans in a format which everyone can use and understand. The presentation of this information will vary in complexity according to who needs it and how it is to be used. In certain types of projects it is often prudent to keep some options available as contingencies if a recognised possible sequence of events does occur.

Step 3: Briefing the team and stakeholders

Having identified all the activities of the plan it is essential you inform everybody involved what has to be done, when things are to be done and the deadlines. This stage is vital to generating 'ownership' in the team and the stakeholders. [. . .]

Step 4: Monitoring progress and support

You must now ensure motivation is maintained at a high level, dealing promptly with problems as they arise. [. . .] This involves you in 'management by walking about' to keep yourself well informed on what is happening and giving support, guidance and assistance where necessary. This visible leadership is essential to encourage the team and show an interest in their welfare and progress. You will not be in a position of control by adopting a distant position – 'management by walking away'. This will lead to poor teamwork and you being poorly informed of the real state of affairs with the project progress.

Step 5: Evaluating results

Evaluation is not a terminal activity! Although you will surely evaluate the performance at the end of the project, you must actively evaluate on a day to day basis. Through regular contact with the team and the stakeholders you determine if the project is on the right track and the results are meeting expectations. Through this active evaluation you can determine if changes are necessary and take steps to implement modifications to your plans. When the project finally reaches the declared point of completion, then you carry out a full post-project evaluation to appraise the performance of yourself and the team throughout the project. It is important to identify the key learning points gained from experience during the project and record these for future reference.

These five steps can be regarded as a cyclic process within the four phases of a project from conception through to termination. They apply to the project in total and any dependent group of tasks. This is shown in Figure 21.2.

In practice the action cycle is a multitude of cycles, each at different stages of progress. At any time blockages can appear to interfere and cause a hold up. This may be due to new information becoming available, poor fact finding initially or just poor communications within the team and between the team and the stakeholders. You may find the objectives revised as one or more stakeholders 'move the goal

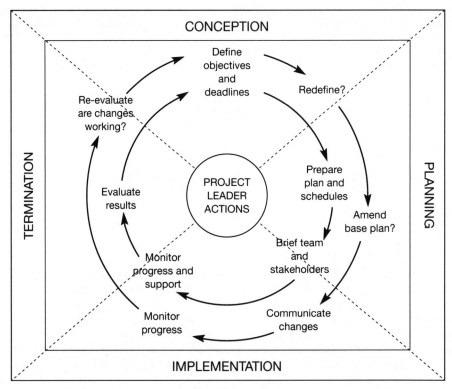

Figure 21.2   The action cycle in the project life cycle

posts' without informing you in good time to prevent wasted effort. Your plans may show shortcomings as the team comes up with better ideas and you must decide whether to modify the schedules.

In fact at any stage of any cycle there is the possibility that the processes may need repeating to resolve problems and derive ways to bypass the blockages. This is a dynamic process that enables you to maintain control and keep the project momentum. These five steps are the key results areas where you take action as project leader to achieve ultimate success. [. . .]

22 Scanning the market: school strategies for discovering parental preferences

CARL BAGLEY, PHILIP WOODS AND RON GLATTER

Introduction

[. . .] Schools have always competed to some degree for the available pupils in an area and undertaken what can be perceived as marketing activities, such as open evenings, fetes, and school shows (Cave and Demick 1990). However, the introduction of more open enrolment and the realisation that under formula funding each new pupil brings in a substantial sum of money have put marketing to parents much higher up the school agenda. This is reflected in general texts on school management, which now invariably cover marketing, and an increasing number deal with the subject exclusively (see for example, Gray 1991; Barnes 1993; Pardey 1994).

Marketing is not considered to be concerned only with presentation, advertising and selling (Gray 1991). It clearly includes communicating and persuading as part of promotion and public relations, but transcends these to embrace qualities such as listening and responding. It is through such processes that marketing is seen as improving the entire quality of service (The Open University 1993). In educational terms this relates to the concept of the 'responsive school' as described, for example, by the National Association of Headteachers (1990).

For marketing to be effective, schools need to have a clear view of what parents think, how they make decisions, and what they look for in a school. It also requires schools to have effective means of acting on this knowledge and understanding.

The Parental and School Choice Interaction (PASCI) Study[1] is investigating the interaction between parental choice of school and school decision-making – how secondary schools respond to competition and how parents react to these responses. Two of the research questions it is seeking to address are the following:

- Are schools making changes of substance (in curriculum, teaching methods, management, planning, and so on) as a result of the heightened competitive environment? (see Woods, Bagley and Glatter 1996).

- If so, do these changes represent what parents are actually looking for in a school, or do they represent only what school decision-makers think parents want?

The second of these questions focuses our thinking on the extent to which schools find out about and consider, or 'scan and interpret', parental perspectives and preferences, an issue to which we turn in the next section. In that section we draw upon interviews with senior managers and teachers which took place in 1993 at 11 secondary schools. These schools are located in three case study areas in which the PASCI Study is concentrating its research activity. A brief outline of the case study areas is given below (names of the areas and schools are fictitious).

Marshampton
Marshampton is a town of approximately 100,000 people with an above-average representation of professional and middle class households. It has a long history of competition between schools (both state and private, though the latter educate less than 10 per cent of pupils in Marshampton). All six, state secondary schools have become grant maintained. Five are comprehensive schools (Bridgerton, Thurcleigh Hill, St Asters Catholic High, Daythorpe and Endswich). One is an academically-selective grammar school (Salix Grammar). Salix Grammar and Bridgerton, and more recently Thurcleigh Hill, are over-subscribed each year. Endswich is in the most difficult position, with the poorest reputation and falling admission numbers.

East Greenvale
East Greenvale (an administrative district of Greenvale Local Education Authority) is a semi-rural area consisting of three small towns and a large number of villages. The education system in the area is organised as a 'pyramid' with an upper school at the pyramid head taking pupils at age 13 from its 'feeder' middle schools and the latter receiving pupils at age 9 from their 'feeder' first schools. There are three upper schools in East Greenvale (Molehill, Dellway and Elderfield), one in each of the small towns.

Northern Heights
Northern Heights is an area which displays many of the deprivations characteristic of many parts of urban Britain, with above-average levels of working class households, poor housing, unemployment, and so on. There is an identifiable ethnic minority community (approximately 5% of the population), which is predominantly of Bangladeshi origin. Northern Heights is not a distinct administrative area (it is a part of Northborough Local Education Authority) but appears to resemble in many respects a local competitive arena. It contains three secondary schools: Braelands (on the edge of the area in a semi-rural setting), Leaside (in a run-down housing estate set apart from the main urban area), and Newcrest (located in the main urban area and near to the ethnic minority community).

Scanning and interpretation

In considering the strategies adopted by schools, Daft and Weick's (1984) model of organisational 'scanning and interpretation' provides a useful tool for approaching the study of schools and their environments. According to this, model organisations vary in their stance towards environments which they may perceive as either fixed, measurable and understandable through rational analysis, or as being more or less flexible, requiring a more spontaneous, intuitive, less prepared form of analysis.

Similarly, the degree of organisational activity aimed at understanding the environment varies. Some organisations will be pro-active, conducting systematic research, while others will be more laissez-faire in their approach, receiving information as it happens to come their way.

In the context of the PASCI Study scanning and interpretation refers to whether and in what ways the research schools conduct activities aimed at knowing more about their environment. The report of our data presented here focuses on the ways by which the research schools gain more knowledge about parents, the major stakeholder group in terms of the schooling quasi-market created in recent years.

Following Daft and Weick's general approach, we report this data under the headings 'systematic and planned feedback' and 'ad hoc feedback'.

Systematic and planned feedback

The following examples of systematic and planned attempts by schools to identify and interpret parental viewpoints were found amongst the PASCI Study's research schools: surveys by means of questionnaire; use of secondary source survey data; a school strengths and weaknesses exercise; selective monitoring of pupils' primary school origins; monitoring of baptismal records and numbers of children in primary schools.

Three years ago Braelands undertook a one-off public opinion survey. This involved Year 11 (16-year-old) pupils with questionnaires stopping and asking the public in the town centre for their views of the school. The Deputy Headteacher at Braelands admitted that in relation to marketing the school 'market research was the weakest area'. While he acknowledged its importance as a strategy, systematic and planned attempts at obtaining feedback were seen as too time consuming and complex. He believed staff did not have either the time or the necessary skill to draft questionnaires and analyse the results to make sure they were valid.

The school does however monitor the views of parents who had chosen the school. Parents who have selected and whose children will be attending Braelands are asked to complete a form indicating the reasons for their choice. As a popular oversubscribed school this exercise is not undertaken to identify areas for change but to ensure that the school's existing standards are maintained and its popularity with parents (particularly middle class parents of more academically able children) continues.

Neither Newcrest nor Leaside schools engage in any systematic or planned scanning of parental perspectives. Nevertheless, senior staff in both schools indicated that they had made use of findings arising from other surveys which involved their schools. They had participated in LEA-wide research on school attendance, which included interviews with a cross section of parents eliciting their views on the school. The findings of the study surprised the Headteacher at Leaside as parents' 'vision of the school was better than the vision of quite a few of our staff'. Parents did however express concern about discipline.

As a result Leaside hopes to improve the school's reputation with the introduction of an assertive discipline policy. Moreover, the Headteacher states:

If we are going for assertive discipline then we're going to have to say to parents, right, this is what we want to do, do you agree with this? If we don't ask then we don't know what they think about it, and invite them in if they're interested enough to come and have a look at videos about assertive discipline. Talk to them about it. Get their agreement and then say right, we've got this in place . . . It will make us a better school.

(Headteacher, Leaside)

The school having picked up on an issue which parents deem to be important is seeking to meet that demand not just by introducing an assertive discipline policy, but by involving parents in its development. Whilst this initiative involves existing as distinct from prospective parents, the Headteacher hopes that by showing his school to be responsive on the issue of discipline it will not only improve the school but make what is at present an under-subscribed school more popular.

Ensuring a good school reputation also featured as the rationale behind a systematic attempt at Braelands to identify the school's strengths and weaknesses. Teaching and ancillary staff participated in a brainstorming exercise to identify major internal threats to the school's reputation and areas of the school that could benefit from improvement. Issues such as the prevalence of litter around the school, chewing gum on school seats and pupil behaviour on buses were raised rather than any substantive curriculum or organisational matters. These responses were based on the staff's own perceptions about the school and their assumptions about what might influence parental choice.

In Marshampton, there has been little to report in relation to systematic and planned efforts at scanning and interpretation. Most effort has been put in by St Asters (a Roman Catholic comprehensive). The Headteacher explains some of the efforts that have been made, and also illustrates how such systematic approaches inter-weave with less formal ones:

I've done it [finding out what parents want] by talking to people, talking to the staff, talking to the clergy and listening to any comments the parents make when they visit on, say, open evenings. Also the year before I came here [Headteacher started in 1992] a number of efforts were made to try and judge what the public opinion was of the school. Questionnaires went out to prospective parents through the primary schools asking for views as to how the school was perceived, and also the previous Headteacher wrote individually to Catholic parents who had not chosen this school for their children and asked them why, and that elicited a number of very direct and frank answers, and I've spoken to parents too as to why they didn't want their children to come here.

(Headteacher, St Asters)

Asked if any of this had resulted in changes to the school, he replied:

I think it's led to a higher profile being given to disciplinary matters and uniforms since these are the most obvious visual ways in which a school's reputation is judged. It certainly focused minds on the importance of academic attainment as well and a great deal is currently going into analysing the examination results each year, discussing them with departmental heads, looking at ways in which these can be sustained and improved, and also in increasing an awareness on the part of all the staff that it's very important to hold up high expectations for children.

(Headteacher, St Asters)

In addition, one of St Asters' Deputy Headteachers has undertaken a research study of parents' perceptions of communication between parents and school.

There is evidence of strong interest in monitoring which primary schools pupils are coming from. Senior teachers perceive certain primary schools as providing a higher percentage of more academically able pupils from predominantly middle-class households. This is based on checking the primary school from which those pupils achieving the best results at GCSE (General Certificate of Secondary Education) came. As the Headteacher at Newcrest observes, 'We monitor that very very closely'. For senior staff at Newcrest hoping to increase the schools league table position (its published performance in public examination results compared to other schools in the area), attracting pupils from these primary schools is seen as crucially important. Similarly, at Braelands, which wants to maintain its academic reputation, the Headteacher remarks, 'We've tracked them (the high achieving pupils) down and linked up with their junior schools'. Newcrest and Braelands, having decided the sort of parents and pupils they wish to attract, systematically identify the primary schools in which they are located in order to target promotional activity.

Being a Catholic school, St Asters is particularly keen to ensure that it receives a high proportion of children from Catholic families in Marshampton. Most Catholic children are concentrated in two primary schools in the town, one of which is close to St Asters and from which it receives a high proportion of the children transferring to secondary education. However, it obtains a smaller proportion of children leaving the other Catholic primary school. St Asters, therefore, monitors both numbers in primary schools and baptismal records to see how well it is doing in terms of attracting Catholic pupils and to assess demand for places in future years.

Ad hoc feedback

Interviewees often referred to the informal feedback that they obtained from parents and other people in the school's community. This is sometimes gained through chance conversations or contact initiated by parents. As one of the East Greenvale Headteachers explained:

> I get two kinds of feedback. The feedback that comes back from parents who are here for another reason than to give me feedback . . . and they pay the school a compliment . . . We all like to say things that please someone else so I try not to be too influenced by that. The other feedback of course I get is from the grossly dissatisfied parents who ring up to complain and there's as much danger that I get that out of perspective as well.

(Headteacher, Elderfield)

Instances of parental pressure leading to changes in schools have been found in relation to homework policy (at Thurcleigh Hill and Bridgerton schools), examination policy and the introduction of the Duke of Edinburgh Award scheme (these last two at Thurcleigh Hill).

We introduced a Duke of Edinburgh award scheme [in 1992] at the suggestion of a group of parents which I'm pleased about. I was a bit anti it at first. I saw it as very much a middle class activity . . . I still think it's got a touch of the middle classes about it but if children are genuinely benefiting from it and it's also improving relationships between staff and pupils, then so be it.

(Headteacher, Bridgerton)

More often ad hoc feedback arises by means of events, policies or institutions that are primarily concerned with other purposes. These include primary/middle school visits, open evenings, open door policies, and via parent–teacher associations, which we discuss in turn below.

As part of promotional exercises to publicise open evenings and distribute the school brochures, members of staff from secondary schools in Northern Heights visit primary schools in the Autumn term. Senior staff say that such visits provide a valuable opportunity to obtain feedback about the school from primary teachers and pupils. As the Deputy at Newcrest claims:

We have such strong primary-secondary links our primary colleagues talk to us and tell us why it is that parents sometimes don't choose us.

(Deputy Headteacher, Newcrest)

A similar emphasis on obtaining feedback from primary school staff was given by the teacher responsible for marketing at Braelands. He admits that parental perspectives are 'sometimes very difficult to pick up'. He continues:

I mean I pick it up from the primaries in particular because I find that parents will talk to primary teachers. They don't talk to us . . . because there is a tradition in secondary school, isn't there, it isn't that easy to go in and talk to teachers, you've got to make an appointment. The primary teachers, I know them all quite well.

(Teacher responsible for marketing, Braelands)

The implication is that a secondary school's inaccessibility to parents necessitates increasing the emphasis placed on other channels – such as primary school visits – to ascertain parental perspectives.

In addition to primary school teachers, the perspectives of primary school pupils were cited as an important source of information. Senior staff at Newcrest report visits to local primary schools revealing an awareness amongst Year 6 (11 year old) pupils of the school's poor league position. In this case an analogy is drawn with the football league, pupils saying they do not want to go to the bottom of the league school in much the same way as they do not want to support the bottom of the league teams. This perspective reinforces the already held general assumption amongst teachers at Newcrest that league tables are an important factor in determining parental and pupil choice (though our own data from parents does not support this view, Woods 1994). [. . .]

Although open evenings provide opportunities for questions and feedback, they are nevertheless often seen by senior teachers as simply enabling prospective parents to consider what their schools already offer:

I say to parents when they are choosing the schools, if the image we present doesn't fit your child or your aspirations for your child, that's the object of these consultations and open evenings so that you can find the right school.

(Headteacher, Braelands)

Consultation in this guise means the school informing parents of its position and giving them the choice of taking or leaving it. Parents visiting Braelands' open evening may well raise issues, but it cannot be claimed that these are being actively sought by the school. Moreover, when they are presented they are filtered out according to their congruence with the existing professional and managerial perspectives of senior teachers about the school. The Headteacher acknowledges that when issues are raised by parents staff ask themselves 'are they the criticisms we expect to hear because we can't be everything to all parents'. Implicit in this response is the notion that the school is prepared to be responsive to some parents but not others. In Braelands' case it is likely to be those from middle class backgrounds with academically able children, as these are the type senior staff are keen to attract in order to maintain the school's academic reputation and standing.

Open evenings at Newcrest frequently elicit feedback from prospective parents. In this case it tends to be negative and relates to the multi-racial nature of the school. White parents ask about the number of Asian children in each class and whether their child will be in a class with Asian children.

They'll come for the night and they'll say, well this is the best open night anywhere, I'm just telling you, well done, but we're not sending our kid here because you've got too many blacks in. That comes up every open night. I always say, well I'm delighted you told me because I'm glad you're not sending your kid to us, I don't want your kid. I only want those people who understand we are about integration.

(Headteacher, Newcrest)

It is perhaps significant, and alarming, that one of the major identifiable parental perspectives being presented directly to the research schools in Northern Heights is on the issue of 'race'. One of the possible explanations for parents' willingness to present their views on 'race' to the Headteacher at Newcrest, and by the same token his forthrightness in rejecting them, derives from the school's close relationship with the multiracial community in which it is located. This is represented most clearly by its open door policy.

The open door policy of Newcrest (and also Leaside) involves not only immediate access for parents to visit the school but also teachers frequently going to parents' homes:

The school's open because they (the parents) always have access. At a moment's notice somebody will see a parent, they don't have to phone and ask for an appointment like they do at Braelands. If they want to see the Head at Braelands they'll see him in two weeks' time. If they want to see me and I can't see them there and then I'll see them at 6.00 pm, somebody else will see them right away.

(Headteacher, Newcrest)

Such strong links with parents means that senior teachers claim the school knows its parents and the local community 'very, very well'. Consequently, when the Deputy at

Newcrest was asked why she believed the school's recent emphasis on technology would be attractive to prospective parents, she replied:

> For the same reason that a chocolate factory knows what the public will buy. We talk to our parents and we convince them that that's what they want . . . people are malleable. If you've got a product to sell you can mould people into receiving that product.
>
> (Deputy Headteacher, Newcrest)

The close relationship between the school and the community may well provide invaluable insights into parental viewpoints. Nevertheless, the Deputy's comment suggests that the relationship is still a top down one with the school convincing parents what it believes it is in their best interest to have.

At Endswich and at Braelands reference was made to the importance of feedback from their respective parent-teacher associations (PTAs): 'The parents association is brilliant at bringing in information for us because they're all actively involved in the local area' (Deputy Headteacher, Endswich).

Many parents who have been active on their child's primary school join Braelands PTA at the same time as their children join the school. In developing the school as an academic institution the Headteacher reported that feedback from these parents was and continues to be influential in understanding the type of education parents want.

Concluding observations

Attention to scanning and interpretation in relation to parents is not a high priority for the case study schools. Indeed, our fieldwork suggests that, overall in the case study areas, much less attention is given to this than to promotional activities, and that school managers are often more concerned to monitor the actions of competing schools than to discover the preferences of users directly (Woods *et al.* 1996). This places a major question mark over the claims that schools immersed in a market culture will be more 'consumer responsive'.

The picture is not uniform, however, and some schools are more open than others to the receipt of parental viewpoints. This would seem to be related to a number of factors, including the school's popularity, culture and organisation. At Thurcleigh Hill, for example, the Deputy Headteacher explained the school's practice of relying on informal contact and not going in for more systematic approaches, such as surveying, in the following terms (referring to the marked increase in admission numbers there in recent years):

> . . . that would be silly, wouldn't it? From our point of view we don't need it, do we? . . . I mean our measurement is based on numbers coming every year . . . it's the best measurement we can have.
>
> (Deputy Headteacher, Thurcleigh Hill)

In Northern Heights, the academic nature of Braelands creates an exclusive environment, which does not engender or encourage parental day-to-day access. This is in marked contrast to the dominant pastoral approach of Newcrest and Leaside schools, both of which describe themselves as having an open door policy for parents. The more isolated geographical location of Braelands may also be a factor limiting accessibility.

School managers place a great deal of reliance upon informal and ad hoc means of feedback. This emphasis upon 'soft' information, often in the form of anecdote and hearsay, should not automatically be dismissed as less valid than more systematic or planned feedback. For example, Mintzberg (1989) warns of an excessively detailed and technical approach to this activity, which runs the risk of a form of 'analysis paralysis'. So much attention might be given to monitoring the environment 'when nothing is happening that when something really does, it may not even be noticed. The trick of course is to pick out the discontinuities that matter, and . . . that seems to have more to do with informed intuition than anything else' (pp. 126–7). Commenting on the work of managers in a range of organisations. Mintzberg (1990) highlighted the significance of 'soft information' in shaping strategic managerial decisions.

It should not be assumed that use of more systematic methods of data collection, such as the adoption of complex, expensive and time consuming market research techniques, is crucial for schools seeking to be more responsive to parental needs. It does however need to be recognised that an over-reliance on ad hoc feedback can have its limitations. For instance:

- *Lack of clear purpose or hypothesis.* Ad hoc data collected at random are very difficult to interpret.
- *Lack of credibility.* School managers may feel uneasy about basing decisions on gossip or hearsay.
- *Irrelevance.* School managers may talk to everyone except the actual users or prospective parents.
- *Bias.* School managers may be over enthusiastic about their own ideas, not listening to what parents say, asking loaded questions, or giving undue weight to those perspectives they wish to hear; they may ask parents questions that are not about the issues that parents want to raise.
- *Inequalities.* An ad hoc approach might only empower certain parents, namely those who know or are able to find out about the system, while others get overlooked and have no opportunity to be heard.

In relation to this last point, professional and middle class parents are arguably more likely to have the confidence, skills and belief to put pressure on schools. We have not to date found clear evidence to suggest that any particular group of parents is more likely to make representations to schools in our case study areas (with the possible exception of racist white parents, from all classes). Social class differences are, however, unlikely to be neutral in this regard (a study of parental choice in Israel, for example, found that 'upper-status' parents were much more likely than 'lower-status' parents to expect to be involved in school decision-making; Goldring and Shapira 1993).

It is not, however, simply a question of only certain parents being confident or skilled enough to make their views known. In a more market-like system some groups of parents may be seen as more attractive to schools: for example, parents with higher incomes (attractive to school decision-makers who need to raise significant voluntary sums) and families likely to provide children who will do well in examinations. There are indications from the PASCI Study of senior staff in the case study schools giving emphasis to middle class parental perspectives, by making changes which it is assumed will be attractive to them. These responses are not all as a direct result of pressure from parents, but arise from the decisions of senior staff about the type of school they want to remain or become.

An important principle in marketing is that of positioning in the market. Companies realise that they will be unable to satisfy all the demands placed upon them. In order to be effective and survive they make careful and informed decisions about the audiences at which their products are aimed and the markets in which they will compete. This process of market segmentation and selection determines the design, promotion and distribution of the product. Products are customised and targeted to meet the backgrounds, expectations and purchasing power of consumer sub-groups. The possibility thus exists for schools submerged in a market-like culture to begin similarly to segment the market, deciding what sort of school they are or want to become and which types of parents and pupils they will try to attract (Webster *et al.* 1993).

In the case of Braelands the Headteacher wants to consolidate and expand the academic reputation of the school. At Newcrest the Headteacher wants to improve the standing of the school in the academic league table, by attracting more academically able pupils from middle class families to the school. This has to be achieved without alienating the majority of existing parents who choose the school for pastoral rather than academic reasons. Whether Newcrest is able to put together what could be termed a successful marketing mix – appealing to one segment of the market while not alienating another – remains to be seen. The point is that the school, along with Braelands, is choosing to be responsive to a certain group of parents – those who tend to be already-advantaged in society at large – and not others. In Marshampton, tendencies to emphasise what might be termed 'traditional academic' issues have been evident (Woods 1993; Woods *et al.* 1996), re-enforcing the concern that changes are being brought about – at least in some schools – with specific groups of parents in mind, and that other developments (certain schools emphasising vocational studies, which may also be a trend in Marshampton) could be leading to a more sharply 'tiered' system (Glatter 1993; Woods *et al.* 1996). If this is indicative of a wider trend then the introduction of a quasi-market in education will exacerbate social inequalities.

Might more systematic methods of feedback help reduce the dangers of inequalities in school responsiveness? A school in West Yorkshire, for example, in developing its marketing strategy, analysed the cultural and racial composition of its local community and identified a high proportion of Urdu and Punjabi speakers and of illiteracy in these languages and in English. As a result a strategy for communicating with parents primarily through speech and the development of a self-help interpreting service was initiated (Maden 1990).

Similarly, a school in Dorset conducted an extensive external relations audit to identify parental concerns to inform a strategy for raising awareness of what the school had to offer, and to develop a strategy which would make the local school community more responsive to a financial appeal (Waller 1993). Other examples include two schools, one in Devon and another in Derbyshire, which undertake scanning and interpretation exercises on a continual basis. Each year the schools interview a random sample of parents and (in the case of the Derbyshire school) pupils to obtain their views on current practice and possible future developments (Harrison 1991; Bush *et al.* 1992).

Such examples (taken from a databank of school responses to choice and competition which is maintained as part of the PASCI Study; Bagley 1994) could suggest a possible trend towards the use of more systematic methods of obtaining parental feedback – though this is not reflected in the case study areas. Their introduction, however, does not necessarily mean more broad-based parental empowerment. Schools positioning themselves in the quasi-market can choose to use systematic and more sophisticated market research techniques to facilitate more successful market segmentation and targeting, i.e. to respond more effectively to the middle class and professional parents who tend to be already-advantaged in society. In such circumstances, the already-disadvantaged will become more marginalised.

For those schools with an intake which is skewed towards the lower end of the ability range, it could be said that there are strong *educational* arguments for trying to attract more academically able (and hence often middle class) pupils. School effectiveness research has tended to show the importance of the 'balance' of the pupil intake in terms of ability in raising or lowering pupils' expected performance levels. It suggests (not surprisingly) that schools with a preponderance of students of lower ability face particular problems in achieving satisfactory educational outcomes (Reynolds 1992). Changes in the balance of pupil intake, which in the light of these arguments could be educationally beneficial, may be happening in Daythorpe and Newcrest. Nevertheless, the danger remains of these schools biasing their responsiveness in favour of one group of parents at the expense of others.

It is clear that the issue of responsiveness cannot be reduced to a matter of technique. There are wider factors – in particular, the incentives and pressures of the quasi-market within which schools operate – which form the context for decisions by school managers and the ends to which techniques (formal or informal) are meant to contribute. There is, too, the process of interpretation (which of course is integral to scanning and interpretation) which cannot be taken for granted. How people interpret what they are told, or find out through systematic information-gathering, or observe in the form of information (such as admission numbers) that is presented to them, is not a straightforward matter. The values, biases and knowledge-base of the school manager are likely to interact with the wider contextual factors referred to above and with specific pieces of information and feedback. Thus, school managers will not automatically go along with the kind of racial views expressed by parents and reported above: not all parental feedback is or should necessarily be acted upon. Also a school's internal dynamics, culture, style and structure of management will affect the process of interpretation. The impact of feedback may well be affected by the position of the person who receives it (whether it is the Headteacher or class teacher, for example) and the opportunities that different levels of personnel have for contributing information. Finally, the perceived success or vulnerability of the school in the local quasi-market will be a factor – whether, for example, school managers see their school as 'failing' to attract sufficient of certain types of pupil.

The whole process of interpretation requires more intensive and critical attention. It may be helpful to think in terms of two kinds of scanning and interpretation policies, each driven by different motives, values and aims. The one is market-driven, aimed at attracting more pupils or different types of pupils, and is often exclusive (i.e. targeted at a particular 'market segment'); the other is 'school community'-orientated, aimed at ensuring that the school is meeting the needs and aspirations of its existing parents and pupils, and is inclusive (involves all those parents and pupils).

The kind of scanning and interpretation policy pursued at school-level is crucial to the question of who exactly benefits from the responsive school. Parents who are already-disadvantaged in society may find the market-like system unresponsive to their needs and preferences (Glatter and Woods 1995). The clear danger is that the values, perspectives and definitions which help to inform and shape school effectiveness will be those of the already-advantaged middle class parental stakeholders with whom many schools – under market pressures – may increasingly elect to engage and align themselves.

Notes

1 The PASCI Study is funded by the UK Economic and Social Research Council (ESRC) (ref. R000234079).

References

Bagley, C. (1994) Life in the marketplace. How are schools responding to increased competition and choice? *Managing Schools Today*, 3(9).

Barnes, C. (1993) *Practical Marketing for Schools*. Oxford: Blackwell.

Bush, T., Coleman, M. and Glover, D. (1992) Life after opt-out, *Times Educational Supplement*, 4 December.

Cave, E. and Demick, D. (1990) 'Marketing the school' in E. Cave and C. Wilkinson (eds) *Local Management of Schools: Some practical issues*. London: Routledge.

Daft, R. L. and Weick, K. E. (1984) Towards a model of organisations as interpretations systems, *Academy of Management Review*, 9(2): 284–95.

Glatter, R. (1993) Choice of What? *Education*, 29th October.

Glatter, R. and Woods, P. A. (1995) Parental choice and school decision-making: Operating in a market-like environment in A. K. C. Wong and K. M. Cheng (eds) *Educational Leaders and Change*. Hong Kong: Hong Kong University Press.

Goldring, E. B. and Shapira, R. (1993) Choice, empowerment and involvement: What satisfies parents, *Educational Evaluation and Policy Analysis* 15(4): 396–409.

Gray, L. (1991) *Marketing in Education*. Buckingham: Open University Press.

Harrison, P. (1991) Pupils must come first, *Times Educational Supplement*, 31 May.

Maden, M. (1990) In search of a quick fix, *Times Educational Supplement*, 8 June.

Mintzberg, H. (1989) *Mintzberg on Management: Inside our strange world of organisations*. New York: Free Press.

Mintzberg, H. (1990) The manager's job: Folklore and fact, *Harvard Business Review*, March–April, No. 2: 163–76.

National Association of Head Teachers (NAHT) (1990) *The Marketing of Schools*. Council Memorandum. Haywards Heath: NAHT.

Pardey, D. (1994) *Marketing for Schools*. London: Kogan Page.

Reynolds, D. (1992) 'School effectiveness and school improvement: an updated review of the British literature' in D. Reynolds and P. Cuttance (eds) *School Effectiveness: Research, policy and practice*. London: Cassell.

The Open University (1993) Unit 5: The school in its environment, Part 1: The developing context. *E326 Module 2 Managing for School Effectiveness*. Milton Keynes: The Open University.

Waller, H. (1993) Primary perceptions, *Managing Schools Today*, September.

Webster, A., Owen, G. and Crome, D. (1993) *School Marketing: Making it easy for parents to select a school*. Bristol: Avec Designs Limited.

Woods, P. A. (1993) Responding to the consumer: Parental choice and school effectiveness, *School Effectiveness and School Improvement*, 4(3): 205–9.

Woods, P. A. (1994) Parents and choice in local competitive arenas: First findings from the main phase of the PASCI Study. Paper presented at American Educational Research Association Annual Meeting, New Orleans.

Woods, P. A., Bagley, C. and Glatter, R. (1996) Dynamics of competition: The effects of local competitive arenas on schools, in C. Pole and R. Chalwa-Duggan (eds) *Reshaping Education in the 1990s: Perspectives on secondary schooling*. London: Falmer.

23 | The practice of educational marketing in schools

CHRIS JAMES AND PETER PHILLIPS

Introduction

Recent changes in government policy have been designed to establish a market in education in England and Wales (Demaine 1988; Maclure 1992; Whitty 1989). One consequence of this has been the increased priority being given to the marketing of educational organisations. Conferences and courses have been held and texts published (for example, Davies and Ellison 1991; Devlin and Knight 1990; Gray 1991; Hanson and Henry 1992; Marland and Rogers 1991; Pardey 1991; Stott and Parr 1991; Tomlinson 1993) for the purpose of offering those with management responsibility in schools and colleges the opportunity of improving their marketing knowledge and enhancing their marketing practice. In the future, educational marketing is certain to be an important aspect of educational management.

At present, much of the literature in the field of educational marketing is characterised by ideas, suggestions, guidance and strategies which are founded on marketing models taken from non-educational settings. These are based on a variety of models, the most useful of which draw on the approaches used in the marketing of services. Education can be viewed as a service (James 1993; Lovelock 1988) and service marketing models can therefore provide a helpful starting point. It must however be remembered that the concept of the service remains problematic (Cowell 1984) and attempts to locate education in a service concept remain relatively limited and unsophisticated (see, for example, Lovelock 1988).

This study looks at different activities which make up the marketing of services and focuses in particular on those activities which make up the so-called 'marketing mix'. It looks at the practice of marketing in a number of schools in England and Wales and uses the elements of the marketing mix to analyse the different aspects of practice. The account presented here represents the first stage of a more extensive study of the practice of educational marketing.

Background

In essence, a service organisation is generally accepted to be one where the activity or benefit that the organisation offers to the [consumer], the service, is essentially intangible (see for example, Cowell 1984; Lovelock 1988). Kotler (1986) defines services by explaining that 'they cannot be seen, tasted, felt, heard or smelled before they are bought' (Kotler 1986: 681). This clear-cut definition is questioned by some authors who stress a goods–service continuum (see, for example, Rathmell 1966; Shostak 1977) but nonetheless the notion of intangibility remains.

Most of the standard textbooks, for example, Kotler (1986) or Cameron *et al.* (1988) describe a range of activities which fall within the marketing of services. These are often viewed as a sequence which has been summarised by Gray (1991: 13) as follows:

1 Marketing needs/problems
2 Marketing research/audit
3 Marketing planning
4 The marketing mix
5 Marketing strategies and tactics.

Although this model has been questioned, principally because it is essentially concerned with the marketing of goods as opposed to services (Cowell 1984), it nonetheless provides a helpful framework for examining service marketing.

There are a number of techniques available to service industries for dealing with the identification of marketing needs and/or problems (see, for example, Cannon 1980; Lovelock 1984). These include the frequently used SWOT analysis where the organisation's strengths, weaknesses, opportunities and threats are analysed. These techniques, together with marketing research/audit methods are an important focus in recently-published texts on educational marketing (for example, Davies and Ellison 1991; Gray 1991; Marland and Rogers 1991; Pardey 1991; Stott and Parr 1991).

Good practice in managing the planning process involves a coherent, staged approach to establishing the current market position, setting objectives and formulating strategies. Advice on doing this in educational contexts is readily available (see, for example, Devlin and Knight 1990; Puffit *et al.* 1992).

The early stages in the marketing process especially the marketing audit provide a basic starting point (the 'where are we now?') for the planning process. In an educational context, an explicit mission statement (Murgatroyd 1989; West-Burnham 1992) together with the other various institutional policies can provide a guide to the future direction (the 'where are we going?') of the institution, processes embodied in the practice of development planning (Hargreaves and Hopkins 1991). The challenge for schools is not these two basic notions, rather it is the need for particular strategies which schools will have to generate to get from the one to the other (the 'how do we get there?'). The process can be facilitated using various tried and tested analytical tools to aid the marketing process. Examples of such tools include the Ansoff, BCG and 3X3 (business screen) matrices and are well documented in an educational context in Pardey (1991). These enable the data from the market audit to be analysed systematically and assist in the identification of strategies. Murgatroyd (1989) and West-Burnham (1992) also provide helpful strategies.

One of the complicating factors in the practice of educational marketing is the range of recipients of the service provided, or stakeholders, and the terms used to describe them (see Murgatroyd and Morgan 1993). In this study the term customer is used predominantly in reporting the findings with the intended meaning of those with whom the organisation has dealings. The term was not used in the data collection phase. This issue of the variety of stakeholders in educational organisations is taken up again in the discussion.

The importance of the marketing mix

The concept of the marketing mix is central in marketing for it is the key in marketing terms to an organisation moving from the 'where it is' to 'where it wants to be'. It is concerned with understanding how marketing operates in practice, as opposed to why it is necessary. It represents the domains of marketing practice in which marketing strategies and tactics will be deployed and as such it offers a framework for the analysis of the process of marketing. It is for this reason that we have used the notion of the marketing mix to analyse the practice of educational marketing in schools.

The marketing mix can be separated into different components and is a feature of many management texts (see, for example, Christopher and MacDonald 1991; Cowell 1984) and is frequently cited in texts on educational marketing (see, for example, Gray 1991; Tomlinson, 1993). There is some debate over the number and kind of components of the marketing mix. Within the marketing mix for manufacturing industries four components are typically identified:

- product
- place
- price
- promotion.

These are often referred to as the 'four Ps' (see, for example, Borden 1984). For the marketing of services, additional components have been suggested:

- people
- processes
- proof.

This gives a service marketing mix model often referred to as the 'seven Ps' (Cowell 1984). Interestingly, Gray (1991) considers that only 'five Ps' should be included in the educational marketing mix – product, place, price, promotion and people. He argues that processes and proof are 'an unnecessary complication' (p. 31) and that they can be accommodated within the 'five Ps' model. For the purposes of this study however, we have used the 'seven Ps' model, since it offers the most detailed tool for the analysis of the marketing mix in educational settings.

The purpose of this study

The overall purpose of this study was to explore and document marketing practice in schools. This paper uses the components of the marketing mix as a framework for the analysis of practice. It examines in turn each of the seven Ps that make up the service marketing mix. For each of the seven Ps, data is presented to illuminate the ways that schools in the study perceive and act in relation to that aspect of marketing. Data has been collected from a group of 11 schools in the primary and secondary phases across both the private and public sectors. The schools were selected because they were judged to be in a competitive environment and should therefore be actively considering marketing and their market position. They were of the following kinds:

- two 11–18 co-educational secondary comprehensive schools (maintained);
- two 11–16 co-educational secondary comprehensive schools (maintained);
- two 4–13 boys preparatory schools (private);
- two 11–18 boys secondary (private);
- three 7–11 co-educational primary (maintained).

Data was collected by means of interviews with senior teachers in the schools, typically the headteacher, using a semi-structured interview schedule. The interview questions were designed to explore the respondents' conceptualisation of marketing and the marketing practice in that particular school. Data was also collected by means of documents provided by the schools. The interviews were transcribed and standard data reduction techniques were used (see Miles and Huberman 1984) to reduce and analyse the data. Follow-up interviews were carried out in most cases and in all cases the data collected was validated by the respondents. In some cases, teachers in addition to the headteacher were interviewed.

Results: An overview

It must be said at the outset that while all those interviewed recognised the importance of marketing, their understanding of marketing and marketing theory was generally limited, as was their ability to articulate rationales in terms of marketing theories for aspects of their practice which could be interpreted as marketing. This can in part be explained by the fact that none of those interviewed had received any management training in marketing. There was a confusion between marketing and selling as these two responses indicated: 'Marketing is selling – a deliberate act', and 'I market my school by selling the school to parents'.

None of those interviewed, for example, indicated any specialised knowledge of the concept of the marketing mix and none of the schools studied had any documented marketing policy. Much of the data collection process focused on exploring with respondents aspects of their management practice which could be interpreted as marketing, even if this was not recognised as such.

All those spoken to were able to articulate what they saw as their market although often it was a restricted view. Typically, parents were identified as those in the market to whom the service was provided as the second quotation above indicates. Not unexpectedly, private schools tended to describe their market in terms of parents' ability to pay, and had some understanding of how the market was developing as this example indicates: 'The market for this school is changing, there is no doubt about that. Gone are the days when all of your parents are doctors and lawyers and other professions . . . We now have builders, decorators, shop owners, salesmen and those kind of people and they all get involved in the private school system now . . . We have people who are prepared to sacrifice more now in order to be able to afford private education'.

In maintained schools the market was described in terms of the proximity of the parents to the school – the catchment area – despite open enrolment. One respondent who was clear that parents were the service recipients and who recognised the potential impact of open enrolment considered that 'My market is my catchment area – I feel it still exists'. Another took a similar view, also alluding to the impact of open enrolment, 'the market of this place is the area around the school, the old catchment area'.

Some respondents considered that the market was wider than the parents. One state school headteacher, for example, was emphatic that 'the market . . . it is the children and their parents'. Typically, however, parents were seen as the service recipients and for the respondents the complications resulting from the multiplicity of recipients of the service of educational organisations was not seen as an issue. Marketing the organisation to 'provider stakeholders (suppliers)' (Murgatroyd and Morgan 1993: 5) was not raised as an issue.

Product – the services being offered to the market

Answering the question 'What is a product?' is not particularly easy (Maxwell 1989). Kotler (1986: 296) defines it as 'anything that can be offered to the market for attention, acquisition, use or consumption that might satisfy a want or need. It includes physical objects, services, persons, places, organisations and ideas'. Service organisations in a market setting offer a service 'product' to the market. The product in education is consistently described as the range of services provided by the school, college or university (see, for example, Barnes, 1993, p. 49). Primarily, the services provided by schools are the courses offered to students but the services will extend beyond the curriculum. Frequently cited examples of other services include twilight computer clubs, restaurant meals for adults, consultancy for businesses and contract research programmes, care of children while parents work and so on (see Gray 1991: 81 and 82; Marland and Rogers 1991: 15; Stott and Parr 1991: 65 and 66).

A number of issues are significant in relation to the product element of the marketing mix.

Product range

This is the range of goods or services offered by the organisation and is sometimes referred to as the 'product mix'. Within the range, some products will be considered to be more central than others and will be viewed as 'core products'. Regular review of the 'product mix' is important.

Product benefits

All marketing texts stress the importance of viewing products in terms of their benefits (see, for example, Kotler 1986). There is a danger when attempting to market a service that the service itself is described rather than the benefit the customer gains from the service. This is particularly relevant to education where historically we have been conditioned to describe the courses and programmes taught by a school or college rather than to identify the gains and benefits. There has been a tendency for course development to be product and/or producer-led.

Product life

Often a provider-led approach in the marketing of services carries with it a failure to recognise the finite 'life-cycle' of a service. In education, for a variety of reasons – for example, the limited resources for course development – courses can be continued long after they may be deemed appropriate by the recipients.

Product quality

The notion of quality is related to the service's strengths and the demands of the market. Whilst optimum quality throughout the whole range of the product may be unrealistic, it is important that the central features of the product conform to the customer's requirements (Crosby 1979). The extensive literature on enhancing quality in the provision of services stresses the importance of all the members of the organisation being committed to it (see, for example, Hopson and Scally 1989).

Practice in the schools

Product range

All the schools in the study had a good understanding of what it was that they offered to their customers. Although they did not refer to this explicitly as their product; in marketing terms, this is what it was they were describing, and not surprisingly they described it confidently and unambiguously. One school for example, while confusing selling and marketing, clearly had a view of the product: 'I sell the caring environment we are trying to nurture. I sell ethos. I sell the SAT results, the standards and our league table position'.

Although the quotation above includes more than one product (that is, caring environment, ethos and academic standards) typically respondents referred to a single quality described in general terms, such as 'a traditional school' or a 'good school' and made no explicit reference to the range of products they offered. Indeed the terms product-mix and product-portfolio were viewed by all the schools with suspicion.

Significantly though, almost all the schools realised that there was a need to highlight various aspects of their provision. Examples they chose to cite included the school's dyslexia unit, expertise in technology, the pupils' examination results in science, the music provision in the school and home-school links. There was a clear desire expressed by all the respondents to highlight a particular aspect of their product to make their provision special, different and therefore appealing to their market but none had any systematic procedures for reviewing their product mix. [. . .]

Product benefits

In their marketing literature and during the data collection, all of the schools in the study referred to the service they offered in descriptive terms as typified in the quotation above. None of the state schools described the services they offered in terms of the benefits. The private schools tended to infer that there was something to be gained from their particular service but failed to be specific about its benefits.

Product life

There was no evidence that course developments in any of the institutions was other than curriculum-led (product-led); certainly none were deliberately market-led. There were corollaries of this in other aspects of marketing practice. In all schools, including the private schools, there was an:

(a) unclear recognition of market segments;
(b) absence of data on market needs; and
(c) inadequate marketing links (as a general rule) with the recipients.

The issue that a course/activity may have a finite life was not recognised and the 'new' was thought of, and explained in terms of, the extra or additional provision continually being developed in the institution.

Product quality

The notion of quality was referred to in all schools and, in most (but not all) it was related to the school's strengths and the demands of the parents. Examination results and other statements of claim (for example 'this is a high status school with a good catchment') were given to reinforce claims of high quality provision. However, there was little to suggest that any of the schools and the service products they provide are becoming customer oriented in terms of how quality was viewed. Quality explicitly as conformance to recipients' requirements did not figure. In addition, there was no evidence of building a quality culture throughout the institution, a strategy which is a central thread of many quality management approaches. In a number of cases the teaching staff appeared to be excluded (either by accident or design) from discussions about improvement of quality. In all the schools the headteachers clearly saw the 'quality crusader' role as an important part of their total leadership role but had not extended this to creating crusader teams (Murgatroyd and Morgan, 1993).

Price – the resources needed by customers to obtain the goods/services

The price element of the marketing mix comprises of two distinct components: costing and pricing.

Costing

The key task on the costing side is to seek a close match between institutional spending and benefits to the customer.

Pricing

On the pricing side the key task is to ensure that recipients are charged sums in line with the institution's objectives. There are a number of aspects of service price which are significant in relation to the price element of the marketing mix.

Differentiation

In many sectors of the commercial world, there is greater differentiation of products with consequently more freedom to set prices.

Pricing factors

When making a pricing decision there is a need to take account of the value of the product to the customer, the price as an indicator of quality, the ability of the person to pay, the volume of sales required, the market saturation of the product and the price customers are prepared to pay.

The cost of product development

It is important to recognise that developments of the package – the product mix – provided by any institution are almost always expensive. This applies to all service organisations including schools. In educational settings, the pertinence of this to managers, staff, parents and pupils has to be realised and it should be a factor in the change process.

Practice in the schools

Not unexpectedly, in the private sector schools, there was considerable evidence to underline the importance of this aspect of the marketing mix. It was particularly significant in those schools which offered a boarding service. The competition for boarders is fierce because boarding is not as popular with parents as previously and for the schools it is very expensive to administer. Schools which offered boarding were acutely aware of the price element of their marketing mix. Another more general issue is to do with the requirement on the private schools to respond to parents if they voiced their dissatisfaction with provision lest they exercise their exit option (Hirschman 1970; Pfeffer and Coote 1991). The private schools were acutely aware of this exit option which they thought was stronger in the parents of their pupils because those parents 'were spending their own money' and recognised the 'sacrifice' many parents made. The private schools identified the price as a major influence in parents deciding to switch their child's school and considered it to be relatively common if not high in percentage terms. There was some preliminary evidence from the private schools to suggest that moves from the 'expensive private' school to the 'good free state' school is entering the parents' agenda although in the past they had benefited from the reverse effect.

In the state sector recent legislation has facilitated the movement of students (and the income in the form of 'age weighted pupil units' for each student) from one school to another. Those in the state schools in this survey generally recognised this and acknowledged it to be a factor in their thinking. However, as yet there was no evidence to suggest that parents and/or pupils were actually exercising the exit/switching option to any significant extent other than at the transfer ages of 7, 11 and 16. A number of the schools considered that the frequent exercising of this option may become a reality and such a possibility although not yet planned for (in marketing terms) was being discussed in a number of schools.

In both state and private sectors, the cost/benefit analysis of promotional activities (see below) was articulated in terms of additional numbers of pupils attracted. One state school head considered that: 'If I attracted 10 extra pupils and each one brought in £1500 and if the advertisement cost so much less, say £500, then I could live with that'.

The responses in the interviews indicated that sponsorship by external agencies is becoming accepted and is being actively considered in some schools. There was also clear evidence of intention to develop the idea further in due course. The notion of joint school and commerce/industry projects was considered to be a marginally more acceptable form of sponsorship in some of the schools and at the time of the interviews was being actively considered.

In the state schools there was clear evidence that the previous casual thinking on funding is beginning to develop into a more structured approach to financial planning. One school was paying particular attention to detailed forward planning which involved the specific targeting of additional funds (from an increased 'number on roll' – actual and projected – and sponsorship – existing and planned) towards a major capital building project to be realised over a period of three years. Another example of a pro-active response to financial planning was the intention of one school to raise a capital sum in excess of £2 million by the competitive auctioning of part of the school grounds between a number of supermarket groups each seeking a new store site.

In the private sector there was some evidence of 'loss leaders' being deployed to increase uptake. An example of this practice was the offering of one week's free boarding as a strategy to tempt day-pupils to become weekly boarders. Untried innovative schemes were being explored, for example, offering parents a discount of 10 per cent on the fees if they introduced another parent and child to the school and a 'sale period' which gives a 10 per cent discount if enrolment is completed within a given period. All the boarding schools used occasional boarding in response to parental demand and also as a response to 'perishability' (Kotler 1986) although the schools did not articulate it in those terms. Significantly there was little evidence of concern among those who were employing or considering employing 'loss leader' strategies about creating a contrary perspective, 'there must be something wrong with a place that requires all these gimmicks'.

There was a contrast between the private and maintained schools in the way they view financial matters. In the private sector both the pricing and the costing aspects of the price element of the marketing mix (the fees) are actively considered. The dominant concern was to make a profit. One of the private schools, the smallest of those visited, aimed to make a profit of £10,000 and included in its annual budget a bad debt provision of £20,000. In the maintained schools in the study, pricing was not an issue, but there was considerable evidence that the costing aspect is receiving increasing attention. The dominant budgetary concern is with 'breaking even' and not with making a profit.

All of the private schools in the study claimed they would never be able to survive on fees alone. All of the fee income is used meeting 'day-to-day' running costs. They relied on parental donations and other fund-raising projects for all major capital expenditure. Surpluses on fee income was not adequate for funding such expenditure.

In the maintained schools, parental support in the form of voluntary contributions was considered to be essential for curriculum enrichment or extra-curricular activities. One of the schools which had what it described as a 'middle class catchment area' was at pains to suggest that this did not necessarily mean that all the funding problems associated with organising activities of this kind were solved. This difficulty has implications for marketing planning, particularly in terms of the extra-curricular aspects of the 'product' component of the marketing mix.

Place – the location and accessibility of the services

This particular element of the marketing mix is concerned with the location, appearance and the facilities of the place where the service is delivered, which influence the accessibility and availability of the service. Important aspects of 'place' in service marketing include the following.

Appearance and condition

In almost every case the appearance and condition of the service location is an important aspect of marketing that service.

Customers and other visitors

In a customer-orientated culture, the customer, the potential customer and other visitors will warrant attention that reflects that orientation. Examples of this include reserved parking spaces for visitors, good signposting and a welcoming environment.

First contact and accessibility

This aspect of place is about how an individual makes the first contact with the organisation and about how easy it is for them to make it. The importance and potential value of the first contact is significant.

The challenge of improving the 'place' component of the marketing mix can be daunting and can require creative and radical thinking. Improvements include a range of activities from the simple and inexpensive to more complicated and potentially costly. In a school/college setting, an example of the former would be a telephone answer machine which received messages *and* gave explicit information (such as emergency contact numbers) in use outside normal hours and during any days in the school holidays when the office was not staffed. An example of the latter would be where the head and other senior staff routinely hold clinic or surgery sessions at a number of off-site venues such as local primary schools, or the local welfare club. This attempt to improve accessibility is potentially expensive not solely because of the time used but because of the cost incurred following up quickly all enquiries, complaints and so on.

Practice in the schools

All the state schools visited had diverted a significant proportion of any surplus funds, through the flexibility given by locally-managed status, into improvements in the appearance and condition of the school. There was clear evidence that all the state schools have improved significantly their facilities and procedures for dealing with all visitors and prospective parents. Examples included making the reception areas more welcoming, decorating corridors, erecting new notice boards in 'public' areas and erecting welcoming/informative signposts to assist visitors. The private schools had also diverted resources into improving the appearance of the school especially those areas visible to visitors or prospective parents. [. . .]

To a significant extent all the schools, and particularly one which had falling rolls, expressed a wish to make substantial changes to the school environment. All were constrained, typically financially, in making these changes but none of the schools had an explicit strategy for overcoming the constraints.

Promotion – the activities which communicate the benefits of the services to potential customers

Promotion can be used to inform the market and persuade those in it to choose the service that is being offered. Typically this is best done by identifying the key feature which will appeal to the market, the unique selling proposition (see, for example, Gray 1991: 126 and 127), and supporting this message through the design and content of publicity material.

Important aspects of this element of the marketing mix include the following.

Communication

The promotion part of marketing is the phase which most people understand and come into contact with. In its simplest form the promotional plan is the communication between the producer and the customer. Stott and Parr (1991) have reviewed the factors which influence the decision on the most appropriate type of promotion such as: What has to be achieved? Over what time scale? What resources are available? Which customer group is being addressed?

The key features of promotional material are as follows:

- attract *attention* of potential customers;
- arouse *interest* in the product;
- create *desire* for its benefits;
- prompt *action* from potential customers.

These are usually referred to by the acronym 'AIDA' (see, for example, Gray 1991). Marland and Rogers (1991) have added the feature 'conviction' to the list to give the acronym AID(C)A. It is added to ask the question 'How do you convince the viewer/listener/reader that what you are saying is true?'.

Promotional tools

Many authors (see, for example, Stott and Parr, 1991) identify the three main types of promotion. These are as follows.

Advertising using television, cinema, radio, posters and the press. Important considerations here include: cost, target market, timing and consistency of the advertising medium with the ethos of the organisation.

Public relations (PR) both press and non-press. The aim of press PR is to achieve editorial coverage which can be secured by building up trusting relationships. Its main advantages are that it is a reinforcing mechanism and cheaper usually than an advertisement.

Non-press PR will include the usual special events in the school calendar together with a limited number of receptions and/or exhibitions. The claim that whilst advertising costs money, PR is free is not true, although typically PR is very cost-effective. Some of the PR mechanisms will involve consultation processes and all of the social events become important ingredients in the school's PR portfolio. Off-site displays may be of limited use on their own but coupled with other frequent exposure are positive. Exhibitions can also be useful but there are cost implications in terms of time, effort and money. In a school context maintaining a customer orientation requires regular consultation with parents and others (employers and so on) about improvements which can be made.

Outreach material includes all material which is produced to communicate with a specific audience. Examples include the prospectus, leaflets, letters, Christmas cards, direct mail, promotional videos and any 'giveaways' (such as pens, carrier bags, badges, etc.). There are important design considerations, the elements of which can collectively help to establish a corporate identity.

Practice in the schools

All of those interviewed believed they were committed to promoting their school and from their responses saw this as the dominant element of their marketing practice. Most considered that their practice of communicating with customers was effective although none of them carried out any systematic evaluation of it. None of those interviewed indicated any knowledge or were able to articulate any knowledge of the elements of communication practice, for example, AIDA or AID(C)A (see above).

Over half of the schools had never advertised and one state school headteacher claimed to be strongly philosophically against it and avowed that he would never do it whatever the circumstances: 'I get very upset when people appoint a marketing manager. The school should sell itself and once you have to employ someone to sell it there is something wrong. I'm against advertising; it is unprofessional. I telephoned a headteacher who did it and told him he was an idiot'.

Paradoxically, from the information given by this headteacher, and from the documents he provided, the public relations strategy and practice of his school were among the more sophisticated and developed of those in the study. The only advertisements used by any of the schools, state or private, were placed in the local press. The prohibitive cost was cited as the reason for not advertising more widely.

All schools engaged in press and non-press PR and considered that this aspect of their marketing was effective. No school had a documented PR policy but almost half were able to describe the key elements of the PR strategy used by the head or designated 'press officer'.

All the private schools regularly used various exhibitions and off-site displays. No state school did more than engage in very limited off-site display and then often as part of a joint venture with another school (often one with which it was in competition). The schools considered that their links with feeder schools were generally good but surprisingly, considering the importance of these schools in terms of their ability to influence pupil choice, not universally so.

All the schools were developing outreach materials as a matter of priority. In most, this development was from a low base line, whilst in others (mostly, but not exclusively, the private schools) developments were concerned with making current practice more sophisticated. Four of the schools were developing promotional videos using either in-house or outside expertise (in almost equal ratio). Although those schools with videos considered that they were pleased with them, they all signalled negative feedback from the target audience. This reinforces the point that the production of such resources must be carefully planned.

All of the schools between them have used all the usual promotional tools available (as cited above) but the most common is the prospectus. All the schools considered this to be the most effective means of promoting the school.

There was evidence that the notion of the unique selling proposition (USP) was better understood by private schools than by state schools. This understanding was apparently intuitive and is perhaps the result of not having a captive (that is locally residing) catchment. This is the comment of a preparatory school head. 'Parents will understand that it is not only a prep school but it has a special facet to it that it is going to actually give the school something special. The moment parents feel that they are going to a school which actually has something special, as well as it being an ordinary traditional prep school they are going to feel a little more tempted to go and see it and what it has to offer.'

In the maintained schools there was little reference to the USP. All the schools gave broadly the same messages of what they were offering.

People – over 90 per cent of 'services' personnel come into contact with customers

The 'people' element of the marketing mix is concerned with those involved in selling and performing the service and with the interaction of customers receiving the service.

Important aspects of this component of the marketing mix include the following.

The people are the service

Gray (1991) claims that any service industry is to a substantial extent the people who deliver it. For example, 90 per cent of service staff are involved in customer contact in contrast to only 10 per cent in manufacturing. However, he observes that in both tourism and banking the staff are recruited for technical or administrative skills rather than customer contact skills. There is a danger where employees do not feel responsible and agree with customers that any problems are the fault of 'the management'. This is accentuated if the way the service is provided means that staff take responsibility for only one part of the service.

Good motivation is good organisation

Service industries need both organisation structures and staff motivation policies. Hence there is a need for training, involvement, staff development and incentives to motivate staff.

Quality and codes of conduct

Gray (1991) makes the point that in service industries, the staff codes of conduct replace the quality control of manufacturing industry as the bench-mark. He asserts that education is no exception in this.

Corporate strategy

Since all service organisations are wholly dependent upon the success of their marketing, the marketing function is the central management function. When this is the case a 'marketing strategy', and a 'corporate strategy' are one and the same. Again schools are no exception in this.

Practice in the schools

A number, but not all, of the headteachers of the sample schools recognised the importance of internal marketing and that they should be marketing their school (the product) to the staff who in turn should market it, in partnership, to the catchment area (the market place). It is evident however, indeed it was even articulated by a number of the heads, that staff do not always carry the same messages to the parents and to other customer groups outside the school. In the words of one headteacher: 'One of the concerns that I have . . . is that what ever good is going on in the school I don't think the staff push it enough outside the school'.

A number of reasons were cited for this, many of them not unexpected. For example if staff felt unable to influence key issues of policy and practice, or had no sense of ownership they were happy 'to blame management'. In one specific case, the head was recently appointed and had yet to 'win over' some of the staff. He considered that until he does so, it is inevitable that some confused messages will emerge from the school.

There was little evidence generally to support the belief that the cultures of the schools in this study have changed and taken on a market-oriented approach nor had they changed so that a market-oriented approach might be more easily adopted. Certainly moving to a customer-oriented culture will represent a significant change in most of the schools studied and will require sophisticated management of change (Whitaker 1993). One headteacher expressed a view that he had deliberately moved to a more participative management style and considered that moving to a market-oriented culture within the organisation would be more straightforward because of this.

Some of those interviewed from both private and state sectors considered that problems could arise when the school governors became more involved in marketing and became themselves 'people' in the marketing mix. A view was expressed that the governors can become too involved and unthinkingly accepting of the school's philosophy. One headteacher, new to the school, said there was a reluctance on the part of the governors to 'step back a little' and take a more detached and constructively critical view.

Processes – the operational system by which marketing is managed within the organisation

This aspect of the marketing mix, the processes of marketing, is concerned with the management of marketing within the organisation. It should not be confused with other marketing activities and is not part of the marketing strategies and tactics. In educational settings Shreeve et al. (1989) suggest that this aspect of the marketing mix should be the responsibility of one individual who 'co-ordinates the marketing efforts of the college staff'. Marland and Rogers (1991) suggest a range of options for those individuals who might take on this role. Their suggestions include a 'freelance' (for example, a parent), members of staff at all levels and the chair of governors.

There are significant financial implications of marketing. In a school context, Pardey (1991) points out that the budget for marketing should not be determined by arbitrary percentages of the total school budget but by reference to the strategies required to achieve the objectives set for the school's marketing operations. If these strategies are necessary for those objectives to be achieved, then the resources they require provide the means for setting the budget. However, all resources should be included; not just the items which are clearly identifiable but also the resources 'borrowed' from other budget headings. These resources are controlled most effectively by delegating responsibility for them to those who will be involved in achieving the specific market objectives. By locating the responsibility for operations and budgets together and setting up clear lines of accountability, management can be made more effective – which means outcomes are more likely to be achieved.

The other management issues subsumed within this particular element of the marketing mix call for a detailed consideration of the organisational framework and its culture. As with the people element of the marketing mix, bringing about a market orientation in the processes elements of the school could be a challenging task for the educational manager. Those with management responsibility in schools can draw on other management systems, however, as there are clear links here between management of this element of the marketing mix and approaches such as total quality management (Murgatroyd and Morgan 1993; West-Burnham 1992) and other management devices employed presently to move schools forward (Hargreaves and Hopkins 1991; Murgatroyd 1989).

Practice in the schools

In none of the schools did anyone other than the headteacher have explicit responsibility for marketing. One headteacher explained why this should be so: 'It's my school and I will do it (organise marketing) my way in the same way as I do everything else. The staff would not like such a position. They would be suspicious'.

It is hardly surprising with the limited amount of intuitive and/or accidental marketing – a key theme of this study (see below) – that there is as yet no evidence to indicate that any other aspects of an operational system for marketing is in place in any of the schools. In almost half of the schools development planning is sufficiently advanced that incorporating a marketing strategy will be straightforward and be found to be supportive to what already applies. In the other schools explicit planning was less advanced suggesting a bigger step might be needed to move to a customer-orientated service and to climb onto the marketing ladder. There was no significant difference between private schools and state schools in this respect.

In the majority of maintained schools there was a genuine concern about funding marketing particularly the promotion element. This was less apparent in the private sector. The concern in all maintained schools, often left unchallenged and unreconciled, was the short-term belief that these are funds which should be spent on children's education and to do otherwise is to cheat them in some way.

Proof – what actual evidence is there to confirm that customers have received service appropriate to their needs?

The proof of the sale of a manufactured product is easily obtained and unambiguous. The proof of benefit from a service is less easily obtained. Education is no exception to this 'service problem'. The challenge is to devise systematic procedures to monitor and evaluate all aspects of the marketing strategy. Within the mix this element is therefore to do with all the physical evidence that supports service delivery and any physical items which may go with the service.

Interestingly, none of those interviewed were able to articulate aspects of their practice which revealed evidence of the benefits of the services they provided. (A simple example would be the qualifications gained by the pupils and the certificates which prove those benefits.) One interpretation of this is that the schools do not view established aspects of their practice from a marketing perspective and further to this see marketing principally as promotion. (This issue is discussed below.) This is confirmed in the responses of those interviewed to questions which explored the issue of proving that the marketing strategy worked. All the answers were couched in terms of the evidence of the success of their promotion/PR practice although even for this element of the marketing mix evidence was not gathered systematically in any of the schools.

Discussion

The dominant theme of this research was the general lack of coherent marketing practice in the schools visited, despite the fact that the schools were chosen because they were considered to be in a competitive environment. This can be explained in part by the fact that none of those interviewed had received any management training in educational marketing. The lack of coherent practice does not mean that there were no activities in the schools that could be construed as marketing in the way it is viewed in non-educational services. It was however only after probing and exploration that the respondents revealed aspects of their management practice that could be viewed as marketing in its widest sense. In fact, all the schools were active in the various elements of the marketing mix albeit in an inconsistent and intuitive way. However, the practice revealed should not necessarily be interpreted as indicating a marketing orientation in the way it is conventionally viewed. This notion of marketing as a customer-driven response to a competitive market requires a different approach to that revealed in the schools visited. Adopting this approach is not simply a matter of adjusting and supplementing current practice. It is about adopting an entirely different 'mind-set' which sees *all* the organisation's activities in terms of the customers' requirements. This approach was not evident in any of those interviewed, indeed there was considerable resistance to the idea.

One explanation for this resistance is that it is a manifestation of professional responsibility. There is a special quality and complexity to the educational relationship which makes the marketing of it as a service problematic. Teaching is not simply about responding to customer wants; it is also about meeting customer needs and it is in understanding customer wants and needs and distinguishing between them that professional judgement is required. It has to be added however that there is a balance to be struck between understanding customer wants and needs and responding appropriately, and perpetuating a quality of service provision that is totally provider/producer led.

One further outcome of the ignorance of marketing and the absence of an internalised market orientation, is that marketing is seen as simply an 'add on extra' to current practice. This interpretation could in part explain the over-emphasis on the promotional aspects of marketing as revealed in this study. Promotion is what most lay people would guess that marketing is and it is the aspect of marketing that can be most easily taken on and added to current practice. Those who take this view respond to being in a competitive environment by promoting their wares – 'All that's needed is some advertising and public relations'. Furthermore, the creative nature of the aspects of this element of the marketing mix possibly has particular appeal.

All the schools had a very limited view of who their stakeholders or customers were. Almost all considered that parents were the focus for their marketing activities, with a minority including the pupils as well. A more sophisticated view of educational marketing would encompass marketing the organisation to the wide range of stakeholders (James 1993; Murgatroyd and Morgan 1993).

At the moment, some schools appear to be seeing educational marketing as an aspect of crisis management. That is, they are viewing marketing as being all about ensuring survival as opposed to ensuring that schools meet the needs of clients in both the short and long term. In a sense these schools are responding to a relatively sudden realisation that they are in a competitive environment by taking up quickly those aspects of marketing practice which involve little change in current practice and in which it is most easy to make progress. It is possible that as expertise becomes more sophisticated and the education market develops other aspects of the marketing mix will be addressed and a more explicit customer-driven orientation will be adopted.

The absence of a coherent marketing strategy and the piecemeal approach to marketing planning is possibly a consequence of the wide range of imposed changes that many schools are facing and the turbulent environment in which they exist. Of course, it is highly unlikely that the schools will ever exist in a stable environment, but the extent and range of change are possibly making it difficult for schools to plan. These factors, turbulence and imposed change, make it very difficult too for schools to behave pro-actively; they are forced to be solely reactive.

Essentially the stance taken by texts on courses and texts on educational marketing draw on principles derived from the marketing of goods such as cars and consumer durables which have been adapted for service industries. One outcome of this research has been a realisation of the complex task that those with responsibility for marketing schools and colleges face. A variety of factors, such as the range of stakeholders, the changing characteristics of the pupil customers with age and the wide range of different facets of the service provided, combine to make educational marketing a very sophisticated activity. This [chapter] has deliberately not addressed the issue of the rightness or wrongness of creating a market in education and it is as yet unclear what an educational market place may look like. As the market develops so will the distinctive field of educational marketing which will in all probability draw on elements of service marketing but will almost certainly contain features which are unique to the field.

References

Barnes, B. (1993) *Practical Marketing for Schools*. Oxford: Blackwell.

Borden, N. H. (1965) The concept of the marketing mix, in G. Schwartz (ed.) *Science in Marketing*, Chichester: John Wiley.

Cameron, M., Rushton, R. and Carson, D. (1988) *Marketing*. Harmondsworth: Penguin.

Cannon, T. (1980) *Basic Marketing: Principles and practice*. Eastbourne: Holt, Rinehart and Winston.

Christopher, M. and McDonald, M. (1991) *Marketing: An introduction*. London: Pan Books.

Cowell, D. (1984) *The Marketing of Services*. Oxford: Heinemann Educational.

Crosby, W. (1979) *Quality is Free*. London: McGraw-Hill.

Davies, B. and Ellison, L. (1991) *Marketing the Secondary School*. Harlow: Longman.

Demaine, J. (1988) Teacher's work, curriculum and the new right, *British Journal of Sociology of Education*, 9(3): 247–63.

Devlin, T. and Knight, B. (1990) *Public Relations and Marketing in Schools*. Harlow: Longman.

Gray, L. (1991) *Marketing Education*. Buckingham: Open University Press.

Hanson, E. M. and Henry, W. (1992) Strategic marketing for educational systems, *School Organisation*, 12(3): 255–67.

Hargreaves, D. and Hopkins, D. (1991) *The Empowered School: The management and practice of development planning*. Cassell: London.

Hirschman, A. O. (1970) *Exit, Voice and Loyalty. Response to Decline in Firms, Organisations and States*. Cambridge: Harvard University Press.

Hopson, B. and Scally, M. (1989) *Twelve Steps to Success through Service*. Leeds: Lifeskills Communications.

James, C. R. (1993) Education as a service, in C. R. James, D. Payne, I. M. Jamieson and A. Loxley, *Managing Accountability*. Bath: University of Bath.

Kotler, P. (1986) *The Principles of Marketing*. Englewood Cliffs: Prentice-Hall.

Lovelock, C. H. (1984) *Services Marketing*. Englewood Cliffs: Prentice-Hall.

Lovelock, C. H. (1988) Classifying services to gain strategic marketing insights, in C. H. Lovelock (ed.) *Managing Services: Marketing operations and human resources*. Englewood Cliffs: Prentice-Hall.

Maclure, S. (1992) *Education Reformed*. Buckingham: Open University Press.

Marland, M. and Rogers, R. (1991) *Marketing the School*. Oxford: Heinemann Educational.

Maxwell, R. I. G. (1989) *Marketing*. Basingstoke: Macmillan Educational.

Miles, M. B. and Huberman, A. M. (1984) *Qualitative Data Analysis*. Sage: Beverly Hills.

Murgatroyd, S. (1989) KAIZEN: school-wide quality improvement, *School Organisation*, 9(2): 241–60.

Murgatroyd, S. and Morgan, C. (1993) *Total Quality Management and the School*. Buckingham: Open University Press.

Pardey, D. (1991) *Marketing for Schools*. London: Kogan Page.

Pfeffer, N. and Coote, A. (1991) *Is Quality Good for You?* London: Institute for Public Policy Research.

Puffit, R., Stoten, B. and Winkley, D. (1992) *Business Planning for Schools*. Harlow: Longman.

Rathmell, J. M. (1966) What is meant by services?, *Journal of Marketing*, 30(4): 32–6.

Shostak, G. L. (1977) Breaking free from product marketing, *Journal of Marketing*, 41(4): 73–80.

Shreeve, R., Thorp, J. and Rickett, J. (1989) *Marketing Hertfordshire Colleges*, Ware, Herts: Herts County Council/Ware College Marketing and Information Unit.

Stott, K. and Parr, H. (1991) *Marketing your School*. Sevenoaks: Hodder and Stoughton.

Tomlinson, H. (1993) *Marketing the School. Bulletin No. 2: The Head's Legal Guide*. Kingston upon Thames: Croner Publishers.

West-Burnham, J. (1992) *Managing Quality in Schools: A TQM approach*. Harlow: Longman.

Whitaker, P. (1993) *Managing Change in Schools*. Buckingham: Open University Press.

Whitty, G. (1989) The new right and the national curriculum: state control or market forces?, *Journal of Educational Policy*, 4(4): 329–41.

24 | Educational leadership: schools, environments and boundary spanning*

ELLEN B. GOLDRING

Introduction

Recent reform efforts and calls for school restructuring are changing the nature of the relationships between principals and their constituencies as environments change. Principals must measure accountability, recruit students and teachers, include parents in decision-making and mobilize resources. All of these changes link schools with their environments, ultimately increasing the impact of the external environment on the management and control of the internal functioning of schools.

This chapter is based on the assertion that principals must pay increased attention to managing their schools' external environments. Only schools with sufficient adaptive capacity will flourish with new environmental realities. Environmental impacts on schools have grown so great that it is imperative for principals to understand environmental leadership strategies.

Organizational behavior literature also reflects the increasing importance of the environment for all types of organizations, moving from a closed-systems to an open-systems perspective. The open systems view does not suggest that organizations do not have boundaries, but rather suggests that the boundaries are permeable. Boundaries serve as the barriers between personnel and activities under the responsibility and control of the organization and those outside these domains. They also indicate the borders of the organization's discretion regarding its activities (Pfeffer and Salancik 1978). For example, school principals encounter limits in the extent of the changes they can advocate, depending upon the community surrounding the school.

Boundaries have a filtering function: they screen inputs and outputs because organizations cannot deal with all elements from the environment. Boundaries also serve as mechanisms to secure a certain amount of organizational independence from the

* Adapted version of 'Striking a balance: boundary spanning and environmental management in schools' (1995) in S. Bacharach and B. Mundell (eds), *Images of Schools*. Thousand Oaks, CA: Corwin Press.

environment. In essence, boundaries contribute to organizational rationality (Scott 1981). They help insulate schools from their environments so that a balance is reached between the constantly changing external environment and the need for stability in the school's internal functioning.

It is important to note that organizations differ in the permeability of their boundaries (Katz and Kahn 1978). Permeability is defined as 'the extent to which marginal outsiders participate in or influence organizational activities' (Corwin and Wagenaar 1976: 472). The main function of environmental leaders is to manage the permeability of the boundaries. Certain types of organizations, however, have less leeway in managing this permeability. Schools have very permeable boundaries. For instance, parents as outsiders have considerable influence on school activities. Principals cannot insist that parents stay out of the school, although they may require specific procedures during their visits (a boundary spanning strategy).

The guiding premise throughout this chapter is that although leaders are constrained in their actions regarding the environment, they have considerable latitude for making choices. In fact, organizations have the power to manipulate and control their environments (Child 1972). The ultimate tension between schools as organizations and their environments, and the challenge to their leaders, is ensuring a balance that affords the school both the necessary resources and relationships which require a certain level of environmental dependence, while simultaneously achieving enough independence to adapt and ensure change. For instance, schools that receive grant money for a special project from a local business do not want the business to begin to intervene regarding the way in which the teachers implement the program in the classroom.

This chapter considers two aspects of environmental leadership. The first part of the chapter presents specific environmental leadership strategies, strategies for designing and positioning the school to ensure the proper balance between autonomy and dependence. The second part of the chapter reviews specific boundary spanning power tactics. Principals utilize these tactics to manoeuvre the school in the environment as they balance autonomy and dependency. A third, final section discusses the role that environmental perceptions play and interrelationships between these components.

Throughout the chapter two terms are used interchangeably to describe the function which school leaders, typically principals, fulfil: environmental leader and boundary spanner. The boundary spanner function in organizations is essential to manage organization–environment relations. While boundary spanning is carried out by many people in the organization simultaneously, it is important to focus on the boundary spanning of leaders, including principals, who typically set policy and manage many of the crucial relationships *vis-à-vis* the environment.

Environmental management strategies

Principals employ various strategies to respond to their environments. Strategies are long-term courses of action, which usually imply the allocation of resources to reach certain goals (Chandler 1962). Environmental management strategies require broad-based planning and action. These strategies are tools that aid leaders in adapting to their environments and in modifying themselves to thrive in a given environment.

The strategies can be grouped into three broad categories: (1) those aimed at reducing the dependencies between organizations and their environment (independent strategies); (2) those aimed at environmental adaptation to promote organization–environment relations (cooperative strategies); and (3) those aimed at changing the environment to maintain the organization (strategic manoeuvring, socialization).

Strategies aimed at reducing dependencies

Independent strategies are directed at responding to the environment to increase the organization's own independence and autonomy in relation to its environment. Three independent strategies are most prevalent: *competition, public relations* and *buffering*. A competitive response is often useful when an organization faces uncertainty regarding environmental support. In this case an organization can compete for that support by seeking alternatives. Competition reduces organizational dependency by providing alternative means of acquiring resources. School leaders who are attuned to alternative sources of funding, such as special grant programs, demonstrate a competitive response. They are no longer solely dependent on resource allocation from central government.

Highly related to the competitive response, and often a connected aspect, is the public relations response. Organizational leaders apply public relations strategies to control and manage their environments by trying to influence the environment's perceptions of, and knowledge about, the organization. This is crucial in attracting support and resources, but also necessary to maintain clients and personnel. Organizations vary in the amount of public relations expenditures, but Thompson (1967) suggests that this strategy reduces environmental dependency by gaining prestige at a relatively low cost.

For instance, the central role of public relations as an independent strategy can be seen when examining the impact of national reports calling for educational reform. Entities in the schools' environments, including state and federal governments, the public at large, businesses, and parents, began to pay closer attention to schools when these reports focused attention on the numerous problems facing schools. In response to this external attention, those school leaders indicating progress towards school improvement will be more independent from external involvement and pressures than those that either do not report their efforts or do not engage in such efforts.

In many cases, the environmental leader's preferred strategy is to reduce environmental influence as much as possible, that is '. . . to seal off core technologies from environmental influences' (Thompson 1967: 19). This strategy is termed 'buffering'. For instance, principals usually achieve this by creating formal procedures to respond to parental requests. Hollister (1979) found that schools with high parental demands adopted rationalistic,bureaucratic controls to deflect these demands. Formal controls, rules and regulations often serve as buffers. Buffering includes principals' insistence that local agencies, businesses, or other groups (including parents) contact them first before approaching teachers.

Independent strategies aim at responding to the environment through organizational self-control. That is, the organization's leader acts to increase its own independence and status in relation to its environment. Insufficient independent strategies, such as poor public relations, can often result in a vocal opposition group's success at blocking a proposed innovation. This type of situation indicates a high level of dependency between the school and the environment.

Strategies aimed at environmental adaptation

Through adaptive strategies leaders attempt to increase cooperation and joint action between the organization and the environment. These strategies generally require that the organization relinquish some autonomy in order to adjust to the environment. Contracting, cooptation and coalition building are useful adaptive strategies.

Contracting is an adaptive strategy. When the leader of the organization negotiates directly with elements in the environment to reach an explicit agreement, then a contract of cooperation occurs. Usually, contracting occurs after a lengthy exchange of information and communication. Contracts allow environmental leaders to coordinate the organization's future activities with environmental elements in order to reduce uncertainty in a changing environment (Scott 1981).

Cooptation occurs when the organization absorbs elements from the environment in order to reduce threats. 'The strategy of cooptation involves exchanging some degree of control and privacy of information for some commitment of continued support from the external organization' (Pfeffer 1972: 222). Through cooptation, leaders establish links with environmental elements upon which the organization is highly dependent. The cost of cooptation to the organization is great since elements from the environment gain control and influence concerning the organization's internal functioning. Coopted elements carry more influence than do those elements involved in a contracting relationship with organizations because cooptation allows influence in a wide range of activities and topics, whereas contracting is usually confined to specific domains. Consequently, it seems that boundary spanners would engage in cooptation when other boundary strategies are not sufficient. When the organization faces high dependency and uncertainty in regard to an external group, and other boundary mechanisms are unavailable, then cooptation seems a viable option.

Cooptation also benefits the organization as it allows organizational leaders more control over the environmental element than if it were completely outside the organization's realm of norms and authority. In fact, often the coopted element begins to identify with the focal organization and therefore becomes less of an adversary. Furthermore, having taken part in the decision-making processes of the focal organization, the coopted element may show commitment to the policies which were formed. For example, principals generally coopt parents through dominating the Parent–Teacher Association (PTA) and using it as a support group for their own decisions (Vidich and Bensman 1960; Gracey 1972; Wolcott 1973).

Coalition building is another form of adaptation used by boundary spanners. In this case the leader joins elements from the focal organization and the environment for a common purpose. Each unit retains its independence and the organization retains some control over the means used to achieve the common goals with their environmental partners (Corwin 1965).

Principals use coalition forming, aimed at complete cooperation between the school and the parents, when the principal and parents work together to achieve common goals. In this case, principals view parents as important allies due to similar aims and interests, and seek to involve them. This can be contrasted to the principal who coopts the PTA. In the former case, the principal and PTA work on common agendas in a collaborative atmosphere. In the latter, the principal tries to manoeuvre the PTA to support the school's agenda. The productivity of the coalition stems from the members sharing a common perspective on particular issues (Scott 1981). Hence, including representatives from parent or community groups on school decision-making teams can be either coalescing or cooptation.

Strategies aimed at redefining environments

The strategies presented thus far are directed at managing relationships with the environment. Under certain circumstances, however, it is either too costly or too difficult to manage such relationships; instead, environmental leaders employ a strategy to try to change environments or redefine domains. Strategic manoeuvring is utilized to influence the nature of the environment in which an organization is situated. These strategies endeavor to afford the organization more autonomy and less dependence on the present environment (Galbraith 1977). Thus, for example, some schools may redefine their missions completely to attract a totally different student clientele. The net result of this change is that the school is now competing in a new environment.

Principals have crucial roles in defining the school's domain and ensuring smooth environmental interactions. As they utilize their knowledge of and connections with the environment, principals not only provide valuable insights on program offerings, but help establish coordinating ties with the school's new constituencies resulting from changes (Goldring and Rallis 1993). Principals also are key in maintaining the legitimacy of the 'new' structure. Keeping the organization visible and informing constituents about the organization enhances environmental ties. Strategic manoeuvring, therefore, allows the school to realign and widen its support system (Sizer 1984; Goldring and Rallis 1993).

Strategic manoeuvring often demands that principals use an entrepreneurial approach to achieve their plans. Seeking external funding from a foundation or a corporation requires that they communicate the school's newly defined mission both to the immediate funding sources as well as to the community constituents who can influence funding decisions.

Environmental leaders utilize an additional strategy to 'redesign' their environments. This is referred to as 'socialization'. Through socialization leaders attempt to socialize elements of the environment into accepting the norms, values, and operating procedures of the organization. This is similar to cooptation, but no formal role is given to the elements representing the environment. Principals engage in socialization to channel and mould parental involvement into acceptable, manageable styles by creating congruence between the school's resources and parental expectations. Through socialization, principals encourage parents to accept the school's goals and methods as they '. . . de-educate the public about the school's capabilities and re-educate it about what it can reasonably expect from the school' (Morris et al. 1984: 116). Socialization is crucial when engaging in strategic manoeuvring, as constituencies should be socialized to accept the changes impacting on them.

Summary

This section presented three broad environmental management strategy dimensions. The first includes strategies used by organizations to protect their independence *vis-à-vis* their environments. The second strategy provides leaders with tools to help organizations adapt to the external environment, while the third suggests strategies used by organizations to change their environments.

Surveying all the strategies together, it is clear that they may be categorized as either reducing or increasing organization–environment interactions. Some appear to be more costly, difficult, and complex than others. Consequently, when the aim is increasing the organization–environment relationship, coalition building may be a proper strategy only after public relations strategies have been unsuccessful. Correspondingly, when the goal is reducing this relationship, competition may be best employed after buffering strategies do not remove sufficient environmental influence on the organization.

Clearly, organizations do not always use a single strategy. The ultimate challenge to leaders is achieving an ongoing balance between independence and dependence: independence for change and autonomy, dependence for support and resources. The organization–environment interchange is reciprocal; 'organizations not only adapt and change in response to their environments, they also act upon and change their environments' (Trice and Beyer 1993: 301).

Boundary spanning power tactics

As in other aspects of leadership, success in the boundary spanning role requires an ability to access and use power. Boundary spanners access power according to their relationships with external forces and their ability to handle environmental contingencies, such as lack of adequate resources (Hickson *et al.* 1971). Sources of power that emerge from relations with the external environment include resource control, decision premises control and institutional relationships.

Resource control provides a central source of power for boundary spanners. To serve as a basis for power, a resource can be expert knowledge or skills essential for organizational functioning (Mintzberg 1983). Knowledge about the environment is important because it increases the likelihood that a person or subunit controls or reduces uncertainty for the organization (Crozier 1964; Pondy 1977). Since environmental leaders function at the apex of the organization facing environmental uncertainties, their expertise affords them power from this aspect of their role.

Access to information represents another important source of power (Mintzberg 1983). By controlling the flow of information into the organization, an environmental leader assumes the role of 'gatekeeper'. A 'gatekeeper' enjoys access to external information channelled into the organization. The person strategically located to control information as it flows in and out of an organization makes crucial decisions as to what information to send to whom, or how much information should be given to whom, thus allowing attention to be focused where the environmental leader has directed it through the manipulation of the information flow. By controlling information, environmental leaders protect the organization from stress and other external interferences. For example, principals report using information from their district superintendents about forthcoming state mandates to prepare their schools before the mandate passes (Goldring and Rallis 1993).

Schools and other organizations ultimately obtain most tangible resources from the environment. Resources seen as the most critical or the most scarce afford the greatest power (Miles 1980). Consequently, environmental leaders who acquire the most crucial resources, and especially those difficult to secure, acquire the most power within organizations. For example, in a school system where 'effective' teachers are hard to find, principals successful in luring this scarce resource to the school may be viewed as having power.

An additional source of power related to controlling resources is control of decision-making premises. It is possible for the environmental leader to wield power because of the ability to affect the decision-making process (Pfeffer 1981). When one person confines the decisions of another person to limited areas, the person making the decision faces less uncertainty and the person who has confined the decision acquires power. Principals often lead teachers in decisions about implementing new curricular guidelines, capitalizing on their knowledge of parents' views about the new guidelines. Principals are using their external relationships to guide the decisions of teachers to head-off possible conflictual decisions.

This type of control of information and decision-making premises is a function of network centrality. By controlling decisions and information within an organization, the environmental leader gains network centrality.

The environmental leader centrally located in the network gains legitimacy in the eyes of organizational members and external elements due to the ability to fulfill the linking person role (Litwak and Meyer 1966). The linking person role allows environmental leaders to mediate between a wider base of persons in the organization, as well as between the organization and the environment, thus allowing them to represent a wider circle of organizational interests. Together, knowledge of the organization and environment, and the utilization of this knowledge to link organization and environment, increase the environmental leader's base of power.

Environmental leaders also gain power from external environments irrespective of their ability to contribute to internal operations. They often gain power from their connections and supporters in their environments (Scott 1981). This has been referred to as the institutional perspective (Meyer and Rowan 1978: 357): '. . . Organizations and their internal units derive legitimacy, power and authority from their status in social environments'. Environmental leaders who are highly valued by institutions in the organization's environment or who develop important relationships with these institutions, especially those that are important constituencies for the organization, gain power based on legitimacy. Legitimacy, in turn, is gained by accepting the institutional environment's norms. Principals who are highly regarded by a local university educational administration department, for example, bring legitimacy to their schools because of their connections with the university. These relationships facilitate principals' efforts when they engage in internal change. They gain status and legitimacy in the eyes of their teachers and parent clientele due to their standing in the university community.

Summary

Environmental leaders link organizations with the environment by using various sources of power. Centrally located within the organization, they procure and control resources from the environment in order to facilitate the internal operations of the organization. Acknowledging and developing these power sources are essential tools when planning and implementing environmental management strategies.

Environmental leadership and environmental perception

The organization–environment relationship, facilitated by the environmental leader, is affected by how individuals perceive the environment, rather than the objective state of an environment: 'The environment which members of an organization respond to and act upon is the environment they perceive' (Trice and Beyer 1993: 303).

Daft and Weick (1984) suggest that organizations in general, and environmental leaders in particular, must interpret their environments. Environmental leaders must formulate the organization's interpretation of the environment and design an appropriate response. In other words, only through perception or interpretation of the environmental leader can environments become 'known' to organizations.

This does not mean that boundary spanning and environmental perceptions are influenced by a single person or organizational function. Boundary spanning roles are highly cross-functional (Hambrick 1981). Some boundary roles, i.e. collecting information, may be carried out by many people in an organization while others, i.e. domain identification, may be carried out only by individuals in specific organizational functions. For example, both principals and teachers gather information from parents, while principals only may engage in resource mobilization. In some organizations, boundary roles are concentrated in the hands of specific people; in other organizations, boundary roles cut across many functions. In every case, individuals are called upon to interpret, decipher and understand their environments.

Organizational members construct or invent their environments according to their perceptions. For instance, a principal perceiving the environment as hostile and disapproving may react defensively, while another principal in the same environment may view the criticisms as a source of help in promoting an agenda for change.

Conclusion

This chapter began by claiming that a new context of schooling, often associated with reform efforts, is altering the external boundaries of schools. As schools attempt to include more diverse voices in policy decisions, meet the needs of all student bodies, and respond to external mandates and demands, leaders must not only attend to the internal functioning of their schools, but must also assume an environmental leadership role.

Environmental leadership implies taking an active role in engaging with the environment. This can be accomplished through reducing dependencies, adapting to the environment to promote organization–environment relations, and changing the environment. Rather than reacting to environmental changes and pressures, the leader initiates and plans strategies to help the organization reach an equilibrium with the environment. To reach this equilibrium, leaders serve as the catalyst for change within the environmental context.

The tensions facing leaders as organizations interact with their environments are rooted in the need for organizations to be autonomous and independent from excessive demands, yet simultaneously develop ongoing interrelationships to ensure continued support, such as resources and legitimacy. Hence, environmental leadership aims at meeting both goals of independence and dependence.

Principals who assume the boundary spanning role must guide their schools using boundary spanning strategies to create an appropriate balance between the school's dependence and independence relative to the environment. Principals may control and manipulate many of the forces impacting on the school utilizing resource control, decision premises control and institutional relationships. Only through such active leadership will schools be able to adapt sufficiently to survive, much less thrive, in the emerging dynamic environments.

The principal's role as environmental leader constitutes an entirely new framework for operating, one that proves both challenging and stimulating. In such environments, positioning and strategizing assume the same significance as the moves in a game of chess. Much like a chess master, the principal must exhibit the courage to take risks and seize opportunities that benefit the school today, while utilizing the vision to leap ahead in positioning the school to take advantage of future challenges.

References

Chandler, A. D. (1962) *Strategy and Structure*. Cambridge: MIT.

Child, J. (1972) Organizational structure, environment, and performance: The role of strategic choice. *Sociology*, 63(1): 2–22.

Corwin, R. G. (1965) *A Sociology of Education*. New York: Appleton Century Crofts.

Corwin, R. G. and Wagenaar, T. C. (1976) Boundary interaction between service organizations and their publics: A study of teacher–parent relationships. *Social Forces*, 55: 471–92.

Crozier, M. (1964) *The Bureaucratic Phenomenon*. Chicago: University of Chicago.

Daft, R. L. and Weick, K. E. (1984) Toward a model of organizations as interpretation systems. *Academy of Management Review*, 9(2): 284–95.

Galbraith, J. (1977) *Organization Design*. Reading, MA: Addison-Wesley.

Goldring, E. B. and Rallis, S. F. (1993) *Principals of Dynamic Schools: taking charge of change*. New York: Corwin/Sage.

Gracey, H. L. (1972) *Curriculum or Craftsmanship?* Chicago: University of Chicago Press.

Hambrick, D. C. (1981) Specialization of environmental scanning activities among upper level executives. *Journal of Management Studies*, 18: 299–320.

Hickson, D. J., Hinings, C. R., Lee, C. A., Schneck, R. E. and Pennings, J. M. (1971) A strategic contingencies theory of intraorganizational power. *Administrative Science Quarterly*, 16: 216–27.

Hollister, C. D. (1979) School bureaucratization as a response to parents' demands. *Urban Education*, 14: 221–35.

Katz, D. and Kahn, R. L. (1978) *Social Psychology of Organizations*. New York: Wiley.

Litwak, E. and Meyer, H. J. (1966) A balance theory of coordination between bureaucratic organizations and community primary groups. *Administrative Science Quarterly*, 2: 31–58.

Meyer, J. W. and Rowan, B. (1978) The structure of educational organizations, in W. M. Meyer et al. (eds), *Environments and Organizations*. San Francisco: Jossey-Bass.

Miles, R. H. (1980) *Macro Organizational Behavior*. Glenview, IL: Scott, Foresman.

Mintzberg, H. (1983) *Power in and around Organizations*. Englewood Cliffs, NJ: Prentice-Hall.

Morris, V. C., Crowson, R. L., Porter-Gehrie, C. and Hurwitz, E. Jr. (1984) *Principals in Actions: the reality of managing schools*. Columbus, OH: Charles E. Merrill.

Pfeffer, J. (1972) Size and composition of corporate boards of directors: The organization and its environment. *Administrative Science Quarterly*, 17: 218–28.

Pfeffer, J. (1981) *Power in Organizations*. Marshfield, MA: Pitman.

Pfeffer, J. and Salancik, G. (1978) *The External Control of Organizations*. New York: Harper and Row.

Pondy, L. E. (1977) The other hand clapping: An information processing approach to organizational power, in T. H. Hammer and S. B. Bacharach (eds), *Reward Systems and Power Distribution*. Ithaca, NY: Cornell University.

Scott, W. R. (1981) *Organizations, Rational, Natural and Open Systems*. Englewood Cliffs, NJ: Prentice-Hall.

Sizer, T. R. (1984) *Horace's Compromise: the dilemma of the American high school*. Boston: Houghton-Mifflin.

Staff (1992, Summer) The AAEPP umbrella: enterprising educators. *Private Practice Educator*, 2(1): 1.

Thompson, J. D. (1967) *Organizations in Action*. New York: McGraw-Hill.

Trice, H. M. and Beyer, J. M. (1993) *The Cultures of Work Organizations*. Englewood Cliffs, NJ: Prentice-Hall.

Vidich, A. and Bensman, J. (1960) *Small Town in Mass Society*. New York: Doubleday.

Wolcott, H. F. (1973) *The Man in the Principal's Office*. New York: Holt, Rinehart and Winston.

Index

Autori sistema Šahovskog informatora • Авторы система Шахматного информатора • The Inventors of the Chess Informant systems • Die Autoren des Systems des Schach-informators • Auteurs des systèmes de l'Informateur d'échecs • Autores del sistema de Informador ajedrecistico • Autori dei sistemi del Informatore scacchistico • Författarna till Schackinformationssystemet • واضعو أنظمة دليل الشطرنج • チェス新報システム開発

ALEKSANDAR MATANOVIĆ, BRASLAV RABAR, MILIVOJE MOLEROVIĆ, ALEKSANDAR BOŽIĆ, BORISLAV MILIĆ

Odgovorni urednik • Главный редактор • Editor-in-chief • Chefredakteur • Rédacteur en chef • Redactor en jefe • Redattore Capo • Chefredaktör • 編集長 • رئيس التحرير

ALEKSANDAR MATANOVIĆ

Zamenik odgovornog urednika • Заместитель главного редактора • Assistant of the Editor-in--chief • Assistent des Chefredakteurs • Assistant du Rédacteur en chef • Asistente del redactor en jefe • Vice Redattore • Vice Chefredaktör • 編集次長 • مساعد رئيس التحرير

DRAGAN UGRINOVIĆ

Redakcija • Редакционная коллегия • Editorial board • Redaktion • Collège de rédaction • Colegio de redacción • Collegio Redazionale • Redaktion • 編集委員 • هيئة التحرير

MILAN BJELAJAC, BOŽIDAR ĐURAŠEVIĆ, MILUTIN KOSTIĆ, ZDENKO KRNIĆ, MIROSLAV LUKIĆ, ALEKSANDAR MATANOVIĆ, BRUNO PARMA, DRAGAN UGRINOVIĆ, SAŠA VELIČKOVIĆ

YU ISBN 86 7297 016 0

YU ISSN 0351 1375

Izdavač • Издатель • Publisher • Herausgeber • Editeur • Editorial • Editore • Utgivare • 出版社 • الناشر

ŠAHOVSKI INFORMATOR

11001 Beograd, Francuska 31, PO Box 739, Yugoslavia

Tel. (38 11) 186-498, 630-109; Telex 72677 CH INF YU; Telefax (38 11) 626-583

ШАХМАТНЫЙ
ИНФОРМАТОР

CHESS
INFORMANT

SCHACH-
INFORMATOR

INFORMATEUR
D'ECHECS

INFORMADOR
AJEDRECISTICO

INFORMATORE
SCACCHISTICO

SCHACK-
INFORMATOR

チェス新報

دليـــل الشـطرنج

šahovski informator

47

I–VI 1989